T0225055

App Development Recipes for iOS and watchOS

A Problem-Solution Approach

Molly K. Maskrey

Apress®

App Development Recipes for iOS and watchOS

Molly K. Maskrey
Parker, Colorado, USA

ISBN-13 (pbk): 978-1-4842-1819-8   ISBN-13 (electronic): 978-1-4842-1820-4
DOI 10.1007/978-1-4842-1820-4

Library of Congress Control Number: 2016943972

Copyright © 2016 by Molly K. Maskrey

This work is subject to copyright. All rights are reserved by the Publisher, whether the whole or part of the material is concerned, specifically the rights of translation, reprinting, reuse of illustrations, recitation, broadcasting, reproduction on microfilms or in any other physical way, and transmission or information storage and retrieval, electronic adaptation, computer software, or by similar or dissimilar methodology now known or hereafter developed. Exempted from this legal reservation are brief excerpts in connection with reviews or scholarly analysis or material supplied specifically for the purpose of being entered and executed on a computer system, for exclusive use by the purchaser of the work. Duplication of this publication or parts thereof is permitted only under the provisions of the Copyright Law of the Publisher's location, in its current version, and permission for use must always be obtained from Springer. Permissions for use may be obtained through RightsLink at the Copyright Clearance Center. Violations are liable to prosecution under the respective Copyright Law.

Trademarked names, logos, and images may appear in this book. Rather than use a trademark symbol with every occurrence of a trademarked name, logo, or image we use the names, logos, and images only in an editorial fashion and to the benefit of the trademark owner, with no intention of infringement of the trademark.

The use in this publication of trade names, trademarks, service marks, and similar terms, even if they are not identified as such, is not to be taken as an expression of opinion as to whether or not they are subject to proprietary rights.

While the advice and information in this book are believed to be true and accurate at the date of publication, neither the authors nor the editors nor the publisher can accept any legal responsibility for any errors or omissions that may be made. The publisher makes no warranty, express or implied, with respect to the material contained herein.

Managing Director: Welmoed Spahr
Lead Editors: Michelle Lowman and Steve Anglin
Technical Reviewer: Charles Cruz
Editorial Board: Steve Anglin, Pramila Balan, Louise Corrigan, Jonathan Gennick, Robert Hutchinson, Celestin Suresh John, Michelle Lowman, James Markham, Susan McDermott, Matthew Moodie, Jeffrey Pepper, Douglas Pundick, Ben Renow-Clarke, Gwenan Spearing
Coordinating Editor: Mark Powers
Copy Editor: April Rondeau
Compositor: SPi Global
Indexer: SPi Global
Artist: SPi Global

Distributed to the book trade worldwide by Springer Science+Business Media New York, 233 Spring Street, 6th Floor, New York, NY 10013. Phone 1-800-SPRINGER, fax (201) 348-4505, e-mail orders-ny@springer-sbm.com, or visit www.springeronline.com. Apress Media, LLC is a California LLC and the sole member (owner) is Springer Science + Business Media Finance Inc (SSBM Finance Inc). SSBM Finance Inc is a Delaware corporation.

For information on translations, please e-mail rights@apress.com, or visit www.apress.com.

Apress and friends of ED books may be purchased in bulk for academic, corporate, or promotional use. eBook versions and licenses are also available for most titles. For more information, reference our Special Bulk Sales–eBook Licensing web page at www.apress.com/bulk-sales.

Any source code or other supplementary materials referenced by the author in this text is available to readers at www.apress.com/9781484218198. For detailed information about how to locate your book's source code, go to www.apress.com/source-code/. Readers can also access source code at SpringerLink in the Supplementary Material section for each chapter.

Printed on acid-free paper

This work is dedicated to all my friends whom I truly consider family. First, to John, who helped me though so many tough times and helped me to become the person I am today, and with whom I hope to co-author a book in the future.

To Erin, who sat with me until the wee hours of the morning when I needed a friend the most.

To my Jess, whom I call Goldi now because she's like the Goldilocks of friends—just right. She comes and listens to me speak on topics of very little interest to most normal people, she takes me out dancing into the early morning hours even on "school nights," and she honored me as my wonderful, beautiful maid of honor.

To KP, you opened my heart and helped me realize that the simplest of times can be the most cherished and that laughing hysterically, without regard for who might be sitting at the next table, is great for the soul.

Finally, to my partner for so many years, Jennifer. You stuck by me, helped with ideas, fixed my grammar, put up with my drama, and still proposed to me and actually went through with the wedding and let me wear white. Here's to many more decades of fun together.

Contents at a Glance

Contents

About the Author

Molly K. Maskrey first learned about software while a sophomore in high school on a Wang punch card computer, where you manually created an octal machine-language program by popping out chads on a single card. While getting her undergraduate degree, she programmed COBOL on IBM System/360 computers at banks in and around Tampa, Florida, moving on, in her twenties and thirties, to work for various large aerospace companies including IBM Federal Systems, TRW (now Northrup-Grumman), Loral Systems, Lockheed-Martin, and Boeing. As the lure and romance of working in big companies (was there ever such a thing?) started to wear off, she realized that a break was in order, so she took several years off, moved to Maui, and taught windsurfing at the beautiful Kanaha Beach Park.

Never one to stay still, Molly moved to Denver, Colorado, in 2005, where she jumped on the iPhone bandwagon by opening one of the first screen repair companies, specializing in ten-minute screen repair. People came from nearby states to have their babies put back into pristine condition, and she made enough money to begin working in not only app development, but iOS accessory design as well. In 2009 she, along with her life and business partner, Jennifer, received approval from the Apple MFi (Made for iPod/iPhone/iPad) program for their first accessory, a credit-card reader that connected through the thirty-pin dock of iPod and iPhone devices, a good six months ahead of Square. In 2010 she and Jennifer founded Global Tek Labs, an iOS development and accessory design-services company that is now one of the leading consulting services for new designers looking to create smart attachments to Apple devices.

That same year, Molly, under her previous persona, published through Apress the first book on how to create accessories for the iPhone operating system; it is still to this day the only major description of the process.

In 2014 Molly and Jennifer formed Quantitative Bioanalytics Laboratories, a wholly-owned subsidiary of Global Tek, to bring high-resolution mobile sensor technology to physical therapy, elder balance and fall prevention, sports performance quantification, and instrumented gait analysis (IGA).

Ms. Maskrey enjoys working on new and interesting technical projects, hosting wine and cheese parties for her friends, and her greatest passion—ballroom dancing. Talk technical projects with her and it will certainly be time well spent, but bring up international cha-cha or Viennese waltz and not only will she become vigorously animated, but she also may start moving while talking . . . even if there is not a dance floor. She's been known to spontaneously start samba line dances at various big box retail stores on quiet Monday afternoons.

Molly lives in Parker, Colorado, with Jennifer, her partner of 26 years, and their two Labradors and basement dance practice floor.

About the Technical Reviewer

Charles Cruz is a mobile application developer for the iOS, Windows Phone, and Android platforms. He graduated from Stanford University with B.S. and M.S. degrees in engineering. He lives in Southern California and runs a photography business with his wife (www.bellalentestudios.com). When not doing technical things, he plays lead guitar in an original metal band (www.taintedsociety.com). Charles can be reached at codingandpicking@gmail.com and @CodingNPicking on Twitter.

Acknowledgments

First, I want to acknowledge all my friends who gave me the support to persevere and go through with writing when it would have been so easy to just give up, most especially my six bridesmaids and dearest friends: Ashley, Lizzy, Erin, KP, Lauren, and Jess. You have made my life complete and without your love and support this would have never happened.

I wrote this book for the thousands of young female engineers and software developers who feel that much of the industry has been exclusive for too long. I want to acknowledge the pioneers who long before my little attempt pushed consistently to create an equal, merit-based system free of any gender or other bias.

I want to acknowledge the Innovation Pavilion and their incubator program for making me a part of something that brings new ideas and products to the world, making it a better place. And I especially want to point out Lindsey Finklang, who provided me with many opportunities to present my work before hundreds of people and get valuable feedback.

Many thanks go to Colorado Dancesport, my home away from home where I can become someone else for several hours each week, and to the instructors, and my friends, who make it happen: Faith, Harmony, Mitch, Robert, and, yes, even Scott.

I also want to acknowledge Children's Hospital Colorado and the Center for Gait and Movement Analysis, who have been so generous with letting me be a part of understanding the significance of what they do for young adults with Cerebral Palsy and other gait disorders; the understanding I've gained drives me to focus efforts to help the many who truly need it.

More thanks go to the clients and friends of Global Tek Labs who so generously allowed me to include some of their projects in this book for illustrative purposes, and to the hundreds of people who have attended my talks over the past year and have given me ideas for what to include, such as John Haley, who told me of his personal woes in understanding Auto Layout in Xcode—those actual experiences helped drive the subject matter I chose to include.

Finally, I want to acknowledge all the authors before me who set the stage for my own little work to fit into a much broader landscape.

Chapter 1

Introduction

I wrote this book for the aspiring app developer who wants to move beyond the level of hobbyist and become a true professional in the field of software. She's discovered that programming, and in particular iOS development, speaks to her (see Figure 1-1). Whether it's solving complex problems, having the freedom to choose when and where to work to make a better life for herself, or just that it's fun—I want everyone to succeed.

Figure 1-1. The creativity of development captures our imagination and draws us in to solve problems the likes of which we never imagined

Electronic supplementary material The online version of this chapter (doi:10.1007/978-1-4842-1820-4_1) contains supplementary material, which is available to authorized users.

© Molly K. Maskrey 2016
M.K. Maskrey, *App Development Recipes for iOS and watchOS*, DOI 10.1007/978-1-4842-1820-4_1

Goals

For me, this is personal. As a business owner, I continually find that there are not enough app developers available to help us grow and expand the business. In particular, finding a capable mobile software engineer with whom I can easily communicate is the most significant problem my company faces. As a bit of background, we design electronics equipment that connects to Apple devices, so we really look to our software contractors to not only understand coding, but also to know how to get the final product, the app, out into the world. We don't want to hire a developer whose end result is to send us an Xcode project file. She needs to take charge, to create the final product as if it were a thing of beauty, an art form extending from her own soul. As such, we assume a more than introductory level of expertise with Xcode, Swift, and, to some extent, Objective C. Many books, online tutorials, video courses, instructor-led courses, and so on exist to help you learn the basics. Apple's own developer portal offers more than enough instructional information and sample applications to take your coding skills to the intermediate level and beyond. More importantly, the real-time, interactive nature of online media lets you stay current and up to date as new features are released and bugs requiring work-arounds are corrected.

This book shows you how to work with all those other pieces of developing an app that you don't typically find in introductory material. Let's look at an example.

You've downloaded Xcode and watched a YouTube video or three on how to write simple apps. After a few easy-to-fix missteps, you not only have your "Hello, World!" app running on the simulator, but you've got a three-level table view and are even displaying jpegs of your cat. Good job. But you want to have it run on your iPhone. What do you do?

> **Note**   This book, unless otherwise noted, uses the term *iPhone* to describe the broader set of Apple devices for which we will be developing, including the iPad and iPod Touch. This serves a couple of purposes. First, it makes the text much more concise. Again, as an intermediate-level developer, you already know that we can create iPhone-only, iPad-only, or Universal apps. Second, our example projects use the iPhone as a target device. In some cases, such as when we're targeting Apple Watch using the currently available tools and frameworks, this is actually required, as Watch can only be paired with an iPhone at this time.

Like just about anything else when creating software projects, all the individual pieces are pretty simple. You follow a predefined sequence of steps to achieve your goal. Just like the first time you became comfortable with the `if-then-else` clause, getting to the point of delivering an iOS app to the Apple App Store requires several actions that become more and more familiar each time you go through them. That's one of the purposes of this book. I want to go through them with you in order for you to gain that familiarity. But more than that, I want to show you the obstacles you might encounter along the way, confront them with you, and work out how to make it to a successful conclusion. In a sense, I'm being a bit selfish. I want to make you into the kind of developer with whom I would choose to work.

So, back to the problem of getting your app into the App Store. We will, of course, go through this in great detail later in the book, but let's look at a simple preview.

You first buy an Apple developer license, log in, and then create and download developer certificates to your computer (Figure 1-2). Next, you create your app identifiers, which are basically the names of your apps, then you add your device or devices on which you intend to execute your code. Next, you create provisioning profiles that you download to your device.

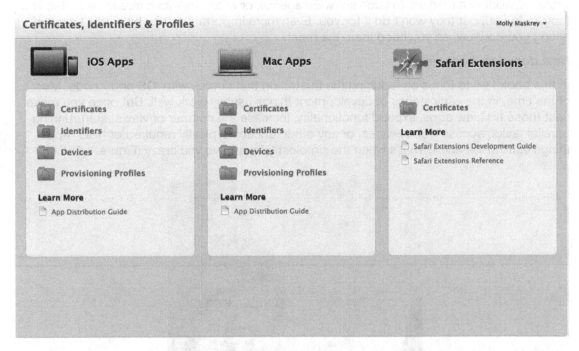

Figure 1-2. While it may seem daunting at first, I'll walk you through a simple, step-by-step procedure to take your app from the simulator to your device in no time

While this may sound like a bunch of gibberish when you've had your head buried in for-loops, alerts, libraries, debuggers, and all that, once the setup steps are done correctly, you can build your app from Xcode and run it on your device. It's no more complicated than learning to effectively use your IDE or the simulator.

As an intermediate developer reading this book, you've most likely done this many times already. If you haven't done it, don't worry; we're going to go through it in agonizing detail in Chapter 3. If you have been through these steps, it probably seemed daunting at first, and some of the things that were supposed to work didn't, but either by perseverance or blind luck you got it to run on your phone. Let's hope it was the former.

But what a sense of pride! You created something that you can take with you to show your friends and family. I'm not being sarcastic; you've truly accomplished something. I remember the first years that Xcode was available for iPhone OS (as it was called back then). Everyone that had seen an iPhone downloaded it to try it out. What happened? It was so complicated to use and the process was so convoluted that the vast majority simply gave up.

Of course, things are much better now. The tools and processes streamline the work flow, and in many cases Xcode can fix most of the common problems associated with not only your code, but the process as well. Just as code hinting provides invaluable assistance in writing correct syntax, and the quick look help delivers just about whatever property and method formats you might need to access, Xcode now includes built-in assistance, much of it automated, to deal with these process problems.

Still, you must understand each of the steps if you're to ever deliver your work to the App Store, or work at a medium to large software agency, or even work as a freelance coder. The tools help you, but they won't do it for you. Even more importantly, they have this knack of letting you down when you need them the most.

How does this book help?

In this book I try to focus on reducing the frustration that comes with iOS and Xcode. Most of the time, in the early stages of development things usually work well. But once you move past those first few apps, expand functionality, increase the number of views, start running parallel tasks, access web services, or any other function typically required of "real" apps, things start to fall apart. That's when the simplest things drive you crazy (Figure 1-3).

Figure 1-3. My number one goal with this book is to reduce the frustration you experience in your early development career

You've worked for two hours to get a view's layout to look good, but when you rotate the simulator screen it falls apart. Or worse, it looks great on the simulator but on a real device it becomes unrecognizable. Similarly, you work through your app's design, coding, functionality, testing, and it's perfect, but when you try to upload it to the App Store, dozens of issues prevent you from leaving your computer to do something else. This and other similar problems create a sense of failure and, more devastatingly, a desire to just give up and do something else. You need to understand that you will never be 100 percent ready for this. If you are and have never experienced any such frustrations, then you're probably not pushing your limits. And to be honest, I really don't want to work with someone who doesn't push themselves. After all, there's not a project that I work on in Xcode where some frustration doesn't send me into a panic thinking I'll never get it to work. I question myself. Did I not think clearly about the design? Did I not understand the description of the framework? Or is this just beyond my capabilities?

There will be problems, and those problems will create frustrations that in turn may create doubt in yourself and in your own abilities to pursue this as a viable career. I often talk to aspiring developers, especially women and girls, who want to pursue software development as a career. Without getting into the socio-political issues surrounding males versus females in technology, quantitative information confirms that such a disparity exists. You can read pretty much any article and find that women are somewhere around 25 percent of the tech workforce. From a purely anecdotal, but personal perspective, I see this as well. At technology meetups, excluding those that are female focused such as Women Who Code, I'll see one or two females at most. When I'm at a software agency interviewing for my own projects or in support of one of my clients, I rarely talk with female engineers. Admittedly, I've become somewhat biased in this and actively seek out female-owned or female-run businesses with which to consult.

And that's not the way it should be. In my company, we want the best, most cost-effective software developers for our projects that we can find and afford. We don't always need the developer with 200 projects under their belt; we may need basic development skills but with the ability to meet tight deadlines. In the latter case, the essence of what I talk about in this book is still critical. The developer still needs to understand how to get the app to market, but she might not have to be an advanced game theory programmer.

As women, many of us see things differently. I can't speak for anyone other than myself, but early in my engineering career I found myself shying away from taking on projects or applying to jobs where I did not think I was 100 percent ready and qualified. I thought I had to meet every single requirement and "nice to have" on the advertisement. Many of my male friends with less experience and, I'd like to think, with less qualifications than I possess applied for and often got the position. This drove me crazy. What made it worse was when they would ask me for advice on how to do something.

Through these frustrations, the idea that I would never be 100 percent ready surfaced. More importantly, I understand now that this is okay. Much of the time, no one meets all the requirements of an advertised job position. In talking to technical people working at various companies as well as some human resources professionals, what the companies look for is the ability to learn and adapt in addition to the basic needs of the job. That said, I came up with this mantra:

1. You're never going to be 100 percent ready.

2. Do it anyway.

3. Just get started.

This works for just about anything where the odds seem like they're against us.

When you see your dream position open up at a company where you'd love to be employed, but you just don't think you have those last two skills, give it a try. While every case is not the same, sometimes your passion for the position or the company might be more important to the interview team than whether you have Scrum certification.

If you're fortunate enough to land that interesting job you discovered and want to excel at it, even if it seems overwhelming at times, just keep going. The information is all out there. Hundreds, if not thousands, have gone before you. You'll get there.

That's a lot of what this book is about. It shows that you are going to encounter problems along the way, but that those problems are solvable. Having been through most of these problems before, how am I going to convince you I know what I'm talking about? I'm going to make my friends suffer. In fact, I personally put in the roadblocks that they will soon encounter. But don't tell them.

For fun, I recruited several of my good friends (or at least they were at the start of all this) as "guinea pigs" to do some app development. These are smart people who understand technology but have never written code—well, not this type of code, anyway (Figure 1-4).

Figure 1-4. To try and understand the actual problems new developers face every day, I recruited friends to start down the path of an app developer. I'm hoping they'll remain friends at the end of all this

One good friend who was recruited as a social media engineer took on website maintenance with a decent familiarity with HTML and CSS, but not much more than that. My friends all use an iPhone, and some have an Apple Watch; even more importantly, they all have ideas for apps they'd like to create. Some are what you might call "power users," while others are just very comfortable with technology.

I decided to help them with their various projects because the ideas were pretty sound and were different enough to cover a broad set of skills and challenges that were reflective of many of the problems that you'll see as you travel down this path. We banged our heads against the keyboard so you don't have to. We explored some of the most common issues of app development. Think of them as the nuances—the subtle things that just seem to show up when working on your project. Not all of the nuances are huge problems or bugs, but if you haven't seen them before or don't have a clue as to how to address them, they have the same head-banging potential as any app crash.

We'll get into each of these issues in the individual chapters that follow, but let's take a look at an example. Many self-employed developers don't use source-code tools or develop unit tests despite the cost and time savings being widely documented. It's just too easy to create a new single-view app project and start prototyping. Before you know it, the app is too far along to consider it just a prototype. It's working fine and you can figure out how to archive the code later. Or, there's so much "meaty" code that it would take too much effort to start developing unit tests. Where would you begin, anyway?

Take any post-secondary development course and two things that are bound to come up are source control and testing. It only makes sense. Lose your project code without a backup and you're nearly back to square one. Or send an app out into the field, even if it's just beta testing, without proper code coverage using unit tests, and the problems will start rolling in. What's worse, you won't really have a place to start.

Source-code control, especially using Xcode's integrated git and Github support, should raise your confidence level. You can work and test and try new things without fearing that you'll lose track of where it last all functioned correctly. It's easy to roll back your project to any stage in your development as long as you follow a few simple rules.

In researching this book, I met with many app developers in the early stages of their iOS careers. Generally, the breakdown was about half looking to get into any technology and thought creating apps sounded like a good idea. The other half included people from different technical disciplines, but mostly web developers who saw more potential in or just liked the idea of mobile software.

This book exists as a combination of two styles. First, the bulk of the writing describes the concrete, the objective scope of the work . . . you need to do this, here's how you do it. But, because this book is not just about fixing problems, but also fixing frustration, I chose to include some of the subjectivity. What does it feel like when you come across a stumbling block or seemingly insurmountable problem? How do you get past it?

At the time of writing this paragraph, I don't know exactly what will happen. As I've said before, I see so many people give up because of the seemingly nonsensical steps a developer must take to accomplish what should be straightforward. Though there are reasons for the complexity, that is no help when you're banging your fist on the keyboard two hours past your bedtime.

This book attempts to help the developer push past those stumbling blocks and move toward a rewarding career that can last a lifetime.

Career

In the previous section, you found references to career opportunities sprinkled throughout the text. Why is that important in this book? Wouldn't everything here be equally applicable no matter where you worked? Before we get to that question, I want to discuss the three basic career paths that I've had the fortune to enjoy.

When apps started appearing in 2008–2009 there were stories of developers, young and old, striking it rich with their great ideas. Games took center stage, but utilities, educational software, and various other categories had their fair share of breakout hits as well. Early on, you didn't see lots of mobile software companies stand out. I remember when I wanted to take a break from working for myself, at home and somewhat alone, it was tough finding companies here in Denver that actually did iOS development. Most companies were in the Bay Area, Los Angeles, Seattle, and on the East Coast.

That, of course, changed pretty quickly. iOS, Android, and Windows development firms exist in Denver, Boulder, Colorado Springs, and everywhere in between. This is most likely the situation you'll find where you live or nearby.

Career Path #1: Employee

Without revealing my age, when I attended college any career other than working for a large company seemed like a second-rate alternative. Big companies offered higher starting salaries, medical insurance, vacation, benefits, retirement, and even bonuses. Working for a company like IBM was the dream of everyone in my engineering class. There was the security of knowing you'd always have a job. I was fortunate to be one of two graduates to actually go to work for IBM, and my mother was so very proud. When I told her a few years later I was leaving for another company she actually cried and told me what a mistake I was making. Back then IBM was a real player in technology. Today, I couldn't tell you what they do.

In the late 1990s dot-com startups were everywhere. I lived in Silicon Valley at the time (Figure 1-5) and had first-hand experience seeing the lavishness, office and housing shortages, and traffic jams. You could leave a job one day and have something new before cocktail hour. I remember banner planes flying over our parking lot displaying URLs of companies that would up your salary no matter what you made.

Figure 1-5. Silicon Valley at the turn of the twenty-first century became the litmus test for ventures capable of survival in the dynamic world of technology

These companies were not like IBM, and nobody expected they would work 30 years and retire from pets.com. Everybody's dream seemed to be to work a few years and cash out when the company was bought out. Most companies failed. At the time I worked for Lockheed-Martin in a very stable but unremarkable career as an aerospace systems engineer. My work interested me, it made an impact in the world, and I was financially comfortable.

Several of my friends joined startups and guess what? None of them made it big. In all cases the startups disappeared after suffering months or even years in a business coma where there were no customers and the funding well that had seemed endless dried up.

Today's software companies offer a seemingly mixed bag. You get the structure and security of a steady paycheck, insurance, and other perks but operate in a mostly startup-like mode. Many companies claim to offer unlimited vacation time. To me, that makes no sense, because if it were true I could get hired and go on vacation for the rest of the year or longer. Now, of course there are limitations to this, but then why advertise unlimited vacation if it is not, in fact, unlimited? It's more like you're not set at two or three weeks when you start and if, say, you finish a major assignment, then get married, your boss will probably let you have an extra week or maybe two. In all cases management has final say on this.

The point is to not be swayed by the promises of job postings or recruiters. Sometimes the people you interview with may give you the facts, but those cases are rare. Just have an open but skeptical mind when interviewing. Assess the good, the bad, and what seems too good to be true.

To get a job with an established software company, from small, locally owned shops to the major players, you want to have the basic set of tools addressed in this book. Everything we cover, except for issues dealing with starting your own business, should be part of your skill set or at least your vocabulary. You may not know exactly how to use Quartz or Metal, but at least by understanding the basic concepts you won't turn a highly interactive interview into one where it seems like they want to push you out the door.

Career Path #2: Entrepreneur

While having a bad boss when working for a larger company can be disheartening, and dealing with traffic two or three hours a day may drive you to madness, neither compares to the stress of doing everything yourself. You still have the constant barrage of bosses (clients) telling you that what they need is not what is written on their contract. You'll suffer constant pleading to reduce your rate, or your hours, or take an equity stake, or some other offer that's not likely to pay the rent or get that new water heater you need.

And on the other side will be the constant paperwork dealing with licenses, tax filings, and investor meetings—if you're lucky enough to get investors. Speaking of investors, unless you have enough free capital to fund your startup, you'll want to use other people's money if you can. That's why having a great idea can boost your potential.

But a great idea is only the seed. You must have a business plan (Figure 1-6) to succeed. And yes, most business plans are not worth the electrons used to create them, but any investor will need to see yours. This brings up the question: What will your business do?

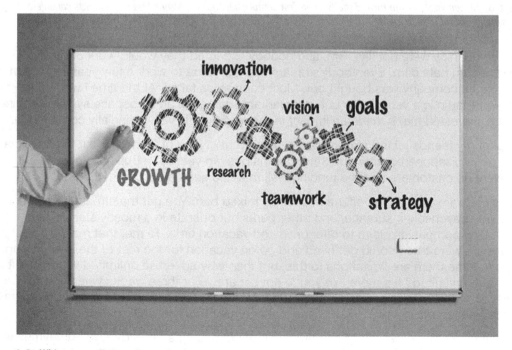

Figure 1-6. Without a well-thought-out business plan, you're setting your company and yourself up for failure

Generally, your best option is to start a consulting business where you take on development projects. Let's say a couple of entrepreneurs come to you with an idea for the latest social media breakout, perhaps Facebook but with a different color scheme. They have a lot of money and really want you to build their app for them. What do you do?

With a consulting company, you'll be hard pressed to find investors to get you started. Money people just won't see the ROI (return on investment) they're looking for via your writing a hundred lines of code or so each day. Luckily, there are other funding options, which we'll talk about in the next chapter.

If you have a great idea for an app, get in line. It's like any diner in Hollywood circa 1960. Every bartender has a script and every waitress is an actress looking to break out. Fortunately, social media tools such as Vimeo and YouTube have leveled the playing field somewhat.

Everyone seems to have a great app concept. Mention yours to a few people and you'll likely hear, "Oh, it's like such-and-such." The good news, I believe, is that there are still a lot of opportunities for mobile software development. In late 2015 Apple introduced the iPhone 6S and 6S Plus along with the iPad Pro. Both device types offer new, unique features that can be leveraged, such as force touch on the iPhone and the larger screen size and stylus capability with the Pro. Coming up with a unique concept that can utilize new features in an exciting and novel manner sets you apart from the crowd. As with the other two types of career paths, we'll discuss this shortly, but if you can create something that provides recurring revenue, such as the in-app purchases of gaming, you might have a chance to attract some investors.

Career Path #3: Contractor

We've talked about starting your own business as an alternative to working for someone else, so think of contracting as the bridge between working as an employee and running your own business. Working as a contractor, like anything, has its plusses and minuses, but it all depends what you're looking to find. I've been on all three paths. For many years early on, I worked at large companies offering lots of job security, but as the economy changed, those promises evaporated quickly.

Being somewhat older, I found myself at loose ends. Should I find another company, participate in the dot-com boom that was happening in the Valley, or do something else? I was fortunate, because the business explosion escalated property values, giving me some choices. I took some time off but stayed current with my skills. Then the iPhone came out and changed everything.

A lot of us in technology at the time were skeptical of Apple getting into the phone business. Sure, the iPod and iTunes were doing incredibly well, but phones were changing so much at that time. The trend was definitely to go smaller, and the iPhone seemed counter to that. Plus, there was the Newton fiasco.

It, of course, took off, and all my non-techie friends had an iPhone long before I did. About a year later Apple opened things up to allow user-created apps, which was about the time I got my iPhone 3G, and things really went crazy. Each day you heard of another app success story.

I developed my iPhone OS skills and created my first app, a slot machine game (Figure 1-7). I was fortunate to have worked in embedded systems for many years, enabling me to quickly understand the concept of running small programs on a phone with limited memory and processing power.

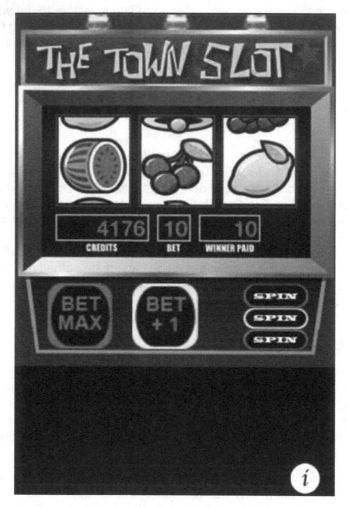

Figure 1-7. Your first app idea can be as simple as this slot machine game developed by the author to gain experience coding for the iPhone in 2009

With some app ideas in hand, none of which seemed all that great—plus I was still at the early stages of developing my Xcode skills—I started looking to work for someone else. There were some opportunities here in Colorado, and I eventually landed a 1099 contract position with an up and coming software agency trying to establish a Denver office.

We'll talk about this more in a later chapter, but even though you're an independent contractor, you have to follow the rules set down by the company but without the perks and benefits. Also, you're not guaranteed a 40-hour work week, so if you're looking for a steady paycheck, this might not be the best choice. It really depends on the company, the projects they have in the queue, and how well you fit in with the culture.

Working as a contractor for a company, however, is not your only option. If you're okay with sporadic income you can create a profile on a freelancing site. Upwork, formerly Elance, allows customers to locate project-based talent directly and choose based on their needs and resources (Figure 1-8). As a developer, you list yourself, your specialty, and any other information you want to advertise on the site to get projects. Much like airbnb, this concept brings together the service provider with the customer, mostly eliminating the middleman and managerial overhead.

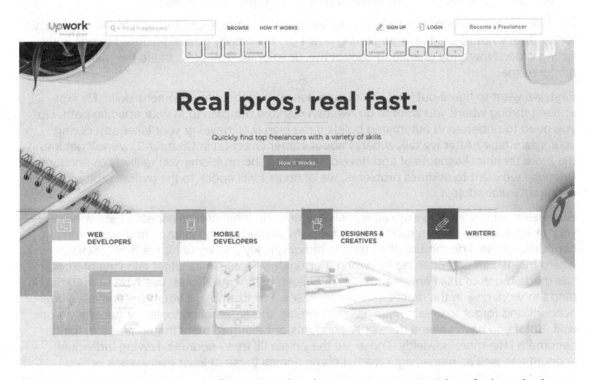

Figure 1-8. Companies such as Upwork offer you the tools and resources to get you started as a freelance developer

As a freelancer you can set your rates and choose which projects would be a good fit for your skills and lifestyle. According to the site, each year freelancers earn over one billion dollars through the online workplace. You can work by the hour or per project, and if you choose to go hourly, the site has tools to let you track your time. If you choose to work on a project basis, then you're paid at completion of milestones you set with your client.

Okay, this connected workspace seems like a really good thing, but it still has a very important point to consider—you still have a boss. Your client is now your boss, and they can be incredibly demanding. When you interview at a company, most of the time you'll meet your boss and co-workers during the interview process. You're able to tell if it's a good fit or not. You won't have that when you're a freelancer. We'll discuss this at length in Chapter 2.

Our Plan

With the understanding that our goal is to develop the skills necessary to further our career in iOS development, how are we going to get there? Attaining a comprehensive set of skills in this area does not lend itself to a linear process. That is, we don't learn source-code control after learning UX skills after setting up our provisioning. It's more of a need-to-learn-it-all-at-once kind of thing. Unfortunately, no one I know can read multiple chapters simultaneously, so we just have to make do with a sequential process.

I'll go through a sequence of instruction based on the experiences that got me to where I am today. That's not to say I'm regurgitating how I did it; in many cases, I learned things in the wrong order. Now's my chance to correct the situation so you don't make the mistakes that hindered me.

First, we want to figure out how you plan to use your mobile development skills. By first understanding where you want to go, we can reshape our plan to fit your specific path. Do you need to understand automated builds if the plan is to develop your killer app during your spare time? After we talk in detail about career direction in Chapter 2, we will get into the more technical aspects of app development and the problems you're likely to encounter. Because we want to address problems, we of course will speak to the overall procedures for each particular subject.

Because getting your app onto an actual device is the most critical aspect of showing off your skills, we take that on early in Chapter 3. As someone who already has a few apps in her portfolio, we'll go through the process rather quickly and try to hit the high points of where things can and often do go wrong. Fortunately, Apple in its latest releases of Xcode has made much of this semi-automatic. But, like most things Xcode, this type of automation tends to work only in the most basic of use cases. For example, if you have one developer account and forgot to create a provisioning profile, the automation tools will generally work well. But if you have several developer accounts or belong to more than one team, things become a little more unwieldy. Those are the points I'll try to address. Having individual accounts as well as managing a team, I come across these at least every week or two.

Chapter 4 presents an overview of the code we'll be developing and referencing throughout the book. We'll tackle four major projects plus a number of smaller, partial ones as we move forward. The four major projects, including source code, are detailed in the last chapters as reference and are included because I have devoted significant time to them over the years. As needed, we'll look at smaller projects, code snippets in some cases, that act as a better reference depending on what we're discussing.

If you're developing apps for profit, whether as a contractor, employee, or running your own business, please get started with source-code control, which we discuss in Chapter 5. A few years ago when Apple first started integrating Git tools into Xcode I was so happy, until I tried to use it and everything broke down and I lost some of my files. I still maintained backups on Github, but I never used Xcode to do it, relying instead on third-party tools such as Tower. Even while I was working at a company a few years ago, Tower was the de facto standard for managing backups and source control.

My writing style, or perhaps it's the way I think and form concepts, causes me to shift around a bit, not necessarily keeping to a purely sequential organization (Figure 1-9), so in Chapter 6 we'll take a step out of the trenches and spend some time talking about methodologies. If you come from large corporate engineering firms you're most likely familiar with the waterfall project design. For years this was the norm. First, you design everything until it's perfect, then you start coding or developing. I must have worked on two dozen projects this way; ISO standards, six-sigma, and all kinds of other buzzwords were tossed around with statistics explaining why this was the best way to do things. Fact of the matter was that of all two dozen projects, or however many it actually turned out to be, none came out on time or on budget.

Figure 1-9. I'll occasionally change up the flow to engage you and keep things from getting too stale or boring

Agile development, while not by any means perfect, provides a completely different mindset to development. To provide a spoiler, you start developing almost immediately and see what happens. This works really well if you're a tinkerer like me. When I see a new feature or framework, I quickly create a simple project and play around. While not exactly the agile process we're looking for, the gist of it is the same; you want to quickly see what works, and more importantly what doesn't work, so your time is better spent during the development process.

For the customer, this results in quicker delivery. For your organization, you spend less time going down paths that don't return good results, which lowers your cost of project development and increases profit, assuming project-oriented pricing. Even if your company bills its clients hourly, and the reduction in number of hours may appear to lower your revenue stream because you're doing less work, in actuality you will almost always wind up using that "found time" for other aspects of the project. This extra effort increases the quality of the project, which in turn gets you more business from the existing client as well as better referrals that let you capture new business.

Chapter 7 takes us back into being hands-on with Xcode and specifically into how we develop the user interfaces and overall user experience. Quite frankly, I am not an expert in UI/UX creation. In most companies you generally find these functions split between two departments or sections. The design group develops the look and feel of the app—the colors, the sizes, and the shapes of the buttons or windows. Think of them as the CSS portion of a website. The engineering group creates the coding; for us, this would be the Swift code using the Xcode development environment. As an interesting crossover, the engineering group also usually instantiates the UI/UX from files delivered from the design group. Basically, you take the design group's "wireframes" and convert them into storyboards and .xib files inside of Xcode.

Continuing our work with Xcode, in Chapter 8 we get serious about building our final products for release into the real world. Specifically, we'll discuss schemes and manual builds. When working in your own business, manual builds are really all you need. But if you intend be employed by, or to act as a contractor for a larger, more established software agency, you'll need a little familiarity with automated code builds. As continuous integration (CI) becomes more and more prevalent at software companies, you'll want to have a handle on the concepts (Figure 1-10). Apple introduced bots a couple years ago in an attempt to supplant the more established Jenkins/Hudson or Travis CI servers. Like all new technology, bots have had their share of issues, and many companies still use one of the other servers as their baseline. But, like what happened with source-code control, the tight integration with Xcode may offer bots an advantage once things become a bit more streamlined.

Figure 1-10. Continuous integration streamlines the testing and distribution processes when multiple developers work on projects together

We won't go into great detail on either option, with the exception of making sure you have enough of a comprehensive understanding to be prepared for your next job interview, either as a direct-hire employee or a contractor.

In Chapter 9 we once again step out of the depths of writing code and look at the world of embedded systems. My experience for the past twenty years focused almost entirely on the embedded space. That's why I was drawn into the world of mobile development. Embedded systems offer a huge variety of real-world things you can interact with. It's no longer just stuff on a display or pulling data from a PHP (PHP: Hypertext Processor) server. With embedded systems, we interact with stuff. For me, this is what it's all about and why I still have passion for the field.

We'll cover how embedded systems began and evolved through the years to become what we now consider everyday devices such as our phones, music players, fitness monitors, tablets, and so on. But then we will move into the world of IoT, the Internet of Things (Figure 1-11). Many see IoT as the next major revolution. We interconnect all the capable devices in our homes and apartments through our mobile devices. We can monitor our doors, feed the dog, start tonight's dinner, track our movement, set the mood, draw the shades, or any of a countless pool of functions that exist today, and many that haven't yet been conceived. As part of a plan creating a modern, connected town, my team uses IoT beacon technology that establishes directed advertising to the consumers in our business district to increase traffic and provide targeted advertising to consumers.

Figure 1-11. We'll cover one of the most exciting new areas of development, the Internet of Things, where we connect and communicate with devices of all kinds including Apple iBeacon technology

Back to the tools in Chapter 10 as we cover getting our app published in the App Store. We'll talk about the App Store in general terms, as anyone familiar with iOS devices must be familiar with the basics if only to update apps and the operating system from time to time. What we're going to focus on are the tools used through each step of the process— specifically, using the iTunes Connect portal to publish our works of art.

Publishing an app really consists of, once we have something we've deemed worthy of putting out into the world, two parts. The first part we mentioned earlier and cover in Chapter 8. We create the archive that gets verified and sent to the App Store. But before that, we need to configure what our app is all about and how it will appear in the store. If you haven't noticed it previously, the non-linearity of the process steps should start to become clearer. We can't publish an app until we have a build to upload, but we can't upload a build until we set up our information in the App Store using the iTunes Connect portal (Figure 1-12). But what if we want to change things a bit before publishing to the App Store? We may want to get a workable build that we can archive and distribute ad hoc before even bothering with iTunes Connect and the App Store. We may not even want to distribute through the App Store if we can distribute through the enterprise.

Figure 1-12. *To publish, advertise, and sell our wonderful application, we'll discover how to work with, and not against, iTunes Connect*

For the most part, once we get to an app build that functions well and is reasonably bug free—we can't find every problem at the start—the steps to get it published in the App Store are pretty straightforward. The problems come in all the details that must be attended to when setting things up to display to the store's subscribers.

One thing you find often in apps other than simple utilities or games is a connection to an external database. Most often we do this through Representational State Transfer Services (REST). Essentially nothing more than reading or writing to a website, our app can share and gather data from any number of users worldwide. We can search business listings, find our way through map databases, or store our own personal information to share with whomever we choose.

As with build automation from Apple trying to supplant the more widely used Jenkins servers, CloudKit (Figure 1-13) provides much of the functionality of REST but is easier to use. The drawback comes from CloudKit currently only working with Apple devices. As such, for the broader mobile ecosystem, it has limited use in its current state. Still, as with other features Apple has added over the years, this will likely change, and it's best that we look at it as an option, especially if you're focusing on iOS only at this time. We'll look at both options and how they might be used in our projects.

Figure 1-13. Apple's CloudKit framework, while limited to iOS and OS X devices, offers a very easy-to-use set of tools for working with information on the Internet

To make a product with which people will interact, testing cannot be overlooked. Just as you wouldn't release a new drug or even food item into the marketplace without testing, neither should you let your apps out into the world unless all the functionality has been rigorously exercised. A few app crashes with cranky customers and your app could be dead before release 1.0 hits the store.

Once your app is ready to go out into the real world, but is not yet available to the general population, you'll distribute your beta release to be tested. Now, with TestFlight integration, you no longer have to create a complex combination of your app bundle and provisioning profile to send to authorized users via email. TestFlight and Xcode have built-in support to make this nearly painless. You have options of either testing internally with your in-house company team or, with a little more work, distributing to a broader set of beta testers.

In Chapter 13, I cover my specialty area, iOS Accessories. We'll look at the various input–output ports by which data can be brought in and sent out of the iPhone. From a simple headphone jack device such as the Square credit card reader (Figure 1-14) to high-speed proprietary connections such as wireless Bluetooth or the wired Lightning connector, the iPhone offers many ways to gather information and provide control capability. I've worked on iOS accessories as part of Apple's MFi program since 2009, when I also developed a credit card reader and companion payment application. Working in the MFi program requires strict adherence to Apple's non-disclosure policies, so many of the details of the plan are, of course, confidential. But the whole point of the plan is to assure customers that a particular device or accessory is compliant with the Apple device to which they intend to connect their purchase. Our discussion of the MFi program, though we'll shy away from the program details and not get into any technical specifics, will look at the types of devices that we can use with our iPhone. We'll look at a wide range of products from personal to B2B (business to business) as well as how we might use the HomeKit framework to integrate devices into our own IoT ecosystem.

Figure 1-14. The Square credit card reader, one of the earliest iPhone accessories, used the headphone jack instead of the 30-pin dock connector, making it cross-platform compatible

In the final few chapters, the projects that we use throughout the text will be described in detail as a reference. I chose four sample projects to cover in their entirety, primarily because they interested me and because they addressed the issues we're discussing in this book. I tried to pick things that I thought would be enjoyable and interesting and spur a sense of creativity and passion but that would also provide useful skills and experience. And, for the most part, I wanted to try to have a little fun by building some things that might be a little different.

Fun

The most important aspect of my life centers on the ability to have fun, so each and every project I take on needs to have an inherent enjoyment to it. I know that, in the early stages of a developer's career, she needs to build her skills and confidence level in order to command a specific salary and work environment. But that doesn't mean I'm going to overwhelm you with writing table view after table view because it's an easy direction to take. As long as I'm running the show, or writing the book anyway, I'm going to do my best to keep you engaged by creating as much interest and enjoyment as I believe possible.

So what are these so-called fun projects I've been going on about? First, we'll tackle a simple conversion from Objective-C to Swift for the slot machine game app that I mentioned earlier. Called Town Slot, a play on words of course, the app contains three spinning wheels, a couple of betting choices, and a spin button. Originally written for the iPhone 3G, the code mostly contains deprecated function calls. In preparation for this book, I converted it to more modern Objective-C and have successfully operated the app on iOS 9 devices. Starting from there we'll make the transformation to a full Swift project.

While this may not seem like that much fun, because Swift is still relatively new, having both Objective-C and Swift coding skills might be the differentiator you need to land that developer position. Eventually, Objective-C will likely become less and less supported, so many companies with existing apps may need to convert their old code into Swift. This in and of itself could be a source of income as a freelance developer. Because the conversion is mostly straightforward, less skilled engineers will likely want to take on such mundane projects. As you are trying to expand your skills while building your own portfolio, this could be just the right job for you to take on.

We want to start playing around with the Apple Watch, as it is currently the "latest and greatest thing." As new and creative uses for the Watch start to reveal themselves, development companies and freelancing sites may rapidly increase their need for skilled Watch coders. My very first Watch app was a simple coin-flip game just to get the feel of how everything works. As I was working through it I was surprised how much it took me back to the early days when I did the slot machine game. I felt a sense of freshness that really drove me to complete the project. My friends were so fascinated with something so simple, a number of them have decided to give app development a chance. Through that simple action, making an almost trivial app that actually does something, I may have given people I know, friends, a chance at a better career and life.

As mentioned previously, the Internet of Things is becoming bigger every day. Someone seems to be coming up with a new connected piece of equipment hourly. So let's have fun with it. Apple's HomeKit framework makes this pretty simple and offers built-in security features not currently found in the vast landscape of IoT products out there today. We'll extend what we cover in the main part of the book with a project that allows us to control a power outlet in our home. Recently, I was asked to give a talk about HomeKit and the Internet of Things and so I created the demo on which this project is based. I could have turned on a simple lamp, but instead chose to start up a flashing, rotating, colored disco ball (Figure 1-15). The audience loved it, and I got so much attention after the talk, the organizers had to shoo us all out of the auditorium. The point again being, have fun in and passion for what you're doing and you'll likely never dread going to work.

Figure 1-15. Using HomeKit to monitor and control devices provides an easy-to-use, flexible, and rational way to control everything from doorbells to disco balls

Our final project incorporates elements near and dear to my heart. I take my experience and interest in embedded systems and combine that with a need to create an impact in the world and form something that could potentially assist thousands, if not millions, of older individuals.

By profession I'm actually an electrical engineer; I took on iOS development to create near off-the-shelf tools that were affordable for a larger percentage of the population. Frankly, as I'll try to continue to stress, I couldn't find developers with the needed skills at an affordable rate. In fact, I couldn't find any developers early on that really understood all the aspects of iOS development needed to make real, interactive hardware systems that were truly useful. I'm not saying I'm special, just that the dictates of the broader market were elsewhere at the time. My concept is to minimize new and complex development to only that which is absolutely required. For everything else—reuse, reuse, reuse. That's what we'll do here.

Last year I designed and built a small sensor that provides information on movement and orientation. It's really just a printed circuit board (PCB) containing what everyone already has in their smartphone or fitness monitor without everything else. We're going to capture a couple pieces of information from that sensor to tell us its orientation. Imagine an XY plane parallel with the ground. If you change the angle in either the X, or the Y, or both axes, we're going to receive that information, really the two angles, and do something with it. Okay, here's where you get to know me a little better. I'm going to measure the angle of the foot. Specifically, I'm going to look at the pitch of the foot and the side to side roll of the foot.

Why? Well, I'm a dancer, a ballroom dancer to be clear, and I was looking for a way to judge how correct or incorrect a student's foot positions were while learning. This sensor could be mounted on a shoe (Figure 1-16) or within an orthotic insert and in real time measure two angles of the dancer's feet. And although we'll look at one sensor to make things easy, multiple sensors are no problem at all. Combined with the haptic feedback provided by using an Apple Watch, the dancer immediately knows whether or not to correct her stance without deviating from her frame.

Figure 1-16. *In one of our projects we'll explore measuring the angles of a dancer's feet in order to quantify and help perfect her artistic performance*

While this is fun, for me anyway, and I hope for you, it's not really taking on the impact feature I mentioned a couple paragraphs ago. What does it do for humankind? Let's extrapolate a bit. What if this same sensor were placed on a person at their core or center of gravity and could determine how much they were in or out of balance. More than just tracking falls—anyone remember, "Help, I've fallen and I can't get up?"—this technology, so simple at its origin, can teach us the *why* of geriatric falls (Figure 1-17). That's the basics of it anyway; the actual implementation is a touch more detailed, this is the space where I find the motivation to get up in the morning and get started. And it's not just my uncle or your grandmother; this type of creativity potentially helps everyone. Quickly, let's look at a few statistics. According to the National Council on Aging, one-third of Americans aged sixty-five and older fall each year. Every thirteen seconds an older adult is treated in the emergency room for a fall, and every twenty minutes an older adult dies from a fall. From a fiscal standpoint the numbers get worse in a few years. In 2013 the total cost of fall injuries was $34 billion and is expected to be over $60 billion in 2020. Passion and impact plus financial opportunity; that's what we want to look for when choosing our future. It's not about just doing what makes you happy or becoming a millionaire. Make the difference that you want to see happen in an occupation that affords you all you need to be happy.

Figure 1-17. More than just work, the things we do, the devices we make, and the software we write can deliver an impact that changes lives for the better. For me, making a difference is why I do what I do

My goal throughout this book is for you to find your motivation, or more specifically, your passion. Maybe it's in sports performance, or rehab because your grandparents are getting older and you care about them. Maybe your passion lies somewhere else altogether that I have no concept of. Whatever it is, wherever it lies, seek it out, and when you can, use your newfound skills to do what you truly love.

You can do it. Just get started.

Chapter 2

Career Direction

As mentioned in the previous chapter, we'll discuss the three basic career options afforded to most app engineers—specifically, to iOS software engineers. There will always be variations that exist, but in general, what follows is a pretty good classification of your options. These are the three options to which I can personally speak, as I've tried them all. Each has its pros and cons, but only you can determine for yourself the differentiators and their importance to your future plans. You may want the consistency of a steady paycheck and are willing to sacrifice choosing what projects you want to take on and give up the freedom of your days. Or, you might go all in deciding to form your own startup to take on the world knowing the risks inherent in that path. I want to give you enough insight to choose wisely or at least to give it some thought before committing.

Option #1: Working as an Employee

The most common track people tend to follow as they develop their software skills seems to be taking a position at an established company. As they finish their training and pass that last examination, the desire surfaces to stop chasing something, take a break, and just get to work. The company pays you a salary and often other benefits such as insurance and vacation. You work a more or less consistent schedule such as 9 to 5, or it could be rotating or even project-based schedule. You'll typically work at their office location, which could be in a hip, cool, and upcoming part of town, or it might be at any of the million or so look-alike industrial complexes from uptown to out in the 'burbs (Figure 2-1). You'll drive to work or take whatever mass transit your town offers. Many companies now offer public transit passes as perks to reduce wear and tear on your vehicles, but more often, they are likely motivated by getting credits for reducing traffic and pollution from the local government. Either way, it's still a nice perk that you can enjoy, and I personally loved taking light rail to town. This option works well for the individual coming from a more traditional background or who is looking for more stability and consistency in her life.

© Molly K. Maskrey 2016

M.K. Maskrey, *App Development Recipes for iOS and watchOS*, DOI 10.1007/978-1-4842-1820-4_2

Figure 2-1. Quite often, as an employee you'll find yourself working at a bland technology park

Even though the trend away from open workspaces is slowly gaining momentum, unless you're a very senior person, you won't have that corner office or cubicle that was such a mainstay of corporate America a few decades ago. Most likely you'll work at a large table with anywhere from four to eight people grouped by department (Figure 2-2). Engineers developing the code sit together with other engineers, as do the designers, quality assurance team, and any other groups. In many cases iOS developers sit with iOS people and the same with Android, Microsoft, or web-based talent. It makes sense. You play with the people with whom you have something in common. You get immediate help and assistance when trying to solve a problem. The inherent synergy of the team spurs on creativity and a sense of teamwork.

Figure 2-2. Typically, software teams work cooperatively in open environments that generally lead to more interaction between members, thus increasing productivity

Because little competitions seem to spontaneously happen (and this happens more among men, or should I say boys), the group may work frequent overtime to best each other and see who can eke out that last few milliseconds in some sort of routine or graphics render. You'll likely have a fridge stocked with soda, snacks, easily heated food, and lots of other amenities to tempt you to continue to stay at the office and produce code. For the younger, more driven engineers, especially those right out of school, this feels like an extension of college life. For the self-taught developer, this may be the college experience they never had. But the seasoned engineer can often feel like a fish out of water. For the female in technology, it can often seem worse, but it's often due to our fewer numbers. Eventually, our quality of work shows through and we become an integral part of the team.

But if this is what you're looking for, it could very well be your dream job. If you're an older engineer, trying to keep up with the developers could give you the opportunity to show off tricks the kids might not have ever considered. You'll be considered the go-to guy for deep technological challenges, typically when algorithms or external hardware becomes involved. You'll participate in beer-pong matches on Fridays and maybe even get invited to the local pub afterward.

For women, things are a little different, and the situation, like everything, can be good or bad. First, I've never found overt discrimination in any organization I've worked for or with in the past ten or so years. Before that, well, I get so mad thinking about it I don't want to even discuss it. That's a subject that matters deeply to me but is meant for a different forum. Many companies welcome women in earnest, but watch out for the ones merely trying to balance out their numbers. If you interview somewhere and there are no women on the development team, I'd consider trying to find out why.

Looking at demographics, the National Center for Women in Information Technology reports that in 2014 only 26 percent of professional computing occupations were held by women. While there may be endless arguing about the why of this and different ways to fix it, my point is that when going for a developer position at a company as a woman, be prepared to be outnumbered by the boys three to one. I don't hold any prejudice here; I simply don't wish anyone, no matter their age, race, gender, preferences, or anything else to go into a situation unprepared. Again, as a business owner, I look for the very best developers I can find.

Whatever you do and however you go about it, be mindful of what the outcome might be. Personally, I pick and choose my battles. If the most important thing to me is getting a job that pays a certain amount, and I really need that to get by, I might make allowances and overlook things that seem to be a bit off. It's up to you and what you're able to deal with, whether you're young and just starting out, older and concerned about keeping up, or a woman in a predominantly male organization. Hey, you could go in, show them how great you are, take on a leadership role, and then make the changes you see are needed.

A good friend of mine works in a position she doesn't really like very much in a company. Working directly for the company, she receives a salary and benefits, including vacation and health insurance. As with any job, there are always good and bad situations. Some you can deal with, others you just have to suck up and learn to take by finding some way to diffuse the situation for yourself without causing bigger problems. It's not a great situation, but it just tends to be the way things turn out for a lot of people (Figure 2-3).

Figure 2-3. A lot of millennials took positions of interest to themselves, but soon discovered the salary wasn't meeting their day-to-day needs. A software development career offers a well-paying and challenging position with opportunities in many different areas that could fill that personal need to make an impact and have fun

She's not in technology nor is she really in the field for which she went to school, studied, and trained. Like so many people in the millennial generation (born roughly between 1980 and 2000) she was told that money didn't matter as much as doing what makes you happy. So, like thousands of others, my friend went to college because it was the thing to do, choosing to study what interested dominated. She worries every month about bills and what she might have to cut out should rent increase or her car breaks down. The sad thing is that it was mostly my generation that sold her that bill of goods. It's not that happiness doesn't matter; it's just that in any situation you have to look at the whole picture and weigh all the options and alternatives. Because she is my friend, I'm helping her to develop a high quality set of iOS and generalized software skills that she can use, hopefully in the near future, to make a change and control her life as she sees fit. There is no one answer to everything, and all I can do is try to help, whether it's my best friend or the anonymous reader who happened to pick up or download a copy of this book.

You've heard me say that I believe passion and fun in what you do, especially in mobile development, are key to achieving happiness in your career. It may not last forever, but when it's no fun anymore, you should really take time to assess what's going on. We'll talk about that later, but for now, you should be a little confused with what I'm saying. On the one hand I'm telling you to seek out and look for happiness in your career, and on the other hand I'm talking about my friend, who was told much the same thing and now finds herself frustrated with her choices.

I want to expand on this to maybe enlighten you as to why this situation exists at all. I mean, there are thousands of software and iOS development jobs going unfulfilled each and every day. At the same time, there are thousands if not tens of thousands of capable young women and men to take these positions and advance themselves and society.

My friend and I are of different generations. She doesn't hold it against me that my generation—teachers, counselors, business people of the day, and so on—essentially screwed her over. What happened was that my "people" told her to not worry about money but rather to shoot for happiness and things would all work out.

The reason why, I believe, is that the same thing happened to us, but in an opposite way. My own mother, as I mentioned earlier, wanted me to take a job with a big company, like I did with IBM (Figure 2-4), and stay there forever. I was rebellious enough not to follow her instruction and continued to move about, getting significant salary increases as I went, but of course losing all that valuable seniority my mother so wanted me to have. I consider myself extremely lucky to have taken that path. Anything even remotely similar to the position I held at IBM was wiped out long ago as the iconic organization faded away. My friends who stayed found themselves with a meager enough retirement to live on, but are still working at odd jobs just to get out of the house or provide a little extra income. I never see them anymore, even though I'm back in Denver, where I had many work friends at IBM. While I've stayed pretty active in the technology scene through networking and meetup events, they've simply vanished.

Figure 2-4. Even former behemoths such as IBM have seen radical changes to their product strategy as technology such as mobile devices becomes commonplace

I have relatives my age who don't know what a tablet is or how to use Pandora or still can't do more than make a call on a smartphone. What happened? I think it's simple and boils down to one word: adaptation. In nature, whether you're a creationist or Darwinian, there exist, without a doubt, forms of adaptation. If you are not a global warming believer, you most likely think that the population will somehow adapt if there are changes really happening. And that's what I'm trying to do in this book; stress the importance of being able to adapt. We want to not just learn the basics of building an archive to upload to iTunes or understand how to move data from a server to a mobile device using MySQL and PHP; we want to be able to adapt when things don't work like they're supposed to. We may want to adapt one methodology to another set of requirements, thereby achieving something totally different. You may find after reading my ramblings that you need to adapt your career expectations a bit, one way or another.

So in each and every chapter I hope that, in addition to seeking fun and passion in whatever you may pursue for a career choice, you'll be ready to adapt. Working in the Apple world should make this second nature. A new device or set of devices get announced two to three times a year. New frameworks, changes, deprecated tools, and so on are commonplace. I believe that once you're in this fast-paced, ever-changing world of mobile, adaptation becomes inherent. You don't even think about it anymore. So, let's get into more about what it would mean and what you might need to land that perfect position at a software company.

Potential Employers

I decided to not include any employer survey information gathered from searching Google, assuming that the data would have grown stale by the time this book went to print. When looking at the top iOS developers, based upon surveys from various online tools, one thing became apparent: the results are, in general, pretty arbitrary. No two surveys I found contain the same list of companies in the top 20 or 10 or even 5. I rarely found two lists that contained more than one or two of the same companies. Upon looking a little deeper I saw that on the top lists that come back from an Internet search, to get on the list the company pays a fee to the survey company. That's when things started to click in my brain. These company rankings, to me anyway, seemed to be nothing more than SEO (search engine optimization) techniques applied to ranking, likely to attract potential clients.

I want to relay something a friend told me just yesterday. If you can, try to pick your boss when you're thinking about accepting a job. This will be the person you work for day in and day out. Even if the money and other perks seem too great to pass up, it won't matter much if each day you dread going to the office or signing into the company's chat service. This story really hit home for me personally.

Years ago I worked for a moderate-size software agency focusing on iOS development. I left within a year because the working conditions, for me, were intolerable. I tend to keep my personal and professional life separate, especially when working for a company. Unfortunately, my manager didn't seem to quite understand this concept and would call me during scheduled off or vacation times. They even went so far as to call my partner because I refused to answer my phone while I was out having dinner. This was way too invasive for me, so I made the decision to leave.

I was fortunate enough at the time to have other opportunities that I could pursue. In your case, you might not be as lucky. So the best advice I can offer is to try and get a sense of the person for whom you'll be working early in the process. Obviously you'll want to meet him or her before accepting any position, and any company that doesn't offer you this opportunity should be considered highly suspect.

We'll be talking about this and other things to watch out for throughout this chapter. Only you can decide which aspect of any opportunity you might encounter is important enough to be "must haves" or "deal breakers." I just want to offer some things to think about as we take this journey—usually based on personal experience.

When looking at assessments you'll find on the web (Figure 2-5), you should consider them suspect and partisan. That is, while a company can't necessarily buy their way to the top of the rankings, all research is subjective based on the criteria used. This is true of any research, whether it be for ranking companies or political candidates. As a math major I've never been a fan of polls. So many factors influence the results, and to say this or that poll is within so much margin of error seems ridiculous. The time of day, or the tone of the pollster's voice, or any of a dozen subtle things can affect the outcome. And that's just from the poll-taking side of things. If I'm in a bad mood, I might answer differently based on emotions rather than subjective thoughts.

Figure 2-5. Always review company rankings you find on the Internet with a bit of suspicion. Look for organizations in the open press or on social evaluation sites such as glassdoor.com to get other viewpoints

While analyzing data from rankings you find on the Internet, it's always best to take the following things under consideration. These rankings are a starting point from which to perform your own in-depth analysis and research. From what you discover, formulate your own analysis and then narrow your scope as needs dictate. Probably the first thing you'll want to do is assess companies based on your own geographical region; what companies are close enough to you?

Although finding local employers of interest, especially if you live outside the mobile development hotspots, might seem daunting, there's a trick you can use. Most public libraries have research associates who are waiting to help. As "real" books continue to go out of fashion, libraries look for new ways to provide community services. In reality, many library employees love to help and will deliver, very quickly, exhaustive reports based on whatever criteria you provide to them. It's an amazing resource that no one seems to know about, and I wholeheartedly recommend giving them a try. Of course, like anything, you can never rely on someone or some organization with whom you haven't yet worked, so I suggest starting with some simple, quantifiable criteria for your directed research. Make sure you can independently and objectively determine the correctness of the results as fits your needs.

Another great resource for locating developer positions nearby would be your local employment resource office. They're usually administered by the county in which you reside in conjunction with the state and federal government, which sometimes offer additional funding for training, particularly in hot job areas. Technology tends to be targeted for extra funding. Through these state and federal programs you can get additional education and support for your continued training.

What's even better when looking for the right position is that these agencies usually have information and job listings for actual positions available in your skill area and geographical location. While you might see two or three times as many positions on a job search site, a lot of those can be duplicates offered by various employment agencies. Companies contract several different agencies to find talent for their open positions. Also, sometimes agencies may have particular individuals in mind for a job submittal and could be fishing for other applicants to make the pool look bigger. This is not to say that agencies are inherently bad—quite the contrary. Their business is to fill open slots, and if they didn't, they wouldn't be in business. But if you want to see what the real jobs are out there, I'd seriously consider starting with your local employment agency.

Now, there seems to be a stigma surrounding these places as being a last resort; they are sometimes referred to as unemployment offices. For older adults it can conjure up images of standing in line looking for a job to feed your family in that one-room apartment in the inner city. Most of the time it's quite different. I actually live in one of the most affluent counties in Colorado and I pay a visit to my local office probably once a quarter to see what's going on. What I've found is that the truly serious employers will always list their open positions with my local agency first. They know that the people sent to them are serious about finding a job. Since the listings often come here first, you could be one of the first people in line for an interview. From the hiring company's perspective, their participation in the county's employment endeavors often qualifies them for tax breaks and other financial incentives. There's motivation on both the employer's part and on the government's behalf to reach high employment in the area.

Now that we've talked a bit about some options of how to find positions, let's take a look at the skills you might need to have to land one of these iOS application developer positions.

Skills

In general, you'll need everything we talk about in this book plus a few other skills according to the specifics of the situation. If you want to develop apps in a formal company setting, whether large or small, you'll need to learn a few tools you might overlook if you were to run your own business.

In this book we focus on the set of mobile development skills with an emphasis on iOS and Xcode. Our technical and process needs include the following:

- Setting up Xcode for device installations
- Source-code control
- Development methodology
- Impressing your user
- Building targets
- Embedded systems
- App publishing
- Web services
- Testing
- iOS accessories

Let's take each one in turn and talk about why we may or may not need that particular skill in our goal of working for an employer. In fact, we'll want to have most of these skills when we interview and should even put them on our resume if appropriate.

First, here are a couple of job descriptions I pulled down just this week to get an idea of what's needed for a typical position. I look at various job sites weekly, out of curiosity mostly, but if the right position came along, I might just have a go at it. I've found that, year after year, the requirements seem to be pretty consistent for iOS development positions.

Sample Job Description #1

```
- Native iOS Application Development
- Core Data
- Autolayout & Size Classes
- Git (creation, push, pull, branching, tagging)
- REST and JSON web service connectivity
- SQLite Administration and Data Caching
- Advanced Location Services
- In-App Purchases
- Analytics, Test Deployment and Crash Logging for Apps
- Beta Testing and issue management

In addition we would also like to see the following from any qualified applicants:

- Knowledge in other areas such as PHP, NodeJS, JavaScript, jQuery, MySQL, Socket.IO, Drupal,
  Cocoapods, Angular.js, and other commonly used web and data technologies is also a plus.
- Always learning/asking questions with a desire to refactor code to always improve current
  projects upon learning new material
```

Sample Job Description #2

```
Type of Engagement: Direct hire

What you'll need:
• 1 or more years of iOS mobile application development
• 5 or more years of experience developing commercial software
• Objective-C, SQLite, Xcode, JSON, XML
• At least one application published in the app store
• Expertise in using both storyboards and xibs
• Demonstrable experience in calling restful APIs to sync phone data with a server
```

One way to learn about a company you might someday come to work for is by looking closely at the specified needs and do a little self-analysis of the position. If you have much web experience, it should become pretty clear that these jobs work with iOS apps that access some host information and store it locally. Because the first position contains a need for "Advanced Location Services," I start thinking that their application might be directed advertising or small-scoped mapping and tracking. Because of the emphasis on analytics, beta testing, and so forth, it's much more likely that this would be a consumer or public-facing application as opposed to an internal enterprise function. However, it might just as easily be a location tracking for a small local delivery company. You won't know for certain until you talk to the team, and even then the exact details of the project may not be made clear for confidentiality reasons.

In general, I find that the most flexible requirement tends to be years of experience. That is, assuming you have demonstrable skills for everything else, the length of time you've worked in the field may not matter. As I alluded to earlier, men seem to understand this and always apply anyway. In fact, based on what I know personally from friends or coworkers, men generally are okay with applying for a job if they meet even less than half the stated criteria. Although it's changing somewhat, women tend to be more compliant to the rules and often won't even send in a resume in the same case. And I can speak from personal experience.

For years and years, I never submitted a resume or applied to a company where I didn't meet every qualification on a job ad, even if they didn't make sense. I mistakenly assumed that the postings were written by the manager or engineering team directly associated with the project(s) and thus were set in stone. I think it was at my third job that things started to click. I realized that in that and the previous two positions, I never used half the skills called for on the job description. Quite the opposite, as a matter of fact; I wound up needing skills that weren't on the posting at all. Some of these I had, such as the ability to use PCB layout tools in one instance, and others I learned on the job or through training. What I came away with was the mantra I stated in Chapter 1 and will continue with throughout this book—do it anyway. I attribute the modest successes I've had over the years to that day and that mantra.

Setting Up Xcode for Device Installations

Before we can go beyond basic apps using the iOS simulator, we must first set up our system, including Xcode, for creating real programs that can be put in the App Store.

We'll cover this in operational detail in a future chapter, but what we're looking for now is *why* you need this skill.

This one should be obvious. When working for a company, part of the requirements for a project to which you'll be assigned will be to validate the functionality of the code on all devices specified by the client. If it's supposed to function on an iPad, you'll most certainly test it on an iPad long before it goes to quality assurance. While the simulator does a good job, nothing functions as a substitute for testing on an actual device. You'll most certainly demonstrate code functionality on actual devices to the client as part of the agile development process. We'll get more into this in Chapter 3, but let me say it again: no matter what path you decide to take with your career plans, you'll always need this skill.

Source-Code Control

Source-code control assures us that all the work we've put into writing our app is protected and can be recovered if a disaster happens or if we make a bunch of mistakes.

The first job description I showed you explicitly calls out the use of Git, a common source-code control technology. In addition, this ad calls out the following specific functions: creation, push, pull, branching, and tagging. When you start a project you create a repository, or storage area, in which to keep and control your source code (Figure 2-6). Pushing sends your code to that area while pulling retrieves it to your local computer. Branching allows you to make a separate copy to work with that does not affect the original source. This allows you to try things out and experiment while always being able to get back to where you were when it all worked properly. Tagging basically sets important points in your project's history as being important. You might, for example, use a tag to mark a specific release or version.

```swift
1  //
2  //  InterfaceController.swift
3  //  CoinToss WatchKit Extension
4  //
5  //  Created by Molly Maskrey on 8/5/15.
6  //  Copyright (c) 2015 Global Tek Labs. All rights reserved.
7  //
8
9  import WatchKit
10 import Foundation
11
12
13 class InterfaceController: WKInterfaceController {
14
15
16    @IBOutlet weak var coinImage: WKInterfaceImage!
17    @IBOutlet weak var button: WKInterfaceButton!
18
19
20    @IBAction func buttonPressed() {
21        self.coinImage.setImageNamed("flip")
22        let randomNumber = arc4random_uniform(2)  // random # between 0 and 1
23        if randomNumber == 0 {
24            self.coinImage.startAnimatingWithImagesInRange(NSRange(location: 1, length: 10), duration: 1,
                    repeatCount: 2)
25            print("HEADS")
26        } else  {
27            self.coinImage.startAnimatingWithImagesInRange(NSRange(location: 1, length: 7), duration: 1,
                    repeatCount: 2)
28            print("TAILS")
29        }
30    }
31
32
33    override func awakeWithContext(context: AnyObject?) {
34        super.awakeWithContext(context)
35
36        // Configure interface objects here.
37        self.coinImage.stopAnimating()
38    }
39
40    override func willActivate() {
41        // This method is called when watch view controller is about to be visible to user
42        super.willActivate()
43    }
44
45    override func didDeactivate() {
46        // This method is called when watch view controller is no longer visible
47        super.didDeactivate()
48    }
49
50 }
```

Figure 2-6. Source-code or version control not only backs up your project files in case of catastrophe, it also tracks changes and modifications during the development process, allowing you to recover to a certain point if you take a wrong turn along the way

When developing software in your home or small office, it's pretty convenient to simply back up projects to local or cloud storage. In the old days we used rewritable DVDs and generally kept them off premises in case of catastrophe. With integrated OS backups and cloud storage the process works much more seamlessly. Using tools such as Apple Time Machine we even have access to earlier versions of our material by scanning back through the various updates. However, these are all based by time; that is, by when the backup occurred. So there exists no key identification or metadata about what each of those backups might be. They're simply organized by date and time. By using version control tools such as Git or SVN we have detailed records and incremental information for each time we made and labeled a specific change. We can access different, earlier versions of our work. We will discuss this in detail in Chapter 5.

Development Methodology

Development methodology refers to the human processes—the thinking, for example—used to go from an idea and a set of requirements to something that can be created and deployed.

Similar to source and version control, when we work all by ourselves, our development methodology fits into the way we've always done things. If we tend to do things in sequence, that's generally how we'll write and test our code. Some people work best by creating a top-down structure and roadmap before writing a single line, while others start banging away on the keyboard long before a clear picture of the project has emerged. It's very similar to writing in general. Take this book for instance; the smart way to write would be to formulate an outline or table of contents for the book, then each chapter continuing on down to each subsection. I, of course, took it upon myself to use a more agile-like process. Writers call it working organically.

A very dear friend of mine is also a writer. Actually, he writes as part of his day job, but doesn't consider himself a "real" author. I've read his work and I couldn't think of anyone I'd rather collaborate with, but that's another story. A week ago he was working on a newsletter for his company while I was simultaneously struggling to find the right voice for Chapter 1. I really hope I succeeded, but anyway, we started talking about our processes. I immediately assumed that he took that top-down structured approach because his writing seems so well thought out. I was mildly surprised to find that he writes much the way I do—organically.

If you come from a formal engineering background, you're most likely an organized, structured thinker. Read most engineering texts and you likely never find out about the author's friends or what they've done. We, on the other hand, will likely want to hang out together at the end of our journey. But, as an engineer, you designed or built things, whether soft- or hardware, starting with a set of requirements or at the very least an idea. You deconstructed the problem down to a design and then moved on to implement something fantastic. Hey, I only want to be friends with great designers.

While this top-down process works for simple, well-contained projects, as our labor content expands and the project size and team size grows, formalizing the process from start to finish becomes critical. The standard for developmental methodology in software is agile, typically either Scrum or extreme programming, but sometimes a combination of the two. We will cover the basic elements of agile in Chapter 6, but as part of our career dissection, at this point we're interested more in what it means to us at the interview and after we're hired.

Because each company implements their own version of agile—I've yet to find one place that follows the process as it is officially defined—I'll only speak from what I've experienced either directly working for a company or as a contractor helping out from time to time. The process functions identically whether you're a direct-hire or freelancer, or at least that's what is supposed to happen.

I visualize the agile process like a party with friends after a few drinks (Figure 2-7). Inhibitions loosen up and team members either become more outspoken or subdued. We would start with a 30–120 second update of what we were doing at a daily stand-up meeting, though we typically sat down in a conference room. Most days it was the team . . . the developers who wrote the code, the designers who created the look and feel of the software, and other people such as QA and the client advocate, which usually turned out to be someone in management.

Figure 2-7. Think of the agile development process as getting together with your "work friends" in an open discussion of how a project should proceed. The best advice I can give would be to leave egos at the door to the conference room

In Scrum, the more prevalent form of agile, you have a Scrum Master. This person acts as facilitator to remove hurdles from the team. What usually happens is that a manager or senior developer takes on this position and often takes charge of the meeting. So, right then and there, the true methodology of Scrum has left the building.

If you're shy or a bit introverted, you'll be overwhelmed during your first few months of working on an agile team. Like writing a book or article, the process moves along organically as ideas and solutions formulate and improve throughout the meeting. Though it's not supposed to work this way, personal dynamics always come into play during the process. Some person or persons typically percolate to the top as the ones to listen to, often stifling criticism or alternative ideas. As females, we're immediately outnumbered three to one based on pure, simple statistics. We see this either as a disadvantage or as an opportunity depending on our inner self. I want to tell you to take it as a challenge rather than a roadblock. I want to say "Just go for it" and let your ideas shine and be heard. But reality must come into play when dealing with our entire professional career, so we carefully analyze the situation and make our moves accordingly. It's not perfect and it's not fair, but this isn't a social justice work on changing the perceived wrongs of society; we're here to get you—no matter who you are—to the position and level at which you want to be. Remember, I want you to become someone I would love to hire to work with me.

A few paragraphs back I mentioned the interview when starting to discuss agile. Interviewing is an art in and of itself. As such, it tends to be very personal. We each handle interviews differently, and most of us adapt to the situation. If talking to someone from HR (Human Resources)—by the way, I often use the term Himalayan Resources because they seem to be so far away from the rest of us—we're very businesslike and sure, and we know exactly where we want to be in five or ten years. I'm thinking all along that all I want to do is be out of here in five or ten minutes. But, it's the price we have to bear to get our chance at the table.

The real interview generally includes a manager or team leader as well as someone with whom you'll most likely be sharing a workspace. It's a two-way street. You want to see if the job fits your needs and the company wants to find out if you'll be a team player. You'll usually get a sense of the company at this point. The questions will tend to focus on how you stand out, what your unique skills are that make you essential to the team. And that's a key word here: essential. If you can make yourself seem as if they'll not succeed unless you're there at the table, the job is yours to refuse.

This can be the turning point, one way or another. With the three or four of you in a room, at a table, focused on a single project—your inclusion or exclusion from the team—the skilled interviewer will often try to trip you up. You'll be led down a path to discuss your strengths and weaknesses like any interview, and you will, of course, come up with some bogus trivial failures that you've learned from. What often catches the interviewee by surprise is that the team will use your enthusiasm about your strengths against you. You're strong, resilient, and innovative, which the team may take as a threat to their position. In the old days the term used was "wild duck." This was someone who wasn't a team player but went off on their own. As always, there's no right answer or way to proceed. Work from your feelings about the situation at the moment.

One of the best pieces of advice I can give right now is to have a number of practice interviews. Go out and apply for positions you don't expect to get or want to take. Start with something that is so far away that the commute would be impossible. You know you're not going to take the job, so experiment with how you handle the process. They will likely mention the distance issue during the interview, but a simple comeback is to do a little research on the area and mention that you've been considering a relocation to the area because of schools, or neighborhood, or nightlife, or whatever. Practice and become an excellent interviewee and you'll be ahead of your competition. And again, the interview will often very closely simulate the agile process used at the company. Take it in and add the experience to your set of skills.

My goal is not to teach you source/version control or how to get Scrum certification; rather, it is to make sure you are familiar enough with these techniques prior to going to interview with a software agency. An interviewee unfamiliar with agile or who doesn't know to what Git refers has little chance of getting past her initial interview.

Impressing Your User

By impressing your user, I mean having a great-looking display for your iPhone interface screen that draws them into the experience immediately.

When working for aerospace companies I was frequently called upon to present my engineering designs to every range of skill and experience level imaginable, from the technical nerd who wanted to go through the schematics circuit by circuit to the high-level decision makers only interested in cost effectiveness—and more often, just cost. Early on I presented as much information as I could fit into my allotted time frame, which, all too often, was nowhere near enough to get the point across. I was one of those tech people so proud of my cleverness at reducing PCB footprint, increasing battery life by 5 percent, or writing self-correcting software subroutines. Thing was, no one understood what I was talking about, or more specifically, no one cared. They just wanted to see the final product.

What they did love to see was the user interface design and prototyping (Figure 2-8). While I may have been developing the key elements of what were sometimes the most advanced systems of the day, the team that put the pretty graphics on the 19" display screens got three times the face time with the customer than I got. Essentially, what they were doing was merely presenting the watered down results of my efforts to some soon-to-be decision maker in the field. The point here is that no matter how cool or how much innovation your idea encapsulates, the user interface (UI) and user experience (UX) set your product apart from the rest, so they need to be perfect. And this is so much more important for mobile apps, and iPhone apps in particular.

Figure 2-8. Like first impressions with people, what a customer sees when they tap on your app, bringing it to life, will immediately draw them in or put them off. Try making it the former

I believe, as do many people, that what drove the success of the iPhone and subsequently the iPad was how users loved to interact with the device. Even the earliest table view controllers, something I now loathe, were super cool in 2009. You could tap a row, the screen would slide over and another row would appear, one more time and you'd see your favorite piece of music or book paragraph. Look at the top selling or free products on the App Store, and they'll all sport these amazing graphics. Sometimes you'll dive into realistic new worlds with games or explore new ideas through easy-to-use educational software. My favorite ideas to use are basic utilities such as timers or maybe a metronome. While possessing a minimalist set of functions, the clean and understated elegance of the UI often makes the tools a must-have.

Years ago, when I attended high school, I wanted to be an artist—jeez, the things we do for love, am I right? I actually painted in acrylics on unique, geometrically shaped canvases of my own design. I won awards—it was a small class—and even had one of my pieces on display at the Kennedy Center in Washington, D.C. Somewhere between then and now, all artistic creativity disappeared. I suspect it evolved into the creativeness I incorporate into engineering solutions—yeah, we're going to go with that explanation. But, to the point, I cannot make those top-tier UI designs in either the gaming world or even the simplest utility function. Later, in Chapter 7, we will cover how all this UI/UX stuff works and some tools that we, the development engineers, use to get our products out there.

The good news is that most companies already recognize this left-versus-right brain limitation. That's why you'll work in conjunction with the design team, the members of which have the innovativeness and creativity to develop these fantastic designs for the client. Because you'll be implementing dozens if not hundreds of these apps over the years, you'll start to get a sense of the process and the tools and soon will be able to make pretty decent designs yourself. You might even find that the design side of the work appeals to you more than writing Swift.

However, if you think this might be something you're interested in, I'd be careful not to discuss it during the interview process. When a company looks for someone for an open position, they're hiring for that position. They don't want to hear that you're looking to move on to something else as soon as you sign your employment paperwork. The hiring manager has made an investment in you and your fellow interviewees long before you saw the job ad. To hire someone who's going to hang with the other team isn't really a motivation for her to put your resume and interview notes at the top of the heap.

Now, in small companies where the employees need to take on multiple roles, this may well be appropriate. Startups, for example, want and need people to take on broad sets of responsibilities that may not fall within their job description. In fact, for these companies there may be no job description at all. But don't get taken advantage of. A good friend of mine finds himself in this very situation. He spends the bulk of his days taking on tasks for which he was not hired and that were not mentioned during the interview. Again, the theme should be caution and adaptability. You'll get a sense of what the company is like during your interview. Most of your fellow employees will be open and honest, telling you the "real story"—at least as how they see it. One question you should definitely ask is how long they have been with the company. They may not have reached the point of saturation yet and are still in the "romance" stage with the company.

In summary, the UI/UX aspects of working for a software company as a developer are most likely not as big of a concern as the other aspects we will discuss throughout the book. You'll find that, as a freelancer or especially when starting your own company, the necessity of these skills become of paramount importance to your success. But most companies already divide the work between the engineering team and design team.

Building Targets

Building to a target means to use Xcode to convert your project into an executable and then to download and run that executable on an actual device.

Employers consider it a given that you know how to build an iOS project from Xcode to a device. You might even be tested on this during a follow-up, or sometimes even during your initial interview. If you don't know how to do this, unless the job description specifically states to the contrary, I'd not even bother sending in a resume. Building and running a project on an actual device is the "must have."

In fact, we're not even talking about building to a specific device in this section but rather will focus on the subject of continuous integration (CI). Companies use CI processes and servers to merge all developer working files into a single set of code known as the *build*. I might work on a sort function while the girl next to me codes a complex I/O routine. CI integrates our work into the final product, or, more specifically, the current version of the final product. This helps to quickly identify issues when an engineer's perfect code causes problems somewhere else in the suite. When this happens it's known as *breaking the build*, and you can get a lot of grief about it from your teammates. Most of the time it's a very friendly and helpful bit of joking around. After all, the problem may not be in your code at all, but in the way someone else's code deals with a method or parameter that you created. But, because you performed the last push to the repository, you'll be the one they come to first.

That's what this CI process was created to do—find and locate issues in the build as early as possible. Unfortunately, in many organizations it's become a sort of hazing or initiation process for the newer developers. Again, frequently it's all in fun and there's nothing vindictive about it.

For you, the developer, the use of CI should be mostly transparent. The integration manager sets what whatever CI server is being used, and when you perform a commit the server generates a new build. As mentioned briefly in Chapter 1, the most common CI systems include Jenkins (formerly Hudson), Travis, and Apple's CI system using Xcode and Mac OS X Server. Let's take the Jenkins system, which I used at my last position. When I did a commit of my changes to the local Git repository, the automated process began. All my changes were integrated into the current project, and the source was compiled into the latest build. Scripts caused automated testing to occur that checked for process errors—this was before UI testing became automated, at least in our organization. If the testing completed successfully, everything was archived and new versioning was created so it could be used. If the testing didn't complete successfully, I was immediately notified so I could start searching for the problem. The vast majority of the time the error was indeed a result of something I did, so the process was really good at driving us toward something without errors.

Since the process works mostly autonomously, if you see in a job description a need for skills and/or experience in a CI process such as Jenkins, the likely reason is that the company might be looking for a developer in the test and integration department, which normally supervises the CI server and tool suite. Now, this is not a bad thing, although the starting pay can be a little bit lower than that for a full-time developer. For some reason, in many organizations QA gets seen as lower in status than developers or designers. As continuous integration technology enters the commercial development world and becomes the de facto method of integration and testing, I think the position salary grids should level out. So the point here is to not discount a position if it's not exactly your ideal job, if it is in the field and has other qualities for which you are searching.

Embedded Systems

An embedded system is a computer that differentiates itself from more general purpose devices such as a desktop or laptop by having a dedicated function; for example, a smartphone or an automated teller machine.

When I started working as an engineer I focused almost primarily on various types of embedded systems. For a year or so while working at IBM in North Carolina I developed software for the 3624 Automated Teller Machine (Figure 2-9). This was the classic definition of an embedded system. It had but one purpose: to allow bank customers to perform transactions without a human teller present. You could get your statement, make a deposit, get cash, and perform account transfers. Now these are second nature to everyone and exist by the dozens in every drug store, grocery store, gas station, and so forth. The nightclub that we go to has a couple of them, as does the gym where I work out.

Figure 2-9. Early inventions such as IBM's 3624 Automated Teller Machine started the revolution of embedded technology in commercial applications. With the exception of getting out cash, an app on your iPhone can perform just about everything that this product does

The device stood about six or seven feet tall and weighed hundreds of pounds in its industrial steel enclosure. There were two money feed mechanisms, usually for five and twenty dollar bills, but they could be customized by the banks. The display was very limited, initially a single-line, orange neon row of characters followed by, as I remember, a 3- or 5-line display, again in neon orange. It had a small processor and very limited memory— we're talking K's of RAM here, not gigabytes or even megabytes. Thus the code had to be extremely efficient. There was no WiFi or Ethernet or other high-speed data connection. Transmission to and from the mainframe (yes, they were mainframe computers, also IBM) was a few thousand bits per second and on a local loop shared with other devices.

This was how I learned to program efficiently and operate mechanical motors, levers, displays, and magnetic stripe interfaces. It was fun and extremely frustrating at the same time.

Now think of an iPhone. While Apple increases the processing capability of iOS devices each and every year, they'll likely never match the power or memory capability of a desktop or laptop computer. While the iPhone 6 now has 1.0GB of RAM, a Mac Pro can have sixty-four times that amount. So you're never likely to get the same huge application you made for the Mac Pro onto your iPhone, at least not without understanding how to program embedded systems. In the dawn of iPhone development, a 3G contained only 128MB of memory. And remember, you don't get all that space. There's this thing called the operating system that takes up much of it.

In most cases, Xcode, Swift, and even Objective-C make software development easy. The source is very wordy and self-documenting, which makes for great maintainability but also eats up space. While you can change a number of "switches" in Xcode to optimize your project for speed, I/O, size, and so on, hand coding critical loops and other functions still happens to this day. Features such as Apple Metal continue to improve performance while mostly maintaining ease of use, but for some very special applications you may have to use human judgment and design skills to get things to work as you need them. By understanding embedded systems, you'll have an insider's view of how these devices work and the tricks that can be incorporated, if needed, to achieve maximum performance.

While this can be useful in many cases, especially when dealing with iOS Accessories, which we'll discuss later, for the most part software development companies don't put much weight on this criterion. But when starting your own company and looking to interface your app with other devices, it's definitely something you'd want to have in your set of skills.

App Publishing

To publish an app means to place it for sale (or free) into the Apple App Store or distribute to only specific users such as employees in an enterprise.

As I stated previously, I wrote this book assuming a level somewhere between experienced novice and newish intermediate. Because the skill set I'm discussing is so critical, I will, from time to time, describe things in a more basic fashion for the sake of clarity and a common frame of reference. Early in the history of the iPhone it was pretty straightforward to submit something to the App Store (Figure 2-10). You created a bundle with all the various pieces, coded algorithms, user interface, database, frameworks, or libraries and submitted it. While, in essence, it's the same amount of stuff that goes to Apple now, much of the mystery surrounding why your app got rejected has been removed.

Figure 2-10. While you still submit the same project files to the App Store, the process has been greatly streamlined over the past few years, making it easier to identify and correct issues earlier

Years ago I submitted an app for a client. A few weeks later I made an update that was rejected by Apple. Okay, easily understood, right? I did something wrong; maybe had a crash or a missing graphic, whatever. Well, it turned out that the app was rejected for something that hadn't changed and was part of the original version that had been approved and was at that time in the store. You've probably heard stories of how hard it is to get into the App Store, but what the problem really revolved around was that developers didn't know all the rules and criteria. Also, humans at Apple were doing the testing rather than automated processes.

Now, long before you get anywhere near having your app go up for sale, myriad tests and evaluations automatically check your app to make sure it meets the vast majority of criteria for submission. The great thing about this is that you know near instantly what you need to fix. It is, in fact, so much easier and clearer to submit an app now than it has ever been.

And whether you work in a company or are an entrepreneur with your own great game or utility idea, you need to understand how to do this. When working for a company, much of the time the integration team will do all of the work distributing the app for the company's client, so it's quite often out of your hands. But in smaller organizations like startups, you'll most likely have to add this to your skill set.

Web Services

Web services allow mobile devices to send and receive data between the specific piece of hardware and the Internet.

To put it succinctly, if you are looking for an iOS development position with a software company, you should know how to get data from the Internet into your iPhone as well as how to send data the other way. It's that simple. Very few apps stand completely on their own and unto themselves. You might be able to get away with this on something like a simple calculator or timer, but even then you might want to be able to provide customizable skins for the app like an animal print or a favorite sports team.

You'll want to brush up on terms like REST (Representational State Transfer), XML (eXtended Markup Language), JSON (JavaScript Object Notation), and PHP, which we mentioned briefly already. Without a doubt, if you can, have something that shows you know how to utilize these technologies either on your public Github account or that you can demonstrate during your interview. Showing the hiring team that you have actual hands-on experience with these will go a long way toward putting you on the top of the candidate list.

At a minimum, study these to understand how they work and when and why you might choose such a technology in your application. Review sample code that can be found throughout the Internet to see how other developers work with data transfers.

We'll cover the most common ways of moving data into and out of your device as well as the more recent introduction by Apple of their CloudKit features, which make data transfers much easier for homogeneous Apple systems, in Chapter 11.

Testing

By *testing* we refer to the unit testing targets generated by Xcode, the ability to perform user interface testing, and using TestFlight integration to send out beta versions to be evaluated by people we know.

I'm going to be honest here; testing is one of those things we clearly should address from the start even before writing the functions in our code, but never do. It's too easy to just focus on our app's UI or the cool new feature we thought of than it is to write unit tests. Even with testing being so intrinsic to creating an Xcode project, we most often just ignore it and silently wish it would go away. And I'm just as guilty as the next person with this.

Apple continues to drive the need for testing into our heads, especially at the yearly developers' conferences, by making it easier and adding cool new features such as UI testing to motivate us. For Apple this makes total sense. The better we test and provide complete code coverage (the amount in percentage of the source that we test), the more likely we'll deliver a solid and near bug-free application. When we fail, such as our app crashing for users, Apple looks bad. Customers complain about Apple's lack of quality assurance in letting such a "buggy" app out into the world.

Software companies are generally divided into two camps: those who test and those who talk about testing but never allocate time to it. Let's talk about that a second. When a company bids on a job for a client, they generally specify an anticipated number of hours for the different parts of a project. Each part is assigned a specialty labor code (designer, developer, architect, tester, etc.) with a specific labor rate; i.e., dollars per hour that get charged to the client. Throw this into the math blender—I so wish I had one of these—and out comes the **expected** cost to the client.

Unless desperate for business, no software company bids a project for a fixed price. Instead, they provide the estimated number of hours and a labor rate. Most of the time unforeseen problems in development, as well as clients changing requirements, force alterations to the plan and therefore make the original estimate obsolete. These type of changes usually happen even as early as the first week of coding. Most often, these changes increase the cost, even when removing functionality from the project, the reason being that the suspect function was likely already coded and was deemed to not be worthy of being in the final version. So all the money set aside for that function was already spent. Additionally, testing becomes one of the necessary tasks that winds up being shorted, resulting in a less reliable product. Likely the project would have gone a little over budget had the company taken the time to determine the severity of the problems, and thus the cost of taking out the buggy function, while not breaking cooperative functions, has to be addressed as well.

While it's good to have unit testing skills and experience, especially for those companies for which it is an integral part of their process, it's not something that is always in high demand. The bad thing is that they may ask you about it and even test you on it, but you might not ever use it in your work.

As for beta testing, which we will cover in Chapter 12, most companies of any reasonable size will have an integration and test department or section. These are usually the same people that manage the continuous integration process and servers. You'll work with them from time to time in order to deal with issues related to your section of the software. You may also be called upon to cover for someone in the event of travel, sickness, or vacation. But, except for small organizations or startups, beta testing usually gets taken care of by someone else.

However, as an entrepreneur or freelancer you'll most likely need to know about beta testing and the use of TestFlight in order to get feedback on your work. We'll talk a little more on this shortly.

iOS Accessories

Accessories attach various external input and output devices with your iPhone in order to interact with the world.

Using an accessory, data moves from the external world into iOS and vice versa through either wired or wireless means. Wired connections include the Lightning connector and headphone jack while wireless can be WiFi, Bluetooth 2.1+EDR, and Bluetooth 4.0 Low Energy (LE). Some of these are very easy to use, where all you need are your developer tools and some skills. Others, specifically Bluetooth 2.1+EDR (standard Bluetooth) or the Lightning connector require having an Apple MFi (Made for iPod/iPhone/iPad) license. I've worked in the MFi program since 2009 developing or helping my clients create fabulous products we call app-enabled accessories (Figure 2-11). I recently helped LiveRowing, a client of my company Global Tek Labs, develop their Concept2 rowing machine interface cable that allows participants to row and collect information about their workout.

Figure 2-11. Working with complex accessories to move information into and out of iOS devices requires specialized skills and acceptance into Apple's MFi program

For me, accessories create amazing opportunities to do interesting things, tackle challenging problems, and create a more connected world for everyone to experience and partake in. In the LiveRowing app, for instance, not only are you able to plan and track your rowing experience by adding the information to your fitness database, you're also able to connect with friends over the Internet and have rowing competitions in real time (Figure 2-12). No matter what amount of distance physically separates you and your friends, the experience becomes the next best thing to being side by side in skulls on the Charles River or wherever you choose.

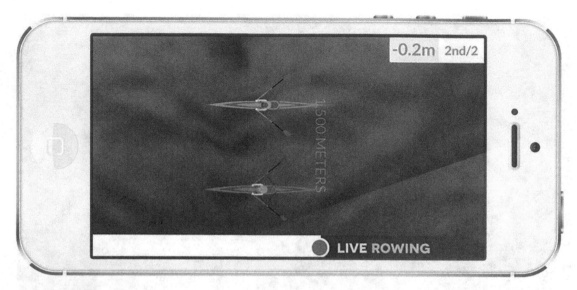

Figure 2-12. Using Apple's External Accessory frameworks allows your app to work with specialized hardware to create interactive user experiences like this real-time boat race from LiveRowing

I've never seen any job posting require skills for the development of accessories. That said, many software agencies work on projects where such devices are involved. In my very first job interview for an iOS development position at a company, my experience came directly into play and got me the position shortly after the interview. Our team was developing an automotive monitoring app for the iPad that allowed the tracking of the vehicle's movement through a transmission interface to create the best profile in order to save gas. For fleet systems, reducing fuel consumption by even a few cents on each vehicle's routes can add up to a tremendous savings. While my app development skills were modest at the time, my experience and knowledge of the Apple MFi program set me apart from pretty much every other candidate.

So, what do you need to know? For the most part, working in the MFi space is not only highly specialized, but as stated previously, is restricted to those possessing a special license from Apple. Unless you own or work for a company that possesses this license, don't worry too much about connecting devices through the Lightning port or using standard Bluetooth.

One skill that would still set you apart and is reasonably easy to learn is Core Bluetooth, which is Apple's iOS framework supporting communications via Bluetooth LE (BTLE). A subset of Bluetooth 4.0, BTLE provides for short-burst secure transmissions to and from Apple devices with the proper Bluetooth radio. Most iPhone and iPad devices for the past several years support BTLE.

So, what types of things use BTLE? Two very key sets of accessories include wireless game controllers and fitness monitors. As games become more immersive and fitness wearables scoop up larger portions of the market, the skills enabling you to work with these devices become something highly sought after. And, really, this technology is very simple to learn and experiment with. If you have any two recent devices such as an iPhone and an iPad as early as iPad 3, you're in business.

For a few years at Apple's Worldwide Developer Conference, Core Bluetooth had its own session discussing the details of and how you could work with the technology. On the developer portal, sample code exists to let you use Core Bluetooth and BTLE to create an interactive two-person tank battle game.

When I talk with clients or at the various meetings to which I am invited, I'll usually have with me a simple, demonstrable device that does something in the real world but connects to my iPhone or iPad to provide visual cues to its operation. In one of our projects we'll take on the challenge of learning how to use this technology and display information from a multi-axis sensor module that I developed about a year ago.

Saying that we're going to write a project that interfaces with a sensor, though straightforward and very accurate, sounds totally boring. It's kind of like saying, "Yeah, I'm a vehicle mechanic," when what you do is design spacecraft. Sure, you work on a vehicle's mechanics, but the perception of what it is that you do can be quite different. I want to expand on our project and try to get across the passion I found when I originally did this.

If you read my bio at the start of the book you may remember I'm a ballroom dancer (Figure 2-13). For me, this activity nearly rules my life as my days are scheduled around lessons, practice, performances, and competitions. At its core, ballroom, for me anyway, combines a complicated set of mental processes with demanding physicality while putting on a visible sense of emotion to impress the judges or my instructors. Most of my friends also dance; some are better than me, but objectively I'm probably at the center of the pack. Right now you should be asking how does this fit into software, and especially into iOS accessories, and how am I going to use this? First, I'll answer the last bit of that question—it all comes down to passion. When applying for a job or just talking to somebody at a meetup, let your passion show through. You'll be engaging, and the person with whom you're speaking will likely want to know more if they see how much something means to you. As for how this all fits together, I took the sensor electronics and placed them on a ballroom dance shoe. This allows real-time monitoring of a dancer's feet so the software can determine, based on the dance style, whether she's executing her movements correctly. Think about that for a moment.

Figure 2-13. *Just as the author combines her love of ballroom dance into the day-to-day world of iOS software and accessory development, by finding your own special passion that fits within your new career choice, you make every day one where you can't wait to get started on whatever might be about to happen*

With some fairly simple electronics, some Swift code, and, oh yeah, I threw in an Apple Watch, I was able to take a purely subjective, artistic form of expression and add in quantitative performance measurement. While I hope this technology is never used in competition, as the artistic expression is what a performance is all about, I hope that it can be used by fellow dancers to improve their practice sessions and develop their routines to perfection. With the Apple Watch and its taptic engine (vibration), I can know—without changing my body position to look around—whether or not I'm doing the routine and especially my foot placement correctly. This is the passion that drives me—to create systems that impact lives—in this case, my own. I truly hope that you can find your passion and incorporate that into your everyday working life at some point, as you'll never hesitate getting up in the morning.

Now that we've talked about how the skills developed and perfected in this book can be used in your job and career search, let's look at how you might go about finding your next, perfect position.

Finding a Job

So, how do you go about finding job? It might be old school, but the first place I go when I'm even remotely interested in working for someone is Craigslist. Why? It's a quick and easy way to get an idea of what's available in your area, but I don't consider it a starting point for true searching. There are various sites you can use to post your resume and get listing of jobs that match your search criteria. But like any site where you post personal information, you're bound to get spam. When searching for a job and you all of a sudden get this great post that says it matches your profile, but it turns out to be a service provider that will help you in your search, you start being a bit more cautious about what you open. I've had friends who received viruses to their systems by just this type of annoying response.

In my area, Indeed.com has been the job search engine on which most of my friends place their resumes and look for positions. Personally, there's nothing wrong with some of the positions on Indeed, I'm just a little leery about posting my resume out there.

LinkedIn is, of course, a reliable and very well-known place to keep and advertise your skills and experience (Figure 2-14). The trouble I have with LinkedIn comes from all the talent acquisition representatives out there. We used to call them headhunters, but now everyone seems to be in the business of finding talent. I suspect most of these individuals are honest and sincerely trying to get you a decent position while, at the same time, satisfying their clients' staffing needs. One of my friends does this and runs the local iOS developer's meetup group. He's been hosting the meetup for over five years, and I was fortunate enough to be in at the formation. While the demographics have changed a bit over the years, and he's changed companies at least once, it's still a great place to get together and talk about iOS development every month or so. Just last month I gave my second presentation at the meeting and got to meet a whole new set of people in the community.

Figure 2-14. While job search platforms come and go, LinkedIn still stands as the way to connect to people with whom you share professional interests

That brings me to the absolute, number one way to get a position for which you're searching. You need to get out there and network. My partner, Jennifer, soon to be my wife, goes out many times a week. Some people call her the queen of networking. I've actually started accompanying her more over the past year and have begun loving meeting new people and exchanging ideas. I've been asked to speak at several different groups as a result. That, in turn, builds my reputation, and you can see that the whole process continues to snowball. A couple months ago, I gave the keynote speech at an IoT gathering in town. From that I met several people with great ideas with whom we've started collaborating. I was asked, as a result, to be on a couple of technology advisory boards where we continue to meet new and interesting people and companies with which to work.

As for Jennifer, her networking and getting to know the technology people in the community who are advisors and decision makers helped her to win the $25,000 grand prize at a new-business competition. It wasn't that she knew the judges or had any inside information, but, by getting to know what people were looking for, she was able to use that to shape her competition package to deliver exactly what was needed to succeed. While other teams just got up on stage and did it the same way they always do, Jennifer developed her idea with a specific target in mind and succeeded admirably.

When networking, make an effort to engage the person with whom you're speaking. Jennifer, after a brief introduction, will try to find out how she can help the other person. This almost always wins them over quickly. Let them know you're offering to help. Later, they may wish to do the same for you. You have a skillset, and so do they. Maybe you're not the best at Xcode or Swift quite yet, but you can put together a WordPress site in your sleep. There are innumerable ways to barter that don't cost you much except time. And the time can be very well spent if you make just the right connection to get you that perfect position or even an interview.

If you're one of those individuals who has trouble initiating a conversation with strangers, there are a few tricks I can offer, but the best advice is to just do it anyway. I was totally the wallflower at school dances and later at networking events. Once I had a crowd, I could talk for hours on end, capturing and engaging my audience. But starting on my own sent chills up my spine. I eventually overcame this fear, mostly, but one great trick is to have someone with you—your networking wing-girl. You know her. She can bring people in just with a look or smile. So take her with you.

Another trick that I actually do use, and for which Jennifer is a total advocate, is to have a short "elevator speech." In a few brief sentences, explain who you are and what you do, plus anything that makes you stand out. Have it roll off your tongue without even thinking. Write it down and practice it daily until it's perfect.

Jennifer's Example Elevator Speech

Hi. I'm Jennifer, founder and CEO of Global Tek Labs. We're a custom electronics consulting firm specializing in guiding our clients' hardware projects through the rigorous Apple approval process. We've been doing this for six years and have helped dozens of products get to market quickly.

Business cards. For some weird reason my millennial friends don't seem to get the purpose of business cards. First, you want to get the contact information for whomever you meet. You never know when you might need their help. I like to write down info on the back of their card about our talk. On my cards, the back side has a predefined area in matte (to enable easy note taking) for just this type of information. The people I usually talk with think it's so cool and wind up incorporating it on their own next set of cards. I got the idea from someone else a long time ago.

Also, use the information on the card to follow up after the meeting. Unless you absolutely know for certain that this is someone whom you'll never need in the future, always send a follow-up note. I go with an email, but it could be whatever you think works best. Even with those people with whom I don't follow up, I keep their information in case it ever comes in handy. You'll likely see them in the future, and it's very polished to remember who they are and what they're all about.

At some meetups, usually in the beginning, the facilitator will go around the room and give each of the attendees thirty seconds or so to speak about themselves. This is where you'll want to have your elevator speech ready to go, plus a couple more sentences. If you're looking for help or a job in your field, say so. Try to be brief and specific. There may be someone in attendance who has just the right connection. Don't pass up any chance you get to make an impression. One word of advice—don't go over your allotted time no matter how wonderful you believe yourself to be, and don't describe your life story. You'll alienate just about everyone attending, except the other people who do exactly what you do, who are, in all honesty, not the people you need to meet.

I occasionally go to these morning meetups for creative people: illustrators, writers, artists, some web designers, and so on. Most people—I'd say 80-ish percent—stick to the plan and hit the thirty-second time limit plus or minus. But the others will ramble on and on about how their service or skill is so unique and that it's never been done before. My thoughts? If it hasn't been or isn't being done ever before, then is it really a marketable service?

The point is, no matter what the outcome of this or that meetup, don't give up. You're not going to find that job at the first meeting you attend. But you will see what's out there and start making connections. You'll meet someone who's at nearly the same place in their development learning process as yourself. You'll talk at meetings, connect on LinkedIn and Facebook, and develop a rapport. She'll find a position at a company closer to her place and, if you'd like, recommend you as her replacement. That's just one of dozens of potential win-win scenarios I've personally seen take place at these meetups. Much of the time Jennifer or I are putting people together that we think make a great match.

Employee Summary

We have covered a lot of material in this section, most of which can be applied to the other two career paths as well. Specifically, with very few exceptions, you'll need each of the ten specified skills developed in this book no matter if you want to work for someone else, start your own company, or straddle the fence as a freelance developer.

Working as an employee helps to get you closer—although nothing in life is certain—to the kind of job security for which many people are searching. All the superfluous stuff—dealing with insurance, equipment purchase and maintenance, finding clients, etc.—gets handled by someone else while you focus on your area of expertise. For that security you sacrifice the ability to pick and choose on which projects you'll work. Someone will oversee and appraise your performance, and there may come a time when there are people with whom you simply can't get along.

To get this position, go out and network. Meet people and make connections. Perfect your elevator speech until it rolls off your tongue without a second thought. Offer to give a presentation at a meetup, and people will come up to you at the end. Don't rely on job-listing sites or talent-acquisition agencies to get you a job; do it yourself. If you're shy, take along one of your friends to break the ice. A little bit of uneasiness at a couple of meetups is well worth the price for getting you started in your new career. Be sure to keep your LinkedIn profile current by continuously growing your connections.

Option #2: Entrepreneur

I love being an entrepreneur. I hate being an entrepreneur.

I could leave it at that, since it's the perfect explanation of what entrepreneurship is all about, but my publisher would not be too happy with me—and I hope to become a writer someday. In all seriousness, nothing is likely to provide you with the excitement and exhilaration of starting your own business, whether you fund it yourself as a small consulting or software development company or seek out millions in angel, an individual who donates money to startups, and venture capital funding. How do you get started?

Getting Started

Falling back on my usual answer, there is no single correct way to start a business, as it depends on multiple factors, from your personality to the laws in your community and everything else in between. Since I'm not a licensed business planner, attorney, accountant, or tax professional, I would not presume to give any advice about the details of forming your company. Further, your situation and the laws in your community certainly vary from mine, so my suggestion would be to do your research and find guidance as to what fits your specific needs and budget.

What I will do is to relate my personal experiences. When I started my first business, I did it on a whim. I read several articles on Limited Liability Corporations (LLCs) and decided that was what I needed to do. After coming up with a cool name and acquiring the domain, I filled out the online form and in maybe thirty minutes I had my own company. But then I realized I had no idea what to do next. My first company produced short and full-length movies, and I thought I would soon be on my way to Hollywood. Without going into the messy details of that disaster, the company eventually folded and the assets were sold off at an auction. I did learn from that experience, though I would have preferred to use the money for a different type of education.

So where did I fail? First and foremost, I mistakenly jumped into execution without any planning. About the only thing encompassing any element of planning was making sure the domain name was available and acquiring it at the start. I didn't even research as to whether any companies with the same name existed.

> **Caution**   Be careful when choosing your company name. I once was contacted by another company with a similar but not exactly the same name. I had been in business over two years. They were not even established in the same state, but their legal counsel claimed that I violated their copyright because my name was similar.

The first thing I recommend would be to create your business plan. Now, I'm not a "suit"; that is, I really don't like working in business lingo or spreadsheets, I prefer to solve problems. I suspect the bulk of you out there reading this are pretty similar, and you're probably already having doubts about going down the entrepreneurial path. Frankly, those doubts could be justified. It's not that I'm intentionally trying to scare you off, but, as always, I want you to succeed. And to that end, I need to give you enough information right at the start for you to make an informed choice and minimize wrong turns.

Start by creating a business plan. What is your business about, and what is the situation surrounding the formation of your business? To put it more simply, what's the problem you're trying to solve?

You want to write software and do it on your own terms, not working a typical 9-to-5 workday. That's a rationale for how you plan to execute, but not the problem. My version of a problem statement might be:

There are not enough iOS developers to handle all the work in the software market.

This not only states the problem of there not being enough iOS developers out there, it also alludes to the fact that there is a viable market for the solution and that people would likely pay someone—hopefully you—for that service. You'll want to do a simple SWOT analysis (Figure 2-15) to determine your strengths, weaknesses, opportunities, and threats. The strengths and weaknesses are part of, or are internal to, your company, while opportunities and threats are external.

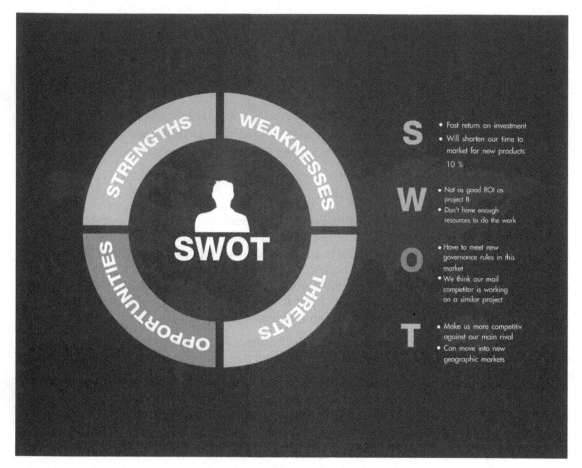

Figure 2-15. *A SWOT analysis can put key aspects of your business in a single, easy-to-access place for reference and to show to potential investors*

For strengths, what sets you apart and what advantages do you have over your potential competition? How do you show those strengths to your potential clients? Conversely, what are the weaknesses on which you need to improve or should avoid altogether? What factors will cause you to lose clients?

What are the opportunities for you to get business? How do you find them? What are the trends out there, and how will they affect you in the near and short term? On the flip side, what are your competitors doing? How are trends and technological changes going to affect you and your business? What is your funding situation, and what is your runway?

> **Note**   A common term tossed about in startups is *runway*. You start with some amount of cash to operate your business. Your burn rate is the pace at which that money is spent, e.g., dollars per month. Your runway is the length of time that you can continue to operate your business based on your burn rate. For example, if you have $120,000 in the bank and spend at a rate of $10,000 per month, your runway is $120,000 / $10,000 per month = 12 months.

The details associated with writing a simple business plan go way beyond the scope of this book. My goal is to get you to think about it right at the start, before going any further and spending money. What's the problem? What's your solution for the problem? How much business is out there, or, rather, what's the market for your services? How are you going to execute the plan? Like anything else you need to know, the information exists, and all you need to do is search for it.

How you create your plan also depends on what type of business you intend to form. Let's look at two mostly opposite ends of the spectrum: consulting versus product-oriented. As a consultant you use your software skills to develop code or apps to your customers' specifications. They give you a problem, some specs, pay you, and you make something for them that they are willing to accept.

Another approach would be to take your own great idea, whether it be an app or some piece of technology that uses your iOS skills, and form the structure based on a product you intend to sell. In that case, the plan will differ since your market may be a little more difficult to define. You must figure out who wants your product, whether there are any competing or even similar products, how much people would pay for your product, what would it cost to make your product, and could anyone else be developing the same product who might beat you to the market and thus render all your effort wasted.

Again, there is no way I'm able to cover all the ins and outs of planning your business. All I'm asking you to do is to think about it before proceeding down any specific path—and document everything! Months from now when you're swamped with work and need to remember why you chose to set something up in a particular fashion, you'll have the answer.

The careful reader will note the irony in what I'm saying here. I'm telling you to plan before getting started, but in a previous section I talked about agile development, where we simply get started and see how things work out. In fact, you could use a process similar to agile when thinking about how you want to form your business. It's really just another way of brainstorming, which can be extremely valuable. Just don't go making decisions like forming a specific type of company structure where you're legally binding yourself without looking carefully at all the options.

Once you've thought it through and documented your tentative plan, let it rest for a few days, then go back and do a thorough review. You may have seen something on the Internet that changes something in your plan or talked to a friend who gave you a different perspective on your product. You might also conduct a little research, subtly asking questions of people you know about what they think of some aspect of your plan, without giving away too many details. If you discover something useful, add it to your planning documents as either a positive or a negative.

Once again, think about as many aspects of your business idea as possible to try and objectively determine if it is viable.

Handling Stress

If you decide to start your own business you will have stress. You'll worry about getting clients and how to generate income. You'll worry about taxes and paying bills. You'll worry about where to best spend your time. You'll essentially worry about everything. What you absolutely cannot afford to do as a business owner is let the stress overwhelm you and destroy your dream from the inside.

Much depends on how you work and deal with difficult situations. Do you multitask well or do you like to sit and write code with a laser-like focus? How do you handle disruptions? Where do you intend to work, and is it conducive to your style of operating? Do you have children or pets that will distract from what you need to accomplish? Are you intending to do this as a second job to get started and would your primary occupation create problems? Are you even allowed by your employer to do something like this?

All I can say on this subject is to identify your potential stressors—you won't get all of them—and think about how you would deal with them if they were to arise. It all goes back to planning, or *being prepared*. Having worked for large aerospace companies throughout my career, I've always been a planner when it comes to projects. In my consulting business, at the first meeting or conference call with a client, I lay out the plan in as much detail as possible, overly stressing the contingencies for when things don't go as expected. Do the same for yourself and your business. While it won't eliminate all the upcoming stress, it might make you a bit more calm knowing that you have plans in place should bad things happen.

Where to Work

I have several friends thinking about starting their own software businesses. A few of them are even helping out with this book by providing me with stories of their challenges and conquests as they move deeper into app development. None have started their own business yet, nor are they anywhere ready to do so, but they've all indicated intentions to work from home. While this sounds appealing, it doesn't work for everyone. I'll even go so far as to say it probably doesn't work for most people.

First, there are often way too many distractions when working from home. Even if you live alone or have significant time by yourself in which to function, all the little commonplace things tug at you. Whether it's a delivery or the landscapers next door or the trucks going down the street, sounds are a common problem. Sounds are my major annoyance. You'd think as I got older my hearing would decrease and sounds would not bother me. I mean, I attended my share of concerts, yet I hear every little nuance in the audible spectrum. Wind bothers me. The rain dripping off the roof right now bothers me. Eventually the kids playing outside in the street—I think it's a school holiday—will bother me. As a solution I use noise-cancelling headphones that work well, but for short periods of up to an hour or so.

Chores such as the laundry can distract you from getting things done. Oh, all I need do is put the laundry in, take it out, and put it in the dryer, etc. Maybe your business isn't starting off as great as you had hoped and you're worried about the stress you're placing on your spouse, so you try to compensate by doing more around the house. What you might be doing in reality is distracting even more from your business.

At home you probably have all your favorite foods steps away from your computer. Just that small bag of chips or soda to get you over that problem you've been dealing with would help a lot. Or maybe it's lunchtime and you take a break and check out the news on TV. Or you see a stain on the carpet and it will only take a few minutes to take care of it. So many distractions are out there trying to prevent you from succeeding.

Now, as always, there is no single correct answer. For some people, working from home will be the correct decision. For many people, working from home may be the only option. You don't have to find and lease space; you save on gas and car wear and tear. But for me there is one big drawback, which is working alone.

When you work at a company, you have a team with whom you can share ideas and ask to help solve problems. You stay up to date on the latest techniques for provisioning or use of CSS styles. When you do take a break, you interact with like-minded people that help to spur your creativity and promote progress. You've become part of a community and may even call them work friends.

So how do you get that sense of community and support when starting your own company? In the past dozen or so years, business incubators have sprung up all around the country to offer just that capability. You rent, by the day, week, month, or longer, a space as small as a single desk up to a complete suite of offices depending on your plan and the amount you wish to spend. I have one incubator nearby that offers daily rates as low as $10 for which you get WiFi, snack bar, printing, fax, a business address, and even 3D printing capability. It's in the business district of the small town where I live on the outskirts of Denver, so it's not the latest in urban chic, but it does offer that sense of community I mentioned earlier. It's quiet and free from most distractions. There are conference rooms in which to meet clients so you don't have to try and sell yourself in a crowded and noisy coffee shop.

Business incubators sometimes offer other incentives as well. Many have people or companies that provide business and marketing advice. The more established incubators also have connections that might possibly get you technical support, advisors, and even funding if you have a viable concept; this is where a great business plan can help immensely.

Incubators now exist in every major city, and more pop up every few months. Most of the technology meetups I attend take place at various incubators around Denver. Some of the larger ones have multiple locations and are almost at capacity on the day they open. Some have dozens of conference rooms, on-site restaurants, and all sorts of other amenities. I've been to incubators built from scratch on razed lots in the hippest part of town that could be mistaken for the trendiest nightclub.

I want to give an example of a very typical business incubator with which I work on occasion. The Innovation Pavilion (Figure 2-16) opened five years ago south of Denver. A key discriminator for this incubator is its geographic location. Here in the Denver area, as I suspect in most major metropolitan areas, certain corridors of town seem to get a certain type of business. Technology startups have tended to form in the Boulder–Denver corridor, most likely due to the university presence; e.g., University of Colorado–Boulder, University of Denver, and Metro State University of Denver. South of the city has come to be the more residential areas where people live.

Figure 2-16. Offering the same basic services and amenities as other incubators, Innovation Pavilion tries to reach the under-represented, more mature founders by locating closer to their homes and offering a live-work-play attitude

The Innovation Pavilion environment fosters the growth of entrepreneurial ideas and helps high-growth companies reach their potential. The ecosystem consists of flexible real estate options, mentorship programs, service provider contacts, corporate relations, and structured funding programs. One of the most valuable aspects of being at IP is sharing a space filled with entrepreneurs eager to exchange ideas and collaborate through productive collisions.

IP's plans include launching ten additional locations over the coming years in cities across the United States, including my own hometown of Parker, Colorado. A major difference from other hip, downtown locations is the theme of live-work-play, which brings a more mature work force into the startup community.

In making your decision, think about your future. If serious about your business, you're likely to be working at it, and on it, for years to come. Are the cost savings of working from home worth the cost of losing out on the day-to-day interactions with like-minded and motivated people? Or is the hour-long commute to that hip incubator downtown worth the help you're going to get? When looking at choosing a potential work location such as a business incubator, in addition to the features they offer, carefully examine their directory. If you're an iOS developer but 90 percent of the companies there are web development startups, will that be a good resource? It might or it might not be. Again, it depends on your plan and the direction in which you want to take your business. As always, think about where you're headed.

Skills

Previously, we discussed the ten basic skills as related to getting a position with a software development company. For the most part, as an entrepreneur we need all those and more. We have to not only do the work, but also run and manage the business at the same time. We have much more perceived control of our life, but at the cost of having to work harder and, most of the time, longer hours.

Without going into detail on each of the ten skills, I prepared Table 2-1, allowing you to quickly see what might be more important about a skill or why a particular one might have less significance as a business owner. Doing everything yourself, you'll have to be very proficient in setting up your system to achieve your client's goal. They may even provide you with specific devices to which you will deploy. This alleviates less savvy clients from having to bother with the technical details. Many clients you will have to handhold at every step.

Table 2-1. Relative Importance of Skills for an Entrepreneur Compared with an Employee

Skill	Importance	Notes
Xcode Setup	Higher	You'll need to set this up on a per-project basis for each client.
Source Control	Same/More Flexible	Keep track of changes and protect your work, but you're not confined to a standardized process such as Svn or Git.
Agile	Lower	You won't have a team other than yourself, so focus on how you do things best; always try to inject new techniques whenever possible, and always keep your client in the loop.
UI/UX	Higher	Unless you're already a skilled designer, you may want to confine your projects to those with minimalistic UI designs. Also consider offloading the design work to someone else in order to save time and effort.
Target Build	Same	
Embedded	Lower	In the early stages of your company, you'll most likely focus on making the best use of Xcode tools, incorporating the extensive built-in support to limit the amount of customization needed in your projects.
App Publishing	Higher	You'll have to do all the work in getting your client's apps into the store. Do it as efficiently and cheaply as possible. Clients don't want to waste money on your mistakes because you haven't prepared.
Web Services	Same	
Testing	Higher	As with getting apps into the store, you want to make sure they get thoroughly tested first. Do unit testing and UI testing, and develop a beta program using TestFlight to get feedback from users so as to eliminate issues after deployment.
Accessories	Likely Lower	Unless you have a hardware engineering background, focus on software-only projects until you become comfortable with all the other skills and code development techniques.

The biggest concern I would have centers on UI/UX design. Remember, the first thing a user sees and reacts to is how the app presents itself. An ugly or hard-to-use UI will turn people off from the very beginning. Unless you have really excellent design tools such as the Adobe Creative Suite, you may want to limit the projects you take on that include complex graphics and user interactions. Another option would be to look for designers with whom you can barter and maybe exchange your skills. Also, be sure to check out freelancing sites such as Upwork where you can hire freelancers (which we'll talk about in the next section) to handle those tasks you want to offload.

In a moderate to large company, as a developer, you may never deal with the actual publishing of the app to the App Store, but this is one task your clients will absolutely expect you to perform. You will be responsible for getting the app into the store and making sure it passes all Apple testing with minimal, preferably zero, rejections. A customer is not going to be happy if you have to ask for more money because you failed in having their app published. At best, you'll likely have to do any rework and resubmissions without getting paid unless you've specified otherwise in your contract with the client. At the same time, putting in too much contingency for mistakes will lead your client to doubt your ability and may lose you the job.

Finally, testing will be another major concern of yours. Put an app into the store that crashes and gets only negative reviews and you'll not only lose your client, but also they're likely to spread the word about the inept developer they hired, calling you out specifically. It's much more common for someone to complain about bad service than it is for them to praise or reward satisfaction. People expect you to do your job well, so prove to them you can. The returns you'll get are repeat customers and referrals.

Entrepreneurial Summary

Starting your own business can be a monumental undertaking. Whether you work from home or a business incubator (Figure 2-17) for the resources and collaboration, you'll likely have some of the best times of your life. Over the past several decades, the traditional business model has skewed toward small businesses, which now in 2011 include 5.68 million employer firms in the United States according to the small business and entrepreneurship council. Firms with fewer than 500 workers accounted for 99.7 percent of those businesses, and businesses with less than 20 workers made up 89.8 percent. So starting your own company is not the far-fetched seeming idea it was a decade or so ago.

Figure 2-17. A business incubator provides you and your company with the kind of person-to-person interactivity you're not likely to get working from home

Without planning, everything can and likely will go wrong. Think about what you offer and if there are people who will pay for your services. Because you're reading this book, you likely fall into one of two categories: 1) writing software for other people in order to make a living but have more control over your day-to-day life, or 2) taking your great idea to market.

For the most part, all the skills we talked about in the employee section still apply, and several become even more important. Starting your own business means you are taking on far more responsibility than either of the other two career choices: working as an employee or as a freelancer. Even beyond the additional technical skill load you now have to have, all the aspects of the business itself, unless you have partners, become yours to manage and deal with. If you enjoy sleeping seven or eight hours a night, then this might not be the right choice, at least until your skills are solid.

Because the workload and risks are much higher, so are the rewards. Working for a company, you might get a quarter or less of the hourly rate they charge to their customers. And if you're a salaried employee—you make a fixed amount per period regardless of the hours you put in—you probably get much less of a percentage than that. As a business owner, barring your company expenses, everything is yours to manage as you see fit. You direct the business and decide the course it will take. You're responsible for the momentous successes as well as the devastating failures.

Option #3: Freelancer

A freelancer or independent contractor is a self-employed person who may or may not work for a company such as a contracting agency, but who is not committed to any specific position for the long term. Basically, you take the jobs you want and you work for clients, but someone else handles all the business overhead, which can range from finding clients to dealing with taxes and business insurance, etc. The downside is that they take a cut of revenue. Think of it like selling your game on the App Store. You offer it for ninety-nine cents, of which 70 percent or about seventy cents comes to you.

Because this position puts you somewhere between being an employee and running your own company, the skills needed are going to vary slightly depending on how close to one of those options you find yourself. Whether you obtain a position with an established company under a contract-to-hire agreement or set up your own shop using a temporary or contracting agency, as a freelancer you have to make some decisions as to how your future will unfold over the coming months or years.

Contract-to-Hire

Often, when looking for a permanent position as a developer, you'll see contract-to-hire, 1099 employee, or something very similar. They're basically starting you off as a freelancer or independent contractor. The hiring company wants to try you out for a while to see if you're a good fit before offering you a permanent position. For you, this can be a good thing or a bad thing. It does get you in the door to work on software development or in whatever position that you've been offered. Much of the time, you'll make more money this way. Because contract-to-hire offers are generally based on an hourly rate, if you wind up working more than 40 hours a week, you'll get paid for it. Depending on local labor laws this may vary, but when I worked this way, I found myself getting a nice paycheck.

Of course you won't get benefits such as vacation, insurance, and so on, and depending on your needs and expectations that could be a major criterion in the decision of whether to accept or reject the position. For the most part, no one on your team will likely treat you any different than a regular employee. One thing I did find was that I wasn't included in company staff meetings related to internal policy. No matter. I never like those meetings anyway, so I saw this as a benefit.

Contract-to-hire positions can range from a couple months to half a year. Mine lasted 90 days before I was picked up as a permanent employee. As with everything else, this can shift around quite a bit, and I've seen people who were made permanent employees a few weeks into their contract.

A contract-to-hire is one version of being a freelancer. You are responsible for all the things a company would normally provide. You usually have a bit more freedom in your work schedule depending on the needs of the company. I was able to shift my start and end times by a couple hours so I could avoid the commute traffic. In some organizations you may see no difference whatsoever between yourself and a permanent employee. This position is really a stepping stone to a full-time position.

General Freelancer

I love using freelancers because they've always given me the results I expect at a very reasonable cost. I use them for everything from web stuff to electrical design depending on my needs and schedule. The key to working as a freelancer is getting the right amount of work assignments to meet your personal goals. Do you want to work on jobs in your spare time in order to supplement your income and improve your skills? Would you like to make this a full-time career choice?

Regardless of how you wish to execute your freelancing decision, you'll need to find projects to take on for which clients will pay you. And, as an aside, payment does not always have to be in cash. I have a great friend who does a lot of our company website and marketing work as an independent contractor. Although we do pay him in cash, he'll barter with other clients with various products and services. It's kind of funny; as I developed more experience in the independent developer space, I found bartering to be more widely prevalent than I had imagined. For me, bartering was something from a couple centuries ago where you brought your corn to market and got a bag of flour and a couple pairs of shoes in return. I guess I watched a little too much *Little House on the Prairie*.

Whether you take payment in cash, products, or services, the key, of course, will be finding those projects, and for that, as with finding a job, the absolute best method is to go out and network. When I give talks at iOS Meetups, about half the crowd work for established companies, and the other half are typically freelancers who have established a loosely coupled network with each other to pass along tips, ideas, skills, and projects. Many of the freelancers I meet are busy working on one or two apps already and can't take on another assignment. If something comes up, they need to have a way to offer the service to that potential client; otherwise, the next time that client has a job they might come away thinking the developer is always too busy. If the developer offers a solution to make the new project happen, even if with someone else, that client will likely come back the next time. This helps the developer keep their supply line of business full. If they are again busy the next time, you might be the first person they look to for help.

We discussed networking and how to go about it in the section on working as an employee, so I won't go into detail again. The key points are to get out there and, if need be, overcome your fear of socializing. Though it's a bit cliché, software people really are a bit introverted. I myself am introverted, though nobody thinks so because when I give talks or speak with people, I project an air of confidence. My introversion comes at the initiation when I have to first go up to someone I don't yet know. Speaking at meetings takes that out of the equation as, after the talk, most people like to come up and chat about something related to what was presented. Volunteering to speak at these events can help a lot. As your confidence builds and you gain visibility at these meetings, you start to know people and eventually reach out to the next set of newcomers.

A few other things. Try to have your "elevator speech" ready to go at a moment's notice. Know who you are and how you want to present yourself to others. This takes it out of their hands and puts it into your own. If, say, you let someone introduce you as an iOS developer, but you do web stuff or Android or something else, you've given up your control. Let them know who you are on exactly your terms. Have business cards ready to go. This may seem old school, but people still take notes on paper when time is short. Mainly though, just be friendly and receptive to lots of different people. If you're looking for a mentor or a job and someone doesn't at first blush fit that bill, don't brush them off too quickly. They may be the person who asks you for help the next time. Always, if it makes sense, offer to help people you meet. My partner does this all the time. One of the things she forever asks of people is how she might help them. They won't forget this, and that's what you want—to be remembered.

Also remember to continually build your LinkedIn network of connections. Don't use it like Facebook or other social media sites and add all your friends. Keep it, as much as possible, to just the relevant connections in your desired areas of interest. Too many party pictures of you and your posse can turn away potential clients or companies interested in bringing on new talent. Focus on the professional. Try to get recommendations from past clients and others with whom you've worked to boost your credibility.

I've talked before about sites like Upwork that can help get you started as a freelancer. Many will take a percentage of the revenue paid by the client while others might charge the freelancer a fee to advertise on the site. While advertising yourself may cost a little up front, getting your bio at the top of the heap can give you a bit of an edge on the competition. It's really nothing more than SEO (search engine optimization) for yourself. If you do decide to invest in a higher placement, if one is even offered, make certain what you put up appeals to potential clients. I've known companies that spend thousands a month on SEO for a website that's clunky and hard to use. All that wound up doing is getting them a faster rejection. Customers didn't have to search long to find out that the company was not what they wanted because the site was too difficult to access.

In addition to online agencies, if you live in a reasonably sized city or town, there will be temporary agencies that you might also consider. Because Denver is a destination city for large conferences, a large number of these exist. When large conferences take place, there's an entire team of IT (information technology) people to operate, manage, and support the function. Many conferences have custom apps just for the duration of the event and need technical help for a few weeks to perform the customization and on-site technical support. I've worked at a few of these events myself and have had a lot of fun and made tremendous connections. It's also a very nice change of pace to get away from the house or office and see what's going on in the world.

Finding work as a freelancer can be challenging as the options are so varied. I think of it like a treasure hunt and look for new and interesting ways to make connections that might eventually turn into paying contracts. To be honest, at best we convert maybe one in thirty or forty contacts into something real, and many of those might be where we barter for service. But the contacts and connections we make almost always lead to something else down the road. Don't dismiss something just because there's no short-term gain or it doesn't look immediately promising. You do have to strike a balance of course. Weigh your urgent need to close some business with the potential for bigger projects later. Being an independent contractor is, in effect, running your own business, so do what's right for that business.

Skills

I'm not going to spend too much time here on skills. As an independent contractor/ freelancer, you already function as an entrepreneur. Effectively, the only real difference is that you've offloaded some of the business details to a company via their website or through your temporary agency. Because you still have to do the job of getting the client's app from the drawing board to the App Store, most of the same skills must be mastered for you to succeed in a way that will net you additional business.

The few exceptions might involve the testing and app publishing. First, someone that uses a freelance developer service may already know about apps and software development. In fact, they may be an expert or even an independent contractor themselves in need of some coding support. You might get tasks for writing a specific number of objects or methods. As such, the client would integrate your code into their own project and you would never have to perform beta testing or build projects to send to the App Store. Each and every case will be unique, so my strong advice is to possess and understand all required skills, practice as much as you can, and follow trends in the general community on changes to how things might be done. Table 2-2 depicts the deviations in skills required for a contractor as compared with an employee.

Table 2-2. Relative Importance of Skills for an Independent Contractor/Freelancer Compared with an Employee

Skill	Importance	Notes
Xcode Setup	Higher	You'll need to set this up on a per-project basis for each client.
Source Control	Same/More Flexible	Keep track of changes and protect your work, but you're not confined to a standardized process such as Svn or Git.
Agile	Lower	You won't have a team other than yourself, so focus on how you do things best; always try to inject new techniques whenever possible, and always keep your client in the loop.
UI/UX	Higher	Unless you're already a skilled designer, you may want to confine your projects to those with minimalistic UI designs. Also consider offloading the design work to someone else in order to save time and effort.
Target Build	Same	
Embedded	Lower	In the early stages of your company, you'll most likely focus on making the best use of Xcode tools, incorporating the extensive built-in support to limit the amount of customization needed in your projects.
App Publishing	Similar	Many customers looking for freelancers already understand the basics of apps and how they get published. Quite often the client only needs help with the coding, so you might do a lot less actual publishing.
Web Services	Same	
Testing	Depends	In many freelance situations, because the client is looking for an inexpensive solution themselves, they may prefer to do testing on their own.
Accessories	Likely Lower	Unless you have a hardware engineering background, focus on software-only projects until you become comfortable with all the other skills and code development techniques.

Career Direction Summary

I spent a lot of time discussing career choices in this chapter because as someone starting out in their development career you'll want to know where to focus your efforts. I've seen so many people give up on trying to becoming a software professional, saying, "There's just too much to learn. I just don't have the time." And it's true. You need to know a wide variety of skills and lots of terminology just to get to the first interview. While it's easy to throw a bunch of buzzwords onto your resume or LinkedIn profile, a trained developer or recruiter can easily spot the difference between someone with actual experience and someone masquerading as a pro. You don't have to be expert in each and every one of the skills we'll cover in the following chapters. It helps, but it's not required or even expected except for the most senior positions.

Focus on which skills are most necessary for the path you want to take. Being honest for a moment, you really should try to have at least a passing familiarity with everything we'll talk about. You may never set up a bot-based continuous integration system, but at least know what it's all about. There's a trick I've used in the past when I know a bit of what something is, but not much more. If an interviewer mentions it or asks about it, I say something like, "I know a little about CI, but I don't understand this concept of bots in the process." This allows the interviewer to describe it to me. They feel good because they get to talk about their work. They spend more time with me so the connection grows and we both become more engaged in the discussion. Even more importantly, I get something tangible from the interview for my time. I learn how something works in an actual functioning organization. If you try this, as soon as you get back to the car or coffee shop, take as many notes about what you learned as you can remember. You can use this in the next interview, whether at the same company or someplace else.

The basic steps I would take if I were starting out would be:

1. Learn what each career path has to offer—its advantages and disadvantages.

2. Decide which skills would be most important to you when choosing that path.

3. Start to learn and develop the skills.

4. Look for meetups that have a direct correlation to that career as well as those that are closely related.

5. Join the meetup and start networking.

6. Offer to do a short presentation on a subject that you think you can quickly master.

7. Start researching for that dream job.

This list is far from all inclusive and certainly should be tailored to your skills, needs, and personality. It's not a formula for success as much as a recipe to get you started down your own, personal journey to be the professional developer that you wish to be.

After a long chapter on preparation, we're ready to dive into each of the skills we need to master to make us great developers.

Chapter 3

Setting Up Xcode

In this chapter we go beyond the initial Xcode setup that most first-time developers experience to the point where we can build apps for sale and distribution. I'll walk you through the step-by-step process of creating and downloading certificates, setting up devices, app naming, and provisioning required for you to begin creating sellable apps for the Apple App Store. While most of the time it's so much simpler just to use the simulator and avoid all the hassles of working with devices, you'll find that you don't want to go too far down that road. What generally happens with newer developers is that the simulators provide a "crutch" that makes many of the real-world problems transparent. Things just tend to work more often, and there's this attitude of, "When I have it perfect, I'll convert it to an App Store product." This does work, of course, but there are so many issues and details you have to take care of that the momentum starts to wane. You become more mired in the details of this app name or that profile or something else, and what's important, the app itself, moves to the background. I'd rather see you work through all this so it's second nature and you can build device-based apps from the start.

First, I want to warn you that this chapter is very dry reading. Because we cover the essentials of how to do specific, necessary steps, I wrote this in a very procedural manner; e.g., do this, then do this, you should see this, click that, and so on. Boring! But necessary. I love to cook and frequently get a new slow cooker or pasta maker, but do I read the manuals? Not likely. I tend to take off and just try something to see how it works. You can, and many people do, work that way in setting up Xcode. Most of the time, however, you will head down the wrong path; there are just too many options where you can go wrong. It's usually possible to back out with only minor effects. The most common mistake people make in this phase is using their ideal app name, making too many errors, and having to start over only to find that because they've already entered the name into the development system it's in there permanently. They wind up having to come up with a new name. So, while it's not that much fun, we just have to wade our way through it all to reach the good stuff.

Let's get started.

© Molly K. Maskrey 2016
M.K. Maskrey, *App Development Recipes for iOS and watchOS*, DOI 10.1007/978-1-4842-1820-4_3

> **Note** Starting with Xcode 7.1, Apple no longer requires you to purchase a developer license, typically $99USD, to load and test your app with actual device hardware. However, at the time of this writing you still need to have a purchased license in order to sell apps in the App Store as well as to distribute them for beta testing using TestFlight. We'll proceed in this chapter as if you fully intend to develop for the App Store.

Joining The Apple Developer Program

Problem

You want to distribute your iOS app, but your Xcode distribution is not set up to let you do so.

Solution

You must join the Apple Developer Program for $99USD per year to get access to the resources needed for app distribution.

How It Works

First, go to the most current Apple Developer Programs website using a search engine, since from time to time Apple may change the actual URL of the site. You should see options for enrolling as either an individual or an organization.

> **Note** Prior to the summer of 2015, Apple offered separate developer programs for iOS and Macintosh OS X. This meant you had to purchase, for $99USD each, different accounts if you wanted to do both iOS and Mac software. Now, one program membership, for one $99USD yearly fee, gives you complete access to both sets of resources.

This is where you want to do a little bit of thinking before you proceed and is why I spent so much time in Chapter 2 discussing career options and the various requirements of your intended path. The most common thing that happens here is that, because it's so easy, most people just go with an individual developer account to quickly get started. What this means is that you're developing, distributing, and selling your apps under your own name, not your company name. Much of the time this works out just fine. But if you want to have a company and use your organization's name on the App Store, you really want to look into enrolling as an organization; that is, use your business name.

It doesn't cost any more than enrolling as an individual, and you get a few benefits when working this way. In addition to using your business name on the App Store and selling your fantastic and unique creations as a business, you can have additional developers work under your account. So, if you and your friends want to develop apps together, things become much easier. You all work under the same Apple portal using the same sets of certificates, app IDs, and so on. Your team doesn't even have to use the same email domain.

In a typical company, everyone would have an email address such as molly@companyname.com or john.Doe@companyname.com. The names would be different but the <something>.com would all be the same. But if you're a bunch of people that just want to work together to create something really cool, you probably want to use your personal email addresses. By enrolling as a company you can still do this. In fact, this is how I've set up the developer account with which we will be working through the course of this book. My friends and teammates work under my umbrella account but use their own individual email addresses for access.

> **Note**   A common source of confusion when setting up a business-based developer account arises when you try to enroll for the enterprise developer program (Figure 3-1). This is used for companies, typically larger companies, that need to distribute apps to employees within their organization. A common use would be to distribute a product catalog app to the entire sales team. This program costs $299USD.

Figure 3-1. The Apple Developer Enterprise Program is for companies that distribute apps internally as opposed to or in addition to in the App Store. You do not need to join this program to develop apps under your own organizational structure

Individual Enrollment

Joining as an individual is pretty straightforward. You only need enter your legal name, address details, and payment information. You typically get taken to the Apple Store and can complete the purchase using your existing account information. Generally, in moments to at most an hour you'll receive a couple of emails. The first will be your purchase confirmation— your receipt for the purchase. Later, you'll receive another email with a link that activates your developer account. In some cases, Apple may have to verify the information you provided. This might happen if, say, your zip code doesn't match, anything was entered incorrectly, or, like me, you have to enter whether you live within or outside town limits.

Organizational Enrollment

Joining the developer program as a company means you have to fill in a few more details and have the information ready and available. The most important thing is that if joining as a company, you have to have a real company. This can't just be the name you came up with and put on your business cards; your company's name should be registered in the state where it was formed.

Most states make forming a company such as a Limited Liability Company pretty easy, but check out all the details and requirements as appropriate. The best advice would be to spend some money to talk with a business attorney and then decide on which type of organization you should form. There are different tax and reporting requirements for each. Once the company is formed, it may take a few days to weeks to have it show up in your state's registry. In my case it showed up on the same day, but I suspect this varies by region.

Registering your business's legal name is only one-half of the equation. You also need to have a DUNS number. This is a nine-digit number provided by Dun & Bradstreet. Filing the legal documentation for your business does not automatically provide you with a DUNS number. You will have to do this yourself and provide the following information:

Legal name

Headquarters name and address for your business

Doing Business As (DBA) or other name by which your business is commonly recognized

Physical address, city, state, and zip code

Mailing address (if separate from headquarters and/or physical address)

Telephone number

Contact name and title

Number of employees at your physical location

Whether you are a home-based business

Since DUNS numbers are typically needed when doing business with the U.S. government, it's a fairly quick method for obtaining a number. You can search for how to do this; you should be taken to the site shown in Figure 3-2, where you can get your number processing started. According to the site's information, it typically takes about a day to process. However, before Apple will issue a developer license they will need to be able to access that number on the D & B servers. Apple has a close relationship with D & B, and there is even a special Apple contact for handling this type of request. So, while it may seem a little overwhelming at first and you may want to give up, it usually turns out well.

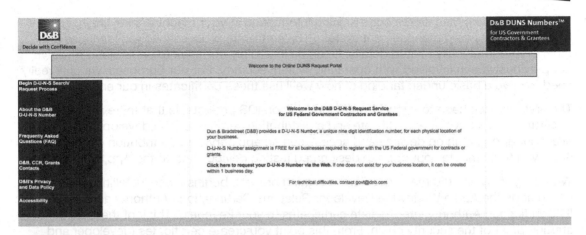

Figure 3-2. *Getting a DUNS number is usually quick and easy if you have a legally formed company within your state. However, the number may take a few days to get into the database so Apple can verify your company in order to issue an organizational developer program license*

Comments

If you never intend to develop iOS (or Mac OS X) software under your own company, then an individual developer account will certainly be enough to get you started and working almost immediately. On the other hand, if you're sure you want to develop as a company or work with others on app projects, consider obtaining an organizational developer license from Apple. It costs no more than an individual membership, but you get so much more flexibility. You will need to make sure your business is legally formed and obtain a DUNS number, but that can be completed within a week.

Developer Certificates

Problem

You've created an app and you want to start the process of getting it into the App Store for distribution and beta testing.

Solution

You must set up your development computer so that the apps you create are code signed and can thus be trusted to execute on Apple devices before you distribute them to the App Store.

How It Works

Code signing is the process that assures everyone downloading your app that it has not been tampered with and will not introduce viruses or other malware onto their devices. In addition to being code signed, your app must be properly provisioned, which we will talk about in a later section of this chapter.

Your development Mac stores code-signing information in your machine's keychain, which is the OS X password management system. The certificate process involves identities and other cryptographically related details. It can be incredibly complex to understand if you've not previously been involved with operating system security. For our purposes, we only really need to have a basic understanding of how we'll use these certificates in our endeavors.

The first thing we need to know, if we're focusing on iOS projects, is that there are two types of certificates: a developer certificate and a distribution certificate. The developer certificates allow our apps to run on devices and access certain app services. Distribution certificates allow you to distribute your apps to designated testing devices and to the App Store.

Without getting into too many details, the signing process begins when installing Xcode, which adds the Apple Worldwide Developer Relations Certifications Authority and Developer ID Certification Authority intermediate certificates to your keychain. Think of these as the starting point of the security chain. From this point you create certificates (developer and distribution) for your team. Each member of your team has their own developer certificate, and as such it will contain their name (Figure 3-3). If you have an individual developer account as opposed to an organization account, your distribution certificate will contain your name. But if developing as an organization, your company's distribution certificate will contain the name of your business as entered when you set up your program's credentials (Figure 3-4).

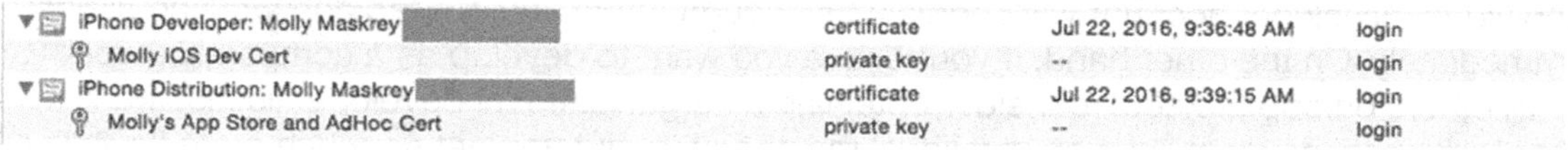

Figure 3-3. *With an individual developer account, both your development and distribution certificates will contain your name, since that is how the account was created*

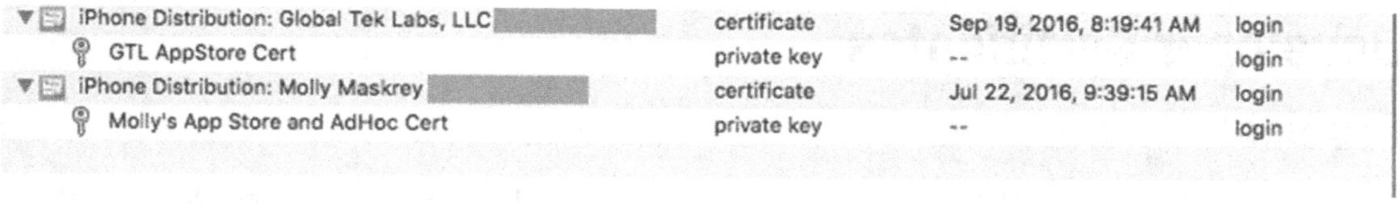

Figure 3-4. *When using an organization developer account, only one distribution certificate is created*

Okay, what I've shown you so far in this section is what we're looking to achieve, but how do we get there? Once we have a valid developer program license from Apple, we head over to the Member Center. As with everything else, the address changes periodically, so you want to search for "Apple developer," and at the bottom of the page there should be a section for the Member Center. Below that you click on the link for "Certs, IDs and Profiles."

At this point you might be taken directly to the page where you can create your certificates, IDs, and profiles. You'll see a taskbar with headers for Certificates, Identifiers, Devices, and Provisioning Profiles. We'll go through each of these in turn, but first we need to get our certificates in order. If there is a pull-down on the taskbar, make sure it is set to "iOS Apps." It may be set to "Overview," "Mac Apps," or "Safari Extensions," but we need "iOS Apps."

Below the Certificates section you'll see the following choices:

- All
- Pending
- Development
- Production

Click on All. It may be already selected, in which case you should see any certificates you already have in the center section of the screen, with a header at the top that should say "iOS Certificates." Along the top will be a '+' button, which is what we click to create new certificates. Click the '+' button.

As we saw before, there will be a listing of options under the Development and Production choices. We first want to get a development certificate, and once this is completed we'll perform the same steps for a production certificate. You should see the following options:

Development

- iOS App Development
- Apple Push Notification SSL (Sandbox)

Production

- App Store and Ad Hoc
- Apple Push Notification SSL Sandbox and (Production)
- Pass Type ID Certificate
- Website Push ID Certificate
- WatchKit Services Certificate
- VoIP Services Certificate
- Apple Pay Certificate
- Intermediate Certificates

Select the radio button to the left of "iOS App Development," then click Continue and you'll be taken to a page that asks you to create a signing certificate. At this point you need to open the Mac Keychain app by locating the icon under Applications that looks like a ring of keys (Figure 3-5). Follow the instructions to create a certificate signing request by selecting Keychain Access ➤ Certificate Assistant ➤ Request a Certificate from a Certificate Authority, as shown in Figure 3-6.

Figure 3-5. Locate and open the Mac Keychain app to create the certificate signing request (CSR)

| Keychain Access | File | Edit | View | Window | Help |

About Keychain Access		Keychain Access
Preferences...	⌘,
Keychain First Aid	⌥⌘A	ACTIONTEC
Certificate Assistant	▶	Open...
Ticket Viewer	⌥⌘K	Create a Certificate...
		Create a Certificate Authority...
Services	▶	Create a Certificate For Someone Else as a Certificate Authority...
		Request a Certificate From a Certificate Authority...
Hide Keychain Access	⌘H	Set the default Certificate Authority...
Hide Others	⌥⌘H	Evaluate a Certificate...
Show All	

Figure 3-6. Using Keychain, create a file and save it to your desktop; this will be used to create your development or production/distribution certificate

Fill out the form so that it looks similar to Figure 3-7, but use the email address associated with your iOS account.

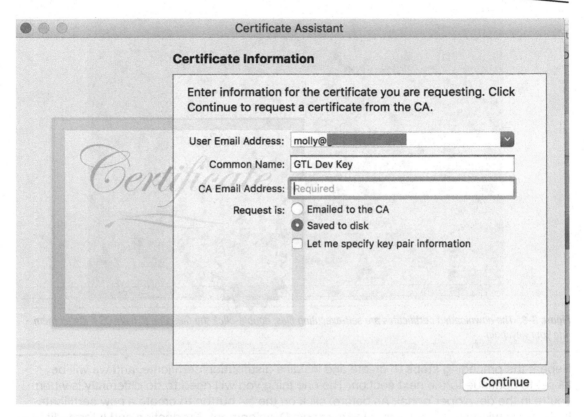

Figure 3-7. *Fill out the form in Keychain and save the file to your desktop*

After saving the file to your desktop—note that you didn't really take any action on this page other than following the directions to use the Keychain app—click Continue, at which point you will be prompted to upload the file you just created. Click Choose File…, and once the upload has completed—it should be very quick—click Generate. All you need do now is go to the next page and download the certificate. The downloaded certificates will have a .cer suffix like those in Figure 3-8. To complete the process, double-click the downloaded file; Mac OS X will install the certificates in your keychain.

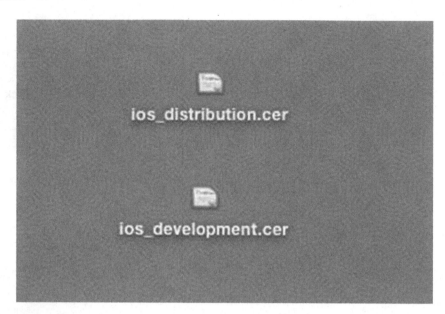

Figure 3-8. The downloaded certificates are self-executing files; double-click the filename to have OS X install them into your keychain

Repeat the preceding steps to create and install a distribution certificate, and we will be all set to continue to the next section. The one thing you will need to do differently is when you're in the developer portal. As before, click on the '+' button to create a new certificate. In the main window you will see three sections: Development, Production and Intermediate. In the Production section, click the radio button for App Store and Ad Hoc. Follow the reset of the steps exactly as before to install the distribution certificate.

Comments

By following this process, you will have accomplished the first step to being able to install apps for beta testing as well as upload your product to the App Store. To verify that this process was successful, use the Keychain app. On the left under Keychains, select "Login," and under Category select "My Certificates." You should see information similar to that shown in Figure 3-4, but for *your* account information.

Certificate Issues

Problem

For some reason your certificates do not show up properly or have a red *X* over the icon.

Solution

You most likely are missing the developer intermediate certificate, so you will need to install it from the iOS developer portal.

How It Works

Go back to the page with headers for Certificates, Identifiers, Devices, and Provisioning Profiles. As before, if there is a pull-down on the taskbar, make sure it is set to "iOS Apps." At the bottom of the page, click on the "World Wide Developer Relations Authority" link to download and install the intermediate certificate as before.

This may or may not correct the issues with your certificates. The first step would be to close everything and reboot your machine if the problem doesn't get corrected. If you reboot and still see a red *X*, use Keychain to delete the two certificates you generated, *not the developer relations certificate just downloaded*, and regenerate your developer and distribution certificates as shown previously.

App IDs

Problem

You've created an app or are ready to begin development, but you want to start the process of getting it into the App Store for distribution and beta testing ahead of time.

Solution

Just as we created our development and distribution certificates, we now want to create an app ID within the iOS developer portal for use in identifying our work throughout the process.

How It Works

We will use one of our project names to work through the app ID process. I'm going to use the name of our Objective-C to Swift conversion project. Originally, I called the app Town Slot as a play on the phrase "town slut." Because you can't generally reuse app names in the App Store, I'm going to go with Town Slot 2.

Back on the Certificates, Identifiers, Devices, and Profiles page, under Identifiers select "App IDs." The screen should change to indicate you are registering an app ID. Click on the '+' button to enter the name of the app; I used Town Slot 2 as my name.

Scroll down to the "App ID Suffix" field. This is where you will enter the specific bundle ID of your app, which you will use when creating an app for distribution to beta testers or to the App Store. The normal thing to enter is your company's reverse DNS domain name followed by the app name. I entered "com.globalteklabs.townslot2."

If you scroll down a little further you will see a section titled App Services. Some of the items may be selected and grayed out, but we don't need to add anything else. Later, we may add services to our other projects, but for this conversion project app, all we need are the default settings.

At the bottom click Continue. If you succeed, you will see a screen similar to Figure 3-9 containing your app's identification information. Beside the Identifier row you will see the app's bundle ID preceded by a ten-digit alphanumeric sequence, which is the bundle seed ID and essentially represents your company. It's used in the App Store to identify the apps your company provides, or that you provide as an individual developer, so that any necessary associations can be made with other apps or MFi accessory hardware if applicable. We'll use this in Xcode later.

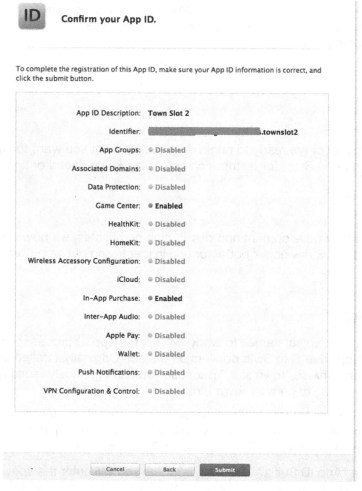

Figure 3-9. *Double check your app information before submitting; otherwise, you may have to start again with a different app name*

After clicking Submit, if everything is entered correctly you'll see "Registration Complete," and by clicking Done you should see this app ID in your list of app IDs, as in Figure 3-10.

2 App IDs Total	
Name ▲	ID
Town Slot 2	townslot2

Figure 3-10. Upon successful registration of your app ID, it should appear in your list of app IDs

Comments

In working through this with the team I assembled to help test out these procedures, the most common issue was using a name that already existed somewhere in the App Store. The app ID in question may not even appear in the store when searching, but most likely someone has used the name previously and the remnants of it have not been removed. More to the point, and from personal experience, I've never been able to reuse an app name that I used previously. There appears to be a long-term storage of app names and IDs somewhere within the iOS developer system that does not permit overlapping or duplicate names. It's similar to not being able to reuse passwords for some lengthy amount of time.

Devices

Problem

You want to test your app on actual iOS hardware.

Solution

In this section we will add our devices to the list of usable devices in the iOS developer system. You are allowed by Apple to add up to one hundred devices throughout the year of your developer program membership.

How It Works

Back on the Certificates, Identifiers, Devices, and Profiles page, under Devices, select "All." If you have any devices already added, you'll see them in the center section under iOS Devices. If you see grayed-out names, those are devices that have been disabled and are not usable within the Xcode system.

Before trying to add any new devices, first we need to get information about the devices we want to use. Let's start with one device, and you can just repeat the process for each additional one you want to add.

> **Note**   As Xcode gets more helpful, processes such as adding devices do become more automated. For example, if you plug in an iPhone on which you wish to install the app you're working on, Xcode will identify that device as not being in your list and will walk you through adding it. However, I've found this works sporadically. The procedures I'm discussing in this section are the primary way that this has been done for years and always works as a fallback, so it's good to know.

You need to get information about your device, and one easy way to do so is to use iTunes. Start iTunes on your computer, connect your device, and click on the device symbol—iPhone if it's an iPhone—at the top to see the display shown in Figure 3-11 or something similar.

Figure 3-11. *Connect the device you wish to work with using iTunes and go to the device information summary*

Make sure you've selected the Summary item on the left-hand Settings bar. Left-click on the serial number itself, not the "Serial Number" title, and the display should change to show the UDID as in Figure 3-12.

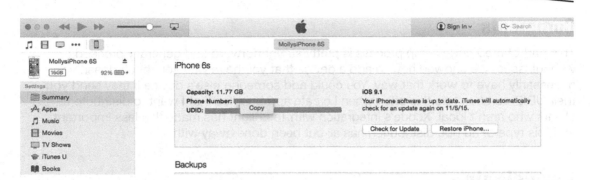

Figure 3-12. *Click on the serial number to change it to display the UDID. Right-click on the UDID number itself and select "Copy" to put the number onto your clipboard*

Right-click on the actual UDID number and select "Copy" to put that number into your computer's clipboard in order to paste it where needed.

Back in the Certificates, Identifiers, Devices, and Profiles section of the developer portal, click the '+' at the top to get to the Registering a New Device or Multiple Devices screen. We'll work with one device at a time for our practice.

Choose a name for your device, and by that I mean think of something that you wish to call your device as it will appear here, In the developer portal, as well as in Xcode when downloading apps to the device. For the most part, I'd suggest just using the name of your device as shown in iTunes, as you named it during the initial setup. But it doesn't have to be the same. It's up to you. Just make sure, especially if you are planning to add multiple devices, that your naming scheme is clear to you. I wouldn't, for example, name something "Test iPad" or even "Test iPad mini 2," because you may get another one—if the first one breaks, for example—and then have to deviate from your naming convention. Think it through early on to make it much simpler later on.

Type the name into the "Name" field, paste the UDID into its spot on the Register Device section of the page, and click the Continue button.

Note   At some point, especially if Xcode is open, you may see a message on your device asking if you want to trust this computer. If this is your device and your computer, of course you'll say yes. A reason you might not want to do so would be if you're logged into the developer portal on a computer that you don't intend to use for Xcode development, such as a friend's Mac.

If the information you entered was valid, you'll advance to a summary page that tells you how many devices you have left in each category. If the information appears correct, click the Register button, and the device should now appear in the summary pane.

At this point you may want to add any additional devices that you expect to use during development and testing.

Comments

This part of the Xcode setup process is pretty straightforward and generally proceeds without issue. We showed how to add a device that you have with you, but it doesn't necessarily have to work that way. You could add someone else's device if they send you their UDID number. I do this often when I create app bundles that I want to distribute to clients who aren't local. Xcode's integration with TestFlight has made this less important, and this type of ad hoc distribution has all but been done away with.

Provisioning

Problem

You've created an app, and you want to start the process of getting it into the App Store for distribution and beta testing.

Solution

The last of the four primary steps in getting ready to work with actual devices is to create provisioning profiles that a device will use to allow that device to execute app builds generated by Xcode. Profiles are used to make sure that the app is signed and is therefore from a trusted, legitimate source.

How It Works

When you generate a provisioning profile, it includes the three items we previously created: signing certificate, app ID, and device IDs. There are two types of provisioning profiles. Development profiles are used during the build and test process, while distribution profiles are needed when delivering your app to the App Store or for beta testing with users. Profiles can be generated by Xcode or manually by the team agent; that is, the main person in charge of the developer account. Later, we'll see how to generate certificates using Xcode, but first let's go through the process of generating a certificate manually.

Back on the Certificates, Identifiers, Devices, and Profiles page, under Provisioning Profiles select "All." Under the section for generating provisioning profiles manually, there should be a link to create manual profiles. Click on the '+' button to add a new item, and you'll be taken to the page for generating your profile.

The first step will be to select the type of profile, either development or distribution. Current choices for development include iOS or tvOS. In the distribution category you also get the choice of iOS or tvOS, but for each of those you need to select either App Store or Ad Hoc. The choices on the page should look like this:

Development

- iOS App Development
- tvOS App Development

Distribution

- App Store
- Apple TV App Store
- Ad Hoc
- tvOS Ad Hoc

Let's walk through creating a development profile for our slot machine game for which we've already created an app ID. Select the radio button next to "iOS App Development," and at the bottom of the page, click Continue.

> **Note** To create any profile, you'll use one of your previously created certificates, either developer or distribution, your set of devices, and your app ID. The key is the app ID. You can't create a provisioning profile until you first set up your app ID in the developer portal.

The next page will ask you to select an app ID via a pull-down that lists the available app IDs. Select the ID for the app of interest. I'm going to select the one for my slot machine game and click on Continue at the bottom of the page.

On the next page you will select the certificate to use for this profile. If the profile will just be used for development, the best option is to select the checkbox next to the development certificate and click the Continue button. Remember that a development certificate will have the names of the different developers on the team, whereas a distribution certificate will show the company name if you set things up as an organization. If you set up your developer account as an individual, then both will show just your name.

The next page will show the list of available devices to which you can attach to this profile. You can click Select All or select individual devices. Selecting all if you only have a small number of devices prevents your having to come back and regenerate the provisioning profile later on. Click Select All and then Continue.

The last page will show you the information so far and provide the opportunity to name your profile. As with other parts of this process, make sure your naming scheme is clear and concise. It also should be easy to identify in a small amount of characters. When we get to Xcode, you'll see that space is at a premium and being able to identify your profiles early in their name makes things easier to manage. For this profile, I use the name "Dev TownSlot2," as it clearly identifies the app for which the profile is intended and that it is a development certificate. Type the name and click the Generate button.

If everything was correct and valid you should get a page with something that looks like Figure 3-13 displayed. Click on Download to save the provisioning profile to your computer.

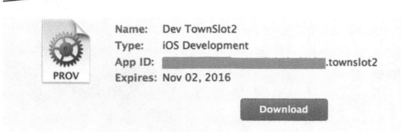

Name: Dev TownSlot2
Type: iOS Development
App ID: ████████████████████.townslot2
Expires: Nov 02, 2016

Download

Figure 3-13. A successfully generated development provisioning profile is valid for a year from its creation date

Caution   Sometimes you may get a message saying that an "unspecified error occurred." This often happens when going back and forth between the developer portal page and other web pages in your browser. Simply try generating the profile again, and it should work okay. Otherwise, validate that all the previous steps have been completed and try again. It also might be that one of the items was generated with undetected errors, in which case go back and step-by-step delete the item and regenerate before trying to create a profile.

Once the provisioning profile is on your computer it will be of the form `<profile name>`. `mobileprovision` and will look similar to that shown in Figure 3-14. Note that any blanks in your profile name have been converted to underscores.

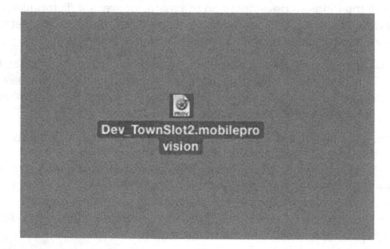

Dev_TownSlot2.mobilepro
vision

Figure 3-14. The downloaded provisioning profile looks like this before being installed into Xcode for use in the development process

Comments

So, what do you do with this? The simplest thing is to just drag and drop it on top of the Xcode icon to install it so that Xcode can use it. In the next section, we'll go into a bit more detail about loading provisioning profiles onto your system so they can be used for app development.

Provisioning Profile Location

Problem

You need to access the actual provisioning profiles installed into Xcode, but you don't know where they are.

Solution

Set up your Mac to see where the provisioning profiles are located.

How It Works

The provisioning profiles are located in the following directory:

`~/Library/MobileDevice/Provisioning Profiles`

The '~' character represents a shortcut to your home directory. This is the starting point that OS X created for you when you set up your computer. It could be anything, but is typically your user name. For my account, my home directory is MollyDev, as shown in Figure 3-15. The first thing that stands out is that there is no Library subfolder. So what do you do?

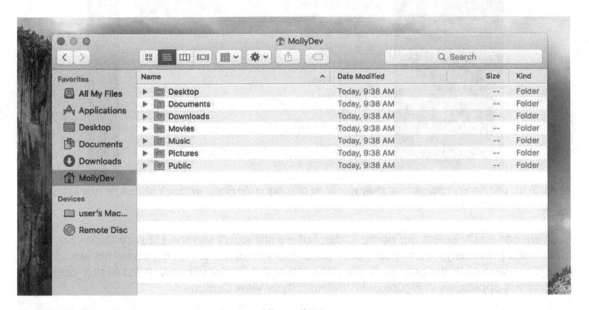

Figure 3-15. The author's home directory shows no Library directory

Throughout the years Apple has endeavored to make their devices more user friendly, but they've also tried a number of ways to prevent the novice user from making simple mistakes that can irrevocably damage their file system. One of these is to hide the user's Library folder. For the vast majority of users this works well. But Xcode developers are, or should be, a bit more savvy, and they occasionally need access to their `Library` folder. Let's get OS X to show us our `~/Library` folder.

In a Finder window, select your home directory in the sidebar. If you don't see your home directory in the sidebar, you need to add that as well. To add your home directory to the sidebar, go to Finder along the topmost menu bar and select "Preferences...," which should result in the Finder Preferences window popping up. Click on the "Sidebar" option at the top and select the checkbox next to the name of your home folder, as shown in Figure 3-16. You can always navigate to this point using any Finder window, but having your home folder in the Finder's sidebar makes things so much easier and faster.

Figure 3-16. *Use Finder Preferences to show your home directory in the Finder window's sidebar for easy access during iOS development*

Now we can easily select our home folder, but we still won't see the `Library` folder. So, as I mentioned previously, select your home folder from the sidebar—in my case this would be `MollyDev`—and click the gear icon along the top of the Finder window. A list of pull-down options will appear, as in Figure 3-17. Select "Show View Options."

Figure 3-17. *Select "Show View Options" to see what OS X will display in a Finder window*

In the View Options window for your home directory, select "Show Library Folder," as shown in Figure 3-18.

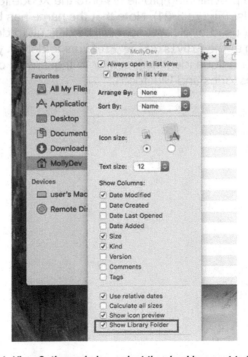

Figure 3-18. *In your home folder's View Options window, select the checkbox next to "Show Library Folder"*

Now, when viewing your home directory you should be able to see your Library folder, as in Figure 3-19.

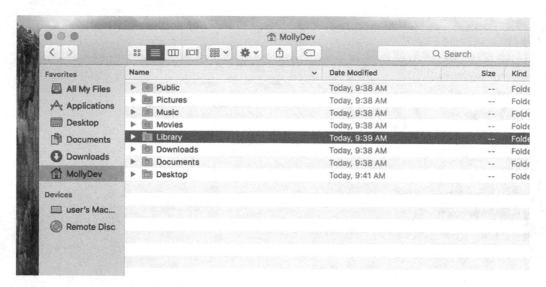

Figure 3-19. Now you should be able to view the Library folder in your home directory

Navigate to the Provisioning Profiles folder as described earlier, and you should see an empty folder as in Figure 3-20 if you haven't yet created any profiles or installed this one into Xcode. When you drag the provisioning profile file onto the Xcode icon to install it, you'll see a profile appear in this folder (Figure 3-21). Note that the name has been changed to a long, seemingly random number used by Xcode, so it will be difficult to determine what profiles are present just by looking at the Provisioning Profiles folder on your Mac. This number is actually a UUID (universally unique identifier), similar to those we'll discuss later in this book in the section on iOS accessories and Bluetooth.

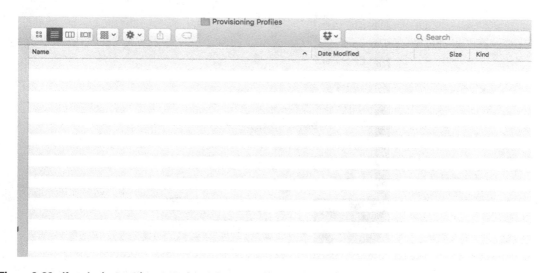

Figure 3-20. If you're just getting started and the computer has not yet been used for iOS or other Xcode development, your Provisioning Profiles folder will be empty

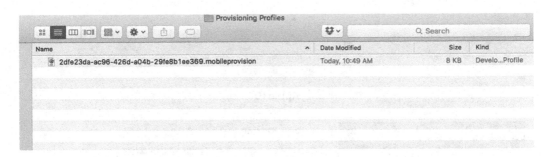

Figure 3-21.   Once installed, the provisioning profile will appear as a UDID for use by Xcode

When you're back at writing code and ready to use the profile, Xcode will automatically handle the task of downloading and installing it for you. You may be prompted for your login credentials, but most of the time it just works. Although we haven't gotten into Xcode yet, I want to show you another way to download provisioning profiles—with the IDE. This saves you from manually downloading profiles from the developer portal and puts the burden of the operation onto Xcode. Sometimes this manual process can be a little flaky. It's become much more solid over the past year or so, but just in case you run into issues, I want to make sure you have an alternate way to download profiles.

Since you should be familiar somewhat with Xcode, after starting, go to Xcode ➤ Preferences then select "Accounts" if that window is not already open. You'll see a window like the one shown in Figure 3-22.

> **Note**   In all of my examples I use the latest beta version of Xcode in order to work with the most current features that are most likely to be present at the time of publishing.

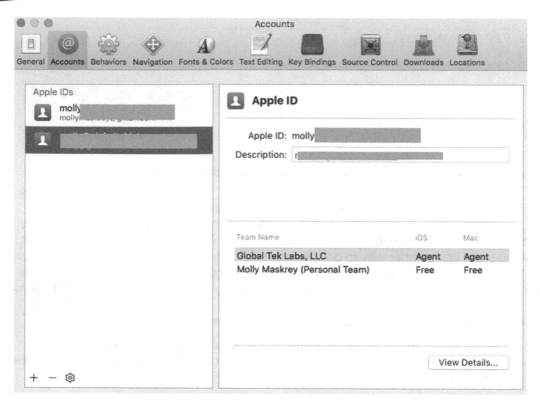

Figure 3-22. The Accounts pane of Xcode for the author's individual and organizational developer accounts

As shown in Figure 3-22, I have two Apple developer accounts. The top one on the left is my individual account, and the other is my organization account. The accounts will initially be identified by the email used to set up your account. The right bottom pane is where you can get information on the details of an account and the available provisioning information. I selected the team name; in this case that's the organization account, not the individual one, since that's how we created the profile earlier. Clicking on the View Details... button reveals the information shown in Figure 3-23. Note that we see the same profile that we created in a previous section.

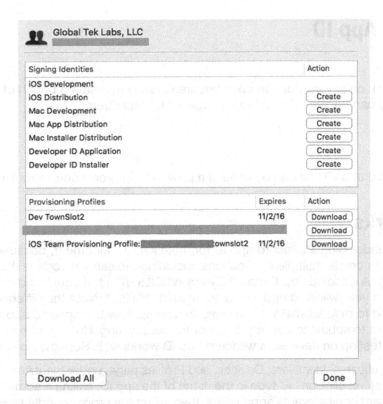

Figure 3-23. Using the Accounts pane of the Xcode organizer, you can create certificates or download provisioning profiles

By clicking Download, you can install any or all profiles within your developer account into Xcode and onto your Mac. Note that you can also generate signing identities for iOS and Mac projects from this pane. There are different options for Mac depending on whether you want to distribute your OS X application directly or through the Mac App Store.

Comments

You've seen in this and the previous section details on creating and installing provisioning profiles. These files are the key to your getting your apps to work on devices, distributing them to others for beta testing, and being able to place your work into the App Store. While this discussion was pretty detailed, it is very straightforward and not easy to mess up. I'd advise going through it a couple times until you have it down, then writing yourself a simple step-by-step procedure for the next time. On my Mac I use Stickies and make sure the topmost line is a relevant title. That way, the next time I have to do this and may have forgotten a step, I have the information readily available.

Wildcard App ID

Problem

You want to work on several apps at once but aren't ready to create a bunch of individual profiles, as they can become difficult to manage in large numbers.

Solution

Create a wildcard app ID that can be used in a provisioning profile across multiple projects.

How It Works

Apple recommends using a wildcard app ID for most iOS development, because this single ID can be used to create multiple applications, including the sample code in the Apple reference library. A wildcard app ID has the form <BUNDLE ID>.*. If your bundle ID were A1B2C3D4E5, then your wildcard app ID would be A1B2C3D4E5.*. Note the difference with something of the form A1B2C3D4E5.com.mycompany.myApp. This is a specific app ID for when you actually want to submit to the App Store or for beta testing. But if you're only interested in learning and testing on devices, a wildcard app ID works well. So, how do we create one?

Back on the Certificates, Identifiers, Devices, and Profiles page, under Identifiers select "App IDs." As before, click on '+,' type in the name of the app ID, calling it something like Company Wildcard or whatever is appropriate, then select the proper bundle seed ID in the drop-down. Further down on the page under App ID Prefix, select the "Wildcard App ID" radio button and type in the bundle ID. The bundle ID would be something like com.mollycompany.*, and then you click the Continue button and carry on as before by reviewing the information and clicking Generate on the next page. This will place another app ID into your developer portal information, which you can use to generate a more widely usable provisioning profile.

> **Note** The bundle seed ID and bundle ID are similar but slightly different. Depending on how it's used, a bundle ID may or may not include the ten-digit value at the start. It's used differently throughout the literature. However, the bundle seed ID always refers to that ten-digit value that references your organization or team.

Comments

If you want to practice a lot with installing apps onto devices, especially ones built from Apple demo code, using a wildcard app ID will make life a lot simpler. Not only will you have to do less prep work to get started, but also later on you won't have as many provisioning profiles that you need to manage and keep track of.

Switching Development Computers

Problem

You want to work on a different Mac but continue developing the same application as you were before. If you try to repeat the preceding steps to create certificates on the new computer, you'll find that things won't work anymore. The problem is that you created a signing request on a different computer, so the development and production certificates won't be the same.

Solution

You need to transfer your development certificate information from your initial development computer to the new computer from within Xcode.

How It Works

This problem always seems to happen at the most inconvenient time. You mostly develop on your large-screen iMac, and for some reason you need to take and show your work to someone else. Perhaps you got stuck and a friend offers to help, or maybe you took my advice in the last chapter and want to give a talk at your local iOS meetup. So you put Xcode onto your laptop, set things up as we talked about, and nothing works; all manner of strange error messages start to appear in the Xcode logs. What happened?

There's an even worse scenario. You go through the same steps as discussed. You give your talk, and it all works perfectly. At home, getting back into the swing of things, it all stops working. What happened?

What happened was that you generated two different signing certificates (or more)—one for each machine. Recall that before creating and downloading certificates you used the Mac Keychain app to create a certificate request on your machine. That request file has built-in references to that Apple-provided developer certificate as well as information about your machine. So these two requests, created on two different machines (even if they use the same developer account), will be different. As such, both can't work.

You need to transfer your credentials from one computer to any other computer you wish to use. This is done from within Xcode itself. Let's work through it. This is another one of those things you should stow away in your quick reference Stickies.

With Xcode in the foreground, select Xcode ➤ Preferences and go to the Accounts pane as we did earlier. At the bottom of the pane (Figure 3-24), click on the gear icon to bring up the export and import options pull-down menu.

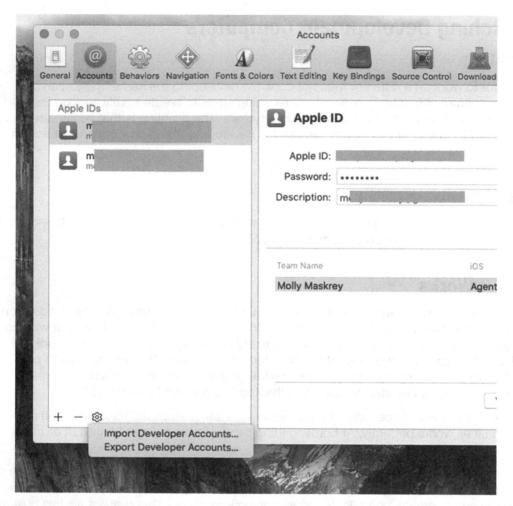

Figure 3-24. *Click on the gear icon at the bottom of the Accounts pane in the Xcode preferences to bring up export and import options*

Selecting "Export Developer Accounts…" brings up the window seen in Figure 3-25, allowing you to name the file for export, provide the location to where it will be saved, and supply a password. Name the file something easy to identify. You can see I named mine myProfileForExport and saved it to my desktop. I usually advise using at least a secure password, but this process doesn't require anything more than a simple set of numbers. Click Save, and the information will be stored in a single file wherever you've requested.

Figure 3-25. Export a single file containing all developer account information from within Xcode. If you're just moving it from one computer to another in your home, you can go with a simple password. But, because this contains such important account information, you want to make sure it is safe no matter what

Because these credentials contain sensitive information, before writing to a file OS X will verify that you are allowing Xcode to export these credentials to a file from the password Keychain on your Mac. In Figures 3-26 and 3-27 you can see this request after I click on Save. Just click Allow to proceed, and the file should appear at the location you specified after a completion message appears (see Figures 3-28 and 3-29).

Figure 3-26. *Xcode requests permission to export your development credentials from Keychain*

Figure 3-27. *Xcode requests permission to export your distribution credentials from Keychain*

Figure 3-28. Upon completion of saving you will be able to see what information was exported

Figure 3-29. Xcode saves the exported information to a single file so that it can be installed on the new development Macintosh computer

Copy the file to a USB drive or move it to the new computer by whatever method works best; place it somewhere that's easy to find, such as the desktop. If you do use a portable drive, make sure to erase the file from the drive when finished. On the computer to which you moved your credentials and plan to continue development on, start Xcode and go to Xcode ➤ Preferences. Select the Accounts pane at the top as we did earlier during export (Figure 3-24). Select the "Import" option, and you will be prompted for the filename and to enter the password. Once the process completes, Xcode will now operate and build apps using the same credentials as the computer on which you began working.

Comments

The process of moving credentials between computers is certainly one you'll need to be familiar with when splitting your time between a desktop and laptop. This comes in handy most when you're operating your own business or as a freelance contractor. When working for a company, either as a direct employee, contract-to-hire position, or 1099 contractor, the IT department will usually set up systems as they see fit. Moving credentials between computers on your own is not permitted except for under special circumstances, such as working from home and using your own equipment.

Summary

As I stated at the beginning, there's not a lot of witty writing in this chapter. We've covered the various situations that you will likely encounter when preparing your Xcode environment to build and run apps on actual Apple devices. Much of the time, Xcode does a lot of the work for you. In fact, if you set up everything on a fresh computer, for example just out of the box with the latest OS X release, just about everything I've talked about is automated. But, there's a problem.

Most of the time iOS developers operate on the edge, so to speak. By that I mean we'll use the latest beta version of Xcode and iOS frameworks so as to include the latest and greatest new features in our products. We have to, because everyone else, our competition, is doing the same thing. Meanwhile, we may have to support existing production-version apps in the App Store. Beta versions of Xcode and frameworks cannot be submitted to the App Store until just before a GM (Gold Master) release or even later. Typically, I get about a week's notice before an official Xcode release that I can now submit apps.

This means that we have to run two different versions of everything; that is, two versions of Xcode and two sets of frameworks. Because of that, especially with beta releases, much of the automated processes can be a little unstable at times. We need to know how to do it the hard way, as we've described in this chapter, to stay current in our skills. It's not that we can't do it the easy way, but we need to make sure it can get done whether it's the easy way or the more difficult, detailed route that I've described.

Chapter 4

Project Descriptions

For the rest of this book I'll be referencing four different types of projects when describing the various problems and solutions that we need to solve. I've purposefully kept these projects as small and self-contained as possible in order to focus on just those elements we need to address.

Our goal with these is not to provide an all-encompassing solution for this or that problem, but rather to provide a working code reference for our needs. To talk about source control, we don't require several tens of thousands of lines of Swift. We don't need a massive database application to cover building deployment targets or using schemes. What we want—no, what we need—is a very basic set of projects with code we can readily understand so we don't spend time unnecessarily worried about this or that syntax item, but rather can direct our attention solely to the task at hand.

Our projects address four key areas:

- Code conversion from Objective-C to Swift
- Using the Apple Watch
- Working with Apple's HomeKit iOS feature and framework
- Interfacing with external devices

Remembering that our goal is not to learn to write Swift, but rather to prepare your iOS experience for the real world, I chose projects that you're likely to encounter as you take your skills out into the real world. There'll always be the boring "Build a Table View" this or "Convert to Core Data" that you will have to deal with, but here, while we can, let's have some fun while learning. Of course, what I think of as fun might significantly differ from your ideals, so we'll just see how it goes.

© Molly K. Maskrey 2016

M.K. Maskrey, *App Development Recipes for iOS and watchOS*, DOI 10.1007/978-1-4842-1820-4_4

Code Conversion

As the popularity and proliferation of Swift continue to grow (despite some holdouts who believe it's not ready for prime time), you're likely as an entry-level developer to be assigned projects where the main goal is to convert an old project into Swift. There are many reasons why this is a good idea. First, as Swift grows and more features are added to support the latest Apple devices, using Swift might be the only way to do things. That is, a desired feature may only be supported in Swift and not in Objective-C. For the short term, I suspect this to be unlikely, but if you make the conversions now you won't be caught off guard if such a time does arrive.

Another reason for converting to the new language is to take advantage of the many safety features built into Swift. The requirement to initialize variables could save you dozens of hours you would have spent tracking down an unnecessary bug because you failed to initialize a property in Objective-C. Like anything else, there are ways around this; optionals allow you to circumvent this restriction by enabling you to indicate an absence of value for any type. Typically, when using existing framework method calls the indiscriminate use of optionals can quickly get you into trouble. First, a returned optional is an optional, not a value. A value is "wrapped" inside an optional, and thus you must unwrap it.

> **Note** We won't be going into the details of the Swift language, so familiarity with the syntax is assumed.

You get into trouble when you try to unwrap an optional for which there is no value; that is, there is an absence of value. Attempting to use an optional for which no value exists by forcing an unwrap causes your app to crash at runtime. This functions just the same as trying to use a nil value with Objective-C.

Figure 4-1 illustrates the basic concept of the app that we will be converting. The code generates a simple three-wheel slot machine where the user is provided with a starting amount of credits and can place bets prior to spinning. The app produces three random positions for where the wheels will land after the spin button is pressed. A method inside the app determines the amount of the win, or that the player loses the spin. The winnings are added or the losses are deducted from the player's bank. If the player uses all her credits, then the game can be reset.

Figure 4-1. Our first project will convert a simple slot machine game from Objective-C to Swift

Originally written in the very early days of iOS when it was still called iPhone OS, the app builds its UI programmatically. On top of the three wheels, which are in reality image strips, lies the graphic image of the slot's faceplate. When originally written, there exlsted only two iPhone types: the original iPhone and the iPhone 3G. The screens were both the same size, so only one image file was required. Because several devices of different sizes and resolutions are in play now, part of the conversion process requires new image files. In order to address this concern, as would be typical in most conversions from Objective-C to Swift, I've included a few, but not all, of the current device sizes.

On top of the front panel image, the app stacks the three buttons and the three labels for credits, current bet, and amount won. While I would not use the same design today if I were creating this app from scratch, the use of Image Views within code should be understood by anyone looking to become proficient in iOS development projects.

Coin Toss

For our second project, we dive into working with Apple Watch. We'll create a simple coin-flipping game called Coin Toss (Figure 4-2). As you can see, I haven't spent a great deal of time on the graphics. That's not what this exercise is about. Our goal is simply to create an app for the watch. That's it. Everything else we can learn from extending our use of the libraries or adding features or even attempting to make it more of a game. We could add more intelligence or use the onboard sensors to skew the probabilities depending on the angle of the watch face relative to the horizontal plane, essentially creating a "weighted" coin.

Figure 4-2. Coin Toss game for the Apple Watch

But again, those enhancements are left up to you. My goal in writing this book in the first place is to inspire to you. I want to push you off the virtual cliff, so to speak, and let you fly on your own.

Home Automation

I call our third sample project Disco Ball because we will remotely, using an iPhone and Apple's HomeKit framework, start our party (Figure 4-3). In reality, we can control power to any device that uses AC power, but turning on or off the table lamp would just be so boring. As with all other projects, I keep this very simple. I want to show you how to access, load, and use HomeKit to create a simple, single-element database and then do nothing more than turn that device on or off. With that simple goal, we'll have the basic operating knowledge to start down the path of a complete home automation system.

Figure 4-3. Our third sample project controls a disco ball, which could be any AC-powered device, using Apple's iOS home automation feature, HomeKit

External Sensor Interface

Our last project will address the use of external devices, typically called accessories, for information input and output. We'll start with a simple, two-part logic board of my own design (Figure 4-4).

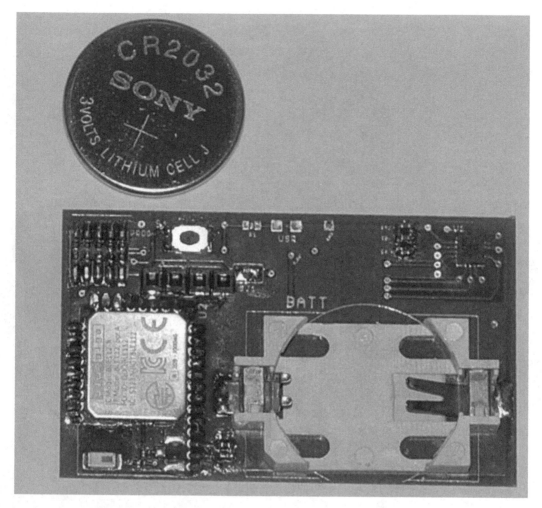

Figure 4-4. Our final project will retrieve orientation information from a remote Bluetooth Low Energy sensor board

The sensor logic board consists of two sections. First, a small MEMS (microelectromechanical systems) integrated circuit measures movement and orientation using accelerometer and magnetometer logic. That information gets passed to a Bluetooth Low Energy (BTLE) module that sends the data out wirelessly.

For our project we assume the sensor will be placed on a human subject's shoe, either externally or internally, using an orthotic type of enclosure. Thus, the data sent by the sensor reflects the orientation of the subject's foot in two dimensions. The foot's pitch refers to the amount above and below the horizontal plane of the toe; that is, how much the toe is up or down relative to the heel. The roll parameter measures the inside or outside roll of the foot, such as when you might twist your ankle when playing sports.

Our app will collect this data and visually display these two parameters of the foot onto an iPad display as shown in Figure 4-5.

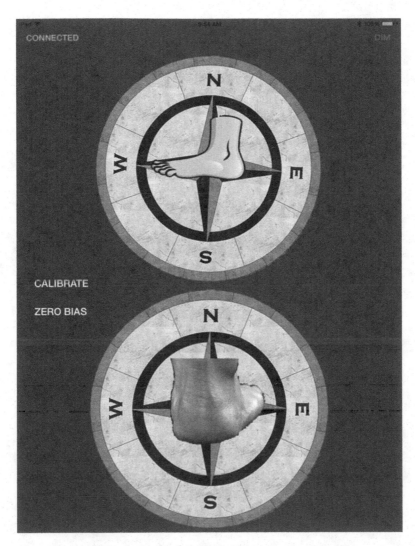

Figure 4-5. Our app project graphically displays the orientation information from the sensor as the pitch and roll parameters of the foot

Sensor data will be read using Apple's Core Bluetooth framework. The raw data will be normalized to reflect a positive or negative angle deviation, which will then be passed to a transform function to rotate the appropriate image in Figure 4-5. While we won't go into detail on angular computations, our visualization of the information will reflect an approximate angle of the foot along either of the two axes.

Chapter 5

Source-Code Control

Without a doubt, protecting the investment you've made developing your iOS application by preventing loss due to a system crash or other mishap has to be done whether you're working for a company or a contractor or running your own business. Not too long ago we backed up our work to floppy disks or separate hard drives, even USB/Flash drives. When cloud storage services such as Dropbox became available, things became a bit easier, but these still did not offer the services required for maintaining more than rudimentary file backups. What we really needed was some type of version control; that is, a way to not only store back-up files but also keep track of changes so that it would be possible to revert to an earlier version if something we tried didn't work out.

Options and History

In this early part of your career, you'll most likely run into two main source-code control systems: SVN and Git. However, while you might find some companies that have been around a while still use SVN, Git, being so tightly integrated with Xcode, has bubbled to the top and has more or less become the de facto standard, at least for iOS projects.

SVN is really the shortened name for Apache Subversion and comes from the command svn used when managing your project. SVN is generally considered the successor to the older CVS system that I actually used in the early 1990s. SVN came onto the scene late 2000/ early 2001. One of the reasons you may find Subversion still in use at your organization is the year when the company was formed. Subversion was for a long time the way you managed source projects and is generally tailored to having multiple developers work on web projects at the same time. Because of its open-source nature, web startups generally went with Subversion to keep costs down while providing security and peace of mind that their intellectual property (IP) would not be lost, stolen, or sabotaged.

Atomic operations (e.g., executing a save function that cannot be interrupted) made Subversion a highly reliable system for source control from its earliest days. Think about this. If you have two or more engineers working on the same project, accessing the same source database, what's to stop them from updating the same file at the same time with two slightly different versions of the source? Which operation (save) would have precedence, and which would be lost? By having an uninterruptable set of commands, every developer's updates are stored without overwriting and losing someone else's changes.

Subversion also maintains version history for deleted or otherwise moved or removed files. This provides a way to go back to some version that worked if a critical bug is discovered; for example, after being deployed to users. It also offers three methods of accessing source repositories: local or network via the `file://<path>` construct, web-based using `http://<path>`, and a custom svn protocol, `svn://<path>`.

Git came onto the scene late 2005/early 2006 when the inventor of Linux, Linus Torvalds, and others wanted a source-control system for that OS. Because of the lightweight nature of the Git code itself, it has very fast performance and is easy to use. Okay, I know what you're thinking: easy to use? I remember hearing about branches, commits, merges, snapshots, and so on and getting so overwhelmed that I avoided Git, Subversion, and any complicated form of source control for far longer than I should have. Just saving backups to the cloud seemed so much easier.

Because you're more likely to see Git used in later iOS and mobile companies, we'll spend most of our time working there, but first, I want to discuss some basic terminology that is generally applicable to all source-control systems.

Basic Terminology and Flow

The basic flow of a project as relating to source-code control, in a generic sense, follows Figure 5-1.

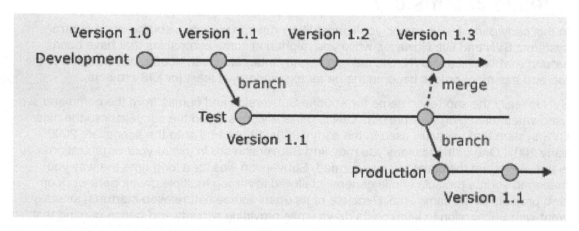

Figure 5-1. Basic source and version control of a software project

We start at the upper left with the bubble labeled "Development"; this is where our project begins. It may happen that, when we first create our project in Xcode, or really in any IDE, we have the option to create the source repository. This generally is referred to the trunk (SVN) or main branch (Git) and is the original set of files that comprise our project. If starting from an Xcode project, it usually contains nothing more than the template files.

Following the main branch to the right as we add code and other functionality to our projects, we'll commit our changes and create new versions. This is where things get confusing. Performing a commit really means that we've saved whatever changes we make in our project to the repository. For example, if we change a plus to a minus, or a greater-than to a less-than in an `if` statement because of an error we found, that would be a commit of those changes to our repository. That's not a new version—not necessarily, anyway. But it might be considered a revision. After all, you are revising the code for whatever reason. In many organizations *revision* is used interchangeably with *version*. So immediately you start to see how this can get confusing. One of the biggest sources of confusion I had when I went to work for an iOS development company as a contractor was that every engineer on the team used slightly different terminology for source control and versioning.

At some point we'll need to add new features, or maybe we want to experiment and see if we can speed up an algorithm or two. At the same time, we don't want to disturb our working version. This is where we perform a branch. In Figure 5-1 at the Version 1.1 bubble you can see that we created a branch to the line called Test. What we have there is another main line of development, but it's not our trunk or main branch. This is a complete copy of the version 1.1 code and project files that we can manipulate as needed to try different things. We now have two working branches—the trunk or main branch and the test branch. This allows one team to continue developing. Should our algorithm changes prove successful we can later merge the branches together. We merge our test branch back into the main branch, which becomes Version 1.3. We can, if we want, continue the Test branch to try more new things, but most likely we'll put it to rest; if we need to make more changes, we can create a new branch off the trunk. I'm purposely trying to use *trunk* and *main branch* interchangeably, not to confuse you, but rather to get you used to what you might hear at your job.

We'll also want to branch off either our trunk or our other main line to create a production version once we begin shipping or even beta testing. Again, this keeps everything nice and clean but maintains consistency and the ability to merge changes that we make to our project. You'll also note in Figure 5-1 that we have versions on each of our main lines or branches that appear not to be consistent with each other. Also consider using prefix designators such as Test Version 1.1, Dev Version 1.1, etc. to add another level of tracking. Again, this goes to the use of the term *version* and it not being a hard and fast term that refers to a single revision within our system.

Subversion/SVN

While most of this chapter will focus on Git, I want to cover a few of the most basic SVN commands just so you'll have some idea of what's going on if and when you encounter its use in the course of your career. You can put SVN on your Mac if you want to play with it and get some experience, but I'd suggest just looking through these commands, only going deeper if your job requires it at some point.

Creating a Repository

In the vast majority of situations, the SVN repository will already be in place and you won't ever likely need to do this, but just in case, here's what you need to know. Repository creation uses the `svnadmin` command in the Terminal application, and generally you would need administrative privileges for its use:

```
svnadmin create <path>
```

This creates a new repository at <path>, assuming you have permissions, using the default filesystem data store (FSFS). There are two filesystem types you can choose from, FSFS and Berkeley-DB, which can be specified using `--fs-type`:

```
svnadmin create --fs-type fsfs <path>
svnadmin create --fs-type bdb <path>
```

For most other operations you'll use the `svn` command, which is more for the engineering user.

SVN Checkout

Probably the first command you'll use will be to check out a branch in which you'll do your engineering work. The format is:

```
svn checkout <PATH>
```

An example of this for the "test" branch stored at `myname/svn/repos` would look like this:

```
svn checkout file://maskrey/svn/repos/test
```

For a project stored in an online database, the format would be similar but would contain the necessary URL information:

```
svn checkout http://svn.mycompany.com/svn/repo/trunk
```

Once you have your branch checked out and stored on your local computer, you can work with it just as if it were created in place. In fact, it really is just a version of what is on the trunk or whichever branch that you used as the source or baseline. This is your "working copy."

SVN Commit

Once you've made the necessary changes to your working copy and want to save them, you use the `commit` command:

```
svn commit -m "notes about your changes go in here"
```

For the most part, these are the three most common commands you would use as a developer getting started using an SVN repository.

SVN GUI

You'll quickly become familiar with branching and merging, but you'll likely never do a lot of command-line operations as I've shown here. Most likely, you'll use a graphical tool like SmartSVN, available in both free and paid professional versions (http://www.smartsvn.com/; Figure 5-2), to do everything you need to do in a much more user-friendly manner.

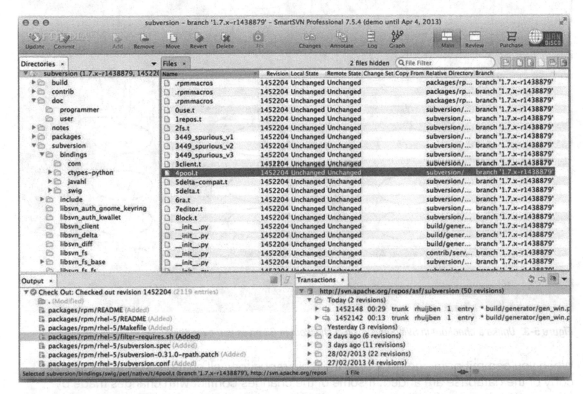

Figure 5-2. A graphical SVN tool such as SmartSVN makes the process of using Subversion much easier for new developers confronted with this Source-code control:subversion/SVN:source- and version-control technology

Git

For the rest of this chapter we'll focus on Git, as that's what you're much more likely to use as you come into iOS development. Unlike in SVN/Subversion, when you check out something using Git, you get everything—not one branch, but rather the whole Git project database—so you have access to everything from the very first commit to the most recent changes and all the branches and versioning (Figure 5-3).

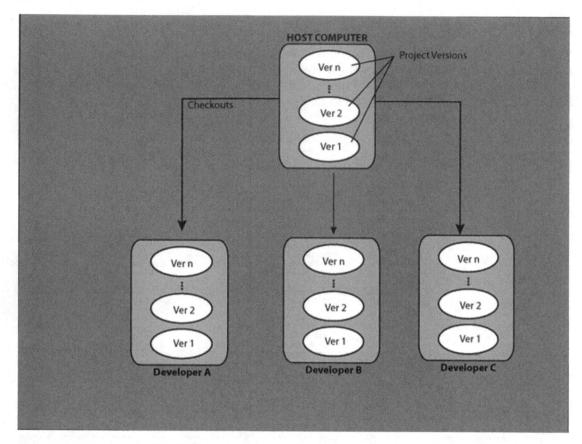

Figure 5-3. Unlike a checkout in SVN/Subversion, a checkout in Git gives you everything

When you commit or merge back onto the main repository, all changes you made to your copy of the database are added. If some of the changes conflict with changes made by others who have modified the source, you'll be asked to reconcile the differences, usually with the assistance of the other developer.

Creating a Repository

To create a repository using Git, use the `init` command. To create a repository of the current directory, in the Terminal application enter:

`git init`

To create a repository of a specific directory:

`git init <directory>`

This operation is only performed once to create the central repository. To create a repository on your local machine from an existing repository you use the `clone` command and not `init`.

Git Clone

To get a working copy from a Git repository, similar to using the checkout command in Subversion, use the clone command:

```
git clone <path>
```

Git Commit

Finally, just as with SVN/Subversion, you use commit to save changes to a Git repository, adding the –m to include comments on the changes:

```
git commit –m "notes about the changes you made"
```

Git GUI

Just as we saw in the last section, you'll most likely never have to enter command-line functions directly, except in some instances that we'll cover shortly, such as when you have an existing project that has not been converted to a Git repository. When I worked at an iOS development company several years ago, our Git interface of choice was Tower at a cost of $69USD per license (https://www.git-tower.com/; Figure 5-4). It was a very easy-to-use GUI that made source control much more accessible.

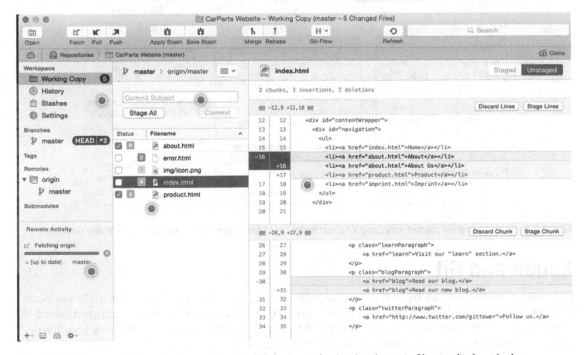

Figure 5-4. Tower provides a simple, easy-to-use GUI for accessing local and remote Git repositories, cloning, committing, merging, and all other necessary source-control functions

You can even find an Xcode "cheat sheet" to using Tower with your iOS projects (Figure 5-5).

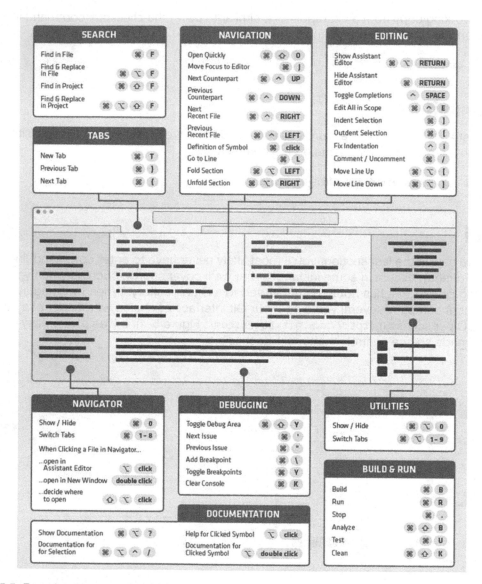

Figure 5-5. *Tower has even started supplying a "cheat sheet" in order to use its GUI interface with Xcode projects*

Xcode and Git

For several years Git has been tightly integrated with the Xcode IDE. However, early versions of Xcode turned out to be difficult to work with, and most companies, mine included, went with Tower rather than deal with the hassle of trying to get Xcode and Git to work together more smoothly. Even today, some companies that develop highly complicated projects with a large number of branches still prefer to use tools like Tower, or even resort to the command line. For us, Xcode and Git integration should satisfy all of our needs, and if you do need a more detailed level of control, work with your engineering team; each company's implementation and usage will vary significantly.

Creating a Project

Problem

You want to start an Xcode project and include Git version control.

Solution

This is probably the simplest thing we'll tackle. All you have to do when creating your initial project is to check the box "Create Git repository on" when you're ready to save the project (Figure 5-6). You can save it locally onto your Mac or to a remote location such as Github, which we'll talk about in the next section.

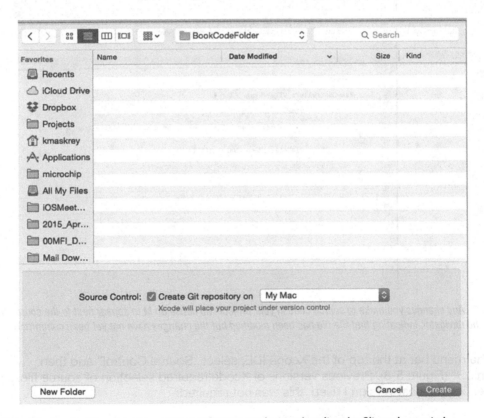

Figure 5-6. Simply select the checkbox when creating your project to place it under Git version control

Modifying Code and Committing Changes

Problem

You need to modify your source code and have Git manage the changes.

Solution

When you create a project and use Git, all you have in your main branch is the template source files that Xcode created with your project. Make a single change like adding a comment and you'll see an *M* to the right of the source file's name in the Xcode Project Navigator (Figure 5-7).

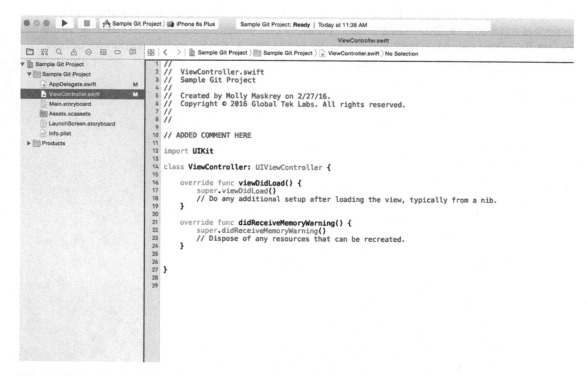

Figure 5-7. *Any changes you make to source code in your project will cause an M to appear next to the source file's name in the navigator, indicating that the file has been modified but the changes have not yet been committed*

From the menu bar at the top of the Xcode IDE, select "Source Control" and then "Commit…" (Figure 5-8). Previous versions of Xcode required selection of source files; however, in the latest version I used, this was not required.

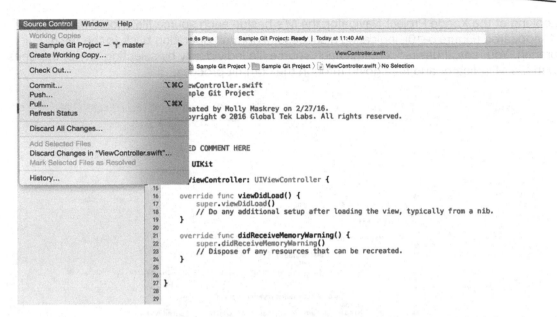

Figure 5-8. Select "Commit..." from the Xcode Source Control pull-down to add the changes to the main branch

When the screen in Figure 5-9 appears, type in your notes regarding the changes you made at the bottom. In most cases you'll enter a summary of what you did and not anything too specific. Also note that you can see the changes you made to the source file highlighted in blue.

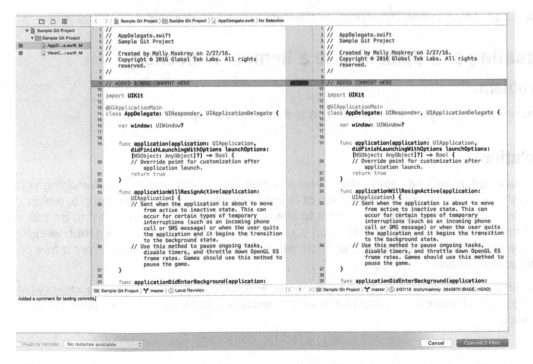

Figure 5-9. When ready to commit, review your changes in the window, add your notes regarding the changes you made, and click the Commit button

Looking at the Xcode Project Navigator, the *M*'s beside each source file should have disappeared (Figure 5-10), indicating a successful commit operation back to the main branch. You may, if desired, commit each source file individually by selecting any of the ones with the *M* indicator and then going through the commit process.

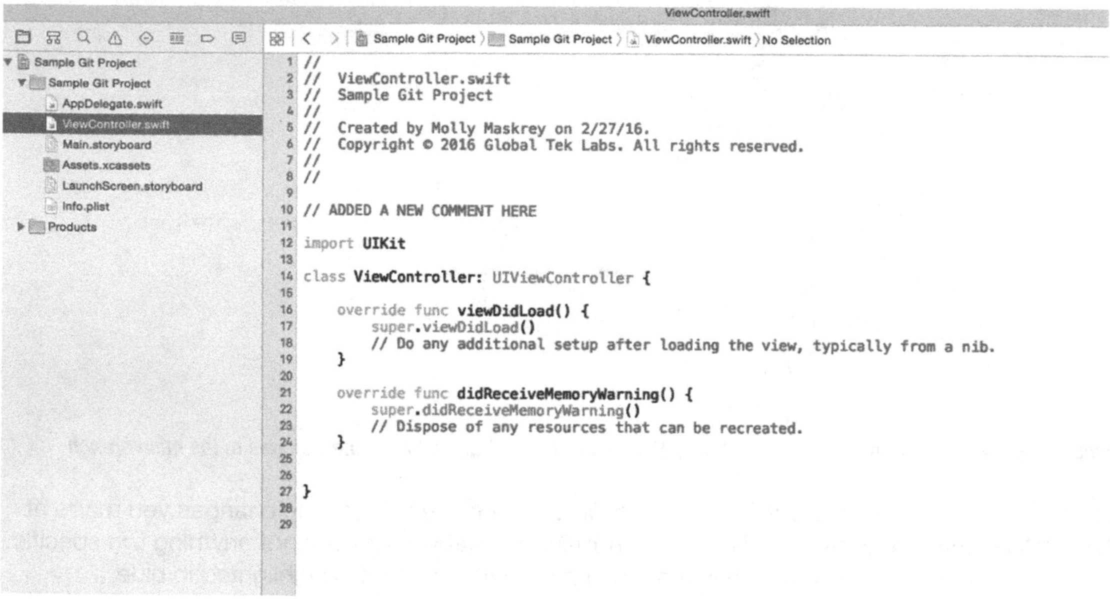

Figure 5-10. After committing your changes, the M indicator should no longer appear

Creating and Uploading to a Remote Repository

Problem

You need to store your Git-managed project in a remote repository.

Solution

In this solution we'll be using github.com, an either free or paid system for managing your repositories. I'm using the free version of Github remote storage in this example, which means the project is visible for anyone to see and download. You won't want to do this with real projects. Instructions for setting up your account can be found on the github website and really just involve entering your information and deciding whether you want a free or paid subscription.

The first step in Xcode is to go to Preferences ➤ Accounts and check your repository list. In Figure 5-11 you can see that I have several available, but we need to add one for this project.

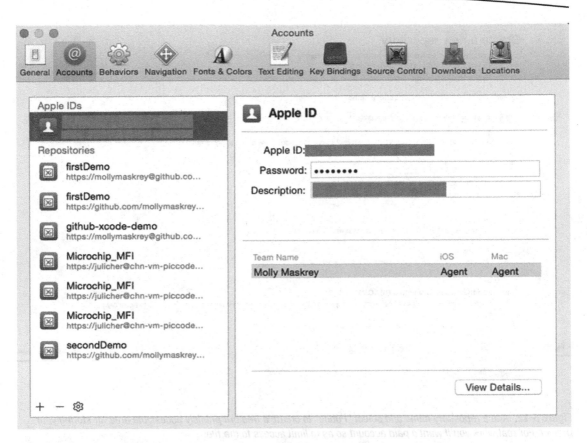

Figure 5-11.   From Xcode Preferences ➤ Accounts you can see your list of remote repositories

In your `github.com` account, add a repository for storing your project. In Figure 5-12 you can see that I added a repository name of `samplegitproject`. This can be any name you want to use. It does not have to be your project name, but should be something you can easily identify.

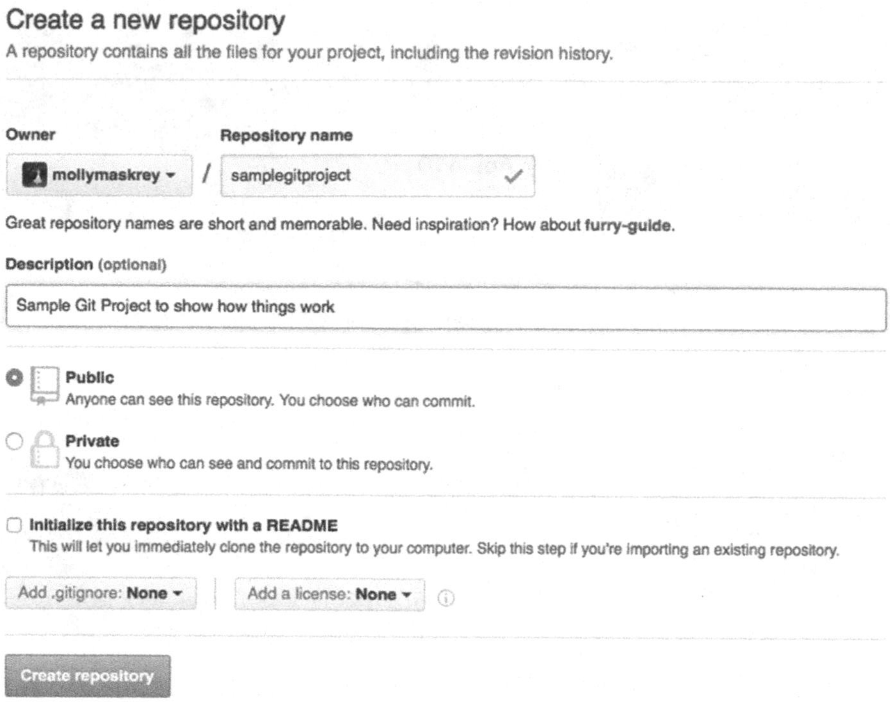

Create a new repository

A repository contains all the files for your project, including the revision history.

Owner   **Repository name**

[mollymaskrey ▾] / [samplegitproject   ✓]

Great repository names are short and memorable. Need inspiration? How about **furry-guide**.

Description (optional)

[Sample Git Project to show how things work   ]

● **Public**
   Anyone can see this repository. You choose who can commit.

○ **Private**
   You choose who can see and commit to this repository.

☐ **Initialize this repository with a README**
   This will let you immediately clone the repository to your computer. Skip this step if you're importing an existing repository.

[Add .gitignore: **None** ▾] [Add a license: **None** ▾] ⓘ

[Create repository]

Figure 5-12. Add a repository name and select "Public" to create a free but publicly accessible area for storing your project. For real work you'll want a paid account so as to limit access to the files

Once you create your repository, github will provide you with the information needed to access the repository from Xcode (Figure 5-13). We're currently interested in the `https://` path name that we'll need to tell Xcode about.

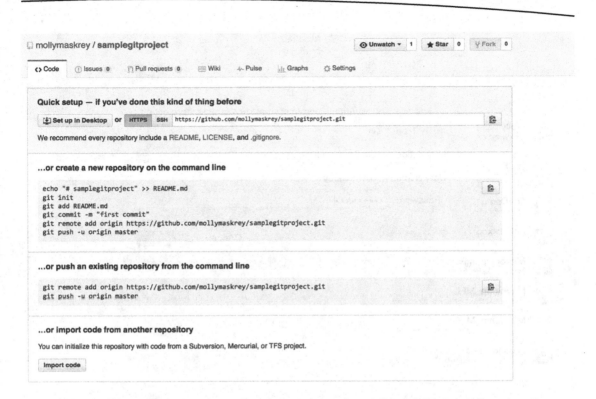

Figure 5-13. *You have many options for accessing your remote repository, but for this Xcode sample project all we need is the https: address*

Back in the Accounts pane of the Xcode Preferences window, provide this pertinent information (Figure 5-14). You'll also need to provide your github user ID and password that you set up when initializing your github account.

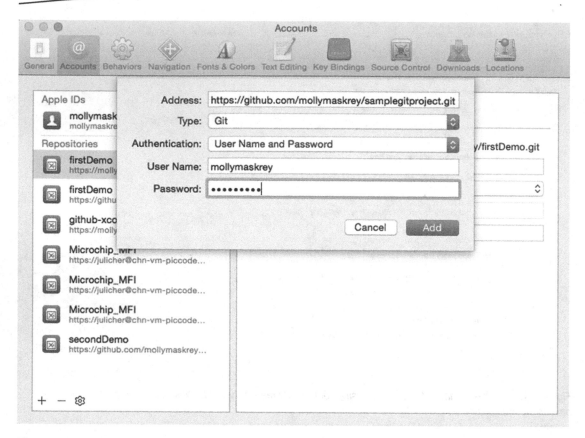

Figure 5-14. *Enter your repository's path name and your account credentials so that Xcode knows about this remote repository*

Then you should see the repository become available in the lower left corner of the Accounts pane (Figure 5-15).

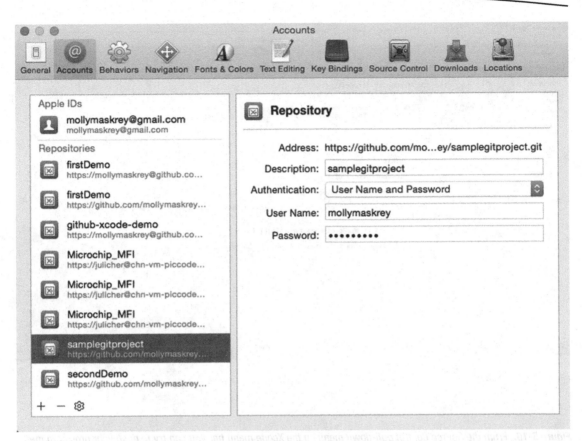

Figure 5-15. *After correctly entering the repository address and account info, the remote repository should be available to Xcode*

However, if you just try to push to the remote repository (Figures 5-16 and 5-17), you won't see it.

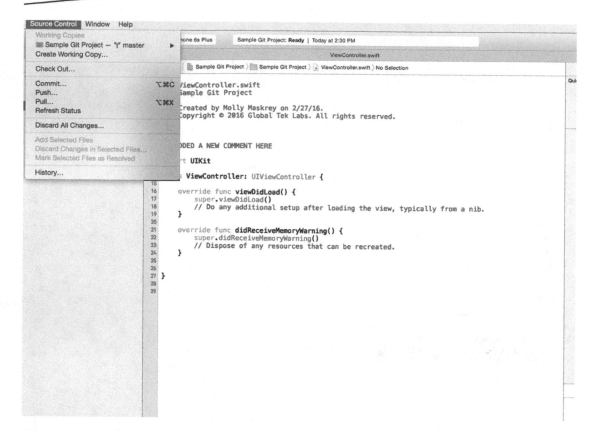

Figure 5-16. *From the Source Control pull-down menu on the Xcode menu bar you can try to push your project to the remote repository*

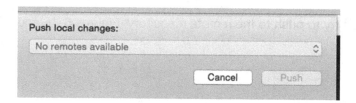

Figure 5-17. *However, you may see that no remotes are available*

The issue at this point is that although you created a repository on github and let Xcode know about it through the Accounts section of Preferences, this project does not know about the repository. You need to configure this project by going to Source Control ➤ (project name) ➤ Configure (project name) Project… (Figure 5-18).

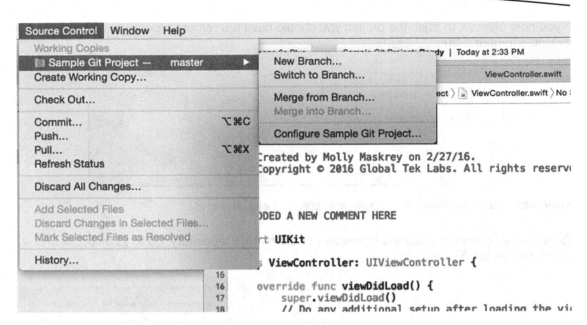

Figure 5-18. You must configure this project to know how to use remote repositories

You'll see a Remotes tab, which is where you need to once again enter the address for the remote repository (Figure 5-19), but since you've already provided the accounting information, the ID and password for your repository, to Xcode, other than the origin remote (which is the main branch), you should be ready to go.

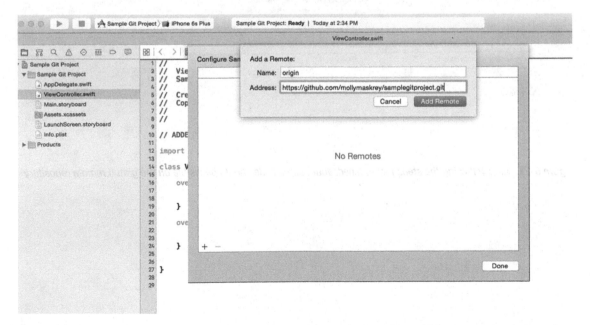

Figure 5-19. Using the typical name of origin as our master branch, enter the address of the remote repository so the project knows about it; we should be just about set to push our code

If you now attempt to push the project you should have the remote repository visible and available (Figure 5-20).

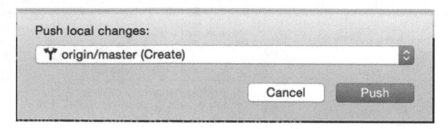

Figure 5-20.   Now the origin/master branch should be available for you to push to

To verify that everything pushed (uploaded) to the remote repository, go to `github.com` and check the file list (Figure 5-21).

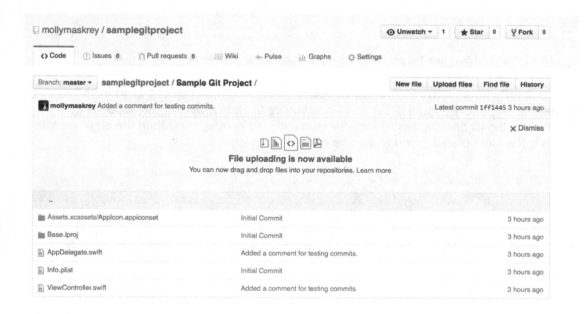

Figure 5-21.   After following the steps just outlined, your source code should be visible on the github remote repository

Cloning and Using a Git-Managed Project

Problem

You have to start working on an already existing Git-managed project and need to maintain source and version control.

Solution

In this solution, we'll use the project we just created. We will start by deleting the working copy of everything from our local computer and go from there. First, open Xcode and close the sample Git project we were just working with. Next, go to the directory where you initially placed (or later subsequently moved) the sample Git project and delete it by moving it to the trash (Figure 5-22).

Figure 5-22. Delete the working copy of the sample Git project from your hard drive

From the Xcode menu bar, select "Source Control" then "Check Out...," which should be the only available option (Figure 5-23).

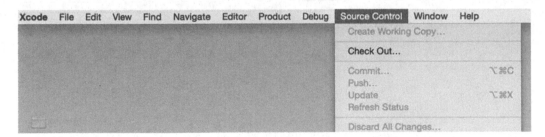

Figure 5-23. From Xcode you can check out a copy of a project with which to begin working

You'll be directed to select the repository from which to load the project (Figure 5-24).

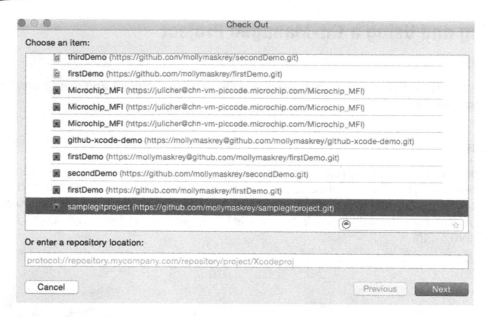

Figure 5-24. After selecting "Check Out…" choose the repository for the project with which you want to work

Once Xcode finds and opens the remote repository, you'll be asked where you want to place the working copy of the project on your computer or network (Figure 5-25).

Figure 5-25. Xcode will ask where you want to save your Git-managed working copy of the project

Finally, just as before, the complete working project with all the latest commits will be available in Xcode for you to continue development (Figure 5-26).

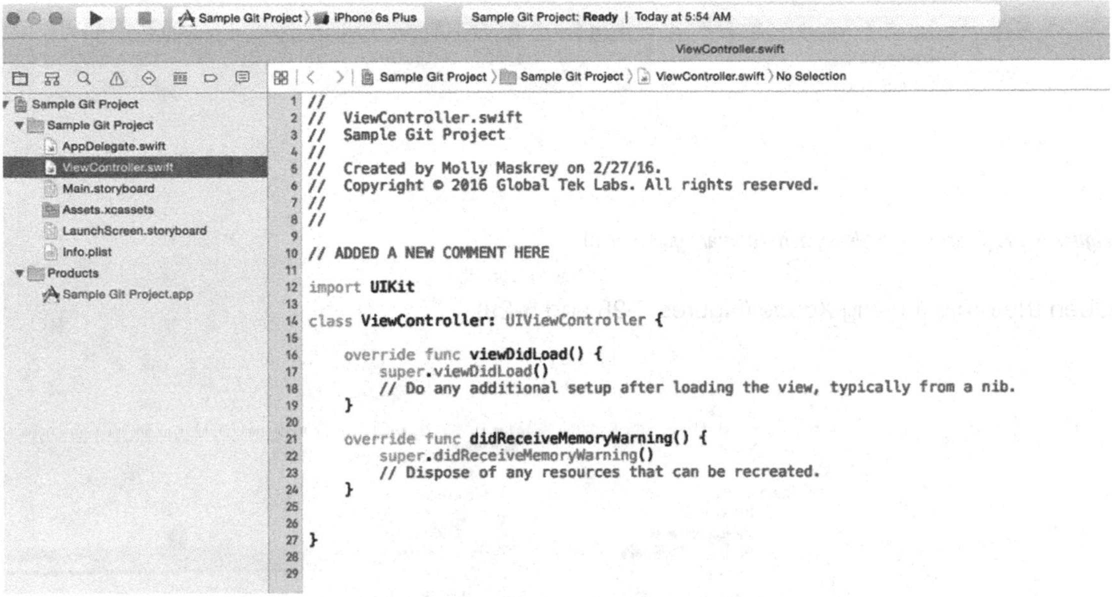

Figure 5-26. *Your checked out project should appear just as it did when we worked with it previously*

Working with Existing Unmanaged Projects

This situation will most likely occur when you're operating your own business or working independently as a consultant. You'll create a project, and either because you forget or maybe because you just want to quickly try something out your project is not managed by Git.

Problem

You have an existing unmanaged (by Git) Xcode project and you want to convert it so it will be under Git source and version control.

Solution

We'll start with the EADemoS project that is described in Chapter 17. The details of the project do not matter, only that we created it without using Git or source control, and it does not exist in my account on github.com. As you can see in Figure 5-27, I actually copied the zip file of the project to our working directory and unzipped it there so we can have a clean starting point.

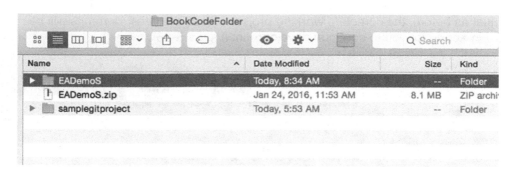

Figure 5-27. *Start with a clean, non–Git managed project*

Open the project using Xcode (Figures 5-28 and 5-29).

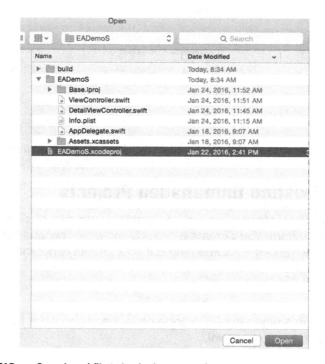

Figure 5-28. *Open the EADemoS.xcodeproj file to begin the conversion*

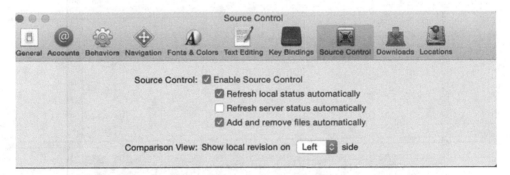

```
1  //
2  //  ViewController.swift
3  //  EADemoS
4  //
5  //  Created by Molly Maskrey on 1/18/16.
6  //  Copyright © 2016 Global Tek Labs. All rights reserved.
7  //
8
9  import UIKit
10 import ExternalAccessory
11
12
13
14 class ViewController: UITableViewController, EAAccessoryDelegate {
15
16 @IBOutlet weak var infoLabel: UILabel!
17
18 // SAMPLE DATA FOR TABLE VIEW
19 //var sampleAccessoryArray:[String] = ["see no accessory", "hear no accessory", "speak no accesory"]
20 var sampleAccessoryArray: [String] = [""]
21
22 // External Accessory Stuff
23
24 var accessoryList:[EAAccessory]?          // our list of accessories, most likely there will only be one
25 let accessoryManager: EAAccessoryManager = EAAccessoryManager.sharedAccessoryManager()
26 var connectedAccessory: EAAccessory?
```

Figure 5-29. Verify that the project and source files appear as you would normally expect

Make sure that in the Source Control pane of the Xcode Preferences window, source control is enabled; if it is not, check the appropriate box (Figure 5-30).

Figure 5-30. Make sure that source control is enabled in the Xcode preferences

You can verify that this project is not yet under Git source control by going to the Source Control pull-down menu (Figure 5-31). Here you can see that normal options such as commit, push, and so forth are not available, indicating that this project is not yet Git managed. What you want to do is to select "Create Working Copy…" from this list of options (Figure 5-32).

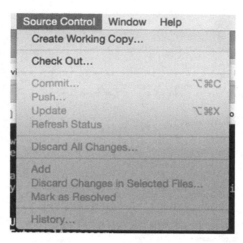

Figure 5-31. *After verifying that the project is not being managed under Git, select the "Create Working Copy..." option*

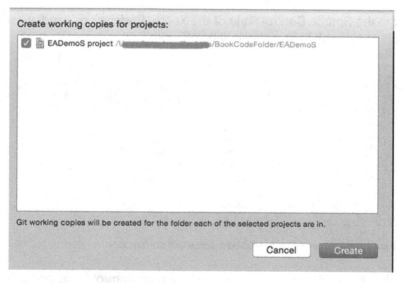

Figure 5-32. *Create the working copy of the project*

At this point your project will be under Git source control. To verify, open a Terminal window and navigate to the project directory. Run the `ls -al` command to see the listing in Figure 5-33. The `.git` directory indicates that this project is now under source control and management. Using the same techniques we explored earlier, you can upload this project and source files to a remote repository such as `github.com`.

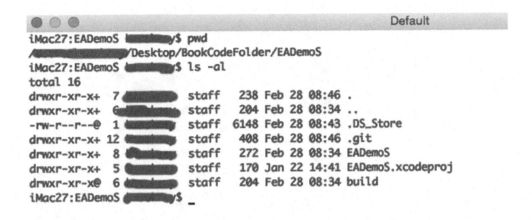

```
● ● ●                                              Default
iMac27:EADemoS ▨▨▨y$ pwd
▨▨▨▨▨▨/Desktop/BookCodeFolder/EADemoS
iMac27:EADemoS ▨▨▨$ ls -al
total 16
drwxr-xr-x+   7 ▨▨▨     staff    238 Feb 28 08:46 .
drwxr-xr-x+   6 ▨▨▨     staff    204 Feb 28 08:34 ..
-rw-r--r--@   1 ▨▨▨     staff   6148 Feb 28 08:43 .DS_Store
drwxr-xr-x+  12 ▨▨▨     staff    408 Feb 28 08:46 .git
drwxr-xr-x+   8 ▨▨▨     staff    272 Feb 28 08:34 EADemoS
drwxr-xr-x+   5 ▨▨▨     staff    170 Jan 22 14:41 EADemoS.xcodeproj
drwxr-xr-x@   6 ▨▨▨     staff    204 Feb 28 08:34 build
iMac27:EADemoS ▨▨▨$ _
```

Figure 5-33. When you see the .git directory you can be assured that this project and all files contained therein are being managed by Git

Summary

In this chapter we covered the basics of source-code control and some of the most common tools you're likely to see and use as you enter your iOS development career. In general, the two most common systems you will encounter are SVN/Subversion and Git.

Early in this chapter I provided a comparison of the four basic, most common functions you might utilize when using either management system. Those operations were to create a repository; to check out or clone a project; to commit changes you make into the management system; and to get away from the command line by using a GUI-based system.

Because Git has become more widely used with Xcode projects, in the previous section we looked at, in detail, how to create projects, commit changes, use a remote repository such as github, clone or check out a project from a remote repository, and work with an existing unmanaged project to bring it under source control.

Going into greater detail on this subject while maintaining a broad coverage of topics would, as most technical subjects would, become a complete book in itself. What I've hoped to do here is to give you enough information to not only get started as you enter your career, but also to assist you with those all-important interviews as you seek your dream job.

Chapter 6

Development Methodology

Development, in the context of our journey, means to create something over a period of time. On Sundays, for example, I really enjoy cooking. I started cooking in earnest just a few years ago. My first projects were soups where I would strictly follow a predetermined set of steps, a recipe. Now, I'm reasonably confident in my ability to understand most things, so cooking to a recipe was no problem. Eventually, after getting a handle on the necessary kitchen skills and being able to work through the typical Sunday afternoon interruptions, I was able to make my chicken soup from memory.

The thing was, however, that the soup was pretty, well, bland. It's not that it wasn't good or healthy or anything like that—it just had no kick. Also, I live at an altitude of 6300 feet. Water boils at a lower temperature than it does at sea level, which is where most recipes tend to be baselined. Like any project, I had to make adjustments to the process. I added this or that spice, varied the types and amounts of primary ingredients—for example, tomato sauce, meat, vegetables, and so forth. This is when cooking started to really become fun. I was experimenting, but not just trying things randomly. I varied the process depending on the needs of where I was in my development. If I didn't think something was spicy enough, I added spice. If I thought the soup was too thick, I'd add broth or a little water. I adjusted on the fly in accordance with the needs of the process.

This is exactly how hardware and software development works in the real world. While I can't teach you to become an expert developer based on any one process—I'm still working on that for myself—I can describe the most common processes that you're likely to see throughout your development career, at least in the short term. The waterfall and functional design methods were the de facto standards when I first became a practicing engineer. Now, they're only spoken of as fond memories by gray-haired men remembering the good ol' days.

© Molly K. Maskrey 2016
M.K. Maskrey, *App Development Recipes for iOS and watchOS*, DOI 10.1007/978-1-4842-1820-4_6

In software, except for highly specific firmware projects that reside on or close to the metal, object-oriented design and development rules the roost.

> **Note**   Writing software that is "close to the metal" refers to code that you write that runs on the processor, typically an embedded microcontroller, without any intervening operating system. You do everything from setting up the registers, handling interrupts, checking and switching clock speeds based on battery levels, and so on directly on the processor. On an iPhone or iPad, iOS provides that intervening layer, and we use the sets of Apple frameworks to make our coding life easier.

If you go to an iOS development firm today without a good understanding of objects, instantiation, classes, inheritance, and so forth, don't expect to be invited back for the second interview. When I was out interviewing at mobile development firms as part of my research for this book, I found that about half of them would give written tests to evaluate my skill level. I've never been a fan of testing, but because I was curious and it was research, I hunkered down and endured the humiliation. You see, tests given at a company are based on what they're doing, not on what you might learn in school or have practiced at your last position. While they do provide an objective way to compare and contrast candidates, they in most cases don't really assess your ability to dynamically grow and learn.

But, back to the point, every single test that I took during this time had at least half or more of its content centered on object-oriented design and development, usually with specifics related to iOS or Android projects.

Another interesting part of the tests was used to determine a candidate's familiarity with the development process, most typically Agile Scrum. Again, we're not here to make you a Scrum Master. Even the Scrum Masters I've talked with don't seem to have an accurate understanding of what that job is really about, and that includes many who passed the certification. I want to give you enough information so you understand what you're getting into and, even more so, what you're lacking. You need to figure out where you need to grow your knowledge, skills, and abilities.

Problem

As you begin to look for a job, you come across terms such as agile, Scrum, waterfall, and others that describe the processes of development, but because these are not directly related to writing software you don't quite get what they mean.

Solution

In the following sections we'll discuss the two most common software development methodologies: waterfall and agile. Even more recently, the process known as lean manufacturing has become more and more prevalent, especially in systems (hardware and software) startups, so we'll talk a little about that as well. You won't become a Scrum Master or expert in any of these, but it should give you the basics to start your research and fill in the gaps in your knowledge and skillset.

Waterfall

Waterfall development isn't new—it's been around since 1970—but most developers still only have a vague idea of what it means. Waterfall methodologies treat the software development process as a manufacturing or construction process. Progress is viewed as a steady flow from project initiation through analysis, design, development, testing, deployment, and, eventually, maintenance (Figure 6-1). In fact, waterfall was originally developed for hardware projects, aircraft design, electronics, a ship, the perfect shoe, pretty much anything and well before writing code was commonplace.

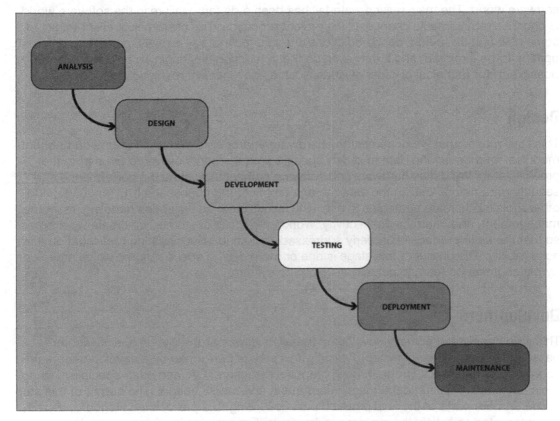

Figure 6-1. With the resemblance of water cascading down a slope, the waterfall methodology proceeds as a sequential series of steps, each assuming the previous step was performed correctly

Analysis of Requirements

This is the most important phase of the waterfall process, as it involves gathering information about what the customer needs and lays out, in the clearest possible terms, the problem that the product is expected to solve. Analysis includes understanding the customer's business context and constraints, the functions the product must perform, the performance levels it must adhere to, and the external systems it must be compatible with. Techniques used to obtain this understanding include customer interviews, use cases, and a desired list of software features. The results of the analysis are typically captured in a formal requirements document that serves as input to the design process.

The skill set for this activity includes problem analysis, goals and objectives definition, cost-benefit analysis, and presentation to senior management. This step can be arduous and boring for the fast-paced, innovative developer. But, if you enjoy interacting with customers and helping to come up with cost-effective solutions for a wide variety of problems, requirements analysis could be the job for you.

Unfortunately, the waterfall process has not translated well from the hardware to the software world. The main reason waterfall has been a de facto failure in the software world is because requirements change as the project proceeds. The customer or client thinks of some new feature to add, cost predictions change, technology evolves, permitting different options to be explored, and it may even be that a functionality originally required is not possible to for technical or other reasons, such as government restrictions on privacy.

Design

This step means that we document the hardware and/or software architecture, components, modules, interfaces, and data to satisfy specified requirements delivered to us from the previous step. We define hardware and software architecture; state the performance and security parameters; design the data-storage architecture; choose the IDE, language, and other tools; and create strategies to deal with issues such as exception handling, resource management, and interface connectivity. Working with our customer, we create wireframes so that the user interface is properly addressed, including issues relating to navigation and accessibility. The output of this stage is one or more design specifications, which are used by the engineering team to actually develop the system.

Development

This step consists of actually developing the product as per the design specifications passed in from the previous step. Typically, this step is performed by a development team consisting of engineers, programmers, graphics designers, QA, and other specialists using tools such as compilers, debuggers, interpreters, and media editors. The output of this step is one or more parts of the final product, built according to a pre-defined standard, tested and integrated to satisfy the system requirements. For projects involving a large team, version and source control, as discussed in Chapter 5, is critical to tracking changes to the code tree and reverting to previous snapshots in case of problems.

Change Management

Once development has begun against a firm set of requirements, it's not too long before something has to change. Typically, customer management has consulted with their marketing team and realized a "needed" feature is missing. It may also be that the development team, particularly members who were not involved in the requirements and/or design phases, discover that something is not possible or, more likely, that the cost and schedule allocated to a task just isn't large enough. This is when change control, or change management, comes into play.

In the waterfall methodology we're discussing, change management can be a very arduous process. Because of the linearity of our method as well as the need for traceability forward and backward, between requirements and maintenance, documentation has to change at pretty much every step of the process. To prevent changes from just happening whenever any team member so desires, a change control board (CCB) is usually part of the process. This team comprised of members of the customer and development companies reviews each change for its necessity and impact in terms of cost and schedule, as well as its benefit to the overall project and the client.

A change request can be approved, denied, or modified. Denying a request doesn't mean that the change isn't warranted; it could be that the engineer who brought it before the board has not provided sufficient information in her request. CCBs can meet with any frequency, but from what I've experienced, they generally happen every one or two weeks until the velocity of requests starts to slow down.

Like any other task when developing a product, the CCB)also costs money. Each member of the review team charges their time against the pool of money set aside in the budget for addressing changes. And, as always happens, there tends to never be enough money in this bucket.

Changes, specifically unplanned changes, have the biggest cost and schedule impact on any project not because they are expensive in and of themselves, but rather because they affect nearly every other part of the process. If the development team initiates a change request and it's approved, the specs have to change, as does the design of the system itself. Testing and implementation plans as well as maintenance schedules may have to be altered.

Testing

Near the end of the development phase we test both individual components and the integrated system to ensure that they are error free and fully meet the criteria within the requirements document. An independent quality assurance (QA) team defines "test cases" to evaluate whether the product fully or partially satisfies the requirements outlined in the first step. Three types of testing typically take place in a software project: unit testing of individual code modules; system testing of the integrated product; and acceptance testing, formally conducted by or on behalf of the customer. Defects, if found, are logged, and feedback is provided to the implementation team to spur correction. This is also the stage at which product documentation, such as a user manual, is prepared, reviewed, and published.

Deployment

Though we describe this as a completely separate stage of the waterfall process, deployment is in a larger sense part of the testing process as well. While many companies may have a proven software or app distribution mechanism, many clients are first-timers looking to figure out what works best for their customers' needs.

Most current software development companies institute a series of progressively more complex deployments. The QA team members become the first responders as they evaluate the functionality delivered to them from engineering as part of testing. QA not only tests the standalone modules, UI, database, web services, functionality, and so on, but also the distribution mechanism for deploying to users.

We'll discuss testing further in Chapter 12, but once a reasonably complete and functionally cohesive system is available that doesn't crash too often, a first round of in-house testing generally happens. Usually, the management and marketing teams carry company devices on which they will test the first deployment prototypes, essentially alpha testing, and render their non-technical verdict(s)—does the UI make sense, did the app become stuck, was it easy to use, are any instructions clear enough to be useful, and so forth.

Next, beta testing allows a small, usually well-defined, set of people to try out the app and provide feedback to the development organization. Chapter 12 talks in greater detail about deployment for testing, specifically using features in the iTunes Connect portal such as TestFlight. Beta testing provides the last chance to find and fix bugs before the app gets into the hands of the general public.

Once all the preceding testing has uncovered any issues and those have been corrected, the app becomes available to its intended market. Apps that are meant to be used by the general public get displayed and sold in the App Store. For those apps that are enterprise in nature— that is, they are only deployed to members of a specific organization or group— they are usually deployed via tools available through the Apple Enterprise Developer Program.

Maintenance

After deployment onto user devices, *maintenance* refers to making modifications to the system or an individual component to alter functionality and/or improve performance. These modifications arise either due to change requests initiated by the customer or defects uncovered during live use of the system. Typically, every change made to the product during the maintenance cycle is recorded and a new product release (called a "maintenance release" and exhibiting an updated revision number) is performed to enable the customer to gain the benefit of the update.

Waterfall Summary

The waterfall model offers some advantages for software developers. First, the staged development cycle enforces discipline: every phase has a defined start and end point, and progress can be conclusively identified by both vendor and client using milestones like any project management system. The emphasis on requirements and design before writing a single line of code ensures minimal waste of time and effort and reduces the risk of schedule slips or customer expectations not being met.

Getting the requirements and design out of the way first also improves quality; it's much easier to catch and correct possible flaws at the design stage than at the testing stage, when all the components have been integrated and tracking down specific errors is more complex. Finally, because the first two phases end in the production of a formal specification, the waterfall model can aid efficient knowledge transfer when team members are dispersed in different locations.

However, despite the seemingly obvious advantages, the waterfall model has gone out of favor in the past decade if not before. The biggest issue revolves around the fact that very often customers don't really know what the requirements are; rather, what they want emerges out of repeated two-way interactions over the course of the project. In this situation, the waterfall model, with its emphasis on up-front requirements capture and design, is seen as somewhat unrealistic and unsuitable for the way we work in the real world. Estimation of time and costs is also extremely difficult. In general, therefore, the model is recommended for use only in projects that are relatively stable or where this process may be required as part of the contract. For example, many large-scale government software development projects still to this day rely on the waterfall process model.

Problem

You keep hearing about lean manufacturing. What is it? Do you need to know about this?

Solution

Lean manufacturing describes a method of iterative product development and testing that solely focuses on solving a customer's problem.

Lean Manufacturing

Too many entrepreneurs believe that if they build a cool new widget and promote the heck out of it, customers will buy it. There are tremendous pressures from team members, advisors, board members, and investors to just hurry up and get something to market. But what happens if your beautiful, full-featured widget just sits on the retailer's shelves? Does it matter much then that you got it to market on time and under budget? Do you really want to pour all your precious time and energy into just keeping busy?

> **Note**   The author, while not hard at work writing this text, runs an engineering department for a tech startup with a very unique value proposition. However, even though her entire team knows what that proposition is, there's still a great sense of urgency to just build something that we can get on the shelves soon.

Lean manufacturing switches the focus from the innovator's dream and outside pressures to what a customer will actually use. Through a rapid series of MVPs (minimum viable products) and well-designed tests (Figure 6-2), any feature that can't be proven to solve a customer's problem is whittled away. And while lean manufacturing is generally targeted toward physical products, this process maps easily to the iterative agile methods we'll talk about shortly.

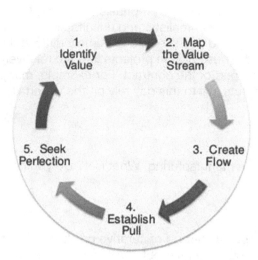

Figure 6-2. Managing the path to perfection with value defined from the customer perspective is the key theme of lean manufacturing

And it is not good enough to rely on hearsay, or what a few customers say they "might buy someday." These are real tests of actual MVPs, or at least tests of marketing material that leads to verifiable actions (email subscriptions, pre-orders, or crowdfunding campaigns).

This is the true scientific method in use, and for a former scientist like myself, these tests are really kind of fun to design. A hypothesis is formed: "The customer will buy dark purple socks." A test is designed: Light purple and dark purple socks are knitted, and a table is put up at a nearby farmer's market. The results are calculated: The dark purple socks sold out within 30 minutes; the light purple socks were ignored. Now, this was a very rudimentary test (and it really just shows my bias toward dark purple). We could have picked the wrong colors, texture, price, location, and even season. But now these can be the next tests to run.

Our aversion to failure can sometimes skew our view of these tests. Each test leads to a failure! (OMG! That means I'm a failure!) But really, each failure is a tremendously valuable lesson. And it's much better to "fail" at a tiny experiment early on than during or after a big product push.

This process can also be essential to a company's growth and continued success. Say your widget has sold very well, but the design team wants to add more features. If you manufacture a full-featured new widget and release it to customers, how can you interpret its success (or failure)? If it doesn't sell, is it due to the higher price? Or could it now be too complicated to easily install and use? In our dark purple sock example, we might respond to advisor pressure to expand the product line by adding silver and gold flecking. Do they not sell because the patterns are too busy? Or do some people not like to mix silver and gold?

The lean manufacturing focus is always on solving a customer problem. But don't develop a product for your perfect average customer. Instead, create a customer archetype of your early adopter. These customers really feel the pain of their problem, and will more quickly grab onto your perfect new solution. Besides, mainstream customers are much less forgiving of early product flaws.

One other key point in your MVP testing is to address the riskiest assumption first. If you can't solve those problems at the start, all the other tests will be meaningless. Again, if you're building a widget that nobody wants, adding features or improving the marketing will not help it to succeed. Success is creating something that solves a problem. Here's to your success!

Problem

So, how does lean manufacturing differ from agile development?

Solution

Agile processes focus on the development of the product and driving waste out of the product itself, while the focus of lean manufacturing is to develop a product that someone will buy and that will return a profit. That's not to say lean manufacturing should replace agile in any sense. Agile works best when a client has decided what needs to be built and your organization has been hired to make that project a reality. Essentially, agile focuses on the key aspects of product development after the product has been decided upon. The client, the ones paying for the development, take on the burden of whether or not the product is something that customers want.

Agile

In general, agile project methods are the set of iterative methodologies in which everything evolves in a collaborative environment. Teams composed of graphics designers, UI/UX experts, engineers, QA, and so forth are supposed to be self-organizing and function across departmental and skill areas, though this is not always the case. What tends to happen, from the author's experience, is that the basic management infrastructure stays in place and the implementation of agile in such an organization can "loosen" it up, creating a more free-flowing set of ideas and tasks.

For the most part, two sub-classes of agile have come to the forefront, and you're likely to see both in action throughout your interview process. In many cases, the two will blend together without a clear distinction between them as to their implementation. That is, a company may say they're doing a sprint (a Scrum term meaning a short one to two week iteration to create a tangible product) but might still allow changes in the design or functionality during the sprint, something not permitted in pure Scrum.

Scrum

Scrum is an agile project management methodology. The key trademark of Scrum is to apply empirical control to the software development process for a project. To implement this type of control system requires transparency, inspection, and adaptation. *Transparency*, as one would expect, means that every part of the development process is open and observable by all the team members. If I, as an engineer (coder), wish to work with the graphics designers to make sure their idea for a control can be implemented, then I just do so. I walk over to the designer and together we work out an amicable solution ahead of time. Transparency allows this and comes in the form of an openly viewable product backlog, highly-visible information such as task boards and burndown charts, a daily standup, sprint reviews, and retrospectives—all of which exists to clearly convey the flow of work through a cross-functional team (Figure 6-3).

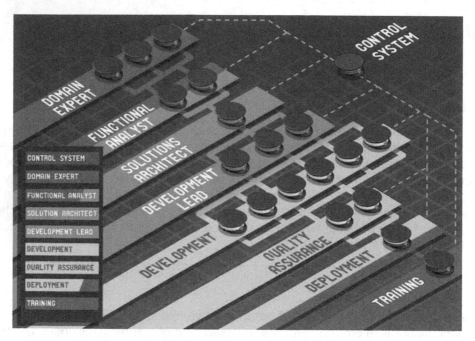

Figure 6-3. The Scrum team and empirical process control

Inspection means you can see how the work flows through the process as a result of the project being open and transparent. Each step or iteration or piece of code or design is critically evaluated by the team in a productive and non-threatening manner. In pretty much any agile process, all team members should leave their egos at the door. You will, more often than not, have your product be criticized for some reason, be it that it did not meet a requirement, is being too complicated, or even is just unnecessary. Don't take it personally. In fact, seek out the counsel of your peers early on, before they come to you. You'll bring them into your space, and they'll give you ideas and provide the criticism you need to do your job not only correctly, but also more efficiently. And that means you're much more likely to go home at five than you are to sleep on the couch at the office.

You then use the knowledge learned from inspection as a basis for making incremental ongoing improvements to the process; this is *adaptation*. This is where your friend the graphics designer might come to you with an idea she'd like you to consider. Perhaps you want to use an out-of-the-box UI control element from the Apple frameworks but, because of the way the customer would actually need to use the app, some amount of customization would make the customer much happier. So her suggestion to you pushes you to adapt your design and development effort for the overall good of the project. This improvement only came about because the entire process was open (transparent), she was able to see and evaluate (inspection) your work, and you were willing to make the change (adaptation) for the overall good of the project.

Once again, as with other topics in this book, I'm not here to make you a Scrum expert, but rather to give you a sense of what all this is about so you can talk intelligently at your upcoming interview.

> **Note**   When Jeff Sutherland created the Scrum process in 1993, he borrowed the term *scrum* from an analogy put forth in a 1986 study by Hirotaka Takeuchi and Ikujiro Nonaka, published in the *Harvard Business Review*. In that study, Takeuchi and Nonaka compared high-performing, cross-functional teams to the scrum formation used by rugby teams.

Roles

Like any software development team, the Scrum team consists of individuals of varying skills and specialty areas. As we saw earlier in Figure 6-3, it takes a range of skills to complete a project in the best manner possible. The domain expert provides the experience and knowledge about a specific area the team is addressing. For example, if the project is to create an online storefront, then a domain expert may provide insight into how payments are processed through banks and intermediaries. Further, a team may need or have multiple domain experts. In our payment example, we may need someone intimately familiar with security since we're dealing with sensitive customer information such as credit card numbers.

While much more common in the earlier days of agile, the functional analyst position's tasks are slowly being brought into the realm of the other team members, such as the developers. Usually, functional analysis is done by the software engineering team during the sprint rather than doing a functional decomposition prior to beginning any coding. There is often a similar, associated role known as the business analyst (BA) who focuses on the business aspects and breakdowns more from a client's perspective.

The solutions or systems architect provides the chief technical oversight of the project. Usually, she has worked directly with the customer prior to the contract award to create a well-defined system, or at least as much as could be achieved that early in the process. Technical development leads report to her, and usually UI/UX, engineering (coding), and QA do as well. From there, the software engineers, designers, QA personnel, deployment experts, and training developers create, through the Scrum process, the final deliverable product.

One role you will always hear about is that of the Scrum Master. Many organizations confuse this positon with the individual that runs the project. In fact, in a true Scrum process, the Scrum Master is the person who should be the least visible. The Scrum Master's role is to facilitate the Scrum process for the rest of the team. The basic idea is that she make things go smoothly for everyone else, removing impediments and roadblocks before they become an issue.

How Does It Work?

In its simplest form, Scrum can be defined as the following seven steps:

1. The product owner, usually the customer rep or person closest to the customers, creates a backlog, or a prioritized wish list of small, well-defined tasks (Figure 6-4).

Figure 6-4. Task board showing the product backlog of tasks to be completed

2. During sprint planning, the team takes from the top of that wish list a sprint backlog and decides how to implement those pieces.

3. The team is given a fixed period of time—a sprint (usually two to four weeks)—to complete its work, but it meets each day to assess its progress (daily Scrum).

4. As described earlier, the Scrum Master keeps the team focused on its goal while removing roadblocks preventing the job from getting done.

5. At the end of a sprint, the completed tasks should ideally be shippable, ready to hand to a customer, put on a store shelf, or show to a stakeholder. Most often, the customer's team would be given the materials for review and assessment.

6. The sprint ends with a sprint review and retrospective; that is, looking at how things went, making evaluations, and noting anything that might need to be altered for the next sprint.

7. The process repeats. As the next sprint begins, the team chooses another chunk of the product backlog, and everything starts over.

Scrum Agile Summary

I've shown you the very rudimentary basics of the Scrum agile process. Essentially, everything is identified as early as possible, much like in the waterfall process, but we don't begin work based on a fully architected, complete design. Scrum works on small, manageable, and well-defined tasks. These tasks should be quantifiable; that is, at the end of a sprint it should be clear whether the completed task is correct or not. And, finally, in the ideal situation the completed tasks (products) should be delivered, or be able to be delivered, to the customer for their inspection, test, and review.

Extreme Programming (XP)

XP is an agile software development methodology or process. How is different from Scrum? If you go back and look at the first line in the first paragraph on the Scrum section, you see Scrum is defined as an agile project management methodology without specifically calling attention to software development. In the very next sentence in that section, we began an in-depth discussion of how Scrum can be and is used in software development, but it's not limited to that. And, more importantly, Scrum is independent of the development process. Again, Scrum is a project management methodology.

XP gives us a process with which to create software in an agile and productive way, which in turn can be managed as a Scrum project. So, very succinctly, the two are not mutually exclusive and usually go hand in hand. XP focuses mostly on the engineering practices required to deliver software with quality. XP provides a set of core practices that are implemented during development of the product (Figure 6-5).

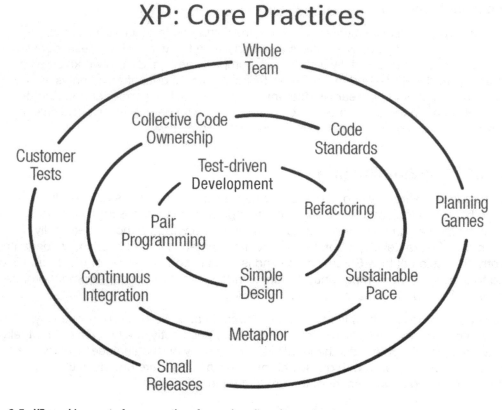

Figure 6-5. XP provides a set of core practices for use in agile software development

I won't go into each and every one of these practices, but I do want to mention the three you're mostly likely to become familiar with. The first is test-driven development (TDD). In TDD, unit tests are created based on the requirements before any functional code is actually written. When the functional code is created, it will be automatically evaluated when the build is performed. Xcode provides excellent support for unit testing and test-driven development, which we will talk about in Chapter 12. Refactoring, or code refactoring, is in essence the reuse of existing, working code with small changes so it can operate successfully in its new intended position in the project. Advantages of refactoring include readability (because it has been used and documented previously), reduced complexity, and maintainability.

Finally, another very important aspect of extreme programming, though not shown in Figure 6-5, is user stories, which are similar to use cases but not exactly. They are similar in that they describe the usage of the project, but are not limited to the user interface. They're generally written by the customer as things that they need the system to do for them and are used to accurately plan and create time estimates for future releases.

Problem

Where do functional design or object-oriented analysis/design (OOA/OOD) fit into this?

Solution

Both functional and OOA/OOD are ways that we as software engineers define the system that we plan to create and write code to implement our design. Neither of these is a methodology, and both are used as freely in the agile process as they are in a waterfall implementation.

We've talked mostly about methodology so far, so let's get a little more into the design of a project—or, more specifically, how you might set out to design your project or software—by looking at both functional and object-oriented design.

Functional

Functional development, or functional software architecture, refers to an implementation where a problem is coded as a series of functions that can be called, typically from a master program. The C language, as originally implemented, supports this. Functions are written separately and called via the `main()` function, which is called by the operating system when the program is loaded and executed on the hardware.

Anyone who has taken an undergraduate software engineering course in the last twenty years or so knows that pretty much everything today is written as a series of objects that interact. We'll discuss that in the next section. However, writing an object-oriented system does, in most cases, create a much larger software image; that is, the actual bits that get loaded onto the hardware. This is because an operating system is most often required to handle the interaction and operation of the objects with the system. You can't simply create objects in code without some way for them to interact and do something. That, most often, is the burden taken on by the operating system and any additional supporting frameworks or libraries.

Where functional development finds its home is primarily in embedded systems, which we will discuss in Chapter 9. For now, an embedded system is a very small, lightweight, and generally single-function device (hardware) that has a program that runs on its microcontroller, or MCU. An MCU is a special-purpose central processing unit (CPU) that contains additional supporting functionality such as timers, serial connections, analog-to-digital (A/D) convertors, and so on. An MCU, because it's typically placed in a larger number of devices—think set-top box, microwave, thermostat, etc.—has to be low cost in order for the manufacturer to make a profit. It will have a very limited memory, and the code must be kept small—only what is actually required. For that reason, most small embedded systems do not have an operating system; they also avoid licensing fees this way so as to avoid raising the cost of the product.

Through the use of a functional design methodology, only those methods absolutely necessary are coded and stored on the processor (MCU). Usually, through a series of interrupts from signals generated by external events, those methods and other sub-functions are called, but only when necessary. This creates a highly efficient, cost-effective hardware-software system that in most cases cannot be achieved using object-oriented design methods.

Object-Oriented Design

Most likely you've already heard about and worked with object-oriented system development. You create a series of classes that represent some object, let's say a vehicle. That class, which is not an instance of an object but rather is a representation of the broad set of similar objects, has properties and methods that you also implement in your coding. For example, a property of a vehicle might be color or number of wheels. A method might be move.

We use the class to instantiate or create actual objects that we can work with in our code. However, a vehicle is a very broad class of object. What is the vehicle like? Does it roll, or go across the water, or fly through the air? So, we can also subclass, or create new, more specific classes of objects from the previous class. Relatively speaking, and not always consistently, one class would be referred to as the parent, the other as the child. The parent is the less specific class, while the child has more specifics designed into it. As an example, a child or subclass of vehicle might be plane, car, motorcycle, or boat. It could be a bicycle or unicycle or hoverboard. Really, it all comes down to what is needed in your specific application.

Because there are so many texts, tutorials, videos, and so forth on object-oriented design, and because if you've done any coding you're most likely already familiar with the basics, I'm not going to go into more detail. By working through the basics of Swift or Objective-C in Xcode you'll quickly get a sense of what this is all about.

Summary

In this chapter we've looked at the different development methodologies you're likely to come across as a software engineer entering the marketplace. While the waterfall method can be found in older organizations, especially those dealing with large government software contracts, you'll encounter way more instances of agile methodologies. You'll want to know the basics of Scrum and what a sprint entails.

Most often, the interviewer—if he is not well versed in the subtle differences between Scrum and extreme programming—will get the two confused. Most often, they will refer to their method as Scrum without any regard for the fact that Scrum is a project management methodology and not specifically directed to software. My suggestion is to let it go and don't correct them. You know what it's all about, and your purpose is to get that job you really, really want, not to come off as a know-it-all.

Finally, we talked about the differences between functional and object-oriented design and when you might want or need to use a functional decomposition of your project in order to have it all fit into a very small-memory MCU in an embedded system.

Chapter 7

UI/UX

The first thing a user sees when she starts your app (Figure 7-1) is the user interface—the screen of stuff that pops up after they launch the app. We all know the value of a first impression and that you never get a second chance at one. Because there will almost always be one or more competitors to your iOS app in the App Store, if you fail to keep the user engaged from the very beginning, chances are she'll just download the next app in the search results.

Figure 7-1. The goal of every commercial or enterprise iOS developer should be to engage your customer from the moment they launch your app

© Molly K. Maskrey 2016
M.K. Maskrey, *App Development Recipes for iOS and watchOS*, DOI 10.1007/978-1-4842-1820-4_7

User Interface and User Experience (UI/UX)

First, let's be clear about what we mean by user interface (UI) as opposed to user experience (UX). The iOS Human Interface Guidelines (HIG) document from Apple should, of course, be your first stop in understanding the differences, but I'll give it my own personal spin. The UI describes all the visuals you see when launching an app on your device. It's the buttons, the labels, the graphics, and everything else you see after the app starts. Think of the camera app (Figure 7-2) and how it gives you a button to take the picture, some options for what type of image or video to capture, and a few editing features. There's a lot of power, but it's clean and easy to understand. I would say that it's so easy anyone can use, except I'm reminded of a specific instance when I was out with my friends and asked a guy to take our picture. It took him several minutes to figure it out. The point is that no matter how perfect you think your UI is, not everyone is going to get it quickly. This is where the user experience aspect comes into play.

Figure 7-2. Even a well-defined and clearly laid out app like the camera can be confusing to some people. With that in mind, you'll force yourself to create the best user experience you can for your customers

To create a good user experience, Apple suggests looking past the UI to the app's core functionality. What is the app trying to do? What is its purpose? What problem is the app solving or trying to solve? With the most recent releases of iOS, specifically iOS 8 and iOS 9, Apple has made more of the physical screen area available for content, and you should take advantage of that. Don't add buttons or colors gratuitously to make things look pretty, however. This will only distract from the user's experience and could get you bad reviews despite how much time and effort you put into making this the most beautiful thing in the store.

One of the key statements Apple makes in the iOS HIG is to defer to the user's content. Essentially, content is king in the world of iOS apps. Although you want a beautiful and easy-to-manage UI, the user's content is the heart of everything in the app. Another way of thinking about the user experience is to call it *navigation*. The user of your app needs to navigate all the controls and indicators and displays you've added to do whatever it is they need to do. Someone using a credit card payment app needs to quickly get their card info in, identify and confirm their purchases, add a tip if necessary, and sign the form. A gamer wants to know what's going on in their field of play to get the best possible score and make it to the top of the leaderboard. Each application will have a different set of information that needs to be addressed, and each user will need to access it in a manner that fits their needs.

To start out, let's look at information architecture and how to create a great experience for the user.

Information Architecture

The information architecture (IA) is more than just the menus you find on a website or the different levels of a table view as you dig down into more details about your content. The Information Architecture Institute (http://www.iainstitute.org/; Figure 7-3), defines *information architecture* as the art and science of organizing and labeling websites, intranets, online communities, and software to support usability. Essentially then, IA is how you show your users the content and the actions that they can take. IA is the backbone of your app's user experience.

Figure 7-3. The IA Institute's goal is to make information clearer, as should yours be when designing your user experience

Your UX encompasses your menus, the items you show on any screen of content, the overall structure of the app's UI, and even the terminology you show your users via the simplest labels and text areas. Your goal is to display this information to your user in a way that feels natural to them and how they normally would think of the content. The navigation through your app should feel natural and blend into the background. You want your user to focus on their task and not on the details of navigation.

Let's be honest with ourselves for a moment. The chances that your app is the only one out there that does what it does is next to zero. Don't be afraid to go out and explore what your competition is doing. What things work well? What things can be improved upon? Most likely, as part of the initial research your project owner will have identified key competitors with the client. As it is part of an open project, since we're using the agile methodology described in Chapter 6, this information should be readily available and easy to access. Take advantage of the work already done by your team.

Talk with your users if at all possible, or at least with the project owner, who would generally be part of your agile team. The first thing you need to understand is how your users categorize their information. Then, very early in the process, using some of the prototyping tools we'll discuss later in this chapter, perform usability testing and get important feedback from your customer to see if your ideas match with theirs. This usability testing is part of the incremental prototyping that is an integral part the Scrum process management methodology.

One thing to keep in mind is that although you can discuss what this looks like or the best way to do that ad infinitum with your team members, you and your team are not the users. So, no matter what you get out of a lunchtime chat, the best results will be obtained by understanding what your customers are looking for. This can be tough, as the software engineering team is usually further down on the org chart, buried in work and not often able to freely interact with clients, but this is where your Scrum Master can help. Her job, after all, is to facilitate your and the rest of your team's creating the best solution possible and to remove impediments to your success. Let her do her job.

Gathering Information

Rather than just sending out a bunch of open-ended questions to your customers and vacuuming up anything and everything they have to say, a common current technique is to use card sorting, derived from when 3 x 5 inch index cards were used to collect information about tasks a client wanted included in their project architecture (Figure 7-4).

Figure 7-4. *Card sorting is a simple method of identifying, categorizing, and organizing your customer's task requirements*

The process is very straightforward. You, based on the requirements handed down through the initial customer interviews, should have a list of tasks that your system needs to perform. Remember, at this point of the process you're playing the role of UI/UX designer. You're not writing code. This is particularly important if you are running your own one-person shop as a company or contract developer. Even if you work for an engineering team in a larger development organization, these techniques and your understanding of them will serve you well in the early stages of development.

You write the name of each of those tasks onto a card. At the end you'll have many cards, potentially hundreds, one for each individual task. Try to make the tasks as simple as possible, and don't pre-organize them. That's what we want our customer to do in order to give us the basic structure of our information architecture.

You give the cards to your participants, generally the customer or their representative, and allow them to organize them into groups of similar tasks. Once the sort has been completed by the participant, look for stacks of cards that have a large number of tasks and break them into smaller groups. Generally, about ten cards per stack should be the upper limit. Once you have a nice breakdown of tasks, let the user name each group to see what they come up with. This gives tremendous insight into how they think about the problem based on the task list that you provided. This is the heart of the interactive feedback that is so integral to the agile process.

Be sure to, as much as you can, watch and learn as your participant arranges and groups her cards. If possible, have another team member take copious notes while you conduct the interview and sorting process (Figure 7-5). Look for areas where things seem easy and also identify where groupings give them pause. Learn from this experience not just what the groupings are but also where there exists difficulty in identifying something. If your customer is having issues, then it's more than likely that a less knowledgeable user of the app will have the same difficulty. Remember, the navigation of your app should be transparent and allow the user to focus on the tasks they need to accomplish.

Figure 7-5. When conducting a card-sorting exercise with your customer, have someone to take notes while you observe and question to get the most out of the time

After working with several participants, identify where groupings are the same, are similar, and differ significantly. Problem areas will, of course, need resolution. In some cases, it might be that one or two individuals were simply not familiar with that part of the architecture and purpose of the tasks. These issues can often be resolved through renaming, a breaking down of a task or tasks into more fundamental levels, or even grouping smaller tasks into a more common set of tasks.

What comes out of all this—that is, the sorted set of cards with task names—is your information architecture, which defines the organization of your user experience.

Organizing and Understanding the Information

After each session with a participant, record the groupings they came up with into a spreadsheet. A simple way to do this is to use the participant name as the column identifier, and below that create a section where you put the name of each group name they came up with into a cell. Below that cell, order the cards by the task name, or card identifier if you used one.

The next thing to do is to rationalize the group names that your participants created from your list of tasks. It might be that several participants used the same group names in their sort exercise. This should give you a sense of when things worked and when they didn't. For example, if just about everybody grouped tasks that dealt with providing information about the company under the category "About Us," then it's quite likely you should consider that as part of your information architecture. Most often you'll see a lot of similarity to existing apps that function similarly. If group names differ, look for synonyms that are used elsewhere or look on a site like thesaurus.com to give you more generalized ideas for your architecture.

Another thing to consider is how most participants described the groupings. Did they label them as actions or as descriptions? You'll then want to consider groupings as either verb-based or noun-based, respectively. Remember, the tasks have already been defined through the early stages of the agile process. What we're doing here is organizing those into the way in which the user will interact with them; we're creating the user experience.

You probably recognize that what we've discussed so far is very success based. By that I mean that we're assuming that most users will do a lot of the work for us by organizing and creating group names that we can use. While that is the ideal situation, it's not always the way things work out. This is where you have to have some flexibility, as well as be able to gauge your participants' understanding of what is going on. If a participant isn't likely to ever use or have understanding of one type of task grouping, don't weigh their organizational structure quite as heavily as you might for someone more knowledgeable in a particular area. Though this may seem a bit counter to the idea of getting everyone to understand how to use the app in all cases, in reality, it's just not always possible to make things perfectly usable for everyone.

Computer-Based Sorting

Though some people find the tactile nature of working with actual index cards to be very beneficial, and I count myself among them, the time involved in converting and entering the data into spreadsheets can be a hassle as well as a potential source of information corruption. Fortunately, applications exist for doing this using a computer.

xSort provides a very simple way to perform card sorting using your Macintosh computer (Figure 7-6). However, you'll need to be with your participant to effectively use xSort. Also, the app does not come from a recognized Apple developer, so you'll need to open your security options to allow it to function (Figure 7-7).

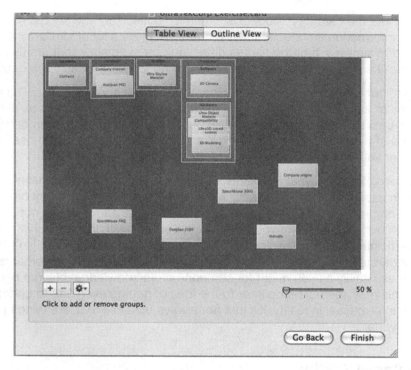

Figure 7-6. *xSort for the Mac provides a free, very simple, and quick way to manage the card-sorting process when you can be face-to-face with your participants*

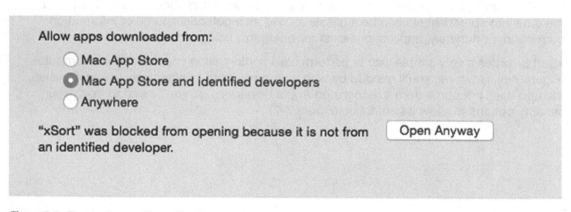

Figure 7-7. *To use xSort you'll need to allow your computer to open the app specifically, which could put your Mac at risk. Personally, I avoid this type of situation*

Most companies that are serious about using the card-sorting process with their customers will use an online subscription service such as OptimalSort from Optimal Workshop (https://www.optimalworkshop.com/). They currently offer pricing monthly, yearly, or by survey (Figure 7-8).

Figure 7-8. OptimalSort offers a variety of pricing options depending on the needs of your analysis

You can go to their website and even work through an example to get a sense of how easy it is to use. Tasks are listed along the left-most column, and all you do is drag and drop each task somewhere in the middle. When you start a new grouping you just label that group as you deem appropriate (Figure 7-9).

Figure 7-9. OptimalSort is easy to use and follows the hands-on card-sort model we've been describing, but also allows remote surveys to be conducted by your team

Remember, the goal of card sorting is to define the information architecture that becomes your user experience. Your goal is to organize the user's interaction with your app so they can access the data they need and perform the tasks they choose while keeping the navigation as transparent as possible. Let the structure of the data, the IA, dictate what the user experiences. Use domain knowledge experts to show you what that architecture is so that your UX is built exactly as it is needed.

Problem

Once we have the user experience, how do we use that to create the user interface (UI)?

Solution

If you've started your own app development company or been hired as an independent contractor whether directly or using an online service, you'll need to handle your customer's user interface needs. If you work for an iOS development organization, then most of the time there will be graphics designers who focus on developing the UI, and you'll only need to interact with them.

In most cases, particularly at major development companies, because of their background the graphic designer will use the tools with which they are most familiar. As you may already suspect, this will likely be products from Adobe such as Photoshop and Illustrator. But, for smaller operations where you need something really fast that is focused on your type of development, a good bet might be something less generic and costly that is tailored specifically for your needs. A non-traditional tool such as Balsamiq Mockups may provide you with an efficient and cost-effective alternative to the hundreds of dollars required to buy the latest copy of Illustrator and/or Photoshop.

Because this book is focused on software development tools and processes that you're likely to encounter throughout your iOS career, I'm not going to teach you how to effectively use any one tool, as there are so many variations as to how things are done in any organization. For example, if you're out on your own as a developer and stick to small projects, there's no reason at all that you can't effectively create your UI using graph paper and a pencil (Figure 7-10). Choose based on your needs, resources, time, and skill set.

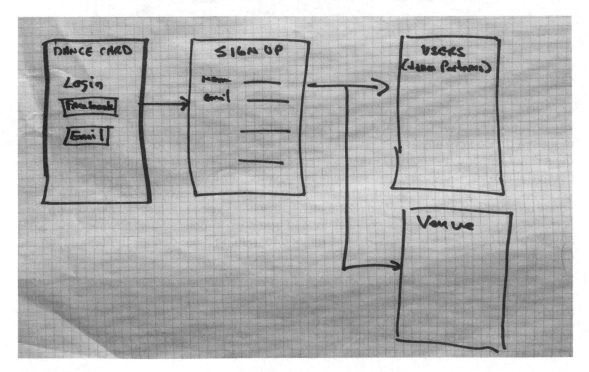

Figure 7-10. A simple UI layout the author created using graph paper and a marker

I recently worked on the development of an app for an online dance card. The first iteration of the UI is shown in Figure 7-10.

If you don't know, a dance card is a form given out at a dance event, usually to the ladies; gentlemen would approach her and pick a dance that they would do together later in the evening (Figure 7-11).

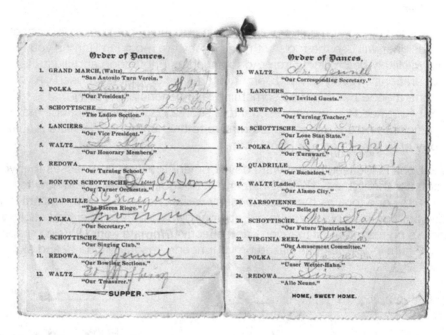

Figure 7-11. A typical paper dance card

My concept was to automate this using smartphone technology, WiFi, and broadband interconnectivity as well as local peer-to-peer (i.e., Bluetooth Low Energy) to allow anyone to request a dance from anyone else at the venue. The music schedule for the evening these days is not set, and quite often people will request a particular song or style that they're comfortable with. Thus, the music list changes dynamically throughout the evening. At my venues, the music is managed on the DJ's laptop and has wireless connectivity, so the songs are available to be identified. Combined with wireless access, a social networking (e.g., Facebook) mechanism for connecting, and true peer-to-peer so that anyone can ask anyone else, I created a very easy-to-use method for getting more dances throughout the evening.

If you were ever at a junior high school dance, then you probably know the feeling of rejection when no one asks you to dance or, if you're a boy, the fear of asking that pretty girl to go out on the floor with you. MyDanceCard, the name of this app, solves that.

As an example of how this might be laid out using traditional tools, Figure 7-12 shows my initial login and signup layout I created using Adobe Illustrator.

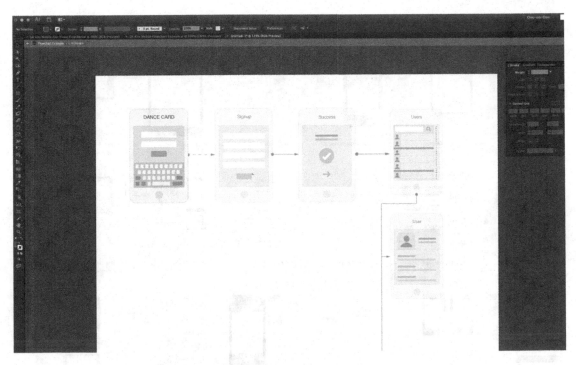

Figure 7-12. *My app's initial login and signup UI layout using Adobe Illustrator*

Going into the details of using Illustrator, even just focusing on iOS UI, is far beyond the scope of this book, and there are so many other resources that include pre-defined illustrator (.ai) elements that you can buy or get for free to lay out your design. Remember, you're not creating the actual UI that runs on an iPhone; you are creating the wireframes—that is, the visual representation—of what the iOS developers will create and build in Xcode.

Balsamiq Mockups for Rapid Prototyping

Years ago at an iOS meetup I attended, I saw a presentation on Balsamiq Mockups, a fast, easy-to-use, low-fidelity tool for creating UI wireframes. Back then it was free, but as of writing, it costs $89USD for a single-use license that allows three users to have access. This is the perfect tool for creating my wireframes, as I operate independently most of the time, and even though I am pretty proficient with Illustrator, Mockups offers some really neat advantages over the Adobe product.

The reason we create wireframes in the first place is to follow our agile process through prototyping and save time by not committing to something too early in our development. With a prebuilt set of components and Mockups-to-Go, an active repository where other Mockup users can contribute their components (Figure 7-13), Balsamiq makes your UI design come together quickly and easily.

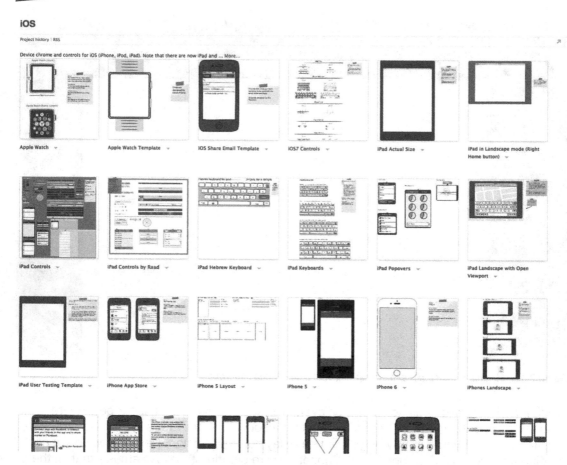

Figure 7-13. *Mockups-to-Go offers a large set of free iOS and Watch components for you to use in your UI design*

Because you're creating a low-fidelity design, the reviewers will be more likely to provide honest feedback, and your work will never be mistaken for a final design. Continuing with the dance card app I've been discussing, you can see how I implemented in Balsamiq the login UI that I previously created with Illustrator (Figure 7-14). Note that in this version I've added actual images of one of the dance venues as well as a Facebook login. Even with actual images as well as the characteristic Facebook appearance, this UI would never be mistaken for a final design.

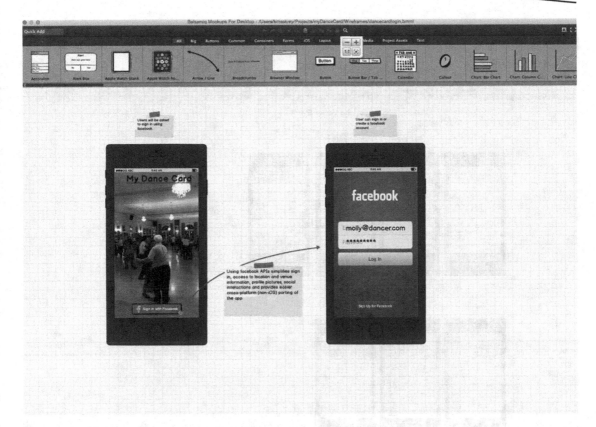

Figure 7-14. The dance card app's login UI design using Balsamiq Mockups

You can add as many screens as you need as well as notes to clearly address the intent of any or all UI elements (Figures 7-15 and 7-16).

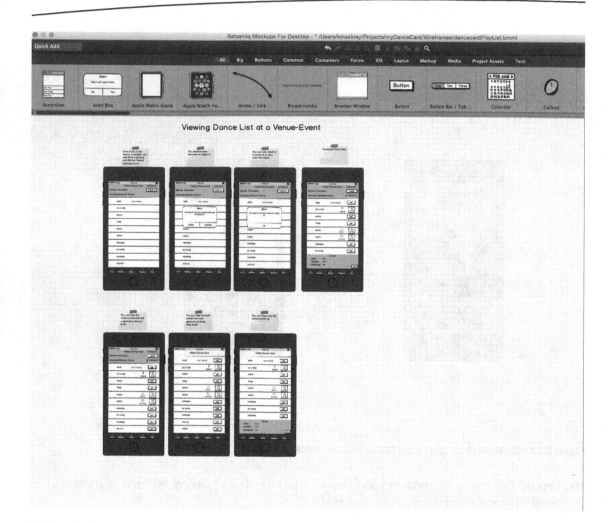

Figure 7-15. *You can create multiple images showing the result of a user action with annotations*

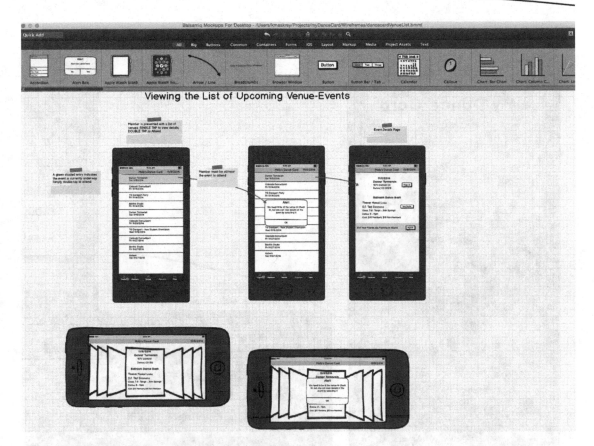

Figure 7-16. You can show both portrait and landscape UI layouts

Finally, Mockups offers a crude simulation capability to allow you to test the movement from one screen to another when activating a control surface. In Figure 7-17 you can see the properties for the selected button element, "Sign in with Facebook." I've defined that link to be the Balsamiq page danceCardPlaylist, which is the page shown in Figure 7-15. So when we run the simulation, pressing that button will take us to the venue list page.

Figure 7-17. You can add links to control elements to create simple UI simulations

You run a simulation in Balsamiq by going to full-screen mode (Figure 7-18), where you get the hand cursor indicating an active control surface that you can use to walk through your UI and, to some extent, your user experience.

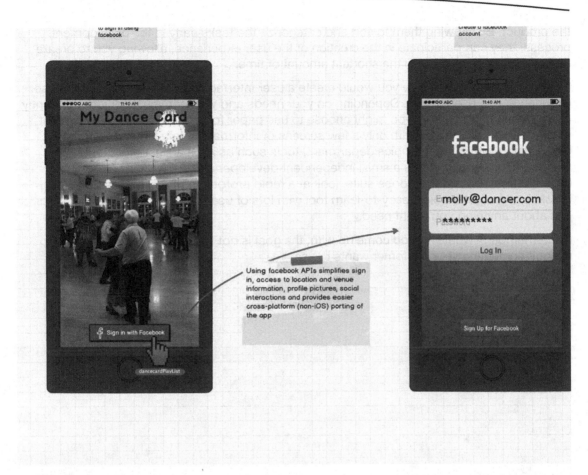

Figure 7-18. Balsamiq Mockups provides a rudimentary but effective way to walk through your UI design to show your reviewers the user experience

Summary

In this chapter we've briefly covered the aspects of user interface and user experience design that you're most likely to come across in your career as an iOS developer.

Because the UI and UX are the first things a customer or user of your app will see, it's critical that you make a good impression. But impression does not equal glitz and fancy colors or pretty control pictures. The impression you want to make is that your app is intuitive and easy to use. Your goal is almost for the user to not notice your hard fought efforts but to simply and easily use the app to get the task done.

While the look and feel of the app is certainly important, you want to achieve the easiest and most understandable user experience possible. Again, you don't want the customer to think about it; you just want them to use it. Taking that into consideration, we focused heavily on information architecture, which is essentially your intended user experience. Through an interactive process with your customer or their representatives using techniques such as card sorting, you get the best information possible from those most knowledgeable about the product. By allowing them to sort and categorize the tasks early in the development process, they can participate in the creation of the user experience, allowing you to create the best product possible in the shortest amount of time.

Finally, we talked about how you would create a user interface from the analysis of the user experience and user stories. Depending on your needs and whether you work independently or for a large organization, you might choose to use paper for a quick design, usually best when dealing with an app with only a few screens of information. In a larger development organization with a true graphics department, tools such as Adobe Illustrator would most likely be used. And, if you're a small independent developer and can't afford or don't have the time to learn the Adobe suite, look at a rapid prototyping tool such as Balsamiq Mockups. You get a quick, easy-to-learn tool with lots of user-contributed components for just about anything you might need.

But remember—whatever you come up with, the goal is not to make it pretty but rather to make it something your customer wants to use.

Chapter 8

Targets and Schemes

In Xcode we create and work with projects that are collections of stuff. A project contains all the files, resources, and other information such as info.plist or build settings to create products. The project also contains the relationships between those elements; for example, source files that may belong to one product but not to others. A *target* specifies the product to be built and how we are going to create it; that is, the instructions for building that target. Each target only builds one product. You can either have multiple targets included when you first create the project or add them later. For each target we use schemes, which define what happens when you build a target. Targets possess multiple schemes, some of which are standard, but you can add and customize them too.

Targets

When you first create a project you are limited to a few specific types of targets, but after the project has been created you have the option to create any number of additional targets. Generally, targets should be useful and focused on the intent of the project. When adding targets, they should provide additional meaning to the project but not deviate from the project's general intent. By that statement I mean that targets should not be used to test out different ideas within a project. For example, you create a project where the primary target uses a simple file structure set up in a specific manner. You decide you want to see if a different file structure might work better, so you create a target for testing this idea.

There are a couple of reasons as to why this is a bad idea. First, within the source code you would need to have some type of build conditionals, e.g., a #IF, to determine which target you are building for so as to only use the appropriate source. You can, of course, do this in the Xcode project settings and not put a lot of #IFs into the source. So, while you've added a target specifically to test your hypothesis, you've added a whole lot of additional code and chances for mistakes at the same time.

An even more valid reason for not doing things this way is that this is what branches are intended for when using source control. We discussed source control in Chapter 5 with a focus on protecting your work in case something bad were to happen, like a system crash, so that you would be able to recover your work.

© Molly K. Maskrey 2016
M.K. Maskrey, *App Development Recipes for iOS and watchOS*, DOI 10.1007/978-1-4842-1820-4_8

We even talked about how branches can be used by different development teams or individual engineers to test out just different types of ideas. Basically, when you want to try something different you create a branch, which in Git is a complete set of all the files and changes so far. From there, you make all the changes you want and test out your ideas. This does not affect the main branch, which is just as you left it. If your ideas don't work out, you can get rid of the branch or just leave it as a note for future work. If it does turn out to be better, then you merge your new work into the main branch to include the changes.

In short, use branches to test new ideas, not targets.

Problem

You understand how to make an Xcode project and add various files, but the concept of targets is still a bit unclear.

Solution

Let's work our way through an Xcode project to see where we might add targets.

When we create an Xcode project from a template (Figure 8-1) there is no clear way to include multiple targets.

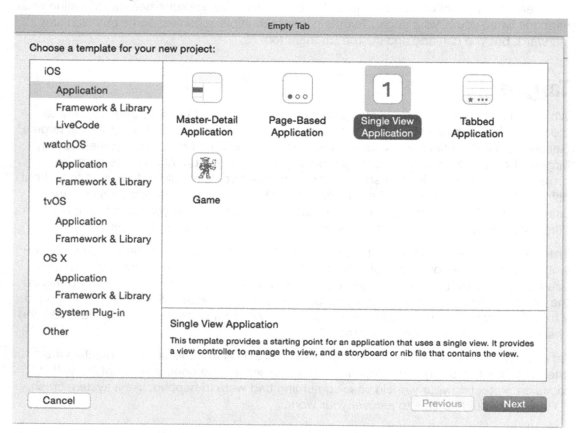

Figure 8-1. Xcode templates do not include targeting options

Adding Tests

When you choose the project options (Figure 8-2), you get options for what will turn out to be new and separate targets in your project. If you look at the bottom of the window, you see options for including unit tests and UI tests. You can select either one of these checkboxes, which will include new targets in your project. We'll show this in a moment.

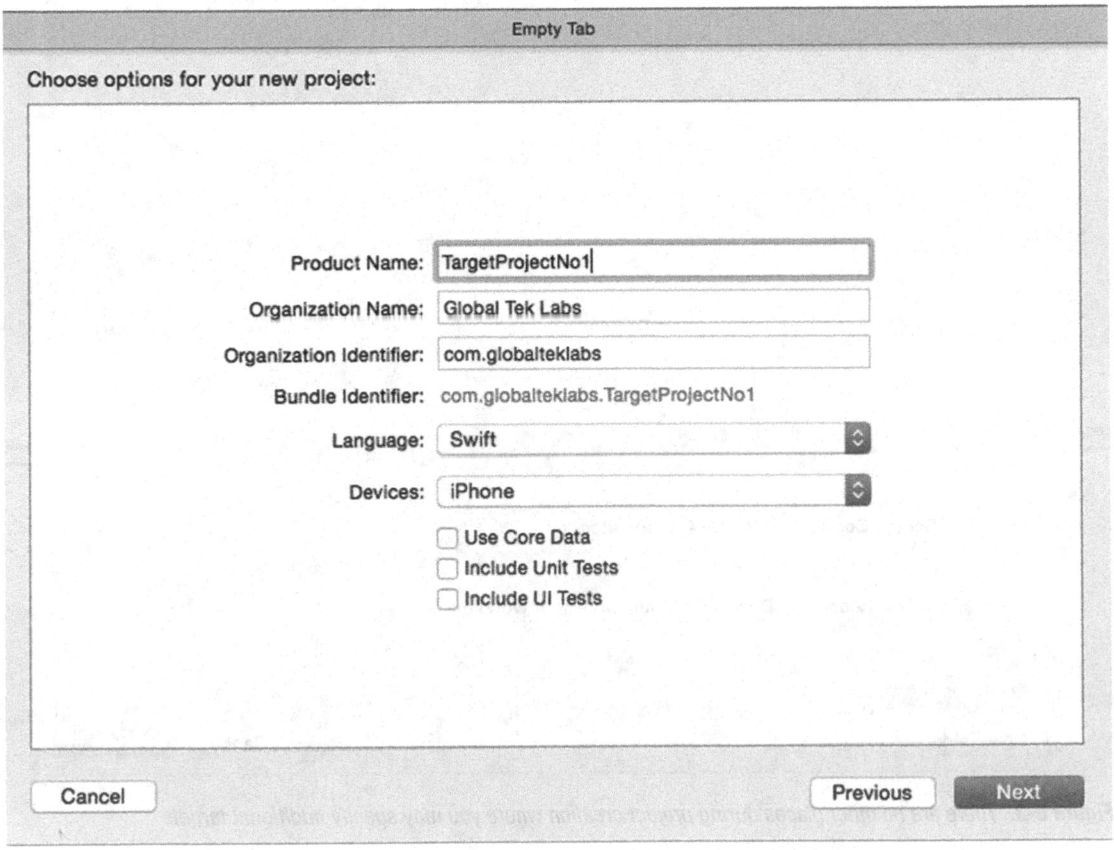

Figure 8-2. *Though not specifically identified as different targets, if you decide to include testing, your project will include one or more test targets*

When you go to the next screen to save your project on your computer (Figure 8-3), note that you have no more options available for creating new targets. Although this is the point where you could specify the use of Git and thus include source code control in your project, that option, in and of itself, will not add any new targets to your project. The general idea is that your project should be focused and not allow for too much variation in its intent or how it is designed. If you want to deviate, use a Git branch. Or, if you want to try something significantly different, create a new, separate project.

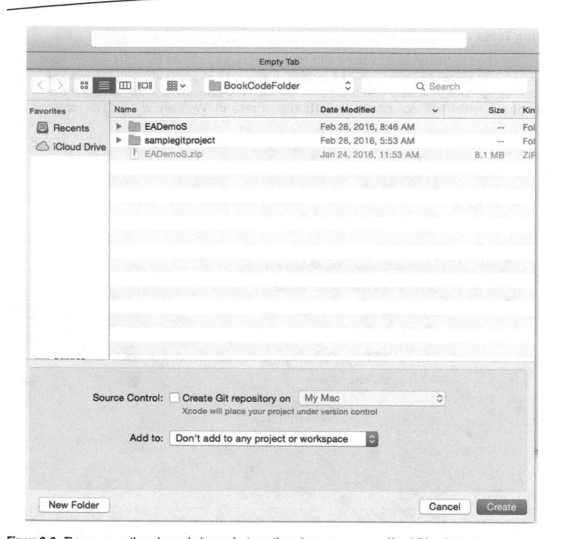

Figure 8-3. There are no other places during project creation where you may specify additional targets

Once the project is created (Figure 8-4), the targets—in this case our single app target—can be clearly seen in the Xcode Project Navigator along with all its appropriate build settings.

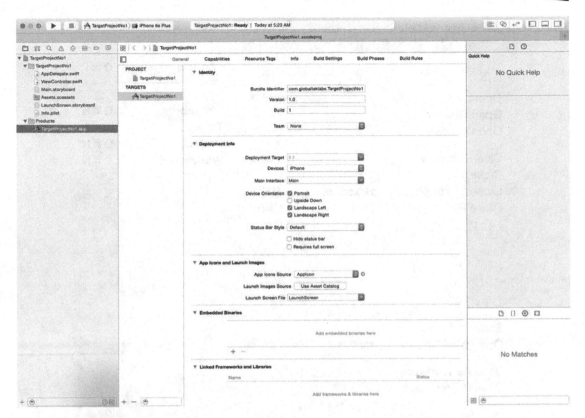

Figure 8-4. *The target of an Xcode project can be selected just like any other project source, UI, or settings file*

Now that we have an active project, we can add additional targets by going to the File menu, choosing "New" (Figure 8-5), and then selecting "Target..."

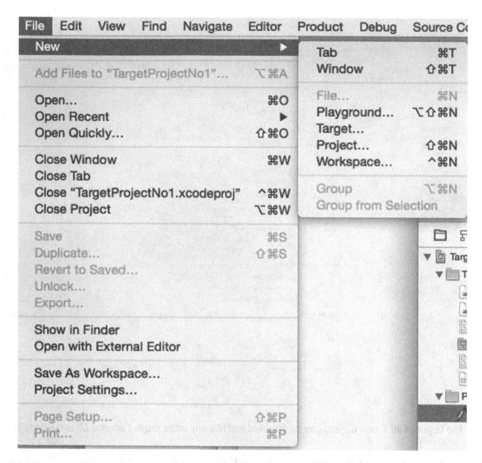

Figure 8-5. Once you have an active project you can add new targets to that project, just as you would add new files

Note that now two additional choices are available, Application Extension and Test (Figure 8-6). Also, to be clear, you can add another application or framework—for example, as an additional target, though, as we discussed, you wouldn't likely do that in most cases. We'll add unit testing to get an idea of how this works.

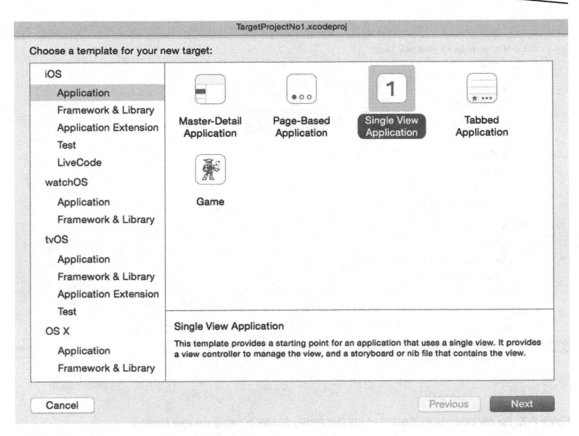

Figure 8-6. *Now, in addition to the previous choices, you can add new targets for testing and application extensions*

Figure 8-7 shows our testing options for either user interface testing or unit testing. We'll select "iOS Unit Testing Bundle."

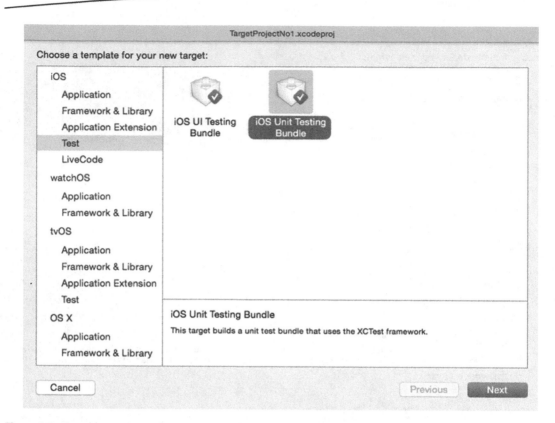

Figure 8-7. *For our example, we'll select an iOS Unit Testing Bundle to create our new target*

Note that we have to now select which project this target belongs to and which target we are intending to test with our unit testing bundle (Figure 8-8).

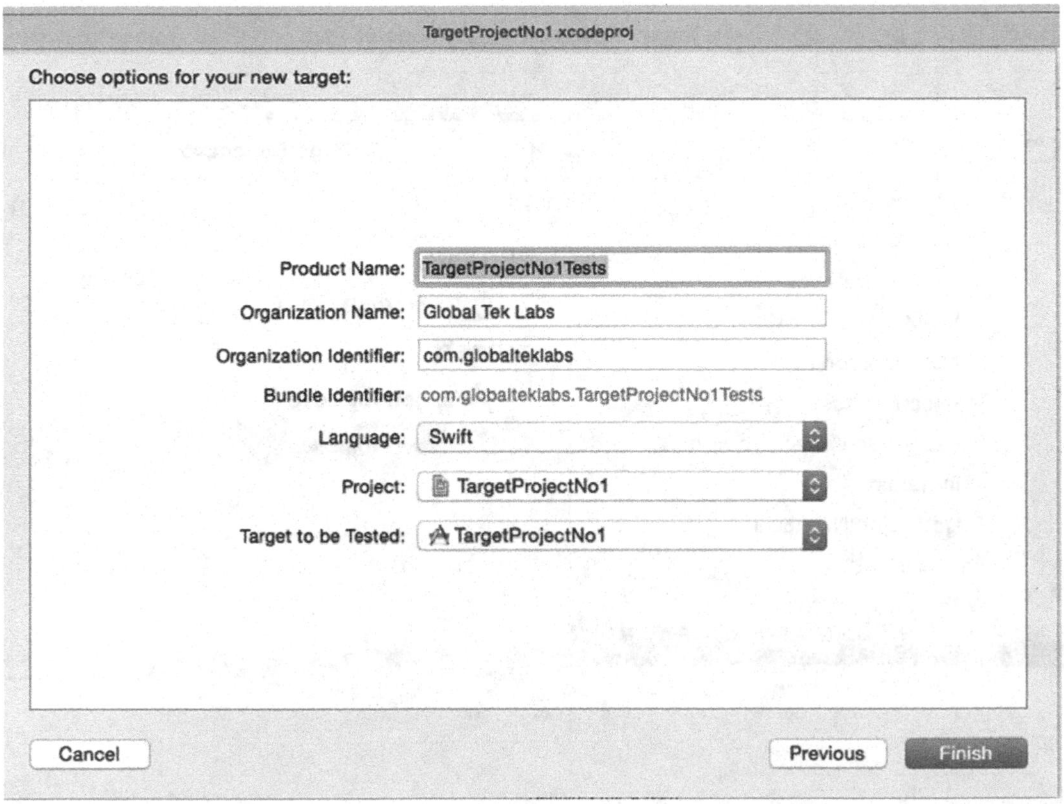

Figure 8-8. *Make sure the correct project and test target have been selected before creating the target so Xcode knows where to place everything*

And finally, in Figure 8-9 we can see in the Project Navigator that Xcode has added the new target for unit testing to our project. Note also that a tests folder called `TargetProjectNo1 Tests` has been added to our project.

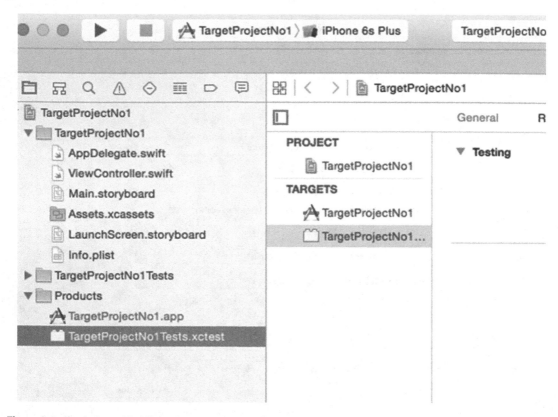

Figure 8-9. Xcode has added the new target to our project

We'll talk about testing later, but you can see that Xcode has added as part of our new target some boiler plate code to get us started using unit testing. See Listing 8-1.

Listing 8-1. Target Boiler Plate Code for Unit Testing

```
//
//  TargetProjectNo1Tests.swift
//  TargetProjectNo1Tests
//
//  Created by Molly Maskrey on 3/15/16.
//  Copyright © 2016 Global Tek Labs. All rights reserved.
//

import XCTest

class TargetProjectNo1Tests: XCTestCase {

    override func setUp() {
        super.setUp()
        // Put setup code here. This method is called before the invocation of each test
        method in the class.
    }
```

```
override func tearDown() {
    // Put teardown code here. This method is called after the invocation of each
    test method in the class.
    super.tearDown()
}

func testExample() {
    // This is an example of a functional test case.
    // Use XCTAssert and related functions to verify that your tests produce the
    correct results.
}

func testPerformanceExample() {
    // This is an example of a performance test case.
    self.measureBlock {
        // Put the code you want to measure the time of here.
    }
}

}
```

Schemes

Problem

You don't quite understand schemes.

Solution

Let's discuss the basics of schemes that you will need to know as a relatively new iOS software engineer.

Schemes define what happens when we select what we want to do by pressing the right arrow (build) button in Xcode (Figure 8-10). Most of the time we just want to run our project, either on the simulator or on an actual device. However, we may want to do other things like test or archive so we can upload our app to the App Store. And though we can select which thing we want to do, it is within the scheme for the target that this is defined.

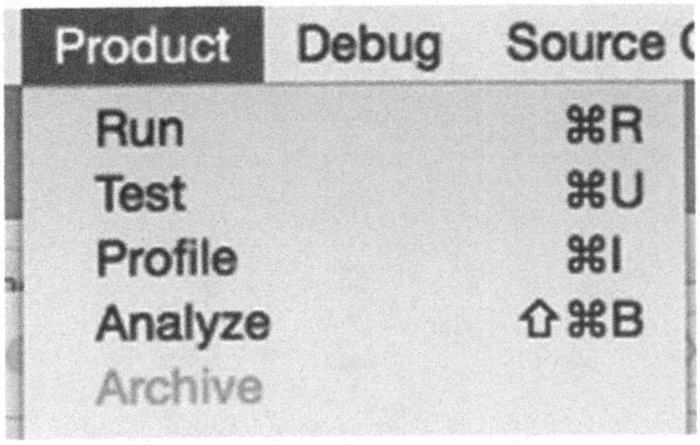

Figure 8-10. Our choices for building a project/target

We can select the scheme to use from the drop-down just to the right of the Xcode Run button (Figure 8-11).

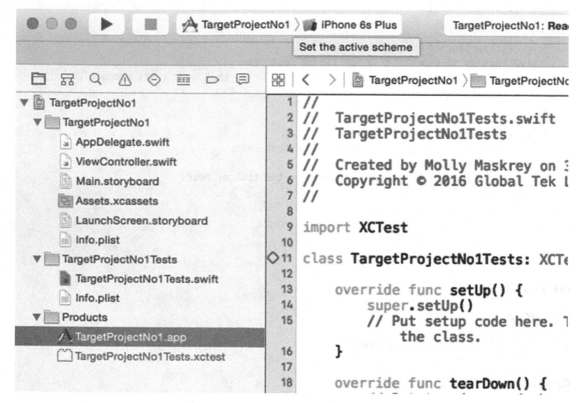

Figure 8-11. *To the right of the Run button you can set the active scheme that Xcode uses when building or running your project*

You can also use the drop-down menu to edit, manage, or create a new scheme (Figure 8-12).

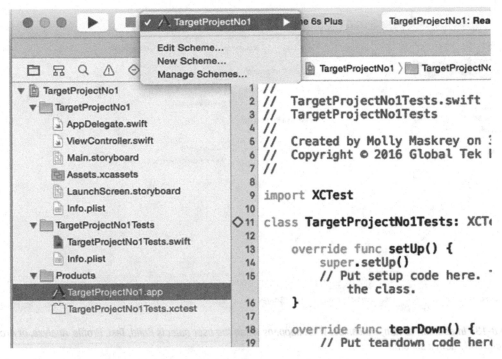

Figure 8-12. You can also manage the different schemes for each of your targets

Problem

What is in a scheme, or what does a scheme do?

Solution

As we said previously, a scheme defines what happens when you select one of the scheme options (by pressing the Run button) in Xcode. Most of the time you just build and run without thinking about it, but schemes offer a few other choices. In the bar across the top of the Xcode IDE window, left-click and hold on the active scheme, then select "Edit Scheme" to get to the screen you see in Figure 8-13. Note that at the top of the figure the build option says there are two targets. These are the app target created with the project and the Unit Test Bundle we just created. To build a target means to go through the whole compilation, linking, etc. process but to not install the app to a device or execute it on the simulator.

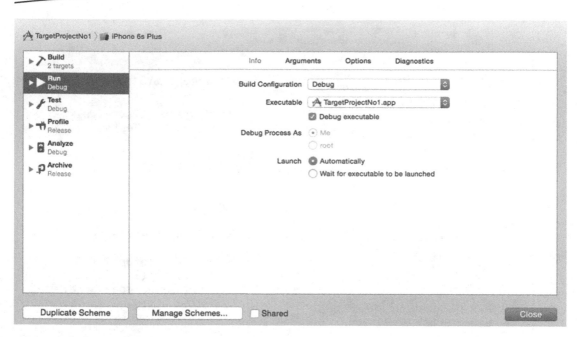

Figure 8-13. *In addition to Run, we can set what happens when the user selects Build, Test, Profile, Analyze, or Archive in our currently active scheme*

By expanding this dialog window, as seen in Figure 8-14, and then opening up each build step as defined in Xcode, you can see that some choices, test and run specifically, offer the option to run the executable while the others do not. While it always makes sense to go through all the available options and to at least have a minimally viable understanding of what you're doing, practically speaking, most developers will only use a handful of these options. The reason for this is that from a company perspective time is money and the more time you spend "messing around" with stuff, regardless of how valuable it might be down the road, the more time it takes to get through the next sprint and deliver the product. As such, you're most likely to use Build and Run. Organizations with the ingrained "Test First" mindset will also use the Test option significantly, but although I do that when working on projects for my clients, I've never been employed at an organization with that way of thinking. We'll talk much more about testing in Chapter 12.

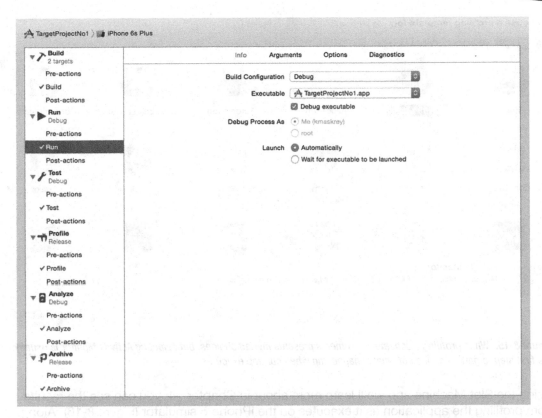

Figure 8-14. Only the Run scheme and Test scheme options offer the ability to execute the project on a simulator or actual device

Profile Scheme

If we use the Profile scheme option we'll be presented with the window in Figure 8-15, which prompts us to select a template for using Instruments. Though beyond the scope of this book simply due to time and space, Instruments provides a way to get data about the execution of a program on a device or in the simulator. One very common use of Instruments is to profile (hence the scheme name) the execution of your app and look for areas where the processing bogs down or to find memory leaks.

Figure 8-15. *When profiling a scheme, Instruments presents myriad choices, but selecting Activity Monitor is usually the first step to getting an idea of what is happening when our app executes*

Using the Slot Machine app we'll learn more about in Chapter 14, you can see the results from profiling the application as it executes on the iPhone 6 simulator (Figure 8-16). Along the top are histograms allowing you to see virtual memory sizes and task loading. One of the first things to look for is a continuously growing VM histogram that never levels off. This would mean there is likely a memory leak somewhere in the code that needs to be dealt with immediately. The next three lines represent processing performance, as does the task list below, where you can readily identify which tasks are consuming the bulk of the processing. On the right side of the Instruments screen you can select and add other performance metrics to monitor during program execution.

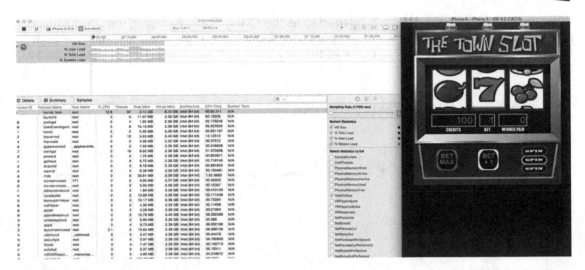

Figure 8-16. Profile analysis of a target

Analysis Scheme

Choosing to run the Analysis scheme (see Figure 8-17) runs your project source through the static analyzer and allows you to find potential memory leaks, dead code paths, variables never read, and so on. Personally, with the introduction of Swift, which corrected many of the vulnerabilities in the older Objective-C language, I rarely use the Analysis scheme. Xcode's built-in, on-the-fly error checking finds most, if not all, of the errors I used to locate with the static analyzer. For example, when we used to have to allocate and initialize variables but could easily forget to manage them down the road, memory leaks were a very common occurrence.

Figure 8-17. Choosing Analyze executes the source static analyzer to find issues in your project

When the static analyzer, originally referred to as the Clang Static Analyzer, was popularized in Xcode 3.2, it was just what we developers were looking for. It provided a visual flow path from where an error was likely to occur all the way back to the offending initial lines of code (Figure 8-18).

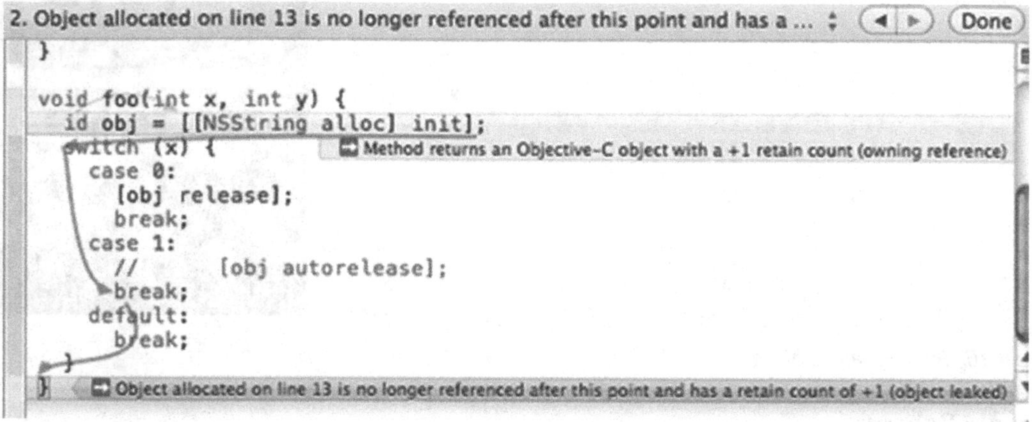

Figure 8-18. *The original static analyzer, popularized in Xcode 3.2, offered the ability to trace a potential error to its origin*

As an example of what we see today, I added an error into our app's viewDidLoad method. The offending line creates and initializes a variable, testVar, that is never used (Figure 8-19). However, it is immediately apparent that Xcode knows this is an issue and so it warns you of the problem.

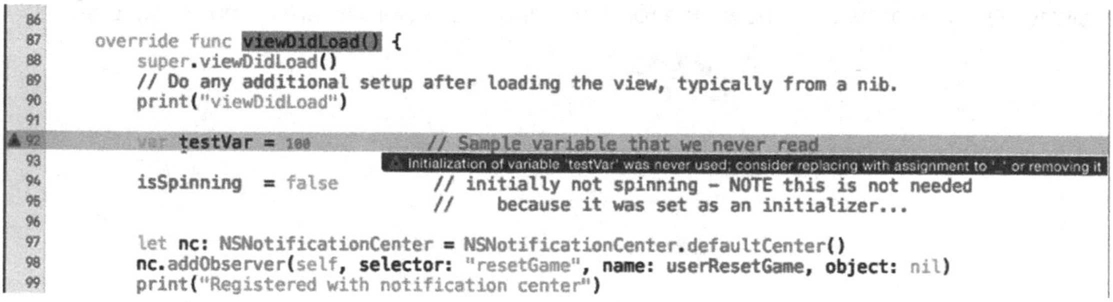

Figure 8-19. *Xcode currently does such a good job of on-the-fly analysis, much of the static analyzer's usefulness, at least for the author, has gone away*

When you run the Analysis scheme you get a detailed report, as shown in Figure 8-20, that gives you the same information already provided by Xcode interactively. With Swift, the flow-path analysis is no longer provided and instead you get this type of report, similar to what you see during a normal project build.

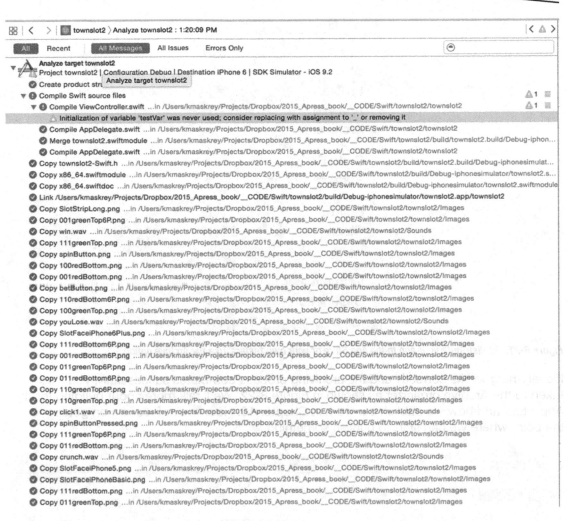

Figure 8-20. Results of a Swift project Analysis scheme

Archive Scheme

When you're ready to place your app into the App Store or to just distribute it to your own set of users for testing, you'll use the Archive scheme option. As we previously did for other scheme options, from the Product menu select "Archive" (Figure 8-21). For this example, we're using the project described in Chapter 15 where we create a simple coin-toss application for the Apple Watch.

Figure 8-21. To distribute your app to the App Store or your own testers, use the Archive option

If everything works correctly and the archiving process completes successfully, you'll be taken to the Archive organizer as shown in Figure 8-22. We'll talk more about building for the App Store and how we publish our work in Chapter 10. Here, we're focusing on getting to the point where we can start to publish something.

Figure 8-22. If your build completes successfully, you'll be taken to the Archive organizer, where you can decide whether to upload to the App Store or to export your app to your testers

You've now successfully created an archive, which is a bundle that includes your product along with symbol information that you submit to the App Store using iTunes Connect.

> **Note** iTunes Connect is the portal, or web interface, where you interact with the controls for setting up, setting pricing, posting graphics, and eventually placing your app for sale. We will discuss it in Chapter 10.

Even though you've created this archive bundle successfully, and without any errors or warnings in your target, the archive still may not be correctly created for submission. The first thing you want to do is to validate the bundle (Figure 8-23) by selecting the Validate... button.

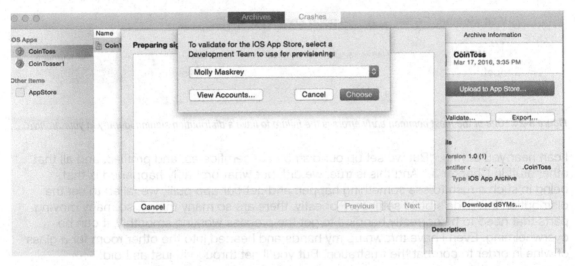

Figure 8-23. Validate your archive, being sure to use the correct developer account if you happen to have more than one

When things work and the archive validates correctly, this takes just a moment or two on the way to submission. And, most of the time, once things get worked out in your process that's usually what happens. However, the first few times through you may encounter a problem or three. Because we're usually in a rush to get something built and tested, we don't always set up everything correctly in our build settings. A common error would be that shown in Figure 8-24 indicating we failed to generate a distribution identity.

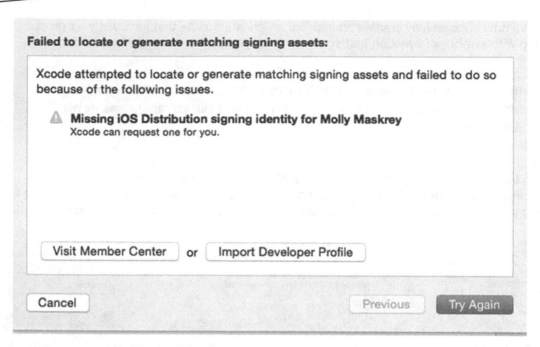

Figure 8-24. *One of the most common early errors is the failure to have a distribution signing identity in your archive*

I can hear you saying, "But we set up our distribution certificates, and profiles, and all that other stuff in Chapter 3." And this is true, we did, but what probably happened is that, being in such a rush to see something happen and get our app built, we failed to set the distribution in Xcode's build settings. Honestly, there are so many things, so many moving parts that need to be correctly handled to get the process working smoothly, it can be overwhelming. Even I have thrown up my hands and headed into the other room for a glass of wine in order to combat the frustration. But you'll get through it, just as I did.

So what happened? If we look through the build settings in Figure 8-25, we can see that our release configuration (we'll discuss configurations later in this chapter) is set to use the Developer identity.

Figure 8-25. *A very common error when validating archives is to have not selected the correct signing identity for your release configuration*

Since we did create our distribution information in Chapter 3, this is an easy fix. You should be able to use the pull-down menu to set it to your distribution identity, as seen in Figure 8-26. You'll want to clean the project by going to the Project pull-down and selecting "Clean," then re-do the Archive operation. You'll see a new archive in the organizer. You can delete the old one that had the error(s).

Figure 8-26. To correct a signing error for your release archive, make sure you've selected your distribution identity

You'll probably come across a few more stumbling blocks on your way to creating an archive that can be submitted to the App Store, but the goal is to get to something like what is shown in Figure 8-27. While it does have warnings, the validation did pass successfully and the archive can now be submitted.

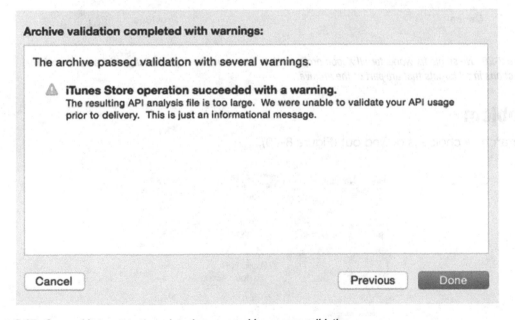

Figure 8-27. Our goal is to get to the point where our archive passes validation

Note   The error shown in Figure 8-27 is a currently well-known problem when using Swift 2 and Xcode 7. It may be that, by the time of publication, this has been corrected by Apple.

Most likely, if you followed the previous few steps and have a very simple app, the steps should work for you. But with more complex projects, such as those that are written for Apple Watch, those steps will not completely fix the problem. The reason is that for Apple Watch you have three targets: the iPhone app, the Watch App, and the Watch extension (Figure 8-28), so make sure any corrections you make in one target are correctly addressed in all targets that are part of the archive.

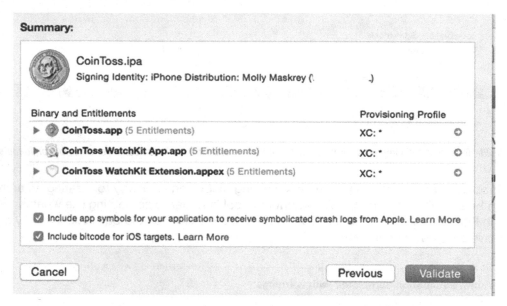

Figure 8-28. *No single fix works for all Xcode projects. With those such as Apple Watch, make sure to perform corrections in all targets that are part of the archive.*

Problem

Your archive choice is grayed out (Figure 8-29).

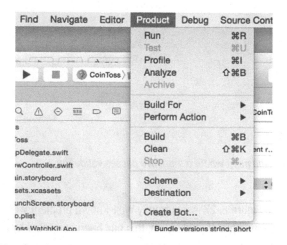

Figure 8-29. *A common problem is to see the "Archive" option grayed out*

Solution

Go to the Xcode selection for the active scheme and check to see for which device or simulator your project is being built. The most common reason is that you've left a simulated device selected (Figure 8-30).

Figure 8-30. If you don't see "Archive" as an available choice, make sure you don't have a simulated device selected

Change it to "Generic iOS Device" as in this example (Figure 8-31), and you should now have "Archive" as a valid option to select.

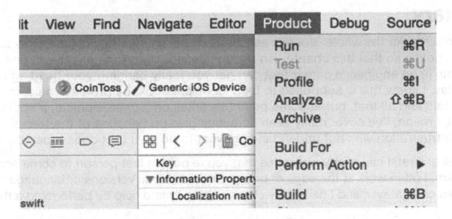

Figure 8-31. Make sure to select "Generic iOS Device" when building your project to an archive

Unfortunately, there's no way I can cover each and every possible problem that you're likely to encounter just with archives—we still have so much more to cover in this book. As you go through a lot of the solutions I offer, the key point you should take away is that the problem is solvable. Most often, if not every single time, you can find what you're looking for "out there" by just conducting a very specific search using whatever warnings or errors or other information Xcode tells you. Try not to get frustrated; I've gotten through them, and you will too. One other thing: There may not always be a fix. I know I said you can find solutions, but the reality is that there can and will be bugs in newer releases of Xcode from time to time, as we saw earlier with the archive warning.

Configurations

One source of confusion for new developers when dealing with schemes is how they differ from configurations. After all, if you look at the previous section, a scheme certainly sounds like something you might call a configuration. In fact, I've had more than one person at various companies use the term *configurations* when they meant *schemes*. So, what's the difference?

It's pretty simple, actually. Whereas a scheme is how Xcode builds your target, a configuration only refers to whether this target is meant for debug or release. You can almost think of configurations as being more closely associated with iTunes Connect, which we'll discuss in Chapter 10 when we talk about publishing your app. Schemes, however, are more of an Xcode thing. That is, we set up (let's not use the word configure, though I have to admit it is tempting) our schemes as needed, just as we've been discussing. We don't see anything to do with schemes outside of the Xcode IDE.

Summary

I wish I could make the whole process as simple as selecting a few checkboxes and pull-down boxes so that this chapter isn't even needed. Unfortunately, this is one of those spots in an engineer's career that can get you really banging your head against your display. I know this is supposed to be a technical book, by professionals, for professionals and all that, but at some point this takes on a philosophical, if not purely emotional. I mean, I've never really seen someone give up because of the technical stuff; it's usually frustration with not understanding what to do next that does a person in.

Some advice: First, I can nearly guarantee that you're not the first person to come across this problem. I often work at the edge of newly released Xcode versions or language or frameworks or whatever, and I never have been unable to find help by performing a thorough search.

In this chapter we covered how to work with targets and schemes and archives. Targets are what your project builds to. You create an app or a test bundle or a Watch extension. You're in control and can add or delete targets as you see fit.

Schemes are the instructions for how Xcode builds your targets. There are several types, such as a simple build, build-and-run, analysis, profile, and archive. You should understand all of these, though analysis and profiling may be something to put off for now if you're feeling overwhelmed.

We talked about a few common issues when working with archives, mostly associated with your project's build settings. A trick I use is to keep the Notes app open on my desktop and keep track of the problems I encounter along the way, along with links to address my most common issues.

In the next chapter, I'm going to take a break and talk a little about embedded systems to give you some inspiration about the really cool things that can be done with iOS projects.

Chapter 9

Embedded Systems

Embedded systems exist at the core of the products we create as iOS software engineers. But ask most app developers about embedded systems and you will likely get either a confused look or something like "Go talk to Jessica. She's the hardware person." While iOS devices have almost exponentially increased in capability each year in terms of speed, screen resolution, memory, and other features, at its core an iPhone is an embedded system. Sure, with its ability to run multiple apps, my iPhone 6S can do a lot of things similar to my iMac, but not nearly as well. As I write this paragraph using my word processing app with four chapters open, I also have my web browser active, a photo editing program, my Photos app, Xcode, and a schematic capture program all available instantly. The power and memory might be present in my phone, but to me it's still a limited-use tool. As such, I'll likely always think of it as an embedded system.

Unfortunately, I can't turn you into an embedded systems developer within the amount of space I have left. Another book idea, perhaps? I can only try to pique your interest and hopefully excite that passion to do great and interesting things with your development career. Embedded systems offer a way for you to do more with your mobile development; you can connect and interact with the real world, not just some semi-artificial intelligent logic battling aliens on your iPad. You can go beyond the simulated to the actual world. You interact with the devices through which you connect with real people.

To take you to that point, I'll offer some basics about embedded systems and some options for you to get started, and will try to connect the dots as to how and why embedded systems mean so much to us as iOS developers.

What Is an Embedded System?

Embedded systems, as opposed to general purpose computers, typically have a narrow scope of functionality. While a laptop or iMac desktop can perform a wide variety of tasks, such as gaming, accounting, art design, medical records management, and just about anything else, an embedded system might do just one thing, such as control your home's temperature or operate your microwave oven.

© Molly K. Maskrey 2016

M.K. Maskrey, *App Development Recipes for iOS and watchOS*, DOI 10.1007/978-1-4842-1820-4_9

One of the first characterizations given when referring to an embedded system is that it's small, or generally of a smaller size, like an Apple Watch, a smart thermostat, or even that old VCR I keep in the closet for some reason I still can't fathom. While this might be true in many cases, take a look at Figure 9-1. On the left is a fairly small printed circuit board (PCB)—smaller than a typical pen. To the right is a huge suite of electronics that stands much larger than the attending engineer. In this case, the left side shows a general purpose computer system while the right depicts a heating, ventilation, and air conditioning (HVAC) embedded system.

Figure 9-1. Size does not determine what kind of system would be classified as embedded

Embedded system devices come in all shapes and sizes. Figure 9-2 shows a sensor I'm currently using in other projects that contains several sensors, including temperature measurement; an accelerometer; as well as a Bluetooth radio. This module could be attached to an electronically controlled window system—a skylight, for example. If the temperature in the room below gets too warm, as detected by the temperature sensor and reported to another controller, a motor could activate, creating the proper size opening to cool the room down appropriately. The accelerometer in the embedded device would then provide data as to whether the skylight was opening or closing or at the proper angle.

Figure 9-2. A small Bluetooth-enabled embedded sensor system

Problem

I want to do more in my software development career than write code, but I have no idea what learning is required in order to use hardware electronics devices such as embedded systems.

Solution

Like anything, embedded systems and electronics engineering in general has its own set of skills and vernacular. If you want to design computer chips that go into the next generation of Apple devices, well, that's way out of scope for this book. But, if you want to work with electronics hardware and connect it with your iPhone or iPad, well, that's doable on a few different levels.

The Details

Designing Hardware

Designing the hardware with all its transistors and milliamps and multilayer boards may seem like the hardest part, but it's really gotten pretty simple over the past few decades. You don't write your app in assembly language, much less enter ones and zeros with switches to create your program, instead using a higher-level language such as C/C++, Objective-C, or, for us, Swift. Additionally, integrated development environments (IDEs) offer many tools for graphics design, source-code management, testing, and creating packages to distribute to users.

Hardware design continues its advance in much the same way. In fact, you could create the system you need to build using a programming language such as C. Many integrated circuit companies offer high-density, reprogrammable electronic devices that can be customized for specific uses. Both graphical and object-oriented languages are available for that customization. However, this design methodology is generally reserved for those specialized devices, and we won't be using it here. In essence, the way we'll consider developing our hardware will be even easier.

The parts that make up electronic devices today can contain a wide range of functionality. In the not too distant past, a DIP (dual inline package) such as that shown in Figure 9-3 might contain a few basic Boolean functions, such as a few NAND or NOR gates (Figure 9-4). Let's be honest though—no one uses that type of package for logic devices. However, it may be used for more specialized functions, typically those related to power management on the circuit. As with our phones and restaurant portions, everything keeps getting smaller. And so it is with electronics and integrated devices.

> **Note**   Because the reader is expected to have a general level of programming knowledge, we will assume a basic understanding of Boolean logic for our discussions.

Figure 9-3. *Integrated circuit devices such as this were commonplace as recently as the mid-1990s and can be found on many aging electronic systems still in use today*

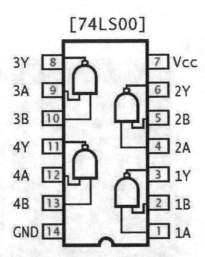

Figure 9-4. Despite the relatively large size of the DIP device, it contains very minimal logic functionality

That's the basic history lesson showing where we started decades ago, upon which are built the technological marvels we take for granted today. Despite the increased complexity today, as well as reduced size and cost, everything still works using a basic reliance on physics and Boolean logic: the electrons still move through traces of copper and at the core, any CPU uses '1' and '0' to perform tasks.

The good news is that vendors of the parts that we typically use want us to succeed. They provide very detailed specifications that can run several hundreds of pages for a single part. Their websites contain application notes on how to use the parts in typical circuits, FAQs covering every aspect of the part, forums to provide user interaction with each other and company representatives, and webinars available any time day or night to view.

While the glut of information can be a problem in and of itself, forcing the designer to look through potentially thousands of pages for information about a single component, most parts in a family tend to work well together. Sticking with a single manufacturer and its recommended product lines provides the novice a good way to get started.

The thing that can best help the beginning designer is to purchase evaluation or prototyping kits, such as that shown in Figure 9-5. I absolutely love this board for development. It comes with pluggable modules for changing to different processors and includes switches, buttons, connectors, a small LED display, a prototyping area, and connectors for extending it even further. Essentially, I've been able to build just about every electronics accessory I've developed over the past five years using this development system. I prototype my idea, work out the bugs, improve things, and write software to work with my design. Only after I'm confident that it's correct, I create my own custom-printed circuit board with just the components needed for my application.

Figure 9-5. A highly robust and flexible embedded prototyping system I use for day-to-day projects

Note   You can find these Microchip development kits at this link: http://www.microchip.com/
Developmenttools/ProductDetails.aspx?PartNO=DM240001

During prototyping, it's basically plug-and-play, with all the effort being exerted in connecting
various off-the-shelf ancillary support modules and programming the firmware on the
board's processor. My first iPhone OS accessory was developed using this prototyping
concept. Through Apple's MFi program, which we'll talk a little about in Chapter 13, I was
even able to connect an iPhone to this system so as to communicate data back and forth.
In fact, Figure 9-6 shows the actual first prototype I created using a similar, but smaller,
development system that connected and functioned with an iPhone 3G running iPhone OS.

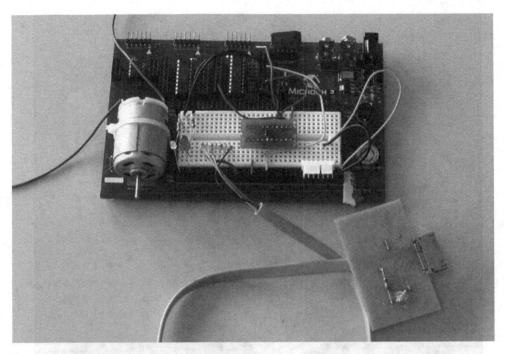

Figure 9-6. The first prototype I created for interfacing with an iPhone 3G in 2009

None of these kits will turn you into an electrical engineer, but they will give you enough knowledge to get you moving in the right direction. The kits range in price from less than a hundred to several hundred dollars.

Using Existing Hardware

Depending on the situation, which includes such factors as time, project complexity, your confidence and skill level, as well as budget, you might also be able to use off-the-shelf parts for your embedded project. A small, single-board computer such as a Raspberry Pi (Figure 9-7) may work well for your needs. These products are a series of credit card–sized single-board computers developed in the United Kingdom by the Raspberry Pi Foundation with the intention of promoting the teaching of basic computer science in schools and developing countries. With support for a wide variety of operating systems and software development tools such as Python, C, C++, Ruby, Pearl, Java, and various IDEs, a Raspberry Pi can be used as a complete personal computer. In fact, it's the fastest-selling personal computer in the United Kingdom.

Figure 9-7. For those embedded systems where cost is a key concern, off-the-shelf modules such as this Raspberry Pi may be all you need

A typical Pi board contains—in addition to the processor—a graphics engine and I/O ports such as HDMI, Ethernet, USB, and power. Many also contain additional connections to add on functionality via daughterboards, such as WiFi, Bluetooth, or pretty much anything else. At this very moment, I have a Raspberry Pi, similar to the one in Figure 9-7, sitting to my right with an attached keyboard, mouse, and 21" display that I use frequently. My system runs RASPBIAN, which is based on the Debian version of Linux. It even contains a version of Mathematica for general use.

So, how would you use this for an embedded systems project? Again, everything depends on multiple factors, such as cost, schedule, complexity, the project requirements, and so on. Let's take a reasonably simple industrial control application. You need to control an environmental regulator such as an air conditioner for a small building. Perhaps this is at a construction site for a temporary office building for site management. Of course, this is a manufactured example, as you'd probably just go to your big box retailer and buy a room air conditioner, but for some reason this is the way we're going to go.

At its simplest, a project such as this could be done using all off-the-shelf components. You set up the Pi, out of the box, as a desktop system. Add a display, keyboard, mouse, and connection to the Internet. Bring up a web browser, go to Amazon, order a USB temperature sensor and USB controllable power strip. When they arrive, plug them in, write a small bit of code, and install it onto the Pi's system build so that it executes on startup and as a continuous loop. Add some code to the mix to notify you via email if something appears wrong, or as the system restarts, or any other notifications you want. Remove the peripheral and place it all into a cabinet somewhere. And with maybe $200 worth of stuff and a couple days of work at best, you've created your own embedded control system.

Now, of course, you wouldn't do this in an actual high-reliability situation with no industrial engineering expertise, but, if you were so inclined, you might do this at home. You might, say, turn on a disco ball when the temperature reaches a certain level. And yes, I still have that obsession with disco balls and it's not going away anytime soon. In fact, later in our projects section, I'm going to walk you through controlling such a device on your own.

The point I am striving to make is that you can address these types of embedded developmental projects on several levels, from do-it-yourself to hiring someone with more expertise and just specifying the requirements, including cost and schedule. If you choose to do it yourself, which I whole-heartedly support, you have a wide range of options as well. You can learn and develop nearly every aspect of the project, elevating your skills and marketability exponentially, or simply buy components off the shelf and lash them together. As with creating a major software application, multiple ways exist to get the job accomplished.

Problem

How do I program these types of embedded systems?

Solution

Just as with iOS, Android, or even Microsoft mobile devices, each vendor as well as third parties provide integrated development environments, software libraries, documentation, starter projects, and technical support to help you every step of the way.

The Details

Diving into hardware, especially if you've focused on software development for most of your career and educational life, can seem daunting and something to avoid. As a woman, it can seem even more like an exclusive boys' club, especially from the outside. After all, guys build stuff and girls use them. Well, that's stupid and really ticks me off. Did you know that Mary Anderson is credited with inventing the windshield wiper years before Ford started automobile production? Over a hundred years ago. Long before the equal rights movement.

> **Note**   There's an awesome site everyone, especially aspiring female engineers, should check out. It's `engineergirl.org` and offers lots of information, interviews, connections, and career ideas.

My point is not political or social, but rather to help you to realize that no matter who you are, you can do this. Yes, it seems hard, and in many cases, for many projects, it can be. But it's doable. And you can do it. So, how? How do you develop hardware?

Essentially, by using the project development kits you get a head start on all the mundane, difficult, and costly development details associated with creating a new and interesting suite of electronics. All the basics are provided, and you just need to tweak it or add a few bits and pieces to make it your own. We've seen this in the previous section.

Most of the work you'll do to develop hardware using this method will be by programming. Think about that for a moment. You use your software skills probably two-thirds or more of the time when developing hardware. Early on in your project, it's probably more like 95 to 100 percent of the time. Again, you're starting with something that already works, has been tested and proven, and has tons of technical support, from companies that want you to succeed. Because if you develop a successful product using their parts and tools, it's great PR for them as well. It's a win–win.

Figure 9-8 depicts the development environment for the prototyping systems I showed in the previous section. While not the same as Xcode, Eclipse, or Android Studio, it should be readily obvious, for the most part, what's what in the layout. To the upper left is a project and file hierarchy. Below that are some specialty windows for specific add-on tools that can be used to configure header and system setup files. To the right is the editing window, and below shows the status of the various operations. Sure, some buttons will be different, the colors won't be the same as you're used to, etc., but as a software engineer you can grasp it and start working in under an hour. Most if not all kit companies offer tutorials to go with the sample project and development kits. Remember—they want you to succeed.

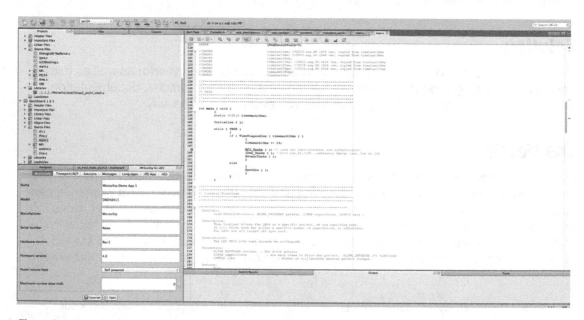

Figure 9-8. *A typical development environment for embedded systems programming operates much like Xcode or any other software tool suite*

So, that's the tool suites, hardware, and software, but how does the actual coding proceed? From an architectural level, it's very similar to programming in iOS, with one exception. For the most part when developing smaller embedded systems, you will not have an operating system to which you make service calls. That is, there's no write-to-disk or load-url OS calls you can use. But all those services are available as long as the hardware and library support is present with the tools. Now, that seems like I'm saying two different things—the services aren't there but they are there. Confusing, right?

Think about Mac OS X for a moment and suppose you're writing an online game that accesses the web for a leaderboard. Your Mac app has to access the Internet, reading and writing, to post and retrieve scores. To do that, you include a reference to a library somewhere in your project code that can execute those operations. But the library doesn't necessarily contain the actual read and write code. That code already exists as part of the operating system, OS X, showing you your desktop, running Safari, and so on. Your game includes references to the hooks in the operating system to access those functions, but they exist in the OS and there is a call to them—a call to the operating system services. It wouldn't make sense to have every program that used the Internet include all the common functionality involved. Add in things like user interface, disk access, and graphics and there wouldn't be enough memory to run more than one or two programs. There would be too much duplication of unnecessary stuff.

With an embedded system, there will usually be just one program running at a time. Remember, an embedded device focuses on doing a single or very small number of tasks and doing them well; that is to say, doing them efficiently. One of the most critical aspects of such a system is its response or latency to stimuli. In a commercial airliner, you wouldn't really want the avionics system to support a lot of unnecessary and mostly unused features. It wouldn't make sense, nor would it be safe. In a more generalized embedded system it's more an issue of cost. These devices are usually commercial, and the manufacturer is trying to make a profit. So the costs need to be as low as possible. A big cost is parts. More memory and more processing speed means more parts and higher costs and thus less profit. So, on something like a microwave oven or smart thermostat, there will be no operating system and no suite of library calls that can be used by apps running on the device.

On these types of products there is one program. For the microwave oven, it's a microwave control program. For a smart thermostat, it's a temperature management program, and so on. Instead of dependence on an underlying OS, the necessary routines are built into the app itself. If the device and the app that runs the device need Internet access, that Internet access library is included when the program is built.

And, getting back to our process of developing embedded systems using an IDE, those necessary libraries, not just the function reference but the actual code itself, gets "baked" into our end product, the code that runs our embedded hardware. Most development system manufacturers, including the ones I use and showed you earlier, include that functionality for use in your and my projects. You don't have to write them from scratch. Again, you get to focus on your new and exciting project using the products of hundreds of others before you. Your ideas build on their work to create newer and better things.

Problem

You like the idea of getting started in developing systems, but the previous section made it seem a little too involved as well as potentially expensive. Is there another easier and cheaper route?

Solution

A very common solution used by many software engineers to gain electronics hardware knowledge and skills is Arduino.

The Details

Everything we discussed in the previous section regarding development kits and systems still applies, but we need to try and make it simpler and even lower in cost. Arduino serves this need and is most non-electrical engineers' start into the dark and mysterious world of hardware. Arduino removes the shroud of mystery and makes it pretty easy.

Arduino is really more than just one thing. It's an open-source community that creates and maintains hardware and software that can be easily used. There is no one Arduino; rather, there are several that use different processors and that are of differing sizes and shapes. Figure 9-9 shows two versions, of which I use both for prototyping projects.

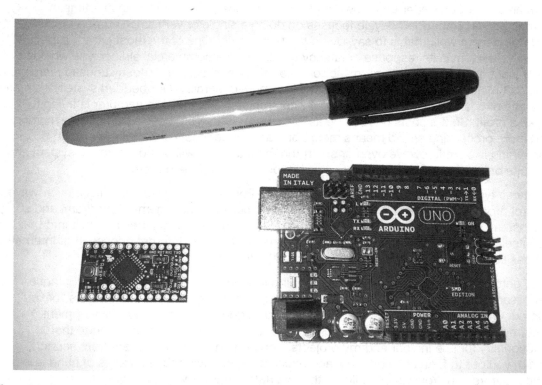

Figure 9-9. Arduino prototyping boards come in various sizes and shapes and with different types of peripherals. One of the most widely used at the time of writing was the UNO, shown on the right

All Arduino boards provide a simple, easy-to-use interface to your computer and work on all operating systems. Because Arduino is open source, you can generally find whatever you need by doing a quick search as well as by checking out the Arduino user groups. Programming is done by writing sketches, which are just C language–style programs, in the cross-platform Arduino IDE as shown in Figure 9-10.

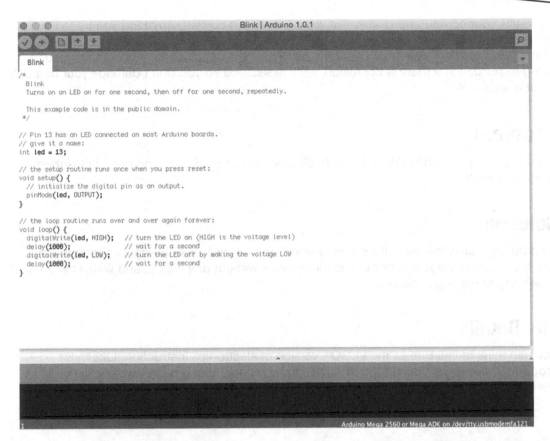

```
/*
 Blink
 Turns on an LED on for one second, then off for one second, repeatedly.

 This example code is in the public domain.
 */

// Pin 13 has an LED connected on most Arduino boards.
// give it a name:
int led = 13;

// the setup routine runs once when you press reset:
void setup() {
  // initialize the digital pin as an output.
  pinMode(led, OUTPUT);
}

// the loop routine runs over and over again forever:
void loop() {
  digitalWrite(led, HIGH);   // turn the LED on (HIGH is the voltage level)
  delay(1000);               // wait for a second
  digitalWrite(led, LOW);    // turn the LED off by making the voltage LOW
  delay(1000);               // wait for a second
}
```

Figure 9-10. You program an Arduino by writing a sketch, or C-like program, that gets downloaded to the board

Although there are many different versions and designs of these boards, you might not find exactly the feature you need. Additional hardware functionality can be added to a base Arduino board through the use of shields, or small attachable daughterboards, that connect to header pins on the main PCB. Many shields offer additional connectors so that you can stack multiple shields to increase the amount of functionality in your project.

Arduino boards can be purchased at many different online shops, such as Amazon or Sparkfun, and computer shops like Micro Center often carry several versions as well. The software and IDE are free to download and use. The main board is generally powered by a USB connection between it and the computer, which also serves as a general-purpose logging interface as well as a means to download sketches to the board itself. The board doesn't actually use USB; instead, a USB-to-serial adapter chip is part of the Arduino design. As a user, you never usually have to worry about this, as it is mostly irrelevant to how you operate the board. Costs for a typical board range from $15 to under $100 depending on the version, processor, and amount of features included.

A common Arduino contains buttons, switches, LEDs, and general-purpose input-output (GPIO) lines that allow you to capture digital input and write digital output. Because the power that operates the Arduino is limited by the amount provided from your computer over the USB cable, you do need to consider how much output drive you are trying to use.

Basically, your computer provides five volts at so much current. Anything you try to control using those GPIO lines must operate under that level minus the amount used by the board itself to power its own circuitry. Just be sure to read the specifications of anything you're trying to build, and if there is confusion, seek assistance so you don't damage your board or other equipment.

Problem

The Arduino approach heads in the right direction in terms of ease and cost, but is there anything simpler?

Solution

A company called littleBits offers a wide selection of easy-to-use pluggable components that can create a huge number of sample projects without any wiring, and with a minimal possibility of making mistakes.

The Details

You can think of littleBits as the LEGO® version of electronics instruction. Like most products these days, you can go to Amazon and order any of a wide variety of littleBits starter kits, like the one I display in Figure 9-11.

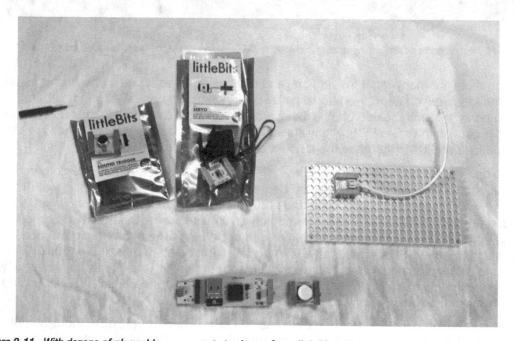

Figure 9-11. With dozens of pluggable components to choose from, littleBits offers an easy way to get started understanding the basics of modularized system design

Using a littleBits development kit, you can create anything from a simple push-button activated LED to a full-on network-enabled IoT (Internet of Things) monitoring device. The modules are color coded and contain magnets so that they snap together only in the way they are meant to be connected. The sides where they attach together are manually keyed so you can't plug them in backward or upside down.

The company offers a cloud-based system as well, allowing access and monitoring of your creation through the browser on your smartphone. There's even an area for sample projects you can try yourself to get started, ranging from automated pet food dispensers to Halloween candy dispensers. I'd definitely recommend starting here if you have no electronics background or are looking to get up and going really quickly. I think this is one of the easiest learning tools available today.

Problem

Why is an understanding of embedded systems important at all if I'm only concerned about programming iOS devices?

Solution

iOS devices, tablets, smartphones, watches, and so on are all, at their core, embedded systems. An iPhone 6S may have more processing speed and memory than ever before, but it's still not a Mac running OS X. While this may eventually change, more than likely something else will become the new "thing" and have limited memory and processing speed. That product is now Apple Watch. In ten years the watch may be just as fast as the iPad mini 2 of today, but likely there will be something else to take its place. As developers and engineers within this space, knowing more than our counterparts, we put ourselves as the ones to go to for these types of projects. Our knowledge and skills of not just development but also the underlying technology can put us ahead of the other person vying for that dream job downtown.

The Details . . . (sort of)

To get into embedded software architecture and its relationship to mobile operation systems and iOS specifically in any depth would take a complete book in itself, so I'm going to be necessarily brief and try to relate it to a basic iOS construct, the run loop.

Embedded Software Architecture

As I discussed earlier, embedded systems are programmed much like any other software project. You work within an IDE; write code in, usually, a high-level language; link in support through libraries and frameworks; and, somehow, download the code to the specific piece of hardware.

What does an embedded systems program contain—that is, what would it look like? At its most fundamental, an embedded program contains (1) setup code, (2) support libraries, (3) interrupt handlers, and (4) a processing loop. I'll discuss interrupts and handlers in a moment, as they are a major part of all this, but let me show you a typical heart of an embedded system program, the main processing loop.

While ridiculously simple, this is actual code, graphically depicted in Figure 9-12, from a simple embedded project:

```
while(true)  {

        statusData = checkStatus();            // Check if any interrupts happened
        processInterrupts(statusData);         // Run any code to handle whatever happened
        performPeriodicMaintenance();          // timers, LEDs, polling, etc.

}
```

> **Note**   I'm going to assume the reader has a basic understanding of C-style high-level languages.

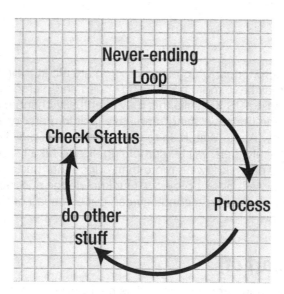

Figure 9-12. *The essence of an embedded system program is nothing more than a continually running loop*

All the code does is execute in a continual loop, never ending and only starting once. This is the main() of a C-language embedded program. So, how does it do anything? The first thing we need to understand is interrupts.

An interrupt, in this context, is an internal or external stimulus. It could be a button being pressed, a smoke detector being activated, a timer expiring, or a credit card being swiped across a magnetic reader. It could be an incoming message from the Internet or a battery-backup system ready to shut down because the wall power has been out for too long. So, in essence, it's no different than that annoying person who comes over and asks me if I saw Kelly's new boyfriend flirting with someone while I'm having a discussion about the election with three friends at a party. You get the idea. It can be good or bad or indifferent, but it is a change in the norm. If nothing happened, then that forever-loop would just run and run and run.

When an interrupt does happen, let's take the button press for example, we need to change things up a bit. The code needs to handle that press and determine if there is an appropriate action and, if necessary, execute some additional code to deal with it.

You may have heard about interrupt service routines (ISRs). These are very, very small routines, functions, or methods that execute upon detection of an interrupt. In a personal computer or Apple device, when something like this happens the OS directs that one of these routines will fire, or execute. But as you should recall, in an embedded system we don't generally have an operating system to count on, though an ISR will still execute. How does the system know?

The processing elements of an embedded system, like the microprocessor in an iPhone, contain a lot of additional functionality. Rather than calling them processors, they are more widely known as microcontrollers because they do more than process logic. They contain timers, analog-to-digital (A/D) converters, digital-to-analog (D/A) convertors, general-purpose I/O (GPIO) lines, and so on. A switch might be connected to a digital I/O line of the microcontroller, as shown in Figure 9-13. The microcontroller manages the processing of the system and has been greatly simplified in this illustration. When the button is open (not pressed) the power is presented to the GPIO #1 input so the code sees a high voltage level. When the button is pressed, the voltage goes to zero because it is shorted to ground, so the code sees a different level. When that change happens, going from positive voltage to zero, the microcontroller detects this and through a series of address registers performed during the setup phase calls that function. The function services the interrupt, thus the name "interrupt service routine." Of course, there is much more circuitry involved, such as resistors to dissipate the current when the switch is pressed as well as other pieces to handle "bounce" between the contacts of the switch, but this gives you the basic idea.

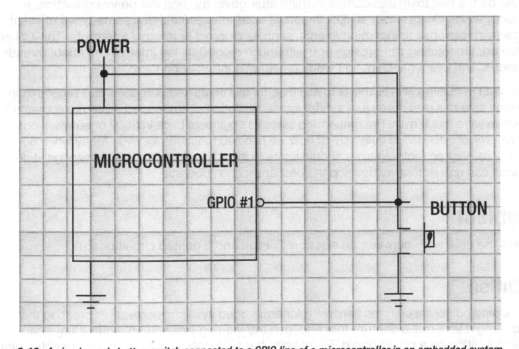

Figure 9-13. A simple push-button switch connected to a GPIO line of a microcontroller in an embedded system

The switch is pressed, the input changes, the microcontroller causes your ISR to execute, and when the ISR finishes the loop continues as before. Here is where many newly initiated engineers make their biggest mistake. The inclination is to handle the button press in the ISR. For example, if the button press is meant to turn a motor ten degrees clockwise, then that code is what happens in the ISR.)This is completely wrong. The ISR should only be used to change a state variable within the structure of your program to indicate the change—that the button was pressed. The actual function to perform the rotation should be handled elsewhere.

There are many reasons for this, but the most important centers on the idea of latency. Many people confuse latency and processing speed, thinking that if you just clock the microcontroller faster, at a higher speed, you're okay. Latency is the time interval between a stimulus (pushing the button) and a response (whatever action needs to happen). By making the ISR very simple, like merely changing a status bit, it helps to maintain the lowest latency, which should be the goal in every embedded system. This way, all the other interrupts that might happen at the same time can also be handled quickly, with the lowest possible latency.

In the processing function, the status can be assessed and a proper order determined for handling the actions that need to be taken. If, for example, a button is pressed twice or more, like when you impatiently call repeatedly for the elevator, only a single response happens. Only that action necessitated by the logical determination of the combined interrupt effects, as determined by evaluating the status, is performed. This is the essence of an embedded system and the process control loops found within the embedded system and its processing architecture.

iOS Architecture

If you've done much iOS reading or looked into game programing in Xcode, then run loops should be the first thing that comes to mind after going through the previous section. A run loop, which exists within an iOS thread, is used to execute these same types of event handlers in response to incoming events, such as external or internal interrupts. The iOS and Xcode documentation can provide you with much more detailed information about threads, run loops, and event handlers so I won't repeat that information here.

The point I'm making with all this is to see that, for all intents and purposes, iOS programming for some time has really been just a different manifestation of embedded systems programming. While we were much more like embedded systems engineers back in 2009 or so when our iPhone projects needed to take care of how we handled functionality, even today when dealing with low-latency projects—games should come to mind here—having this knowledge at our disposal can ensure that we develop the best application possible.

Problem

What's the difference between an electronic circuit and a printed circuit board?

Solution

Developing custom electronic hardware for embedded systems consists of creating the logic using a schematic capture tool and then transferring that schematic to a physical implementation on a circuit board. Essentially, the schematic circuit, or logic, is printed onto the board. Thus, you create a printed circuit board from a schematic.

The Details

Here, we're going to briefly cover the basics of electrical engineering circuit design. It's not something you must know to work with embedded systems per se, but, you may need to work with the designer at some point so it's best to have some common ground.

Circuit Design

I'm sure you'll agree that one section of one chapter is not enough space to teach you electronic circuit design. There are many good introductory texts on the subject, as well as tutorials available free on the Internet.

The main thing here is to not get bogged down in the details. Introductory courses will almost always start with Ohm's law and how it works. The gist of it is a way to define the primary three DC (direct current) parameters in circuits: voltage, current, and resistance. I discussed these earlier, and, for the most part, that little bit is all you need to know.

Think of designing a circuit, like so many other things in life, as using a set of smaller elementary items to make something more complex; the building block approach. In the "old days" we designed using very basic parts such as resistors, capacitors, and transistors, such as in the simple lamp circuit shown in Figure 9-14. We still design using these elements, but through the growth of technology, we've also been given a set of very complex blocks with which to build even more complex things. Consider that, way back when, someone took a bunch of parts and made a car. Now, we as society require cars, buildings, roads, and people to build communities or cities.

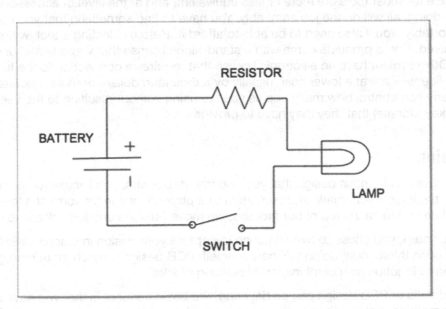

Figure 9-14. Basic elements of a schematic

It should be clear that our embedded system circuits will be much more complicated than the lamp circuit in Figure 9-14. After all, they do so much more than turn a light on or off. On the other hand, if we view them as complex blocks arranged correctly, which is what our product vendors provide us within their development kits, then our job becomes much less daunting. Like when we use the littleBits, our engineering design is more about properly connecting modules together than it is drawing out a complicated schematic from scratch.

The other piece of the circuit design will be creating an electronic representation of your system in some sort of tool. The de facto standard EDA (electronic design automation) tool for some time has been the Cadence/OrCAD suite. Not a single product, but rather a set of individual tools loosely coupled together, the Cadence suite is one of the most widely used products for circuit and PCB design. Another product that increasingly finds its way into engineering houses is the Altium Designer, which like Cadence is set of integrated tools for schematic layout, board layout, and testing.

If you want to try to do it yourself, start with one of the low-cost, quick-turn (quick turnaround time) houses such as ExpressPCB. I found ExpressPCB after researching various electronics and robotics hobbyist sites. Companies like ExpressPCB usually offer a free tool that you can download and use to create your schematic design. The process of going from an idea or hand-drawn circuit is known as *schematic capture*. You're "capturing" your design from paper (or thought) into an electronic format.

After looking at what was offered and what capabilities I needed, I wound up selecting Altium Designer. The tool suite did everything I, as a mid-level designer, needed to do at a reasonable cost. You must do the research yourself, based on your needs and ability and especially budget. The deciding factor in my own case was the extensive set of help available in the form of both PDF and video tutorials.

But let's face it—most tools are more or less equivalent, and at the level of accessory design that we're doing, all will do the job admirably. You have to find something that you can work with comfortably. You'll also need to be able to afford it. Before selecting a tool, weigh the costs involved. Some products come with a stand-alone license that you buy and use on your PC. Others might have an electronic license that requires a connection to the Internet. Electronic licenses are at a lower cost, usually by a thousand dollars or more, because the company can control how many copies you are using without resulting to the use of a hardware key (dongle) that they may have to provide.

PCB Design

Once you have a schematic design that you're comfortable with, you'll make it real by converting the logical schematic representation to a physical one in the form of a logic board. Notice that in each step of our process, we move our idea one step closer to reality.

If, in the last step, you chose to hire someone to capture your design into schematic form, then don't even think about doing this part yourself. PCB design is much more than getting your design to function as a combination of building blocks.

While the details of PCB design can be daunting, the basic concept is that you have a flat piece of something that is painted with copper; it's printed with all the connections of our circuit onto it, and then you remove everything else that you don't need.

More specifically, a sheet of insulator material is coated with copper on the outside of both surfaces. If you remove the unused copper on both sides so that only your circuit remains, then you have a two-layer circuit board. For complex designs, many more layers may be required. The sheets (called laminates) are stacked together with another material separating them. You can therefore have two-, four-, six-, etc., layer PC boards.

Because the unused material is removed before the laminate boards are layered together, as the number of layers grows the precision needed increases. Because the circuits that run on the inner layers have to connect to a part or another layer (otherwise an inner circuit would do nothing because it could never connect to a part) inter-layer connections are needed. Called *vias*, these layer-to-layer connections must line up, otherwise the board won't work.

The good news is that most EDA tools provide mechanisms not only to convert the logical schematic into a mechanical representation, but also help with routing. In essence, you configure the shape and number of layers you want to use, then convert your design to a PCB representation. The tool can either place the parts for you based on some set of rules or you can do it manually; it can also either route the connections for you or let you do it. As always, the higher-end tools provide more functionality at a higher price.

What you wind up with at the end of this process is a board, after the parts are soldered onto it, that looks like that in Figure 9-15, only it is generally much larger for an embedded system project If you rely solely on the autorouter to all the placement for you. In general, an experienced designer can find many ways to make the layout smaller. Designing the logic via a schematic and laying it out onto a representation of a physical board are the two primary steps in this process, but not the only ones. You still need to have the actual boards manufactured from your design, get the parts added, test the resulting product, then install your software. But in this section I wanted to at least get you familiar with the basic processes that most likely would be your burden to bear if you want to design and develop your own hardware system.

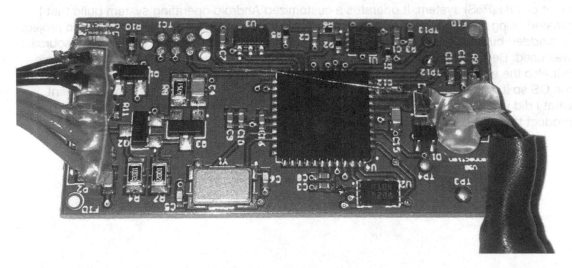

Figure 9-15. A typical printed circuit board with embedded system functionality produced using the steps described above

Summary

Embedded systems form the basis of the iOS devices we program even to this day. By understanding how these systems function, we see that they bear a striking resemblance to the complex and fancy devices we buy online or at our local Apple Store. Though mobile devices get faster and more powerful every few months, it seems, so do those state-of-the-art applications. Give a game developer a more powerful platform and she'll push the immersion experience even further and right to the edge of device capability. As such, because she understands the real-time, low-latency logic underpinnings, her games become state of the art and rise to the top of the charts. Her understanding of the true core architectural nature of the device allows the app to operate right at the limit.

What's more, the architectural direction goes both ways. We've talked about how, as simple embedded devices started, processors developed into microcontrollers to extend the space horizontally, and more smart things started showing up. Our thermostats with springs and mercury switches became small timers to change the temperature over the course of a day. Later those evolved to sensor-based systems throughout our homes to create the best economical balance for our environment. Now smart, completely connected, systems are available at our local Home Depot or Lowes and are just as easy to install and control with our iPhone.

But there's something interesting happening as well. Some smartphones are actually becoming less and less intelligent and are taking on roles previously occupied by embedded systems. Figure 9-16 is a single-board computer system built on a Texas Instruments OMAP (Open Multimedia Applications Platform) processor, the same device that powers many Android tablets and phones. This system was built to function as a smart, Android-based point of sale (PoS) system. It operates a customized Android operating system build that I created using a Linux platform. I removed all those things not needed for this specific project and added built-in security mechanisms to guarantee that only a single trusted data source was used. Because Android is open source, I was able to customize not only the hardware but also the actual operating system. In fact, I actually built the PoS functionality directly into the OS so it could ship as a single, integrated product. If you think about it for a moment, what I did was take a smartphone/tablet device and convert it from a more general-purpose product to a single-use, focused system.

Figure 9-16. *This project began with a basic Android system target that was converted to a single-use, point of sale embedded application, i.e. a cash register*

In fact, this is very common in a lot of devices, such as cable set-top boxes. Built around an OMAP or similar processing core, they run a customized, focused version of the Android OS to provide plenty of system support for downloading and watching cable TV and movies.

Considering that Apple has now opened up Apple TV via tvOS to developers, though it is not open source, Apple seems to see the value in allowing us to access and create new and exciting applications with their version of a set-top box.

In a later chapter we'll expand a little more on this type of engineering as we look into iOS accessories.

Chapter 10

Publishing Our Work

In this chapter we'll work through putting your app into the Apple App Store. We'll use a lot of what we learned in Chapter 8 to create our archives, which will become our product in the App Store. Depending on what you choose as a career path in iOS engineering, it might be a while before this becomes something you do professionally. In most medium or larger software agencies, a separate department often handles distribution to the commercial App Store, to the Business-to-Business (B2B) side, or to the Enterprise, bypassing the App Store altogether.

That said, it cannot hurt to be cognizant of the steps involved in getting your app to market. You may, for example, wish to publish your own game or utility at some time in the future. Also, since working for a large company isn't for everyone, you might decide to go into business for yourself, in which case this is something you'll definitely need to know.

Problem

How do you go from an Xcode project that works to getting your app into the Apple App Store?

Solution

In this chapter we will take one of our sample projects and create an app for the App Store. To keep things simple, we'll use the app from Chapter 14 (Figure 10-1), our simple slot machine game. The details of this project are covered in Chapter 14, so we won't be working through any of the code here. For now, let's assume we got everything to build correctly and go from there.

© Molly K. Maskrey 2016

M.K. Maskrey, *App Development Recipes for iOS and watchOS*, DOI 10.1007/978-1-4842-1820-4_10

Figure 10-1. *We'll use our simple slot machine game to describe publishing an app to the App Store*

Creating the Archive

The first thing we need to do is to create the archive, which contains the app bundle and debug information that we will validate and upload to the App Store. First, in the Xcode project, make sure to select "Generic iOS Device" as the build device (Figure 10-2). This allows you to create the archive and not to run it on the simulator or download it to an actual device.

Figure 10-2. Select "Generic iOS Device" as the Build Only Device in order to create our archive

Next, we create the archive of the project as we did in Chapter 8 (Figure 10-3).

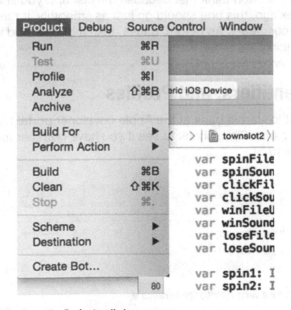

Figure 10-3. Create the archive from the Project pull-down menu

But, skipping ahead to the point where we validate our project and following the steps as we did in Chapter 8, we fail with the error shown in Figure 10-4.

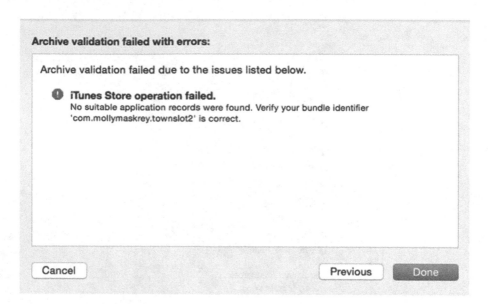

Archive validation failed with errors:

Archive validation failed due to the issues listed below.

⚠ **iTunes Store operation failed.**
No suitable application records were found. Verify your bundle identifier 'com.mollymaskrey.townslot2' is correct.

| Cancel | Previous   Done |

Figure 10-4. Validating our archive fails

We rushed through a lot of steps to try to validate our product for the App Store, and this is not uncommon. You will often think that because the last app you submitted worked and posted correctly a week ago, this one should go just as smoothly. It rarely does, at least in the early stages of your career. As before, pause, take a breath, and work the problem through from the beginning.

Certificates, Identifiers, and Profiles

The first place we want to start is back at the Apple developer portal for the account we are using to distribute this game. First, check to see if you have both certificates—developer and distribution (Figure 10-5).

Certificates	2 Certificates Total		
All	**Name**	**Type**	**Expires**
Pending	Molly Maskrey	iOS Development	Jul 22, 2016
Development	Molly Maskrey	iOS Distribution	Jul 22, 2016
Production			

Figure 10-5. Verify that you have a valid distribution certificate

Since the certificates seem to be okay, let's move on and check the identifiers, specifically whether we have an app identifier for our game. Figure 10-6 shows that we do not, so let's create one.

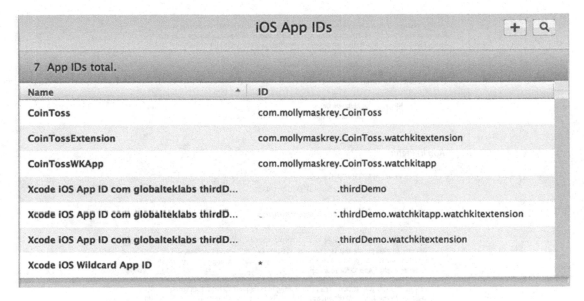

Figure 10-6. Examining our list of app IDs reveals we have no ID for our slot machine game

Click the '+' add button on the top right of the window and fill out the information as shown in Figure 10-7.

Figure 10-7. *Complete the app ID description and, for this example, choose a specific bundle ID for the app*

Leave the rest of the settings as they are (Figure 10-8) and click Continue.

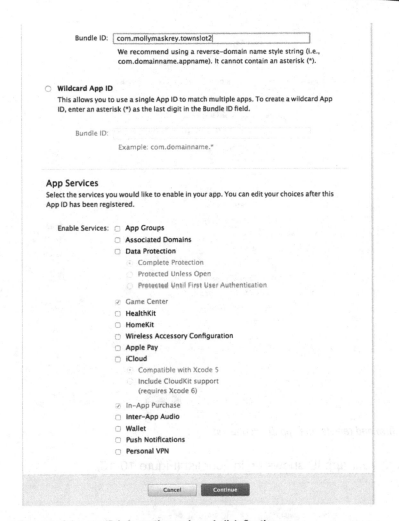

Figure 10-8. Leave the rest of the app ID information as is and click Continue

Confirm the information is correct and register the app ID (Figure 10-9).

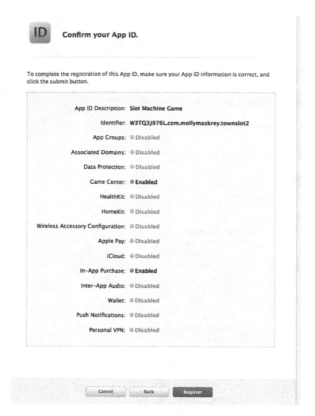

Figure 10-9. Confirm and register the app ID information

Then, verify that your app ID shows up in your list (Figure 10-10).

	iOS App IDs	
8 App IDs total.		
Name	**ID**	
CoinToss	com.mollymaskrey.CoinToss	
CoinTossExtension	com.mollymaskrey.CoinToss.watchkitextension	
CoinTossWKApp	com.mollymaskrey.CoinToss.watchkitapp	
Slot Machine Game	com.mollymaskrey.townslot2	
Xcode iOS App ID com globalteklabs thirdD...	com.globalteklabs.thirdDemo	
Xcode iOS App ID com globalteklabs thirdD...	com.globalteklabs.thirdDemo.watchkitapp.watchkitextension	
Xcode iOS App ID com globalteklabs thirdD...	com.globalteklabs.thirdDemo.watchkitextension	
Xcode iOS Wildcard App ID	*	

Figure 10-10. Verify that your app ID is now available

Let's delete the old archive, retry building, and see what happens. From the menu bar, select Window ➤ Organizer, then the townslot2 app on the left as shown in Figure 10-11.

Figure 10-11. Delete the old archive to keep things neat and try it all again

Also note that we made sure that our build info includes the correct app ID (Figure 10-12).

88	< >	🗎 townslot2							
□		General	Capabilities	Resource Tags	Info	Build Settings	Build Phases	Build Rules	

PROJECT
  🗎 townslot2

▼ **Identity**

TARGETS
  townslot2

Bundle Identifier com.mollymaskrey.townslot2

Version 1.0

Build 1

Team Molly Maskrey (mollymaskrey... ⬍

Figure 10-12. Verify we've set the correct app ID in the build info

Trying to validate our new and improved archive, we get the same error (Figure 10-13).

Archive validation failed with errors:

Archive validation failed due to the issues listed below.

🚫 **iTunes Store operation failed.**
    No suitable application records were found. Verify your bundle identifier
    'com.mollymaskrey.townslot2' is correct.

Cancel   Previous   Done

Figure 10-13. Fixing the app ID alone does not fix the archive problem

Now, let's move on to the last item in our portal, the provisioning profile for distribution. Note that in Figure 10-14 we don't have one set for our app. And really, this should have been obvious when we created our app ID. Since a provisioning profile requires an app ID, it should have been apparent that we needed to create a distribution provisioning profile as well. Let's do it now.

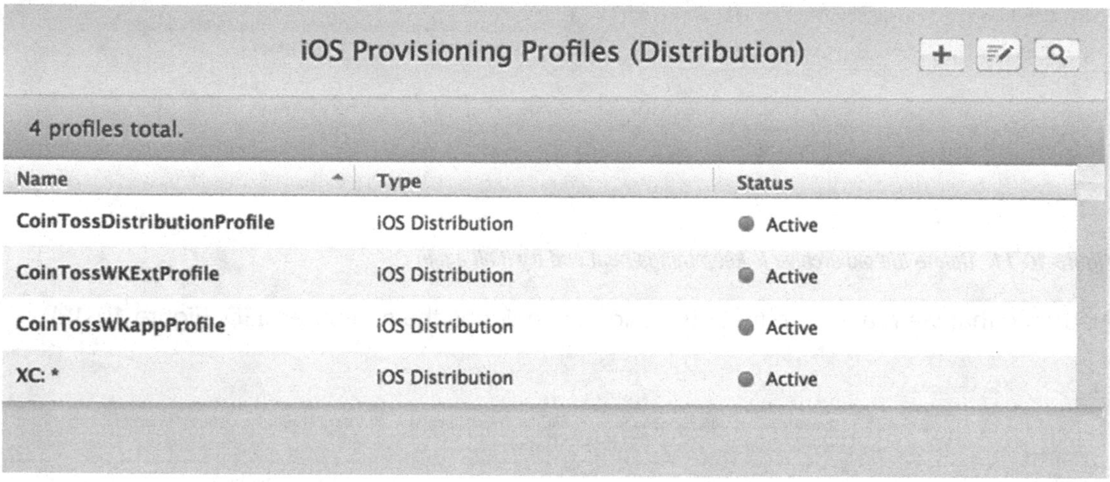

Name	Type	Status
CoinTossDistributionProfile	iOS Distribution	● Active
CoinTossWKExtProfile	iOS Distribution	● Active
CoinTossWKappProfile	iOS Distribution	● Active
XC: *	iOS Distribution	● Active

iOS Provisioning Profiles (Distribution)

4 profiles total.

Figure 10-14. We have no distribution provisioning profile associated with our app

At the top of the window, as we did with the app ID, click the '+' add button and fill out the type of profile, selecting "App Store" under the Distribution heading, then click Continue (Figure 10-15). We'll talk a little about ad hoc distribution options in Chapter 12, where we will cover testing.

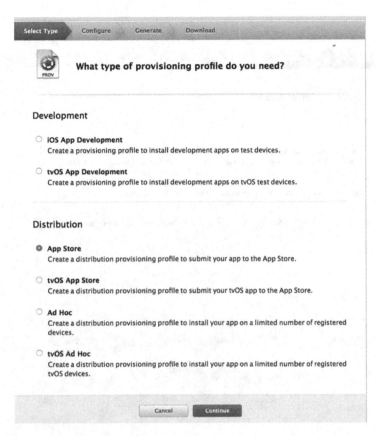

Figure 10-15. Select "App Store" for our distribution option

Select the app ID that we just created from the drop-down menu, then click Continue (Figure 10-16).

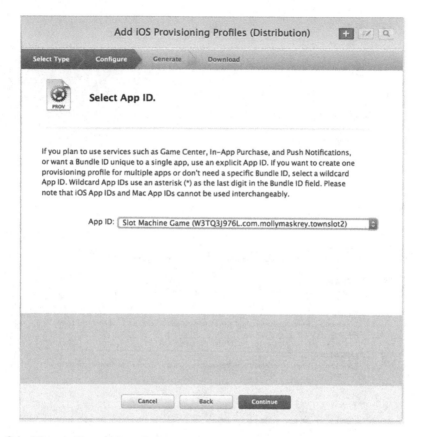

Figure 10-16. *Select the app ID we just created*

Next, make sure to select your account distribution certificate (Figure 10-17). For a simple, single-user account, you'll probably just have one.

Figure 10-17. Select your iOS distribution certificate

Give your profile a name that you recognize for use when building your project (Figure 10-18).

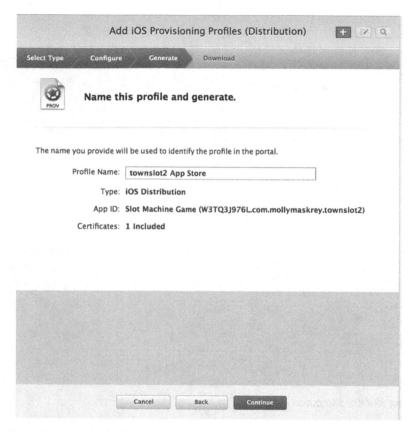

Figure 10-18. Give your profile a good bundle name that you'll recognize

Finally, generate the profile and download it to your computer (Figure 10-19). Once it has been downloaded, just drag it from the Downloads folder and drop it on the Xcode icon so that Xcode can then recognize it.

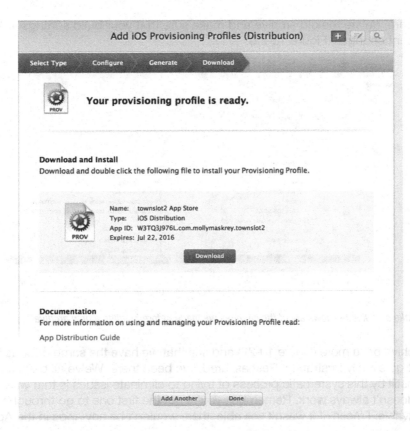

Figure 10-19. After generating your provisioning profile, download it and drag it on top of your Xcode launch icon so the IDE will recognize it

You may want to verify that your profile exists within your Apple developer portal account as a final check (Figure 10-20).

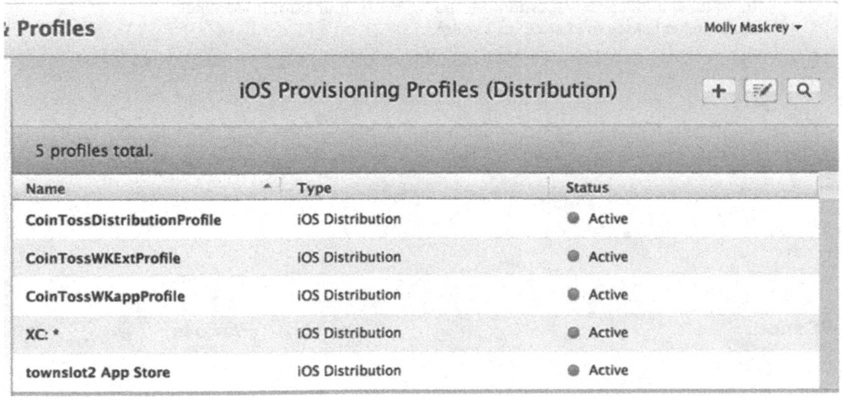

Figure 10-20. Your profile is available for use

As we did before, delete the old archive and make sure that your build settings in Xcode reflect the recent changes (Figure 10-21).

Figure 10-21. Make sure Xcode knows about the changes we made before building a new archive

Create the archive once more (Figure 10-22) and see that we have the same error as before. This is when it gets really frustrating. Rest assured, I've been there. We've all been there. What I'm trying to instill by this systematic process of trying to eliminate issues is that what we think should work doesn't always work. Remember, you're not the first one to go through this, so the problem is solvable. I mean, if it wasn't solvable, there wouldn't be any apps in the App Store.

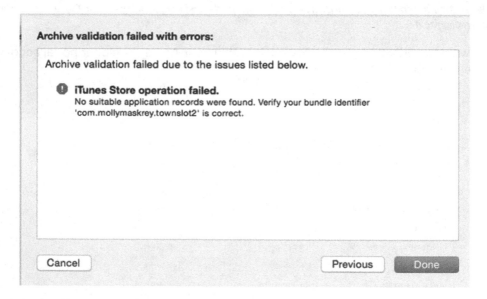

Figure 10-22. Sometimes problems continue long after we expect them to be resolved

Let's think about this. We've gone through all the steps with our developer portal and created the correct certificates, IDs, and profiles. We've modified and set up Xcode to use everything we just did, but we still get the same error. So what is wrong? First, remember Figure 10-15? We selected "App Store." That means that we created a distribution profile indicating that our archive is built for the Apple App Store.

Next, look again at Figure 10-22. It says "No suitable application records were found." Since the validation process couldn't find something, that must mean it was looking for something. And just where was it looking?

iTunes Connect

iTunes Connect provides the portal for you the developer to sell and distribute your iOS and Mac applications. It allows you to organize your portfolio of store content, legal and tax documents, and contact information in addition to collecting information, feedback, and earnings information provided by Apple, helping you to manage your app's sales progress. The process starts by signing up at the iTunes Connect member portal (Figure 10-23; `https://itunesconnect.apple.com/WebObjects/iTunesConnect.woa/wa/apply`).

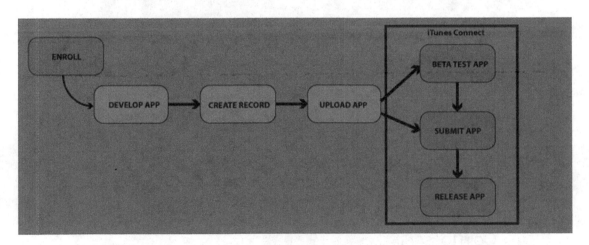

Figure 10-23. The app development and distribution process using iTunes Connect

iTunes Connect Records

Within Xcode, you develop your app, create all the records you need in conjunction with the developer portal, and upload your app using the archive organizer, as we've seen previously. But you need to have a record of the app that you intend to upload "on file" in iTunes Connect. Let's make that happen.

By a "record" we mean an entry into the system that describes the app that you wish to distribute through the App Store. If I go to my existing iTunes Connect login and select "Apps," I only see one entry (Figure 10-24). You can see a coin toss game, which we'll talk about in a later chapter. But there is nothing about our slot machine game. Let's change that.

Figure 10-24. *No current record of our slot machine game exists in iTunes Connect*

Click on the '+' button in the upper left and select "New App" (Figure 10-25).

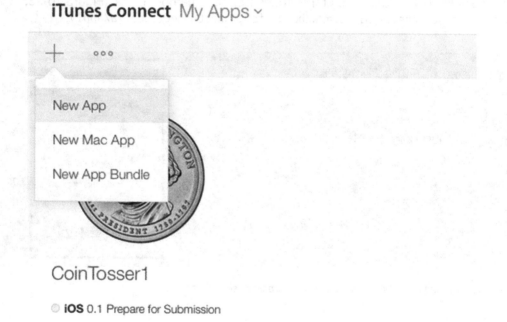

Figure 10-25. *Add new app to your iTunes Connect records*

Fill in the information shown in Figure 10-26, making sure you have the correct and matching bundle ID.

Figure 10-26. *Fill out the new app info, taking care to enter the bundle ID accurately*

Set your pricing information (Figure 10-27). I've set mine to be free. I also set no discounts.

Figure 10-27. *Set up your pricing, including any discounts you choose to allow*

Set up any additional information, such as app category, as you deem appropriate (Figure 10-28).

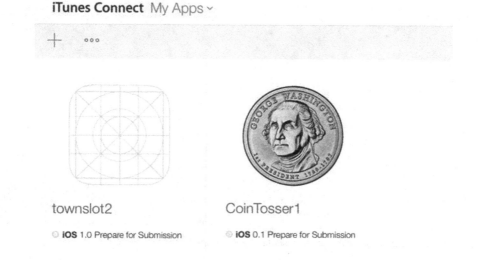

App Information

This information is used for all platforms of this app. Any changes will be released with your next app version.

Localizable Information

Name ?
townslot2

Privacy Policy URL ?
http://example.com (optional)

General Information

Bundle ID ?   Register a new bundle ID.
Slot Machine Game - com.mollymaskrey.townslot2

Your Bundle ID com.mollymaskrey.townslot2

SKU ?
townslot2-001

Apple ID ?
1095730698

Primary Language ?
English (U.S.)

Category ?
Games

Casino

Subcategory (optional)

Secondary (optional)

License Agreement Edit
Apple's Standard License Agreement

Rating ?
No Rating

Figure 10-28. For the slot machine game, I selected a Casino sub-category

When you go back to the Apps dashboard, you should now see this app being displayed (Figure 10-29).

iTunes Connect My Apps ˅

townslot2
◎ **iOS** 1.0 Prepare for Submission

CoinTosser1
◎ **iOS** 0.1 Prepare for Submission

Figure 10-29. Your app now shows up in iTunes Connect

To verify this was the issue, back in the Xcode Archives organizer, delete the old archive, and rebuild it. Then, go to the Archives organizer and validate (Figure 10-30). As you can see, the archive passed first validation. The warning, as we described in Chapter 8, is an issue when using Swift 2 and Xcode 7 and should be cleared up in a future Xcode release.

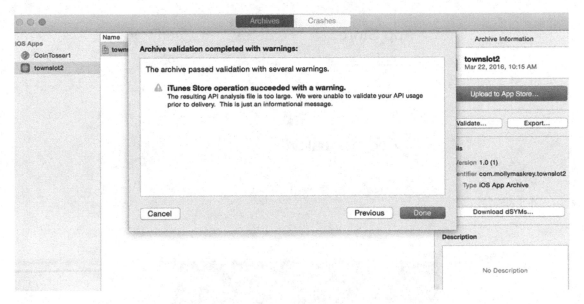

Figure 10-30. Now you should get a successful archive validation

iTunes Connect Graphics

Looking at Figure 10-31, it's quite obvious something's not right. There's no image shown for our slot machine game. Quite likely other metadata is missing as well. Let's fix that.

Figure 10-31. Although our app now appears in iTunes Connect, we still have to add other assets before we can submit it to the App Store

Click on the townslot2 icon and you'll be taken to more detailed information about our app (Figure 10-32). Then click on "1.0 Prepare App for Submission." The 1.0 indicates this is our first version. The yellow ball to the left indicates this section is not yet complete.

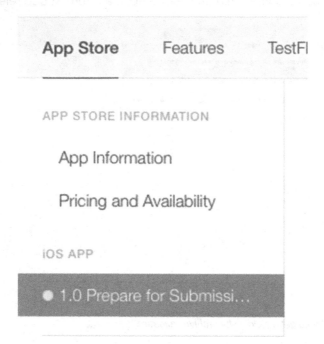

Figure 10-32. *We need to add more information into iTunes Connect before submitting our project to the App Store*

If you look at the first section, you can see that we're missing screenshots of our app (Figure 10-33). These are what you normally see when scanning through the App Store. Note that there are options for iPhones that are 4.7, 5.5, 4, and 3.5 inches as well as iPad and iPad Pro. Reviewing the guidelines at `https://developer.apple.com/library/ios/documentation/LanguagesUtilities/Conceptual/iTunesConnect_Guide/Appendices/Properties.html#//apple_ref/doc/writerid/itc_screenshot_properties`, you will see that the 3.5 and 4 inch are required; that the 4.7 and 5.5 are optional; and that the iPad is required if this app is built for iPad. This happens when you try to save and continue. The areas required will appear a pinkish color, indicating the need for more information. And similarly, if your app is designed for iPad Pro, that is required as well.

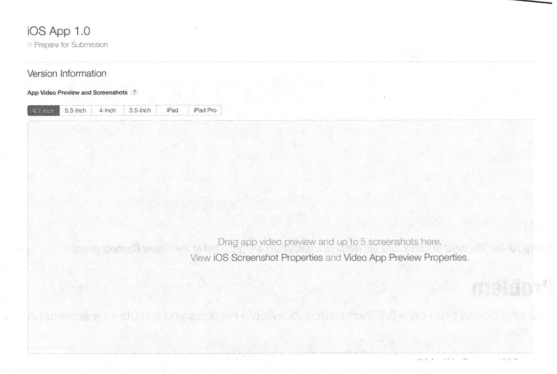

Figure 10-33. Here's where you need to place your screenshots in the iTunes Connect portal

The 4-inch requirement can be met by running our game in the simulator on an iPhone 5. Once the app is executing on the iPhone 5 simulator, make sure the simulator is in the foreground and, using the pull-down (Figure 10-34), select "Save Screen Shot," which should place the screenshot, as a .png, on your desktop.

Figure 10-34. Save your screenshot for the 4-inch requirement in iTunes Connect

If you try to use this image for the 3.5-inch requirement, you'll get the error shown in Figure 10-35. For each requirement, you have to submit an image of the correct dimensions. For the 3.5-inch image, we'll need a screenshot captured on an iPhone 4S. However, as you'll learn in Chapter 14 when we work on this project, we decided not to build for a 4S device. So we've reached a dilemma.

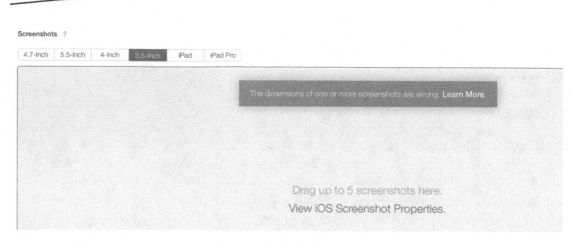

Figure 10-35. We need to make sure the required screenshots are provided in the iTunes Connect portal

Problem

Your app doesn't run on a 3.5-inch device, but Apple requires you to submit a screenshot of this size.

Solution

Because the screenshots are images, there's actually no requirement that they be captured from a device or a simulator. They're only required to be of certain dimensions and image quality. Specific requirements can be seen at `https://developer.apple.com/library/ios/documentation/LanguagesUtilities/Conceptual/iTunesConnect_Guide/Appendices/Properties.html#//apple_ref/doc/writerid/itc_screenshot_properties`.

To get around this in the short term, I opened up the `iphone5.png` file I had saved from earlier and resized it in a graphical editing program such as Adobe Photoshop. I used the option to change image size from 640 x 1096 pixels to 640 x 920 pixels. This made the image a little squat, as you can see in Figure 10-36, but it works for our needs to get our iTunes Connect required information completed.

Version Information

Screenshots ?

| 4.7-Inch | 5.5-Inch | 4-Inch | 3.5-Inch | iPad | iPad Pro |

Figure 10-36. Complete the required entry for the 3.5-inch screenshot

Quickly verifying the build settings (Figure 10-37), we see that this project is indeed designed for iPhone and not iPad.

| | General | Capabilities | Resource Tags | Info | Build Settings | Build Phases | Build Rules |

PROJECT
 townslot2

TARGETS
 townslot2

▼ Identity

Bundle Identifier com.mollymaskrey.townslot2

Version 1.0

Build 1

Team Molly Maskrey (mollymaskrey...)

▼ Deployment Info

Deployment Target 9.1

Devices iPhone

Main Interface Main

Device Orientation ☑ Portrait
                   ☐ Upside Down
                   ☐ Landscape Left
                   ☐ Landscape Right

Status Bar Style Default

                 ☐ Hide status bar
                 ☐ Requires full screen

Figure 10-37. Verify the target is set to iPhone only

There are a few more things we need to take care of. First, we need to add a description of the app itself (Figure 10-38) as well as keywords (Game, Casino, Slots) and a support URL address.

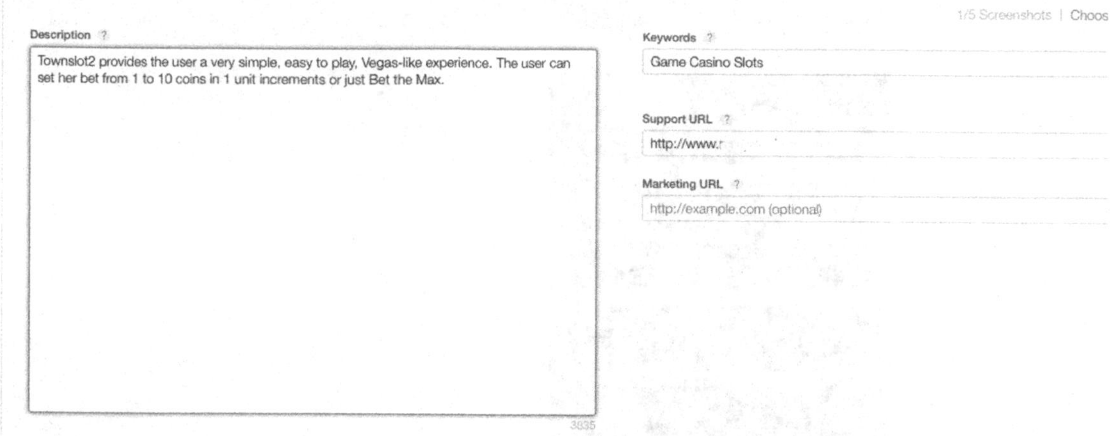

1/5 Screenshots | Choos

Description ?

Townslot2 provides the user a very simple, easy to play, Vegas-like experience. The user can set her bet from 1 to 10 coins in 1 unit increments or just Bet the Max.

Keywords ?

Game Casino Slots

Support URL ?

http://www.r

Marketing URL ?

http://example.com (optional)

3835

Figure 10-38. Add additional information about the app

We also have to add the app icon (Figure 10-39). For iTunes Connect, we have to use a 1024 x 1024 pixel image. Generally, you want to create all your images at this size or greater when developing for the iPad. For now we'll just use Photoshop to scale our 180 x 180 icon up to the necessary size.

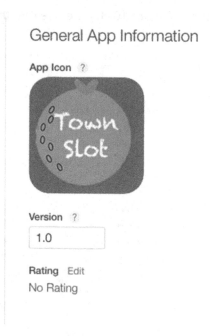

General App Information

App Icon ?

Version ?

1.0

Rating   Edit
No Rating

Figure 10-39. Add the icon and adjust the version number if necessary

Immediately below the icon and version number, select "Edit" by the rating title and fill out the information for your app as appropriate (Figure 10-40).

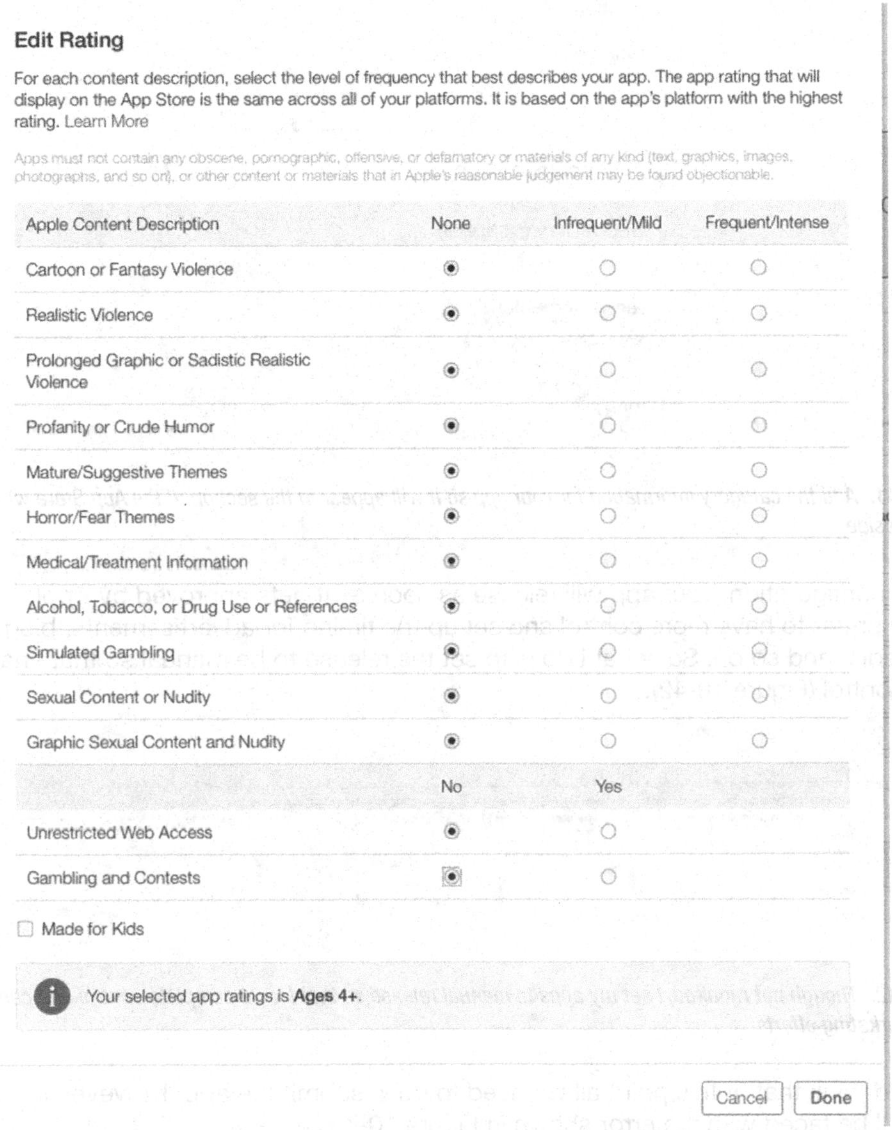

Edit Rating

For each content description, select the level of frequency that best describes your app. The app rating that will display on the App Store is the same across all of your platforms. It is based on the app's platform with the highest rating. Learn More

Apps must not contain any obscene, pornographic, offensive, or defamatory or materials of any kind (text, graphics, images, photographs, and so on), or other content or materials that in Apple's reasonable judgement may be found objectionable.

Apple Content Description	None	Infrequent/Mild	Frequent/Intense
Cartoon or Fantasy Violence	●	○	○
Realistic Violence	●	○	○
Prolonged Graphic or Sadistic Realistic Violence	●	○	○
Profanity or Crude Humor	●	○	○
Mature/Suggestive Themes	●	○	○
Horror/Fear Themes	●	○	○
Medical/Treatment Information	●	○	○
Alcohol, Tobacco, or Drug Use or References	●	○	○
Simulated Gambling	●	○	○
Sexual Content or Nudity	●	○	○
Graphic Sexual Content and Nudity	●	○	○

	No	Yes
Unrestricted Web Access	●	○
Gambling and Contests	●	○

☐ Made for Kids

ⓘ Your selected app ratings is **Ages 4+**.

Cancel   Done

Figure 10-40. Complete the information about your app's rating so this can be displayed in the App Store

If you missed it previously, which I found happens when I save the page, make sure to select the subcategory of your app (Figure 10-41).

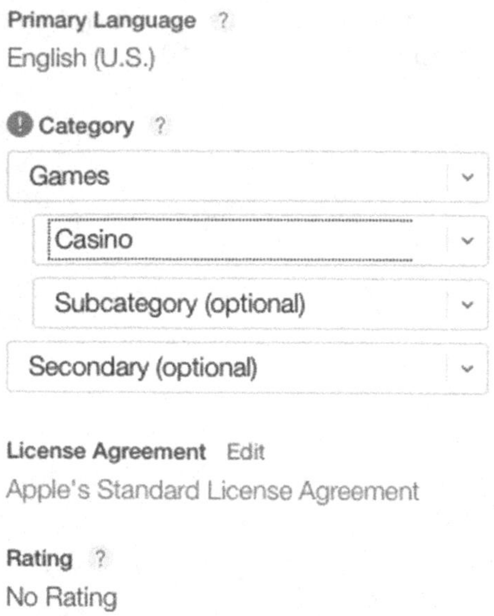

Primary Language ?

English (U.S.)

! Category ?

Games ⌄

Casino ⌄

Subcategory (optional) ⌄

Secondary (optional) ⌄

License Agreement Edit

Apple's Standard License Agreement

Rating ?

No Rating

Figure 10-41. Add the category information for your app so it will appear in the section of the App Store where you need it to reside

With this configuration, your app will release as soon as it gets approved by Apple. I generally prefer to have more control and set up the timing for advertisements, blog entry, social media, and so on. So, what I do is to set the release to be manual so that I have that level of control (Figure 10-42).

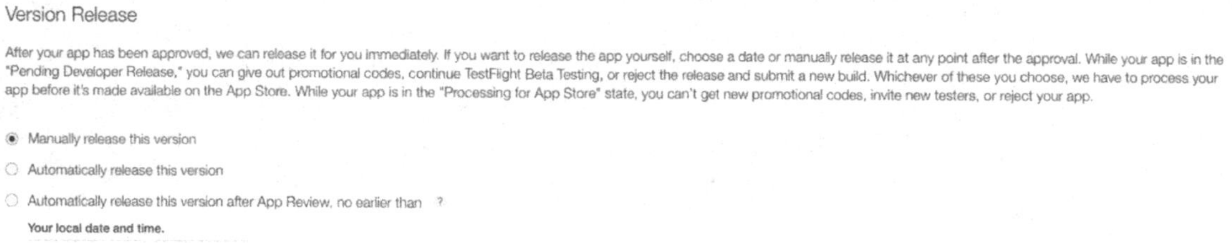

Version Release

After your app has been approved, we can release it for you immediately. If you want to release the app yourself, choose a date or manually release it at any point after the approval. While your app is in the "Pending Developer Release," you can give out promotional codes, continue TestFlight Beta Testing, or reject the release and submit a new build. Whichever of these you choose, we have to process your app before it's made available on the App Store. While your app is in the "Processing for App Store" state, you can't get new promotional codes, invite new testers, or reject your app.

◉ Manually release this version

◯ Automatically release this version

◯ Automatically release this version after App Review, no earlier than ?

   Your local date and time.

Figure 10-42. Though not required, I set my apps to manual release so that I have complete control and can properly time my marketing efforts

You would think that at this point all we need to do is submit the app. However, if you give it a try you'll be faced with the error shown in Figure 10-43.

! There are one or more errors on the page.

Figure 10-43. Though everything seems to be correct, you still cannot submit

In scanning down the page it quickly becomes apparent that the actual app bundle has not yet been uploaded to iTunes Connect (Figure 10-44).

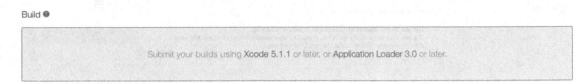

Figure 10-44. *The build that iTunes Connect needs has not yet been uploaded*

Back to Xcode

In the Xcode Organizer, similar to how we previously validated our build, we want to upload it to the App Store (Figure 10-45).

Figure 10-45. *From within the Xcode Organizer you have to upload the build to iTunes Connect*

When it completes, you'll get the same informative message we saw earlier (Figure 10-46). As before, this is an informative message only and you should be able to continue on.

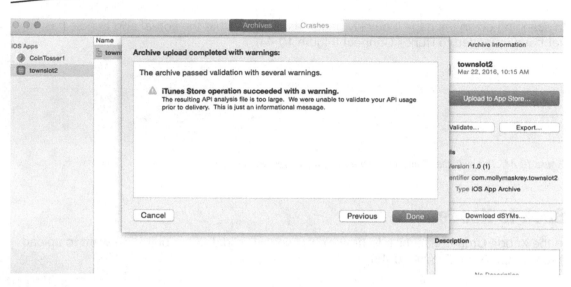

Figure 10-46. The archive uploaded successfully, albeit with an informational message

Here's the next frustrating thing you're going to come across. If you go back to iTunes Connect and try to submit the app, you'll see the same message in Figure 10-47 as we saw earlier. This can drive normal people a little crazy, but take another breath and allow me to explain.

Figure 10-47. Even though we uploaded the build from Xcode, you still can't do anything

The reason you don't see anything is that there is a bit of processing that goes on behind the scenes. There is more validation being performed on your now uploaded build in the background. Shortly—the time can vary up to half an hour—you'll receive an email that tells you things are okay (Figure 10-48). Mine took about ten minutes from the time of submission. If something's wrong, and this usually doesn't happen so long as you pre-validate as we did earlier, the message will let you know.

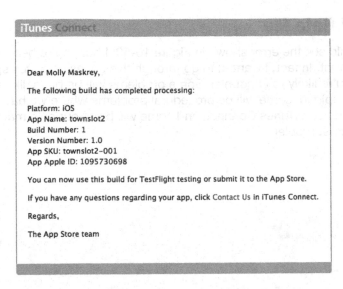

Figure 10-48. *Apple lets you know the build you uploaded has completed processing. We can now try to submit our app to the App Store.*

Go to the section where we had the error before, click on the build, and you can now submit your app, finally (Figure 10-49).

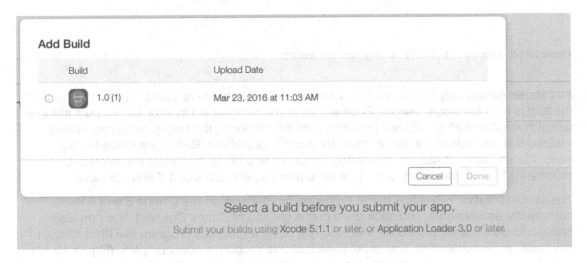

Figure 10-49. *Select the build we just uploaded, click Done, and submit the app*

Please Don't Hate Me

And now you should see the error shown in Figure 10-50. I bet you're becoming really frustrated at this point. In fact, I wanted to go through this series of issues specifically to show you what you're likely to encounter. Some problems will be bugs, like the informational message after our upload, some will be procedural problems where we have to go back and forth between Xcode and iTunes Connect, and some will be of our own making. This last category fits our latest problem.

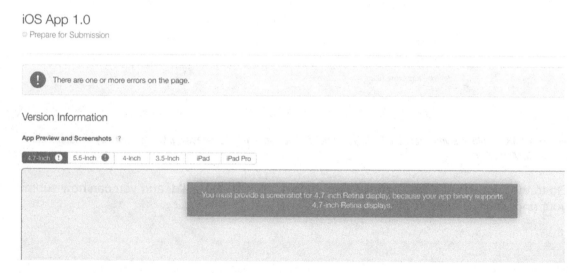

Figure 10-50.   Now we're told we're missing more screenshots

As I stated earlier, only the 3.5-inch and 4-inch screen shots are required. But that's only if the app is built for those devices. Because, as you'll discover in Chapter 14, we built this app with iPhone 6 and iPhone 6 Plus (as well as the 6S versions), the background processing realized this and added the requirement for those screenshots. Before we uploaded our build, iTunes Connect had no knowledge about our app other than what we entered. Once it processed the build file, it knew that we were using screen sizes of 4.7 and 5.5 inches.

The simple solution? Go back to the simulator, run the app on the iPhone 6 and 6 Plus, capture the screenshots, and stick them in this section of iTunes Connect. You can also choose to do what we did earlier and modify it using a graphics program like Photoshop. In any case, once completed, you should see that this section is now complete (Figure 10-51).

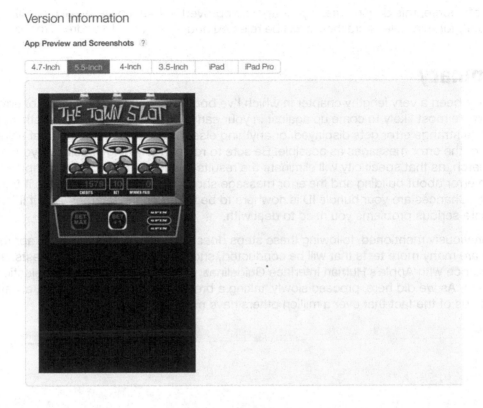

Figure 10-51. *After adding the necessary screenshots as determined by Apple when performing bundle analysis, all errors should be corrected*

If you now press Submit, iTunes Connect will spend some time processing and present you with a few questions that you need to answer concerning export compliance, content rights, and advertising information (Figure 10-52). Check these as appropriate, and if necessary provide any additional details, but now, finally, you can submit your app to the App Store. Hooray. We made it.

Figure 10-52. *The last thing needed is to complete the questions concerning the distribution of your app*

Now, of course, this doesn't mean your app is approved automatically. It will most likely be tested. If, for example, it crashes, it will be rejected and you'll want to address those issues.

Summary

This has been a very lengthy chapter in which I've bombarded you with all kinds of errors that you're most likely to come up against in your early submissions. When something goes wrong, a strange error gets displayed, or anything else, just search on the Internet using as much of the error messages as possible. Be sure to remove anything specific to your app in the search, as that specificity will eliminate the results you need to find. For example, if you get an error about building and the error message shows your bundle ID, remove it from the search. Chances are your bundle ID is nowhere to be found on the Internet. And if it is, there are more serious problems you need to deal with.

As I previously mentioned, following these steps does not mean your app will be approved. There are many more tests that will be conducted, such as performance, crash tests, and compliance with Apple's Human Interface Guidelines, from which most of your rejections will stem. As we did here, proceed slowly, taking a break when it gets frustrating, always conscious of the fact that over a million others have made it before you.

Chapter 11

Web Services

While most of our initial app creations are fairly simple and well contained, within a short period of time we'll need to access external information if we're doing anything serious as an iOS developer. We talk in several places about accessing data from sensor systems or controlling home automation devices using Apple's HomeKit ecosystem. However, if we want to download music or video, upload game scores to our own database, or share files or even small pieces of information, we're going to have to use some type of web services to move data between the cloud and our device.

As a technical professional, you must be aware that the "cloud" is really nothing more than a bunch of computers somewhere also connected to the Internet. But, rather than consisting of MacBooks or Mac desktops, a cloud system is more likely a suite of rack-based computers in a server room somewhere (Figure 11-1).

© Molly K. Maskrey 2016

M.K. Maskrey, *App Development Recipes for iOS and watchOS*, DOI 10.1007/978-1-4842-1820-4_11

Figure 11-1. The cloud is really nothing more than a bunch of computers in a room somewhere, all connected to the Internet, much like your Xcode workstation

In this chapter, we're going to cover two common methods we use in our iOS projects to move data between the cloud and our devices. In the first half of this chapter, the classic web-service access mechanisms will be addressed, while in the latter half we'll review the new CloudKit technology from Apple, specifically for Apple device ecosystems.

Classic Web-Service Access Mechanisms

In this section I'll cover the basics of accessing data residing on servers. You can call it the cloud if you want, but unless you're using a distributed cloud service such as Amazon Web Services (AWS), it's most likely a server that you access via a specific URL. Typically called RESTful services, we move data back and forth using a series of commands such as GET and POST. WE might POST some credit card info up to see if the transaction is authorized, securely of course. We would probably then GET the results of the transaction to see if there were sufficient funds available.

Problem

You need to access a price list for a point-of-sale iOS application, but the client wants to use the same price list for both a web-based solution as well as a different, non-Apple, platform. The price information is mostly static, changing only a few times a year.

Solution

Because we cannot limit the types of devices accessing our cloud data to only Apple equipment, we'll use the more classic RESTful services and a simple XML structure for our price list. While using a database such as MySQL would provide a more forward-looking solution, in some cases a simple, editable file works just as well, shortens the schedule, and keeps the cost to the customer within their reach. This also works well if you don't have the necessary database skills or the time to learn them due to cost and schedule constraints.

RESTful Services

REST stands for REpresentational State Transfer and refers to how communication is performed on the Web, more so than on the Internet in general. You select links or states on web pages that represent other pages of information and get transferred to them. On the Apple website, for example, if you select the state that represents the location of new Macintosh products, then you will be transferred to that new location and presented with a new set of states. A system, such as a website, that implements itself within these constraints is said to be RESTful and thus contains RESTful services.

REST implements a client–server separation of tasks and functionality, some placed at the server or cloud side while others, the ones we'll soon discuss, fall to us to put on our mobile devices. This separation allows for intermediary functionality as well, such as firewalls, gateways, and proxy servers.

Basic Terminology

While most of this will be familiar to those of us who have been around technology for a while (Figure 11-2), we may as well set out some common definitions so that we're all on the same page. If you've developed or worked on websites, many of these should already be familiar.

Figure 11-2. Even to those of us in and around technology day-to-day, terminology can mean different things to different people, at different times, and in different contexts

BROWSER: A browser is the program that resides on and executes on your computer or mobile device that displays information from the Internet. Most often, this will be web sites, but could be file sites or even your local computer files. Safari, Explorer, Chrome and Firefox are all examples of browsers.

URL: A Uniform Resource Locator (URL) is a web address and specifies a location on the Internet to which you might want to connect with your browser. You might also see the term URI, Uniform Resource Identifier, of which URL is a part. URN, Uniform Resource Name, is the other part of a URI. A URI may refer not only to an address out on the Internet, but just as easily a file on your device. By using URIs in your iOS app you can access websites or Internet data just as easily as your local storage.

HTTP: HyperText Transfer Protocol is the communications architecture of the Web. It supports a client–server architecture using a request–response protocol. Think of the website you want to access as the server, the source of information, and the browser on your computer or mobile device as the client. When you enter a URL, your browser is directed to that address on the Web, and the HTTP code executes within your browser to display the website properly. A simple website can be created from nothing but HTTP commands.

HTTPS: This is the secure form of the HyperText Transfer Protocol and is a layered security approach such as TLS (Transport Layer Security) or SSL (Secure Sockets Layer). HTTPS provides secure authorization that the website to which you are trying to connect is actually what it claims to be and uses encrypted data transmission. This type of protocol is critical when sending personal information such as credit card numbers.

CSS: Cascading Style Sheets define a language that works with HTTP for styling the data presented by a website. Because these define the presentation of the site and not the content, they are not relevant for our discussion.

FTP: File Transfer Protocol, or its secure version, SFTP, provides a mechanism similar to HTTP and HTTPS, but is used for transferring files between a client (browser) and a server somewhere.

XML: eXtensible Markup Language is a set of rules and keywords known as tags used for marking up the way data is formatted. XML is typically used to present a consistent format of data to algorithms so they can be parsed easily.

RSS: Really Simple Syndication or Rich Site Summary is a simple way of dispensing news that is periodically updated.

DOM: The Document Object Model is a convention for how data can be organized in a tree structure using primarily HTTP, CSS, and XML. This extends the markup (formatting) of XML into a conventionally used structure known as the DOM-tree that we, as software developers, parse through to get at the information we are seeking.

SOAP: Simple Object Access Protocol provides a specification as to how data is sent across the Internet. It uses the HTTP protocol, and doesn't replace it. Generally, SOAP provides a standardized way to send requests that return, typically, data formatted as XML.

AJAX: Asynchronous JavaScript and XML consists of methods for accessing data and is not a technology itself, but rather uses different technologies.

GET: The HTTP GET method is, just as it sounds, a request to retrieve data from some resource such as a URI.

POST: The HTTP POST method is sometimes seen as the opposite of GET. It sends the data to be processed by a specified resource. Note that POST is not writing data to the resource specifically, but sending data to be processed. As such, a POST command can be used in lieu of GET. In fact, POST is a little more secure because its parameters are not stored in your browser history or web server logs.

PUT: The HTTP PUT method is most often used for creating resources rather than updating an existing resource, for which POST would be commonly used.

DELETE: This one is simple—the DELETE method removes a resource. Use it sparingly.

CRUD: CRUD is an acronym referring to the four basic functions—Create, Read, Update, and Delete—that we will be using to move data between the web and our iOS projects. Another deviation of CRUD, which is SCRUD, adds Search to the set of terms.

Problem

You need to download some data from the Internet to your iOS application but want a simple way to get started in order to understand the process.

Solution

We'll work through the process and the basics of what you need to know. First, we need to have some data and put it onto the Internet somewhere. As an example, let's use the file shown in Listing 11-1, which represents some inventory items for a very small store. You can create this file using a basic text editor such as TextEdit on the Mac or a program such as TextMate that can provide some elementary formatting for file types such as XML.

Listing 11-1. Our Initial Data: An Inventory File in XML Format

```xml
<?xml version="1.0" encoding="UTF-8"?>
<rss  version="2.0">

    <channel>
        <title>Mobile Device Price List</title>
        <description>This is a list of the case options offered at our store.</description>
        <item>
            <title>Blackberry Red Case</title>
            <price>19.00</price>
                    <taxable>YES</taxable>
        </item>

        <item>
            <title>Blackberry Black Case</title>
            <price>19.00</price>
                    <taxable>YES</taxable>
        </item>
```

```
<item>
        <title>Blackberry Green Case</title>
        <price>19.00</price>
                <taxable>YES</taxable>
</item>

        <item>
        <title>iPhone 6 Silver Case</title>
        <price>20.00</price>
                <taxable>YES</taxable>
</item>

        <item>
        <title>iPhone 6S Silver Case</title>
        <price>20.00</price>
                <taxable>YES</taxable>
</item>

        <item>
        <title>iPhone 6 Plus Silver Case</title>
        <price>30.00</price>
                <taxable>YES</taxable>
</item>

        <item>
        <title>iPhone 6S Plus Silver Case</title>
        <price>30.00</price>
                <taxable>YES</taxable>
</item>

    </channel>
</rss>
```

To get the data to the Internet, you'll need to have some knowledge of your provider and how it functions. I use a mostly free service called ecowebhosting (`https://www.ecowebhosting.co.uk/`). After logging in I go to my control panel and select File Manager (Figure 11-3).

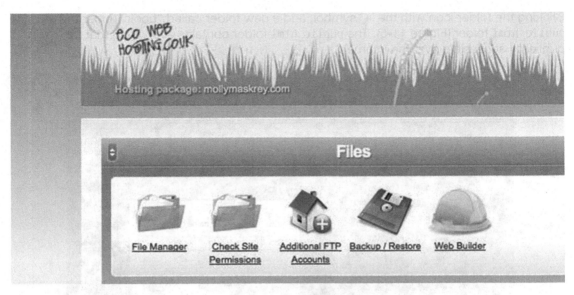

Figure 11-3. Using ecowebhosting, I start at my control panel to access File Manager

My hosting service locks file transfers using FTP by default, so before I can upload new information, I need to unlock the file transfer (Figure 11-4).

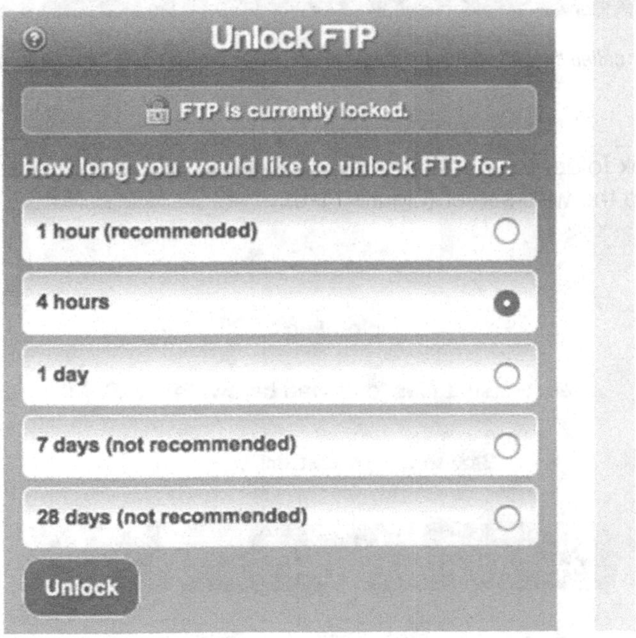

Figure 11-4. If your web service locks file transfers by default, be sure to unlock them before trying to upload your information

Clicking the folder icon with the '+' symbol, add a new folder called "book" under the public_html folder (Figure 11-5). The public_html folder contains everything that is publically accessible over the Internet.

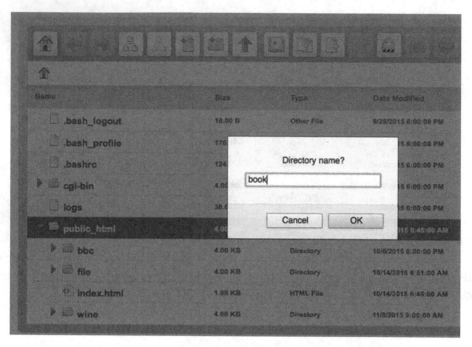

Figure 11-5. *Add a folder called "book" under the public_html folder, which makes your information accessible over the Internet*

After adding the book folder to your hierarchy, click the up arrow to upload the pricelist.xml file to the web server (Figure 11-6).

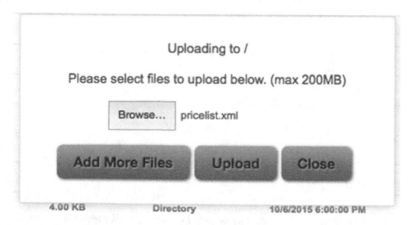

Figure 11-6. *Upload pricelist.xml file to the web server*

Once it completes, you should be able to see the structure with your new book directory and the `pricelist.xml` file contained within (Figure 11-7).

▼ 📁 **public_html**	4.00 KB	Directory
▷ 📁 **bbc**	4.00 KB	Directory
▼ 📁 **book**	4.00 KB	Directory
📄 **pricelist.xml**	1.18 KB	XML File
▷ 📁 **file**	4.00 KB	Directory
⟨⟩ **index.html**	1.98 KB	HTML File
▷ 📁 **wine**	4.00 KB	Directory

Figure 11-7. Our pricelist.xml file is now contained within our web server file hierarchy in the book directory

Pointing your browser to the location—in my case, `www.mollymaskrey.com/book/pricelist.xml`—you will likely see the formatted display as an RSS feed (Figure 11-8). Note that because it is an RSS feed, your browser—I'm using Firefox—should allow you to subscribe to the pricelist.

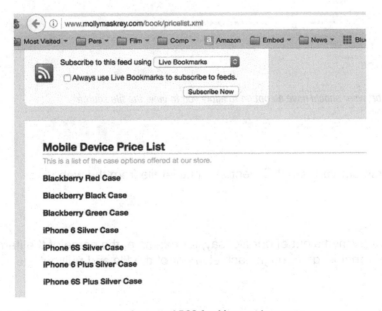

Figure 11-8. Our pricelist should appear as a formatted RSS feed in most browsers

In Firefox, on the formatted web page, I can right click and select “`Show Page Source`” to view the actual contents of the XML file (Figure 11-9). Your browser should offer a similar option.

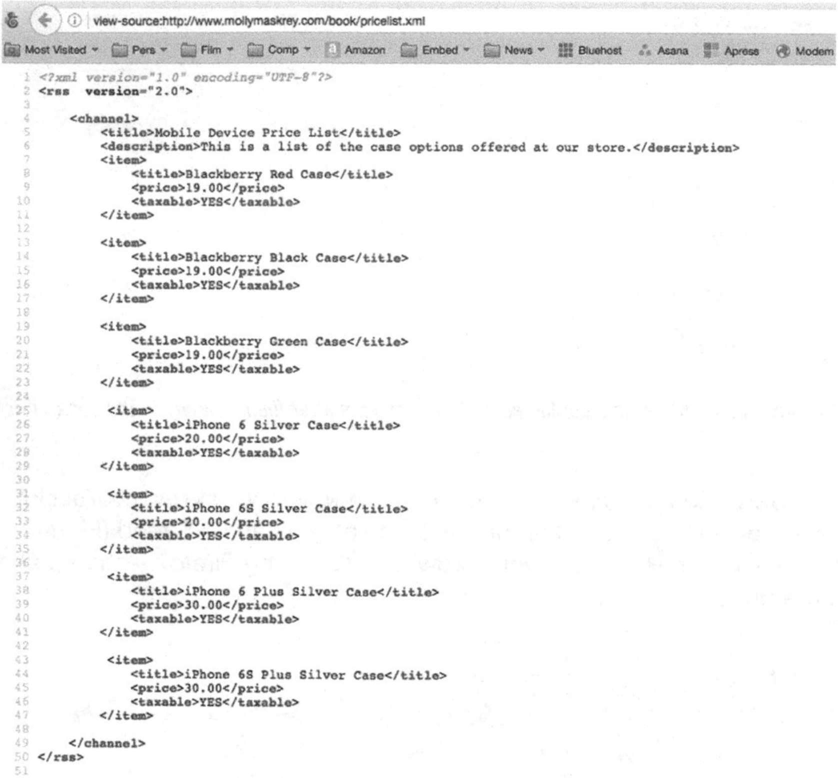


```xml
<?xml version="1.0" encoding="UTF-8"?>
<rss  version="2.0">

    <channel>
        <title>Mobile Device Price List</title>
        <description>This is a list of the case options offered at our store.</description>
        <item>
            <title>Blackberry Red Case</title>
            <price>19.00</price>
            <taxable>YES</taxable>
        </item>

        <item>
            <title>Blackberry Black Case</title>
            <price>19.00</price>
            <taxable>YES</taxable>
        </item>

        <item>
            <title>Blackberry Green Case</title>
            <price>19.00</price>
            <taxable>YES</taxable>
        </item>

         <item>
            <title>iPhone 6 Silver Case</title>
            <price>20.00</price>
            <taxable>YES</taxable>
        </item>

         <item>
            <title>iPhone 6S Silver Case</title>
            <price>20.00</price>
            <taxable>YES</taxable>
        </item>

         <item>
            <title>iPhone 6 Plus Silver Case</title>
            <price>30.00</price>
            <taxable>YES</taxable>
        </item>

         <item>
            <title>iPhone 6S Plus Silver Case</title>
            <price>30.00</price>
            <taxable>YES</taxable>
        </item>

    </channel>
</rss>
```

***Figure 11-9.** Your browser should have an option to allow you to view the file source*

Problem

We need to parse our very simple inventory pricelist file from the web.

Parsing

To get important elements out of our file, say, for example, the name of the item, we need to parse the file—that is, go through each element of the file and pull out the value for our `<title>` tag.

Solution

In Xcode, create a new single view application project: File ➤ New ➤ Project (Figure 11-10).

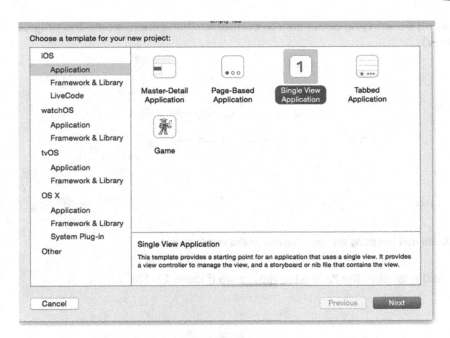

Figure 11-10. Start by creating a single view application project

Give it a name and make sure you're using Swift; don't use Core Data or any testing at this time (Figure 11-11).

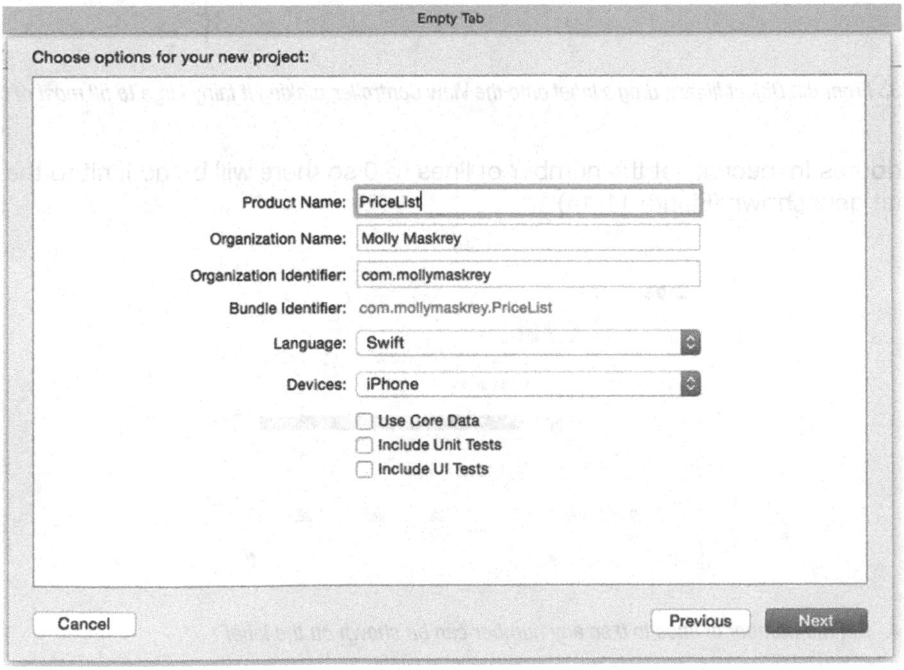

Figure 11-11. I called my project PriceList

Also, we won't be worrying about source control for this; simply create the project (Figure 11-12).

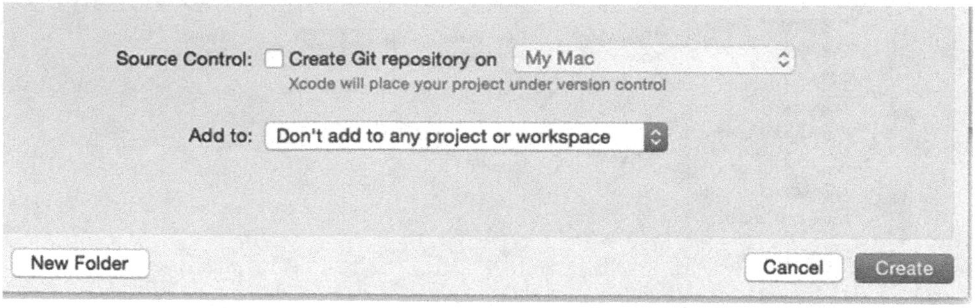

Source Control:
Create Git repository on
My Mac
Xcode will place your project under version control
Add to:
Don't add to any project or workspace
New Folder
Cancel
Create

Figure 11-12. We won't be doing any source control on this simple project

In Xcode, add a label to the `Main.storyboard` file (Figure 11-13).

Label
Label - A variably sized amount of static text.

Figure 11-13. From the Object library, drag a label onto the View Controller, making it fairly large to fill most of the screen

In the Attributes Inspector, set the number of lines to 0 so there will be no limit to the amount of data that gets shown (Figure 11-14).

Label
Text
Plain
Label
Color
Font
System 17.0
Alignment
Lines
0

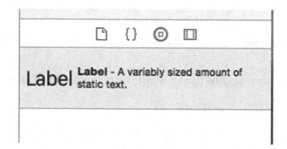

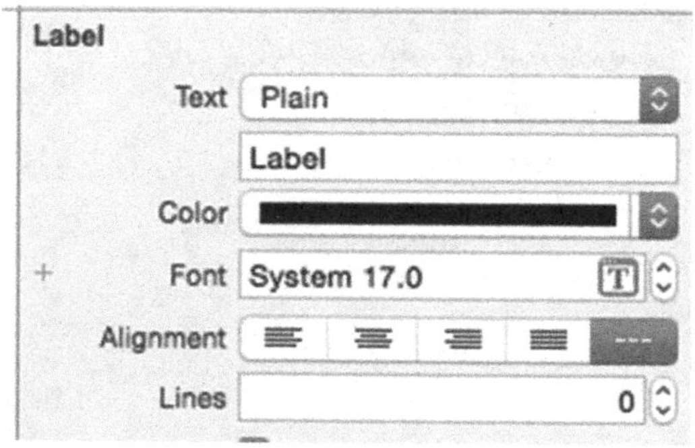

Figure 11-14. Set the number of lines to 0 so any number can be shown on the label

Set the background under the View section of the Attributes Inspector to a color that stands out a little, maybe a light gray color, with the end result looking something like that in Figure 11-15.

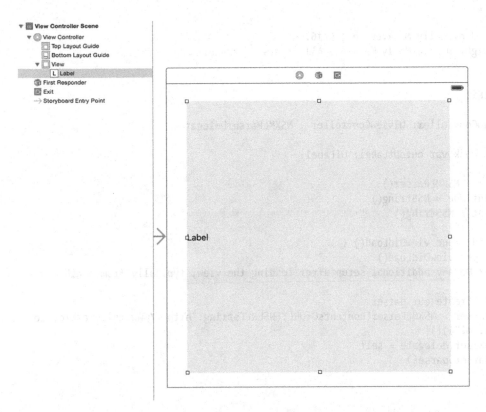

Figure 11-15. Set the label to stand out from the background so we'll know where the information should be

Modify the template ViewController.swift code to that shown in Listing 11-2. First, we've set our View Controller to subscribe to the NSXMLParserDelegate protocol by adding that keyword to the class definition line, which we'll need when we start parsing our file. Next, from the Main.storyboard file, we create an @IBOutlet for the UILabel that we just added called outputLabel. In the class file, I added variables for our parser, an NSXMLParser object, and two strings, one to reference the type of element (elementType) and one for our element data (element) that we will display inside the label on our view.

Finally, we added functionality to the viewDidLoad() method to instantiate our parser object using the NSXMLParser initializer function with the contentsOfURL convenience function that points to the XML inventory file we previously uploaded to the Web. The last two added lines set the delegate of the parser to this file and start the parsing operation using the parse() method of the NSXMLParser class.

Listing 11-2. Our Initial Modification to the Template View Controller Code

```
//
//  ViewController.swift
//  PriceList
//
//  Created by Molly Maskrey on 4/5/16.
//  Copyright © 2016 Molly Maskrey. All rights reserved.
//

import UIKit

class ViewController: UIViewController , NSXMLParserDelegate{

@IBOutlet weak var outputLabel: UILabel!

var parser = NSXMLParser()
var elementType = NSString()
var element = NSString()

    override func viewDidLoad() {
        super.viewDidLoad()
        // Do any additional setup after loading the view, typically from a nib.

        // Create our parser
        parser = NSXMLParser(contentsOfURL:(NSURL(string:"http://www.mollymaskrey.com/book/
pricelist.xml"))!)!
        parser.delegate = self
        parser.parse()

    }

    override func didReceiveMemoryWarning() {
        super.didReceiveMemoryWarning()
        // Dispose of any resources that can be recreated.
    }
}
```

Running this on the simulator—yes, I know we haven't set up to display anything yet—we'll see the error shown in Figure 11-16. We have not yet set up our app to allow the use of a cleartext (http:// and not https://) web address. This prevents apps from maliciously making calls to non-secure sites without exclusively giving the app permission to do so.

```
2016-04-05 10:20:19.078 PriceList[50824:12536867] App Transport Security has blocked a cleartext HTTP (http://) resource load since it is insecure. Temporary
exceptions can be configured via your app's Info.plist file.
<NSXMLParser: 0x7fc9726223c8>
```

Figure 11-16. We cannot access insecure web addresses without modifying our project settings in the Info.plist file

To fix this, add a row in the `Info.plist` file by right clicking the mouse and selecting "Add Row." Change the added row to "App Transport Security Settings" from the pull-down, then click the '+' and select "Allow Arbitrary Loads," changing its value from "NO" to "YES" (Figure 11-17).

	Key	Type	Value
▼ PriceList			
▼ PriceList	▼ Information Property List	Dictionary	(15 items)
AppDelegate.swift	Localization native development r...	String	en
ViewController.swift	Executable file	String	$(EXECUTABLE_NAME)
Main.storyboard	Bundle identifier	String	$(PRODUCT_BUNDLE_IDENTIFIER)
Assets.xcassets	InfoDictionary version	String	6.0
LaunchScreen.storyboard	Bundle name	String	$(PRODUCT_NAME)
Info.plist	Bundle OS Type code	String	APPL
▶ Products	Bundle versions string, short	String	1.0
	Bundle creator OS Type code	String	????
	Bundle version	String	1
	Application requires iPhone envir...	Boolean	YES
	Launch screen interface file base...	String	LaunchScreen
	Main storyboard file base name	String	Main
	▶ Required device capabilities	Array	(1 item)
	▶ Supported interface orientations	Array	(3 items)
	▼ App Transport Security Settings	Dictionary	(1 item)
	Allow Arbitrary Loads	Boolean	YES

Figure 11-17. Add "App Transport Security Settings" to the Info.plist

For kicks, build and run it again using the simulator, and you should no longer see the error. But how do you know anything is happening? Add the two functions in Listing 11-3 to the file. At the start of parsing you should see the "Started Parsing Document" message displayed in the Xcode log. At the end, you should see "Finished Parsing Document."

Listing 11-3. Two Functions Bracket the Start and Stop of Parsing the Web File

```swift
func parserDidStartDocument(parser: NSXMLParser) {
    print("Started Parsing Document")
}

func parserDidEndDocument(parser: NSXMLParser) {
    print("Finished Parsing Document")
}
```

Finally, add the additional code to the `ViewController.swift` file as shown in Listing 11-4, and we should now start to see our parsing functionality begin to take shape. The `didStartElement` delegate function finds the beginning of each element. For us, we are most interested in the item elements that we are intending to sell. Later, we'll see an issue with that. The `foundCharacters` delegate function locates sub-tags within the element we located with the `didStartElement` function.

Listing 11-4. Two Parser Delegate Methods to Identify Elements within the XML Structure and Pull Out to Display the Titles of Our Inventory Items

```
func parser(parser: NSXMLParser, didStartElement elementName: String,
    namespaceURI: String?, qualifiedName qName: String?,
    attributes attributeDict: [String : String])
{
    elementType = elementName
}

func parser(parser: NSXMLParser, foundCharacters string: String) {

    if (elementType.isEqualToString("title")) {
        element = "\(element) \(string)"
        outputLabel.text = element as String
    }
}
```

In the didStartElement function, the only thing we do is set the global variable elementType to contain the type of element that we found. In the foundCharacters function, we use that element type variable as a key to get the title of the element, which is the name of our inventory item, and display it in our view by running the app in the simulator (Figure 11-18).

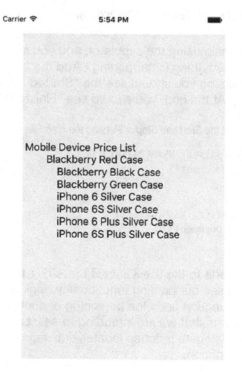

Figure 11-18. Parsed pricelist.xml file from our web server

In this example we created a simple XML-formatted table that contained inventory information. We uploaded it to our web server and then created a simple iOS project that downloaded and parsed that file. For pricelist types of files that don't change very often or that do not have other frequently changing metadata such as inventory count, this works pretty well. In my very first professional app, a point-of-sale Objective-C project that worked with a 30-pin dock connector credit card reader, I set up accounts like this for dozens of smaller clients. From bail bond companies to chiropractors, this model works really well when there's not an inventory stocking issue.

For situations where we do have information such as quantity, we need to be able to delete however many products are sold from the inventory, usually held in a database such as MySQL on the server. What's more, if we make an incorrect sale or a customer returns an item, we may want to restore that item to the stock count. This is especially important where multiple devices may be accessing the same inventory database. That is, you can't sell the same item twice, or that's the goal, anyway.

If we were accessing a database through a server-side PHP script, the code shown in Listing 11-5 would be typical of the interaction that we might develop. The first line sets up the basic URL that points to a script on the server, not a web page, that allows access to the database, whatever form that may take. The second line adds a query to the address using a parameter defined within the PHP code called stockNumber. The \(stockNo!) part converts a stored stock number into the literal part of the string. If the stock number were 123456, for example, the entire URL that we pass to the request would be:

```
http://www.mollymaskrey.com/book/pricelist.php?stockNumber=123456
```

Listing 11-5. Simplified HTTP GET Access to a Data via a PHP Server-Side Application

```
let url = "http://www.mollymaskrey.com/book/pricelist.php"
let urlIncludingID = url + "?stockNumber=\(stockNo!)" // stockNo is a prev loaded item id number

let request = NSMutableURLRequest(URL:urlIncludingID)
request.HTTPMethod = "GET"

let transaction = NSURLSession.sharedSession().dataTaskWithRequest(request) {
                    data, response, error in

        if error != nil {
                print("error = \(error)")
                return
        }

        let responseString = NSString(data: data!, encoding NSUTF8StringEncoding)
        print("responseString = \(responseString)")
}
```

The next two lines instantiate a mutable request and set the method to GET. This could just as easily be POST, PUT, or DELETE but would have to match the capabilities of the PHP code on the server. That is, the PHP code written for what is traditionally called the backend would have to accept the specific HTTP request type.

Finally, we create a transaction that sends the request to the server and expects back some data, a response string and an error code. If the error code is nil, non-existent, meaning no error, then we process the response string by just printing it to the log.

On the server side, we might see code similar to that in Listing 11-6 being used to handle this type of request. Of course, there would be much more to deal with such as a database, the page layout, and formatting, but somewhere on the page or URL address you would see something similar written in a language like PHP.

Listing 11-6. Simplified PHP to Handle Our GET Request

```php
<?php
  if( $_GET["stockNumber"]) {
    echo "You asked for the ". $_GET['stockNumber']. " item from inventory.";

    exit();
  }
?>
```

RESTful Services Summary

Moving data between a server and your iOS app on a mobile device can seem daunting when you're first starting out. I don't want to kid you—it generally always stays fairly complicated. If you work for a moderate- to large-size software agency, this should not be too much of an issue as the teams would be broken up functionally between mobile and host-side engineering. You don't have to know everything, but you do need to understand how to get to the data from your side of the fence.

Web design, web engineering, back-end processing, and database engineering can be and are often complete worlds unto themselves, and in major shops you're likely to find different people specializing in a single skillset. At the development agencies that I worked for, we set up a system of weekly bag lunches where one of the team specialists would talk about topics within their specialty (Figure 11-19). At least once a month we'd have someone from the host side of things describe what they did, how it worked, and what was needed to access data and information. These were always attended by my mobile teammates and made things so much clearer, saving hours if not days on projects.

Figure 11-19. Technical "bag" lunches provide a convenient and fun way to get information from different technical areas within an organization.

CloudKit

Problem

You have an Apple-only system project and need to store/retrieve information from a server on the Internet. The system will never be migrated to a non-Apple system, and you don't have substantial server or backend skills in your organization.

Solution

CloudKit is the transport framework underlying all of Apple's iCloud technologies, including iCloud Drive, iCloud Core Data, and the iCloud Photo Library (Figure 11-20). CloudKit gives your app the same methods to use in your application where one of the other technologies might not be a good fit. CloudKit works with Apple devices, iOS and OS X, and iCloud servers.

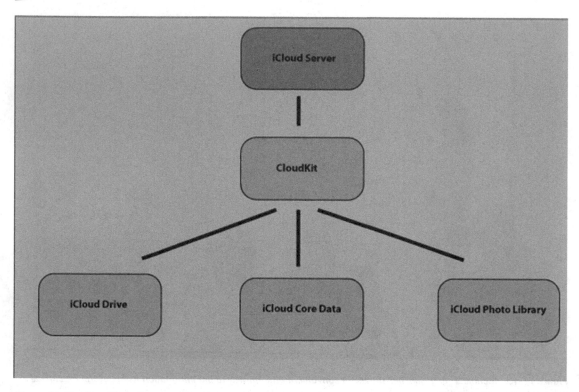

Figure 11-20. *CloudKit is the underlying transport framework allowing access to Apple's iCloud servers*

As with our previous RESTful example, let's start with getting some information into the iCloud server.

The database we want to set up is managed through the iCloud dashboard (https://icloud.developer.apple.com/dashboard/). However, if you try to log in using your developer account credentials AND you have never used the iCloud dashboard previously, you'll see the message shown in Figure 11-21.

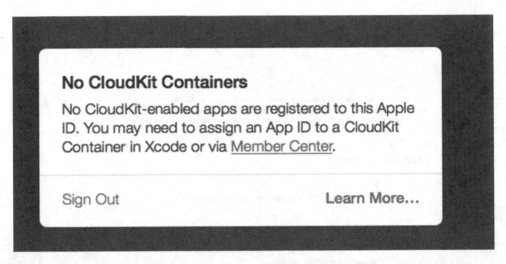

Figure 11-21. You have to do some previous setup, both in your app and on the developer portal, before you can access the iCloud dashboard for the first time

Notice how the message says "You may need to assign an App ID to a CloudKit Container in Xcode…" This tells us we might need an app ID. Let's get that done first. As we talked about in Chapter 3, first go to your developer portal sign-In, then to Certificates, Identifiers, Devices, and Profiles and select "App ID." Click on '+' and start by adding an app description as well as a discrete bundle ID (Figure 11-22).

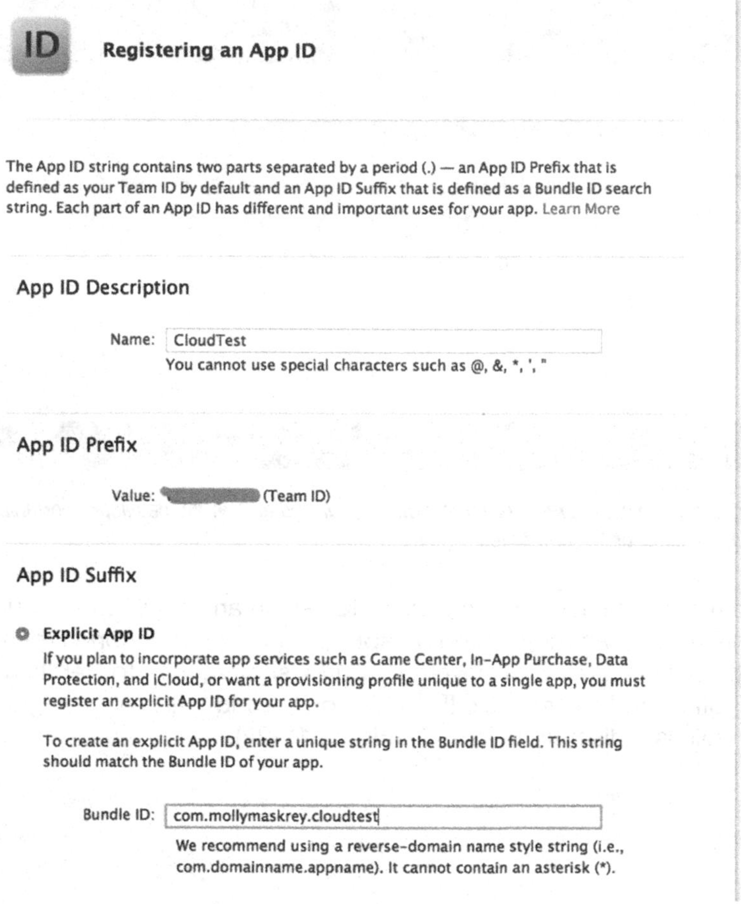

ID   Registering an App ID

The App ID string contains two parts separated by a period (.) — an App ID Prefix that is defined as your Team ID by default and an App ID Suffix that is defined as a Bundle ID search string. Each part of an App ID has different and important uses for your app. Learn More

App ID Description

Name: CloudTest

You cannot use special characters such as @, &, *, ', "

App ID Prefix

Value: ▓▓▓▓▓▓ (Team ID)

App ID Suffix

◉ **Explicit App ID**

If you plan to incorporate app services such as Game Center, In-App Purchase, Data Protection, and iCloud, or want a provisioning profile unique to a single app, you must register an explicit App ID for your app.

To create an explicit App ID, enter a unique string in the Bundle ID field. This string should match the Bundle ID of your app.

Bundle ID: com.mollymaskrey.cloudtest

We recommend using a reverse-domain name style string (i.e., com.domainname.appname). It cannot contain an asterisk (*).

Figure 11-22. Start by creating your new app ID for our cloudtest project

In the App Services section, make sure to select "iCloud" and to add CloudKit support (Figure 11-23).

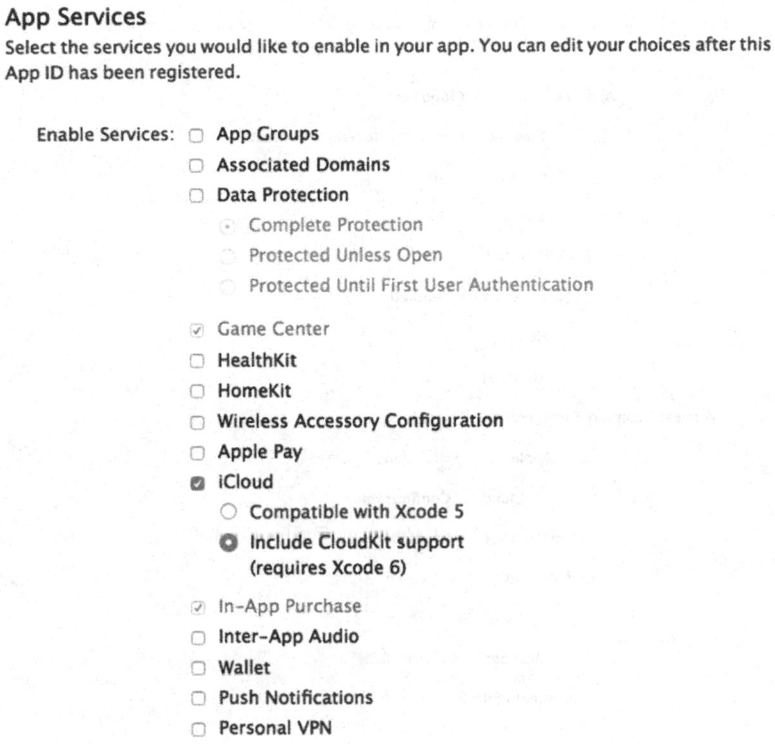

App Services

Select the services you would like to enable in your app. You can edit your choices after this App ID has been registered.

Enable Services:
- ☐ App Groups
- ☐ Associated Domains
- ☐ Data Protection
  - ⦿ Complete Protection
  - ○ Protected Unless Open
  - ○ Protected Until First User Authentication
- ☑ Game Center
- ☐ HealthKit
- ☐ HomeKit
- ☐ Wireless Accessory Configuration
- ☐ Apple Pay
- ☑ iCloud
  - ○ Compatible with Xcode 5
  - ⦿ Include CloudKit support (requires Xcode 6)
- ☑ In-App Purchase
- ☐ Inter-App Audio
- ☐ Wallet
- ☐ Push Notifications
- ☐ Personal VPN

Figure 11-23. Add CloudKit support to your app ID

Complete the creation of your app ID and verify that it looks as you expect it should, with the proper bundle and CloudKit support (Figure 11-24).

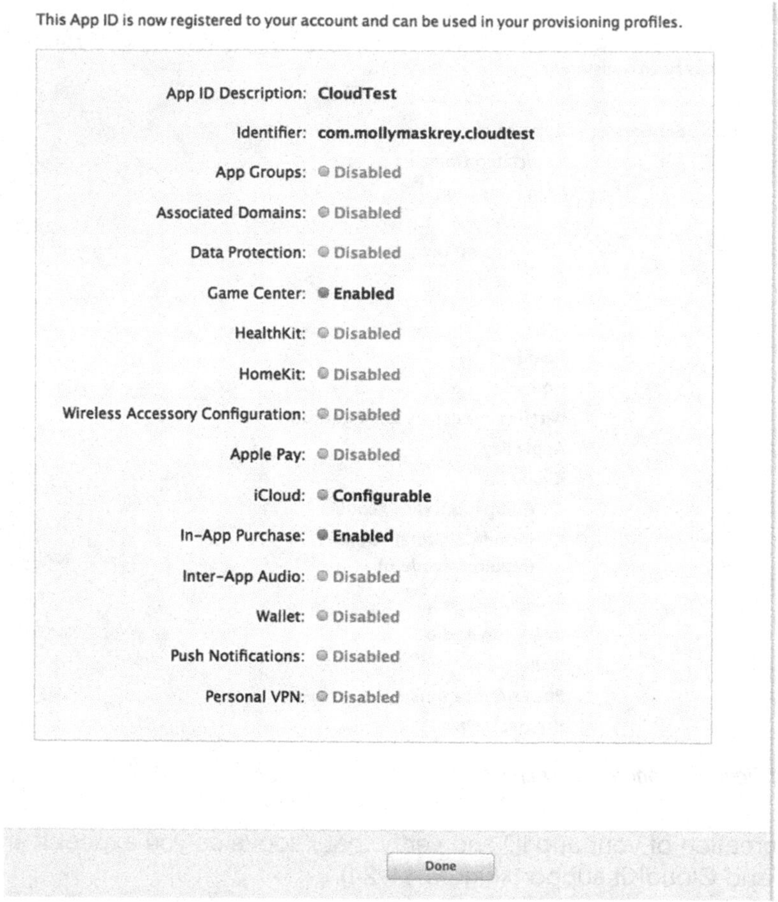

This App ID is now registered to your account and can be used in your provisioning profiles.

App ID Description:	**CloudTest**
Identifier:	**com.mollymaskrey.cloudtest**
App Groups:	⊘ Disabled
Associated Domains:	⊘ Disabled
Data Protection:	⊘ Disabled
Game Center:	⬤ **Enabled**
HealthKit:	⊘ Disabled
HomeKit:	⊘ Disabled
Wireless Accessory Configuration:	⊘ Disabled
Apple Pay:	⊘ Disabled
iCloud:	⊘ **Configurable**
In–App Purchase:	⬤ **Enabled**
Inter–App Audio:	⊘ Disabled
Wallet:	⊘ Disabled
Push Notifications:	⊘ Disabled
Personal VPN:	⊘ Disabled

Done

Figure 11-24. The iCloud parameter should show as "Configurable," meaning we're going to be using CloudKit directly to access the iCloud servers

Also, in the error message we got when we tried to access the iCloud dashboard we saw the thing about containers. So, what is a container? A container is really just the name for your app's iCloud storage area (Figure 11-25). A container includes databases, both a public and a private one, and is represented in the CloudKit framework by the CKContainer class.

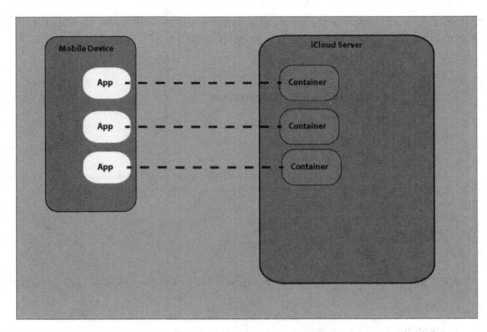

Figure 11-25. Each app has its own container for holding data in the iCloud server

In the Certificates, Identifiers, Devices, and Profiles section, under Identifiers, select "iCloud Containers," click '+', and then click on the "Continue" link in the main window (Figure 11-26).

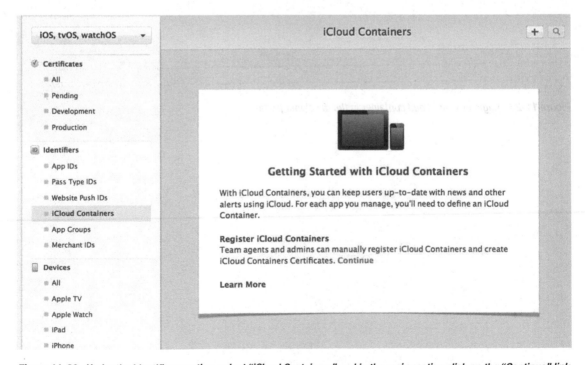

Figure 11-26. Under the Identifiers section, select "iCloud Containers" and in the main section click on the "Continue" link

Register your iCloud container by entering a descriptive name and an identifier that is similar to your app's bundle ID but starts with "iCloud" (Figure 11-27).

Figure 11-27. Register your iCloud container in the developer portal

Confirm and complete your iCloud container registration (Figure 11-28).

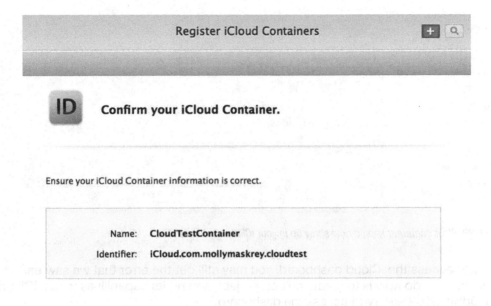

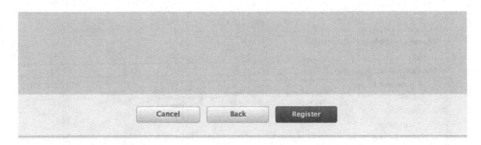

Figure 11-28. Complete your iCloud container registration, verifying the correct identifier you plan to use for your app

It should now show up in your containers list (Figure 11-29).

Figure 11-29. *Your container should now show up in your iCloud containers list*

If you try to access the iCloud dashboard, you may still get the error that we saw earlier. What we have to do now is to create an app project, setting its capabilities to use iCloud and CloudKit, and *then* try to access the dashboard.

Back in Xcode, let's do the usual File ➤ New ➤ Project and create a single view application (Figure 11-30).

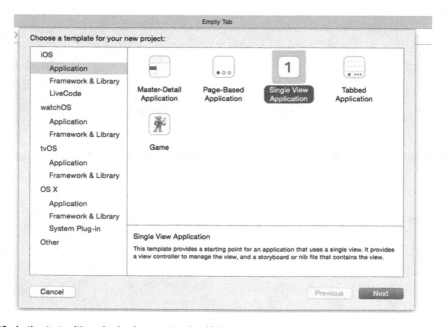

Figure 11-30. *Let's start with a single view application iOS project*

Don't add any tests, and make sure you're writing your app in Swift (Figure 11-31). I called mine cloudtest, being sure to match the names and case sensitivity. Note that we're using all lowercase for the name to match what we did earlier in the developer portal.

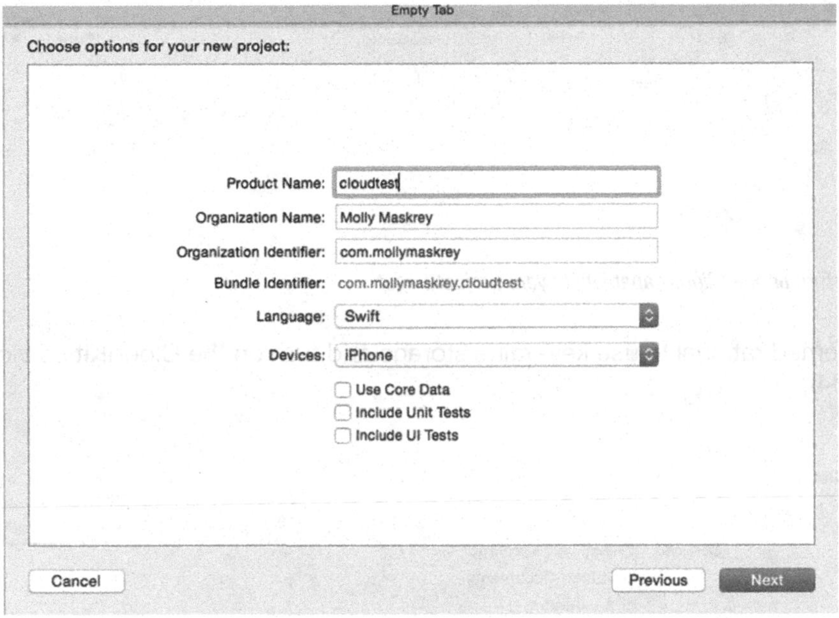

Figure 11-31. We won't be concerned with testing our new app

And since this is a simple demonstration, we won't need to do any source-code control (Figure 11-32).

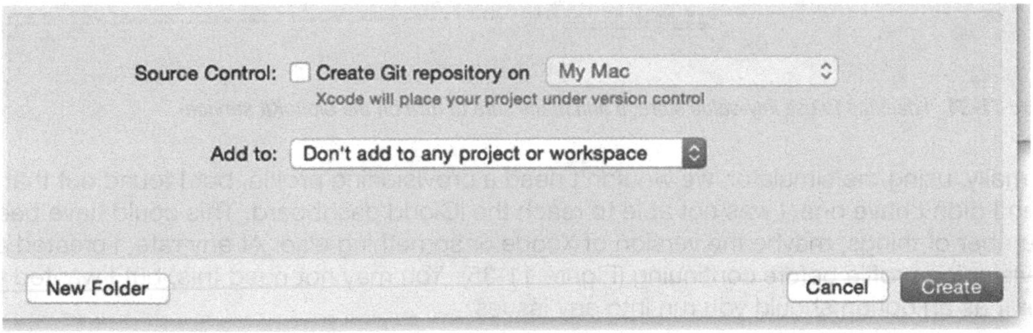

Figure 11-32. We also do not need Git source-code management for now

In the Capabilities tab of the cloudtest target, turn on iCloud (Figure 11-33). You may be asked to choose your development team ID if you have more than one.

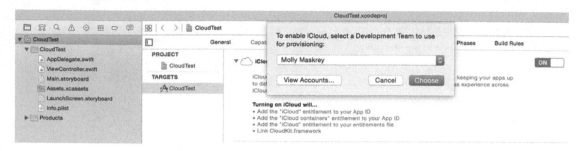

Figure 11-33. Turn on the iCloud capability of your project target

To me, it seemed rational to use key-value storage and turn on the CloudKit service (Figure 11-34).

Figure 11-34. I decided to use key-value storage and made sure to turn on the CloudKit service

Normally, using the simulator, we wouldn't need a provisioning profile, but I found out that when I didn't have one, I was not able to reach the iCloud dashboard. This could have been a number of things, maybe the version of Xcode or something else. At any rate, I created a provisioning profile before continuing (Figure 11-35). You may not need this, but I wanted to offer it as an option should you run into any issues.

Name this profile and generate.

The name you provide will be used to identify the profile in the portal.

Profile Name: | CloudTest Dev Profile|

Type: **iOS Development**

App ID: **CloudTest (▮▮▮▮▮▮▮▮▮▮m.mollymaskrey.cloudtest)**

Certificates: **1 Included**

Devices: **1 Included**

Figure 11-35. If testing on an actual device, you'll want to have a provisioning profile so you have the correct entitlements on your iPhone or iPad

At this point, back in the Capabilities section of Xcode, you should now be able to click the CloudKit Dashboard button (Figure 11-36).

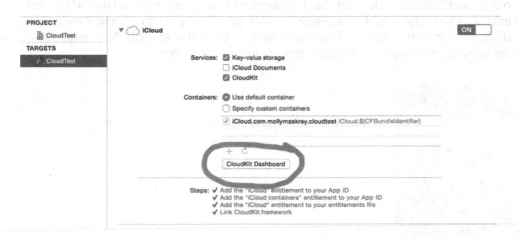

Figure 11-36. Click on the CloudKit Dashboard button to get to the dashboard from Xcode

You should be taken to the iCloud dashboard and the CloudKit section of the dashboard for your app (Figure 11-37). At first, after working in Xcode and the developer portal, the options seem kind of daunting, especially those on the left-hand side. As with any tool, you'll likely find yourself using just a few common options.

Figure 11-37. We should now be able to access the iCloud dashboard and our app's CloudKit section

Saving Data to iCloud Using CloudKit

We have constructed our database and now want to do something with it. I think this is one of those chicken and egg moments. Do we create some "dummy" data and then read it, or do we start by saving data from our app to the cloud? Decisions, decisions.

I opted, this time, for the latter approach, so we'll create a very simple record item and store it to our iCloud database. But first, back at the dashboard, let's click on the '+' at the top and add our inventory record type (Figure 11-38). We'll use the same basic idea as a pricelist database, though here I called it `Inventory`. Since CloudKit is essentially a database in itself, we can use it to manage our inventory and not just a static price list.

Figure 11-38. Start by creating our first record type, Inventory

I designed my record with four fields: the itemName, the itemNumber (a stock number), the itemPrice, and the itemQuantity (how many are in stock; Figure 11-39). For the quantity and price I just went with integers to speed things along. Be sure to click on Save.

Figure 11-39. Add the fields you need to your record format

First, we have to import the CloudKit framework. Note that we aren't subscribing to any delegate protocols. I created static references to our CKContainer and the public database in that container. I also instantiated a record type variable of our Inventory class (Listing 11-7).

Listing 11-7. Our Initial View Controller Code to Save Some Data to Our iCloud Database

```
//
//  ViewController.swift
//  CloudTest
//
//  Created by Molly Maskrey on 4/6/16.
//  Copyright © 2016 Molly Maskrey. All rights reserved.
//

import UIKit
import CloudKit

class ViewController: UIViewController {

    let container = CKContainer.defaultContainer()
    var record = CKRecord(recordType: "Inventory")
    let publicDB = CKContainer.defaultContainer().publicCloudDatabase
```

```
override func viewDidLoad() {
    super.viewDidLoad()
    // Do any additional setup after loading the view, typically from a nib.

    addRecord()
}

//
//  Add records to our iCloud database using the CloudKit framework
func addRecord() {
    record.setValue("1001", forKey: "ItemNumber")
    record.setValue("iPhone 6 Case - Black", forKey: "ItemName")
    record.setValue(20, forKey: "ItemPrice")
    record.setValue(100, forKey: "ItemQuantity")

    publicDB.saveRecord(record) { (savedRecord, error) -> Void in
        if error == nil {
            print("record saved to iCloud database using CloudKit")
        } else {
            print(error)
            return
        }
    }
}

override func didReceiveMemoryWarning() {
    super.didReceiveMemoryWarning()
    // Dispose of any resources that can be recreated.
}

}
```

> **Note** A database is the next level down in the CloudKit hierarchy, below container. In each
> container, by default, there exists a public and a private database. Just as it sounds, public data is
> available to everyone, but the private database is only accessible to the user. And this does mean
> user. As the developer of the app, you do not have access to any user's private database. The
> privacy is maintained via the iCloud user credentials each user sets up on their device.

I created the convenience function addRecord() using the CloudKit framework to localize
the code necessary to add a record to the database here in the app (Listing 11-8). First, set
the values of each of the four fields, then call the asynchronous saveRecord function of the
CKRecord class. In the viewDidLoad() method, call the convenience function.

Listing 11-8. The addRecord() Convenience Function Adds a Single Record of Data to Our Database

```
//
  // Add records to our iCloud database using the CloudKit framework
  func addRecord() {
      record.setValue("1001", forKey: "ItemNumber")
      record.setValue("iPhone 6 Case - Black", forKey: "ItemName")
      record.setValue(20, forKey: "ItemPrice")
      record.setValue(100, forKey: "ItemQuantity")

      publicDB.saveRecord(record) { (savedRecord, error) -> Void in
          if error == nil {
              print("record saved to iCloud database using CloudKit")
          } else {
          print(error)
          return
          }
      }
  }
```

If you run this, guess what? It probably doesn't work, and you get the error message shown in Figure 11-40. This is telling you that you have not yet set up your iCloud account on your simulator, which really means you haven't entered your user ID and password to access iCloud.

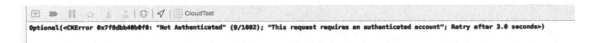

Figure 11-40. You may see this error if you haven't set up your iCloud account on the simulator

In the simulator, go to Settings and iCloud to enter your iCloud user ID and password. Since we've set up everything on our iCloud dashboard, this should work without a problem (Figure 11-41).

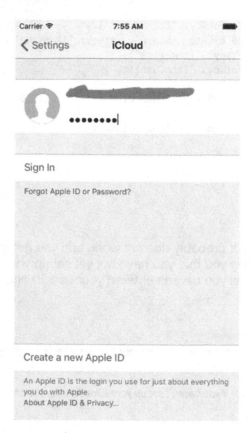

Figure 11-41. *Enter your iCloud account credentials on the simulator you are using*

After accepting the Terms and Conditions from Apple, your iCloud account should be accessible on the simulator (Figure 11-42).

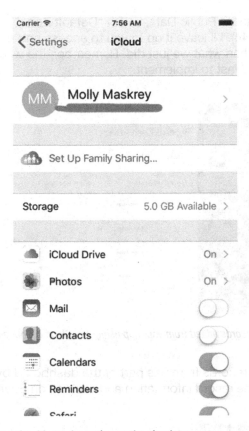

Figure 11-42. Your iCloud account should now be active on the simulator

Try running the code again, and you should now see the successful completion message printed on the console from the addRecord() function (Figure 11-43).

Figure 11-43. We should now have everything working correctly

I can totally hear you saying, "But how do I know it worked?" Well, we could write the other side of the app, something to read and display data, but would that really convince you? I mean, there could be some local buffering that we write to and then read back from, but the data record never makes its way to the server. So instead, let's go back to the iCloud dashboard and look at your actual record.

Back on the dashboard, under Public Data, select "Default Zone"; you should see the record we just added (Figure 11-44). I'll leave it up to you to access and use the private database, but it's really no different than what we just did. Remember, the whole idea of using CloudKit is to make things easy and fast to implement.

Figure 11-44. *You can see any records added from your app using the iCloud dashboard*

What's more, we can add records from this part of the dashboard by clicking the '+' button at the top, then entering the record information and clicking on Save (Figure 11-45).

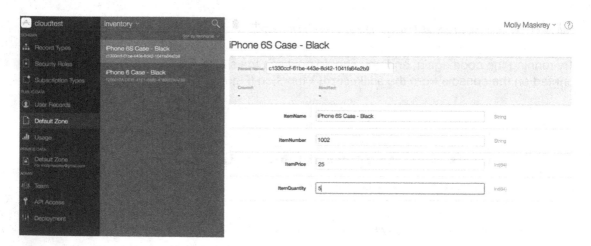

Figure 11-45. *The iCloud dashboard allows us to enter actual record data as well*

Reading Data from iCloud Using CloudKit

For this example, we'll use the private database and enter our initial record into it from the iCloud dashboard. Under the Private Data section, select "Default Zone" and enter a record, then click Save (Figure 11-46). Make a note of the record name ef0fe9e7-bb50-441e-a8f5-8efc257271e4 at the top, as we'll use this in our code. Each record name is generated automatically by the portal, and you must locate your code to enter it into your source file.

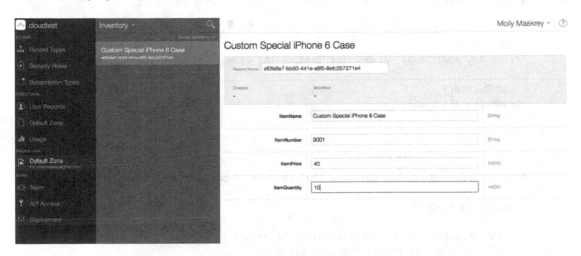

Figure 11-46. Add a record to the private database Default Zone

> **Note**   Zones in CloudKit allow you to segregate private databases into areas of convenience using the CKRecordZone class. Zones are only for private databases and not allowed in the public database.

Modify the code in the ViewController.swift file to that shown in Listing 11-9, adding the readPrivateRecord() function call using the explicit record name from the iCloud dashboard. Comment out the call to addRecord(), but add the call to readPrivateRecord() and execute the app.

Listing 11-9. Modified ViewController.swift File to Support Reading from Our Private Database

```
//
//  ViewController.swift
//  CloudTest
//
//  Created by Molly Maskrey on 4/6/16.
//  Copyright © 2016 Molly Maskrey. All rights reserved.
//

import UIKit
import CloudKit
```

```
class ViewController: UIViewController {

    let container = CKContainer.defaultContainer()
    var record = CKRecord(recordType: "Inventory")
    let publicDB = CKContainer.defaultContainer().publicCloudDatabase

    let privateDB = CKContainer.defaultContainer().privateCloudDatabase      // to read,
we'll us a private DB

    override func viewDidLoad() {
        super.viewDidLoad()
        // Do any additional setup after loading the view, typically from a nib.

//        addRecord()
        readPrivateRecord()

    }

    //
    // Read record from private database that we entered by using the iCloud dashboard
    //
    func readPrivateRecord() {

        privateDB.fetchRecordWithID(CKRecordID(recordName: "ef0fe9e7-bb50-441e-a8f5-
8efc257271e4"), completionHandler: {record, error in
            if error == nil {
                print(record)
            } else {
                print(error)
            }

        })
    }

    //
    //  Add records to our iCloud database using the CloudKit framework
    func addRecord() {
        record.setValue("1001", forKey: "ItemNumber")
        record.setValue("iPhone 6 Case - Black", forKey: "ItemName")
        record.setValue(20, forKey: "ItemPrice")
        record.setValue(100, forKey: "ItemQuantity")

        publicDB.saveRecord(record) { (savedRecord, error) -> Void in
            if error == nil {
                print("record saved to iCloud database using CloudKit")
            } else {
            print(error)
            return
            }
        }
    }
```

```
        override func didReceiveMemoryWarning() {
            super.didReceiveMemoryWarning()
            // Dispose of any resources that can be recreated.
        }
    }
}
```

When the app completes, you should see the record data in the console log (Figure 11-47).

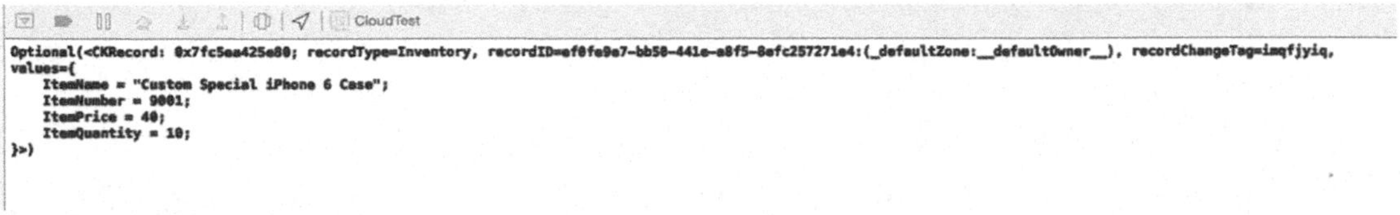

Figure 11-47. *We can see that the app correctly read and displayed the data record we entered using the iCloud dashboard*

CloudKit Summary

In this section we talked about CloudKit and its advantages for setting up a quick and easy web-service system when all we plan to use are Apple devices and the iCloud server. We set up our host side using all Apple tools and created an app to read from and write to both the private and public databases. In our read example, we would not know the exact record name, as that is automatically generated in iCloud, so that example was really just for show. The way we most likely would do this would be to either read all the records in the database if there were not too many of them, or to use NSPredicate and do predicate searches for particular item keywords. The choice really comes down to what you are trying to do and what your needs are for your project.

Summary

In this chapter we covered two types of methods for accessing web services. Most likely, until the CloudKit functionality broadens and, at a minimum, allows access to other types of mobile devices, the usefulness of CloudKit will be very limited.

On the other hand, the complexities of setting up your own web server and programming in HTML, CSS, PHP, MySQL, and potentially other languages will limit your ability to create highly flexible solutions for your project unless you have a diverse, well-skilled team or have the ability to subcontract those services to other contract suppliers.

Chapter 12

Testing

No matter your position, background, education, experience, whatever, we all test our code at some point as we develop our projects (Figure 12-1). You could, at a rudimentary level, consider the build process and even the automatic error detection in Xcode as a form of testing. Long ago, shortly after the invention of the wheel, coding was nothing more than flipping switches on a computer console, hitting a button to enter the instruction, and eventually running the program. Pressing the Run button was the only testing possible. The paradigm shifts in recent years have put testing front and center as we proceed through code development sprints.

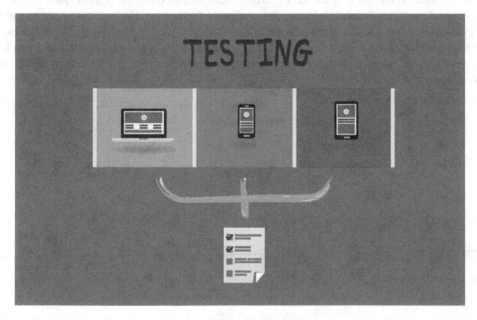

Figure 12-1. We test our apps from before we write a line of Swift until long after we've begun our next assignment

© Molly K. Maskrey 2016
M.K. Maskrey, *App Development Recipes for iOS and watchOS*, DOI 10.1007/978-1-4842-1820-4_12

In this chapter I'll focus on three types of testing. The first two types, Unit and User Interface testing, are integrated into Xcode and are added in when you initially create your project if you've selected them in the appropriate dialog. These are tests managed by you, the iOS software engineer. You create Unit Tests first, knowing what is and is not acceptable behavior in your code. By setting up these behaviors as tests before you code, it's easy to test against your requirements as you code. That's really the point. Don't think of these Unit Tests as something we add on to a project to check off a box somewhere; imagine them as a slightly different way to write the software project requirements. Even the most loosely based development houses manage their requirements in some manner. Using Unit Tests not only provides a convenient centralized spot to do so, but because of their tight integration with Xcode, you get requirements verification basically for free.

User Interface Testing took a leap forward in the summer of 2015 when it was announced at the Apple World Wide Developer Conference that UI Testing was being expanded and tightly integrated into Xcode 7, including recording, so you could now set up a UI sequence as well as have updated reporting. Like Unit Tests, which you may have seen previously, XCTest is the testing framework upon which UI Testing is based. It was introduced in Xcode 5 as the replacement for OCUnit, which was one of the very first testing frameworks designed for Objective-C. In order to actually control UI elements, UI Testing also relies on the Accessibility framework. One thing of note: UI Testing requires iOS 9 or higher to use.

Lastly, we'll address beta testing; that is, giving our app to people to see if it breaks out in the real world, as well as testing every other aspect of how it looks and functions. I love giving my app to my friends to try out (Figure 12-2). While most developers think strangers might offer a more unbiased opinion, I've often found the opposite to be true. Because strangers have no vested interest in your project, they can be a little overly critical. In fact, many will harbor their own bias and criticize your work unnecessarily. I love getting first-pass feedback from friends. Xcode and iTunes Connect are now integrated with TestFlight to allow for much more easily managed testing of your projects.

Figure 12-2. Having a group of friends to take a first look at your project can get you some honest feedback you might not otherwise receive, while maintaining a less adversarial experience

Because testing itself—how it is implemented in conjunction with Xcode—and an individual organization's test philosophies differ widely and are moving targets, I'm going to focus on just the basics of getting started and understanding what's going on. As you develop your skills, as you become more integrated with your development team, and even as the tools themselves become easier to use, you'll find your own way of doing things that works best no matter where you end up practicing your skills.

Unit Testing

Throughout the short history of software development—well, let's call it recent history—testing has evolved from just seeing if it works without causing something to break or explode to planning and writing tests long before coding begins. At about the middle of this historical timeline we began using a lot of C preprocessing and pragma statements, such as #if, #endif, #elseif, and so on, to include code within our code so as to test various functions and boundary conditions and anything else we could think of.

The problem, of course, was that in addition to this strategy of creating a software management nightmare with bits and pieces spread throughout every file in a project, we were also doing testing after the fact. We created tests for the code we developed or were developing. Inherently, what this meant was that we created our tests for our work and not for the project as it was intended to be. We weren't testing the requirements directly; we were testing "how" we implemented those requirements.

Problem

You've heard of Unit Testing but aren't quite sure what it is or how it is different from other types of testing.

Solution

Essentially, we take the smallest parts of an application, called units, and test them individually. A unit is considered to be the smallest piece of code that we can test. That's it. Most often a unit can be mapped to a function or method in your app. When a function or method is too large, maybe taking up several screens worth of real estate, and the testing of that as a unit appears overly complex, you should probably break it up into smaller pieces anyway. Break up the larger task or function into manageable units of work. Really, this is pretty much Development 101—keep things simple and easy to manage from the start.

Some key elements of a good Unit Test would be having the ability to be automated, to not be order dependent, to run in memory and not require database or web access, to be repeatable, and to be fast. There are certainly many others, but these are some of the key aspects and the ones that Xcode can help us with the most.

In both Xcode and iOS development—this is even true for Mac development, which we won't cover here—Unit Tests run as separate targets. This means that we have to add Unit Testing specifically to our project as its own target. This addresses a number of our goals for good Unit Tests. As standalone targets, our testing will most likely be repeatable. They're not dependent on something happening elsewhere to run properly. Since they are targets, they run in memory, and as long as we don't integrate database or remote access into them, leaving that to our primary app, we can keep our tests in memory and generally fast.

There are two ways we add testing to our project: from the start or after the fact. First, let's create a project with Unit Testing built in from the very beginning.

Create a new Xcode project as a single view application (Figure 12-3).

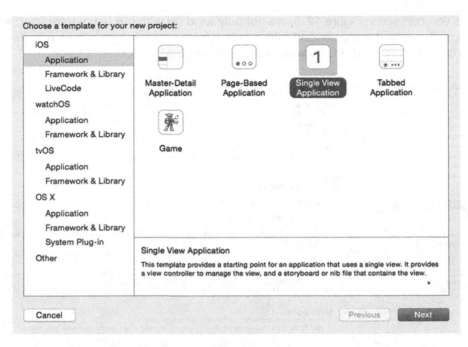

Figure 12-3. Start by creating a simple single view iOS application

In the very next step, add Unit Testing by selecting the "Include Unit Tests" checkbox (Figure 12-4).

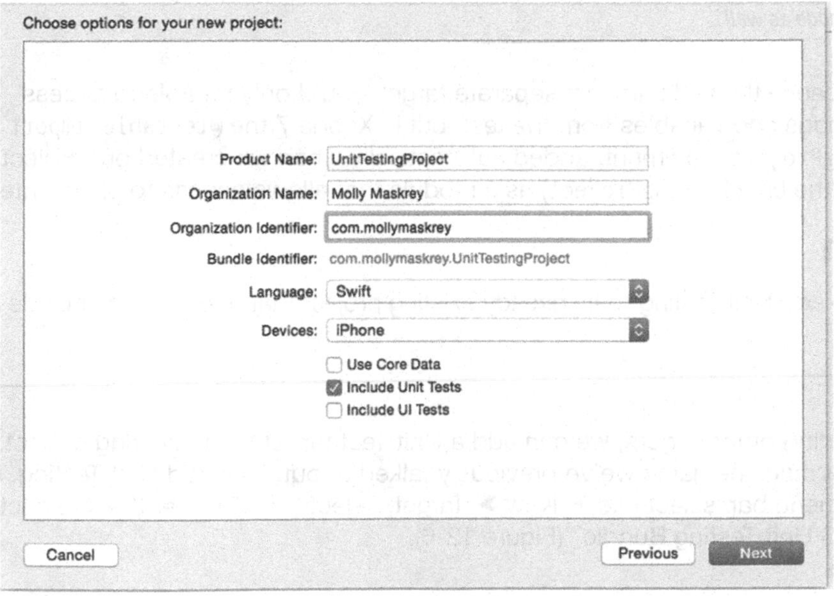

Figure 12-4. To include the Unit Test target, select the "Include Unit Tests" checkbox and complete the project creation

Finally, as you can see in Figure 12-5, we not only wind up with our usual templated single view app, but we also have a second folder called UnitTestingProjectTests with its own template code and info.plist, as well as the UnitTestingProjectTests target.

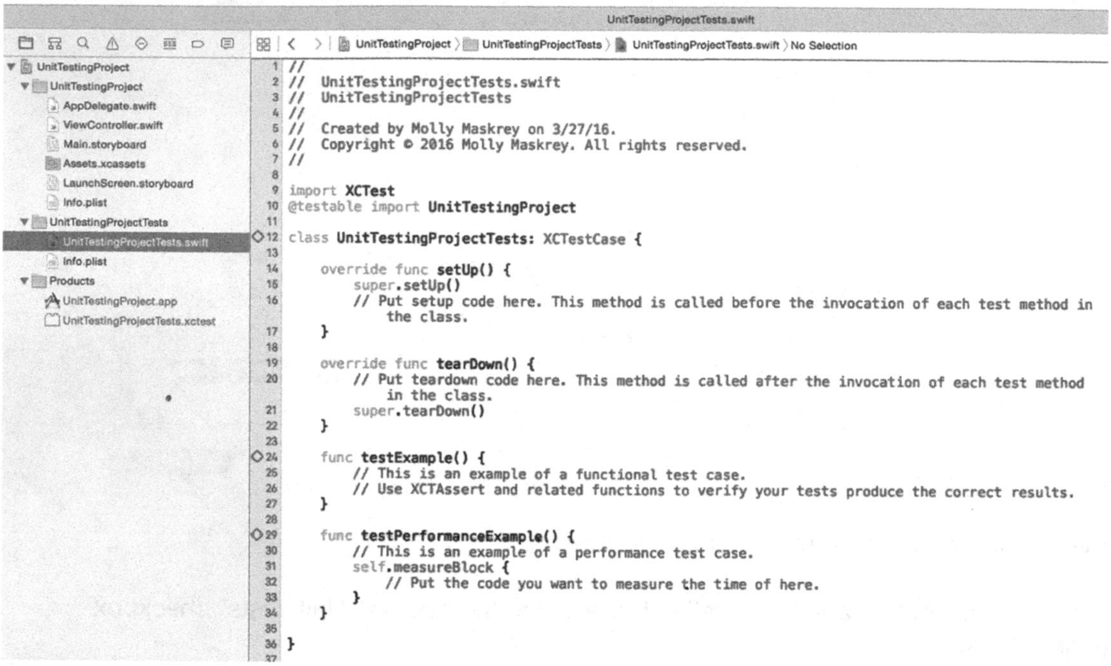

Figure 12-5. In addition to our normal single view iOS application Swift template, we get our Unit Test target and template test code as well

Usually, because the tests are in a separate target, you'd only be able to access public methods and variables from the test, but in Xcode 7 the @testable import UnitTestingProject statement, added automatically when we created our project, adds our whole app (the UnitTestingProject) as a module that allows access to all the internal parts.

Problem

You need to add Unit Testing to an already existing project that does not yet include any testing.

Solution

Just like adding other targets, we can add a Unit Test target to an existing project. Starting with our slot machine game we've previously talked about, let's add Unit Testing. From the Xcode menu bar, select File ➤ New ➤ Target, select "Test" under the iOS section, and choose "iOS Unit Testing Bundle" (Figure 12-6).

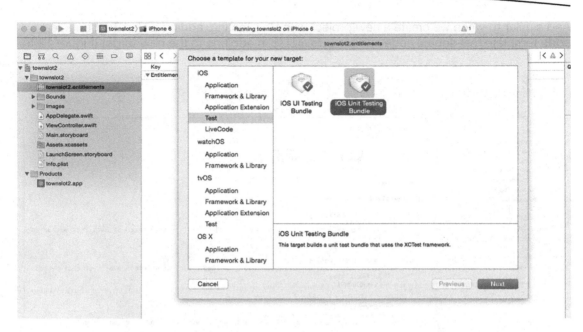

Figure 12-6. *To include Unit Testing in an existing app, add the iOS Unit Testing Bundle as a target to your project*

Verify the target options are correct for what you're trying to do (Figure 12-7) and create the target. In the dialog note the "Project:" and "Target to be Tested:" drop-down menus. If your project already has multiple targets, as it might when working with a WatchKit app, make sure you set the correct target for the Unit Test you're trying to add.

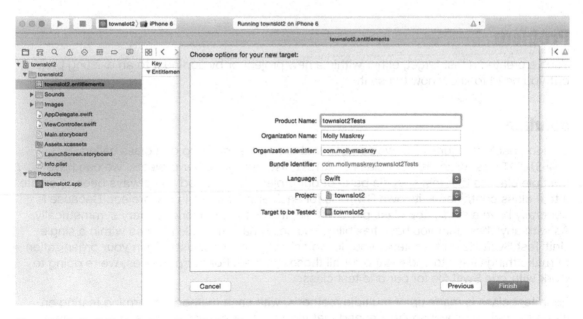

Figure 12-7. *Verify the new target's project settings*

And similar to when we create a new project with Unit Testing, adding a Unit Test bundle adds template test source code and an `info.plist` in addition to the new target (Figure 12-8).

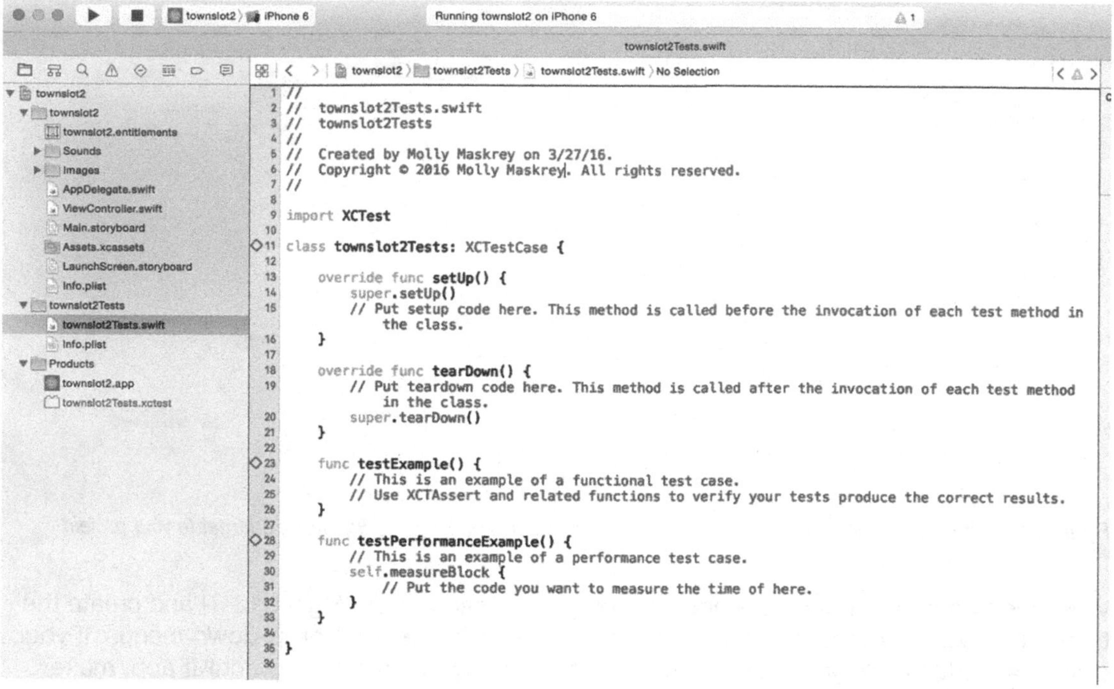

Figure 12-8. When adding a test target to an existing project, we also get template code to go with it

Problem

You've created a test target, either within a new project or by adding it to an existing project, but you need to know how to use it.

Solution

Looking back at Figure 12-8, we can see that our test is made up of a class called TownSlot2Tests, which is a subclass of XCTestCase. As with other projects, we can have multiple classes that test specific parts of our project. My method has always been to create a test class contained in its own Swift file for each app Swift file in my project. Because I generally have a single app class per Swift file, things tend to work out very symmetrically. As with anywhere that you have flexibility, you could have multiple classes within a single Unit Test Swift file, but whatever you do, you should try for consistency in your organization to make things easy to understand for all those involved. For our purposes, we're going to work with one Swift file for our one test class.

Each test class is made up of multiple methods, with each method performing testing on a unit of work, however you've defined that term for your project. The test method names all start with the word "test" so that the code that runs the tests within Xcode knows how to find them. This does not mean that every method in a test class has to start with "test," as you could have supporting methods that are used by different test methods, such as a conversion routine or formatter or any other generic software tool. Those will not be run automatically, nor should they.

Each test method is bracketed by the setUp() and tearDown() methods, so in the code shown in Listing 12-1, to run whatever testing we put into the testExample() method, first the setUp() method will execute, followed by the testExample(), and finally tearDown().

Listing 12-1. Unit Test Class and Methods

```
class UnitTestingProjectTests: XCTestCase {

    override func setUp() {
        super.setUp()
        // Put setup code here. This method is called before the invocation of each test
        method in the class.
    }

    override func tearDown() {
        // Put teardown code here. This method is called after the invocation of each test
        method in the class.
        super.tearDown()
    }

    func testExample() {
        // This is an example of a functional test case.
        // Use XCTAssert and related functions to verify your tests produce the correct
        results.
    }

    func testPerformanceExample() {
        // This is an example of a performance test case.
        self.measureBlock {
            // Put the code you want to measure the time of here.
        }
    }

}
```

Note also that in addition to our testExample() method, which we'll use as a template for functional testing, we also have testPerformanceExample() to serve for measuring throughput as part of our unit tests. The testExample() method is used as a template for creating other tests; that is, we don't generally have an actual testExample() method, though nothing prevents us from doing so. Because they run before and after each test method, setUp() and tearDown() are where you might set up initialization at the start or any other cleanup work that needs to be accomplished after each test runs.

Because our project uses a single view template, and our main—and really, our only—class is the ViewController, we'd likely wind up testing our units of work in that file. Since we're dealing with very small sample programs, these single view/single file demo apps are pretty common. However, with serious application projects we normally have many more classes that are specialized to our needs. We might have several types of classes that relate to our data. For example, if we had an app that dealt with cars, we might have a whole class specific to cars. It wouldn't likely have anything to do with how we visualize the data, just with how we manage cars in our app. This stems from the MVC, or model-view-controller, paradigm central to iOS apps (Figure 12-9).

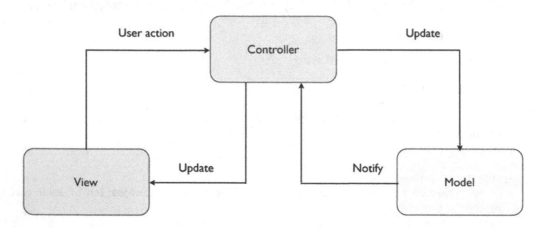

Figure 12-9. *iOS apps follow the standard MVC paradigm where the data and its methods are separate from how the user sees the data— typically through the ViewController (view + controller)*

We're going to look at how to use Unit Testing within the `ViewController` class in a moment, as well as the problems you're likely to encounter, but first let's see how we should probably organize things. First, we'll add a Cocoa Touch class to our project from the Xcode pull-down: File ➤ New ➤ File, then in iOS Source select "Cocoa Touch Class" and create a subclass of NSObject. Add a very simple method as shown in Listing 12-2; because the purpose of this is to represent our data, I've called mine `MyDataClass`.

Listing 12-2. MyDataClass for Separating Data from Our ViewController

```
//  MyDataClass.swift
//  UnitTestProject
//
//  Created by Molly Maskrey on 3/27/16.
//  Copyright © 2016 Molly Maskrey. All rights reserved.
//

import UIKit

public class MyDataClass: NSObject {

    public func divideTwoNumbers (a:Int, b:Int) -> Int {
        return (a/b)
    }
}
```

I've defined my class and the single method as public so our Unit Test bundle can see it, because this is a separate, supporting class. The method only does one thing: it divides two numbers, or integers, and returns the result. In our UnitTestProjectTest.swift file, I've removed the example methods and added the code seen in Listing 12-3.

Listing 12-3. Our Unit Test for the DivideTwoNumbers Method in Our Newly Created MyDataClass

```
//
//  UnitTestProjectTests.swift
//  UnitTestProjectTests
//
//  Copyright © 2016 Molly Maskrey. All rights reserved.
//

import XCTest
@testable import UnitTestProject

class UnitTestProjectTests: XCTestCase {

    var dataClass : MyDataClass!

    override func setUp() {
        super.setUp()
        // Put setup code here. This method is called before the invocation of each test
        method in the class.
         dataClass = MyDataClass()
    }

    override func tearDown() {
        // Put teardown code here. This method is called after the invocation of each test
        method in the class.
        super.tearDown()
    }

    func testDivide() {
        // This is an example of a functional test case.
        // Use XCTAssert and related functions to verify your tests produce the correct results.

        let c = dataClass.divideTwoNumbers(1,b: 1)

        XCTAssert(c == 1)
    }

}
```

The three things to note are the line var dataClass : MyDataClass!, which adds a variable in our test so we can reference the data class. Second, in our setUp() method, the line dataClass = MyDataClass() is where we instantiate the variable for our data class. Finally the testDivide() method is where we actually test that single unit of work—the dividing of two numbers.

The test is very simple. We set c to be the value of dividing 1 by 1, so we would assert that we should get 1 back. The XCTAssert(c == 1) tests the condition c == 1, and if true this test passes. If we run it by selecting and holding down the Run button, then selecting "Test" (Figure 12-10), we see the test passes by looking at the results in Xcode's Test Navigator. You get to that by selecting the Test Navigator icon—the fifth icon right of the Project Navigator icon. Note the green check marks.

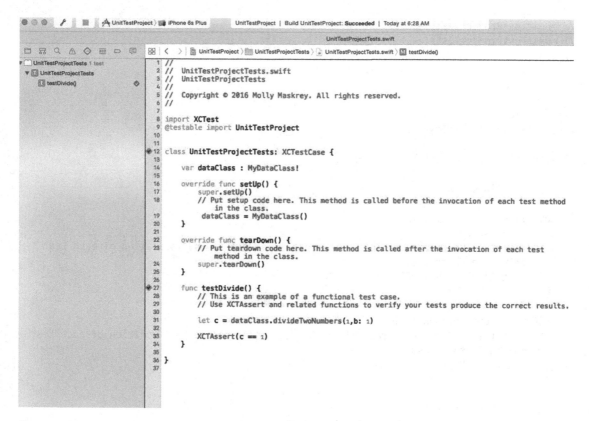

Figure 12-10. We can see that our first Unit Test passed in the Xcode Test Navigator

Let's make a change to the method divideTwoNumbers(a,b) in the UnitTestProjecttests. swift file so that it returns a zero, then let's look at the results (Listing 12-4).

Listing 12-4. Modify Our Method So It Always Returns a Zero

```
// MyDataClass.swift
// UnitTestProject
//
// Created by Molly Maskrey on 3/27/16.
// Copyright © 2016 Molly Maskrey. All rights reserved.
//
```

```
import UIKit

public class MyDataClass: NSObject {

    public func divideTwoNumbers (a:Int, b:Int) -> Int {

//          return (a/b)
    return(0)


    }
}
```

Running the Unit Test, we see that our test, the assertion that the value should be 1, fails
(Figure 12-11).

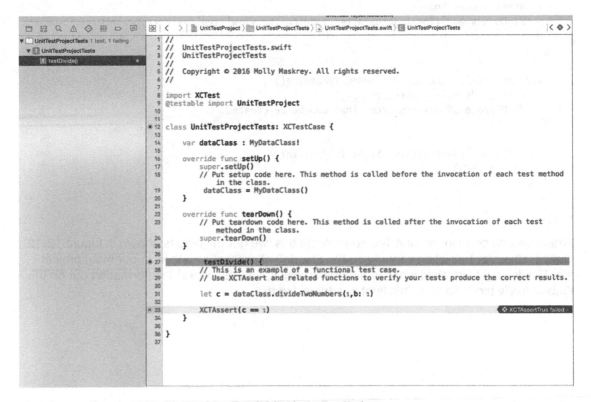

Figure 12-11. *If the assertion fails, we see where it failed in the Test Navigator*

So, that's how it works with our separate MyDataClass Swift file. What often happens, and I'll
admit that this caught me as well, is trying something like this in the UnitTestProjecttests.
swift file (Listing 12-5).

Listing 12-5. Adding a Function to Your Simple ViewController in a Single View iOS Project Like This and Trying to Test It

```
//
//  ViewController.swift
//  UnitTestProject
//
//  Created by Molly Maskrey on 3/27/16.
//  Copyright © 2016 Molly Maskrey. All rights reserved.
//

import UIKit

public class MyViewController: UIViewController {

    override public func viewDidLoad() {
        super.viewDidLoad()
        // Do any additional setup after loading the view, typically from a nib.

    }

    override public func didReceiveMemoryWarning() {
        super.didReceiveMemoryWarning()
        // Dispose of any resources that can be re-created.
    }

     func divideTwoNumbers(a: Int, b: Int) -> Int {
        return (a/b)
    }

}
```

When we add code in the Unit Test to evaluate this, we get the results shown in Figure 12-12. Our testDivide() function cannot see the divideTwoNumbers() method in our main project file. This is very frustrating when you come across it, and the available information out on the Web actually tends to be a little light in addressing this.

```
1   //
2   //   UnitTestProjectTests.swift
3   //   UnitTestProjectTests
4   //
5   //   Copyright © 2016 Molly Maskrey. All rights reserved.
6   //
7
8   import XCTest
9   @testable import UnitTestProject
10
11
12  class UnitTestProjectTests: XCTestCase {
13
14
15      override func setUp() {
16          super.setUp()
17          // Put setup code here. This method is called before the invocation of each test method
                 in the class.
18      }
19
20      override func tearDown() {
21          // Put teardown code here. This method is called after the invocation of each test
                 method in the class.
22          super.tearDown()
23      }
24
25      func testDivide() {
26          // This is an example of a functional test case.
27          // Use XCTAssert and related functions to verify your tests produce the correct results.
28
29          let c = divideTwoNumbers(1,b: 1)          ● Use of unresolved identifier 'divideTwoNumbers'
30
31          XCTAssert(c == 1)
32      }
33
34  }
35
```

Figure 12-12. Even doing things the way Apple says they should work, we get the unresolved identifier error

Because our `MyViewController` class is based on the `UIViewController` parent class, we can extend the parent class in this case to include our method in the `UnitTestProjecttests.swift` file, as shown in Listing 12-6.

Listing 12-6. Extending the UIViewController Parent Class to Include Our New Function

```
extension UIViewController {
    public func divideTwoNumbers (a:Int, b:Int) -> Int {
        return (a/b)
    }
}
```

In Listing 12-7 you can see that I modified my `MyViewController` class to override the extension method and make sure it is public. Although the `@testable` statement in the `UnitTestProjecttests.swift` file is supposed to work, at the time of this writing many people are finding that it is still a bit inconsistent in that sometimes Xcode will report missing methods when the methods are clearly present.

Listing 12-7. Modifying the Function in Our MyViewController Class

```
//   ViewController.swift
//   UnitTestProject
//
//   Created by Molly Maskrey on 3/27/16.
//   Copyright © 2016 Molly Maskrey. All rights reserved.
//
```

```
import UIKit

extension UIViewController {
    public func divideTwoNumbers (a:Int, b:Int) -> Int {
        return (a/b)
    }
}

public class MyViewController: UIViewController {

    override public func viewDidLoad() {
        super.viewDidLoad()
        // Do any additional setup after loading the view, typically from a nib.

    }

    override public func didReceiveMemoryWarning() {
        super.didReceiveMemoryWarning()
        // Dispose of any resources that can be re-created.
    }

    override public func divideTwoNumbers(a: Int, b: Int) -> Int {
        return (a/b)
    }

}
```

Also, make sure to set the Defines Module parameter, which maintains your framework's umbrella header, in the Packaging section to YES. Do this in the build settings for the app target, *not* the test target (Figure 12-13).

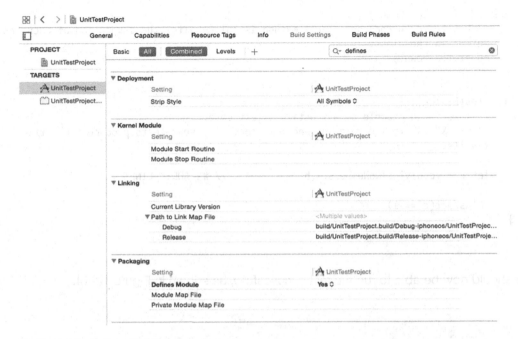

Figure 12-13. Set the Defines Module parameter to Yes

Finally, in the `UnitTestProjectTests.swift` file add the three lines as shown in Listing 12-8.

Listing 12-8. Final Working Version of Our Test for the ViewController Function

```
//  UnitTestProjectTests.swift
//  UnitTestProjectTests
//
//  Copyright © 2016 Molly Maskrey. All rights reserved.
//

import XCTest
@testable import UnitTestProject

class UnitTestProjectTests: XCTestCase {

    var vc : MyViewController!        // #1 ADDED LINE

    override func setUp() {
        super.setUp()
        // Put setup code here. This method is called before the invocation of each test
        method in the class.

        vc = MyViewController()      // #2 ADDED LINE
    }
```

```
override func tearDown() {
    // Put teardown code here. This method is called after the invocation of each test
    method in the class.
    super.tearDown()
}

func testDivide() {
    // This is an example of a functional test case.
    // Use XCTAssert and related functions to verify your tests produce the correct
    results.

    let c = vc.divideTwoNumbers(1,b: 1)              // #3 ADDED LINE

    XCTAssert(c == 1)
}

}
```

You should now be able to run the test successfully, as shown in Figure 12-14.

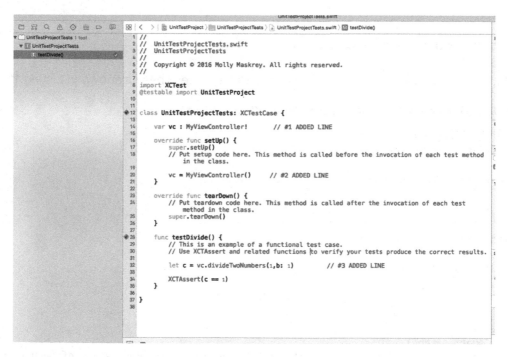

Figure 12-14. Our successful testing of a method within the UIViewController's subclass

Unit Testing Summary

We covered the basic concepts for Unit Testing and the use of XCTAssert(expr), which is the most common statement. However, there are more statements available that you're likely to find useful for more specialized testing.

XCTAssertTrue(expr) is equivalent to XCTAssert but may be a little more obvious in your code. It generates a failure when the assertion is false.

XCTAssertFalse(expr) generates a failure when the assertion is true.

XCTAssertEqualObjects(a, b, format...) generates a failure when {a == b} is false.

XCTAssertEqualWithAccuracy(a, b, accuracy) generates a failure when a1 is not equal to a2 within + or - accuracy. This test is for scalars such as floats and doubles, where small differences could make these items not exactly equal, but works for all numbers.

XCTFail generates a failure unconditionally.

Even more exist for your use and can be found at developer.apple.com, but I've found these work for me most of the time.

User Interface Testing

Problem

Your app has several user interface elements—buttons, labels, text fields, and so on—that need testing, and you cannot see how Unit Testing helps with that.

Solution

User Interface (UI) Testing provides you with the ability to locate and interact with UI elements and validate properties and state. You can also use recording, which will help to automate your test process, as well as integration into Xcode 7 test reports so you can see pass and fail indications.

UI Test contains two core technologies: XCTest, Xcode's testing framework that we covered in the last section on unit testing, and Accessibility, which offers rich semantic data about the UI that XCTest can use to interact with the interface.

UI Test Project from Scratch

To use UI Testing you need iOS 9 or higher for your app project. Let's work through a simple project to get a feel for UI Test.

Start by creating a new single view application project: File ➤ New ➤ Project (Figure 12-15).

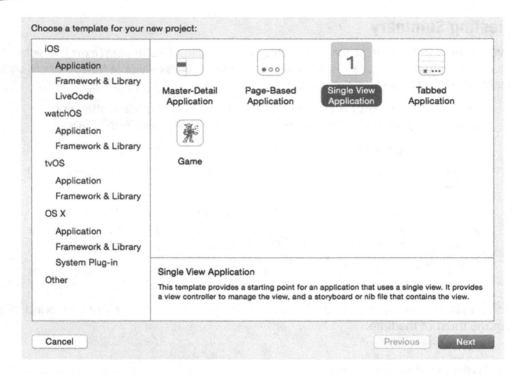

Figure 12-15. Create a single view application project

Name it whatever you'd like, but make sure to check "Include UI Tests" (Figure 12-16).

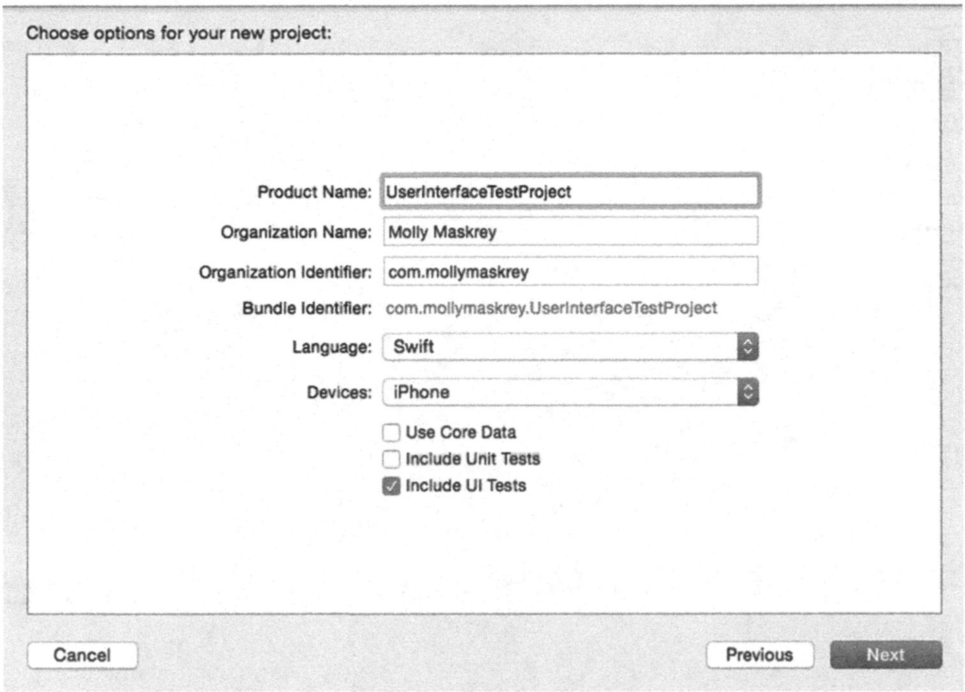

Choose options for your new project:

Product Name:	UserInterfaceTestProject
Organization Name:	Molly Maskrey
Organization Identifier:	com.mollymaskrey
Bundle Identifier:	com.mollymaskrey.UserInterfaceTestProject
Language:	Swift
Devices:	iPhone

☐ Use Core Data
☐ Include Unit Tests
☑ Include UI Tests

Cancel   Previous   Next

Figure 12-16. Name your project and include UI Tests

The first thing I did was create the storyboards (Figure 12-17). Select the view controller, then at the top menu bar choose the following: Editor ➤ Embed in ➤ Navigation Controller. This sets up the navigation controller structure so that the Back button will be automatically available when we add additional view controllers.

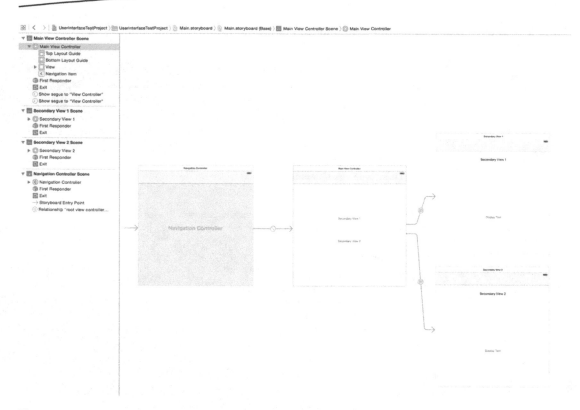

Figure 12-17. Create the main storyboard shown here

Then, add two additional view controllers by dragging and dropping them from the object menu (Figure 12-18). I chose to label my main view controller "Main View Controller" and the additional two view controllers "Secondary View 1" and "Secondary View 2."

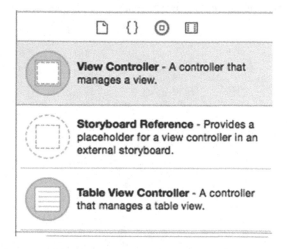

Figure 12-18. From the object menu, add two additional view controllers to the main storyboard

Add two buttons to the main view controller from the object menu, then control-drag from each button to one of the view controllers, selecting "Show" for the Action Segue type (Figure 12-19).

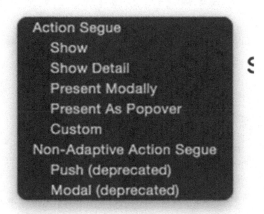

Figure 12-19. Select "Show" for the Action Segue type

On each of the two new view controllers, add a label and a button (Figure 12-20). I called mine showText and displayText, respectively.

Figure 12-20. Add a button and a label to each view controller

Back at the Xcode Organizer, add two new Cocoa Touch classes as subclasses of UIViewController, naming them to relate to the two new view controllers (Figure 12-21). I chose the names SecondaryView1ViewController and SecondaryView2ViewController.

Figure 12-21. Add two new Cocoa Touch class files, one for each view controller

Add an IBOutlet for the label and an IBAction for the button for each associated view controller and add the showText.text = "ALPHA" or showText.text = "BETA" to the action for the first and second controller, respectively. Finally, set the title in the viewDidLoad() method (Figure 12-22). These will be in the SecondaryView1ViewController.swift and SecondaryView2ViewController.swift files. Because we'll be checking the title static text in our test sequence, we'll want to make sure it matches what we test for.

```
//
//  SecondaryView1ViewController.swift
//  UserInterfaceTestProject
//
//  Created by Molly Maskrey on 4/2/16.
//  Copyright © 2016 Molly Maskrey. All rights reserved.
//

import UIKit

class SecondaryView1ViewController: UIViewController {

    @IBOutlet weak var showText: UILabel!
    @IBAction func displayText(sender: AnyObject) {
        showText.text = "ALPHA"
    }


    override func viewDidLoad() {
        super.viewDidLoad()


        // Do any additional setup after loading the view.
        self.title = "Secondary View 1"
    }

    override func didReceiveMemoryWarning() {
        super.didReceiveMemoryWarning()
        // Dispose of any resources that can be recreated.
    }


    /*
    // MARK: - Navigation

    // In a storyboard-based application, you will often want to do a little preparation
        navigation
    override func prepareForSegue(segue: UIStoryboardSegue, sender: AnyObject?) {
        // Get the new view controller using segue.destinationViewController.
        // Pass the selected object to the new view controller.
    }
    */
}
```

Figure 12-22. Adding code to one of the view controllers

Finally, be sure to set the custom class in the Identity Inspector associated with each view controller to the class files we just created and modified (Figure 12-23).

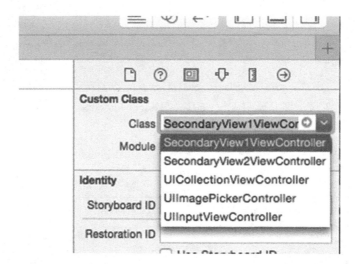

Figure 12-23. Set the custom class of each view controller in the storyboard to the proper Swift file

Connect the outlets and actions from the UI elements on the storyboard to the SecondaryView view controllers by control-dragging as you normally do. When the button is pressed while on one of these view controllers, the text will be displayed in the UILabel. You should now be able to build and run the project, selecting either of the two view controllers from the main screen, then change the label text in either of the individual next-level controllers (Figure 12-24).

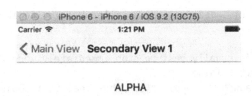

ALPHA

Display Text

Figure 12-24. Build and execute your project on the simulator to verify operation

At this point we have a very basic functioning app with a UI that does something. Looking at our `UserInterfaceTestProjectUITests.swift` file, we see some code has been provided for us already (Listing 12-9).

Listing 12-9. Template UI Test Code

```
//
//  UserInterfaceTestProjectUITests.swift
//  UserInterfaceTestProjectUITests
//
//  Created by Molly Maskrey on 4/2/16.
//  Copyright © 2016 Molly Maskrey. All rights reserved.
//

import XCTest

class UserInterfaceTestProjectUITests: XCTestCase {

    override func setUp() {
        super.setUp()
```

```
    // Put setup code here. This method is called before the invocation of each test
    method in the class.

    // In UI tests it is usually best to stop immediately when a failure occurs.
    continueAfterFailure = false
    // UI tests must launch the application that they test. Doing this in setup will
    make sure it happens for each test method.
    XCUIApplication().launch()

    // In UI tests it's important to set the initial state—such as interface
    orientation—required for your tests before they run. The setUp method is a good
    place to do this.
}

override func tearDown() {
    // Put teardown code here. This method is called after the invocation of each test
    method in the class.
    super.tearDown()
}

func testExample() {
    // Use recording to get started writing UI tests.
    // Use XCTAssert and related functions to verify your tests produce the correct results.
}

}
```

Above the setUp function, add the line `let app = XCUIApplication()` so that we can easily access the application object later in the code. Change the name of the `testExample` function to `testMain` and add the lines shown in Listing 12-10.

Listing 12-10. Modified First Test Case

```
//
//  UserInterfaceTestProjectUITests.swift
//  UserInterfaceTestProjectUITests
//
//  Created by Molly Maskrey on 4/2/16.
//  Copyright © 2016 Molly Maskrey. All rights reserved.
//

import XCTest

class UserInterfaceTestProjectUITests: XCTestCase {

    let app = XCUIApplication()

    override func setUp() {
        super.setUp()

        // Put setup code here. This method is called before the invocation of each test
        method in the class.
```

```
        // In UI tests it is usually best to stop immediately when a failure occurs.
        continueAfterFailure = false
        // UI tests must launch the application that they test. Doing this in setup will
        make sure it happens for each test method.
        XCUIApplication().launch()

        // In UI tests it's important to set the initial state—such as interface
        orientation—required for your tests before they run. The setUp method is a good
        place to do this.
    }

    override func tearDown() {
        // Put teardown code here. This method is called after the invocation of each test
        method in the class.
        super.tearDown()
    }

    func testMain() {
//          // Use recording to get started writing UI tests.
//          // Use XCTAssert and related functions to verify your tests produce the correct
            results.
//
        let mainTitleLabel = app.navigationBars.staticTexts["Main View"]
        XCTAssert(mainTitleLabel.exists)
    }
}
```

However, in the current version of Xcode (7.2.1), when trying to test this build you will most
likely get something like the crash in Figure 12-25.

Figure 12-25. *Trying to test, you're likely to see this exception crash*

To correct this, go to Xcode ➤ Preferences and choose the Locations pane. Change the build location to Custom and Absolute, as shown in Figure 12-26, being sure to click the Advanced button to get these options. Your path settings should fill correctly when making the changes.

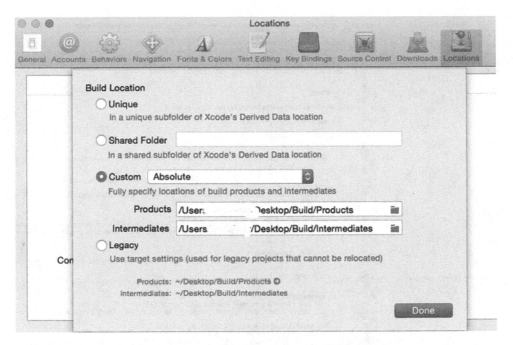

Figure 12-26. Setting the custom build path to Absolute should take care of this exception

Running the test now, you should see it complete successfully (Figure 12-27). What we did here, after creating our convenience constant for the app, was to add the line `let mainTitleLabel = app.navigationBars.staticTexts["Main View"]` in the `testMain` function so as to set a constant to a Nav Bar with the text we expect. Then we do a simple `XCTAssert` to see if it exists, which, of course, it does. What we've done is test our app's main view controller to see if an element exists. We might use this to verify that we are seeing the correct view controller. Since this assert returned `TRUE`, we can continue to do more testing.

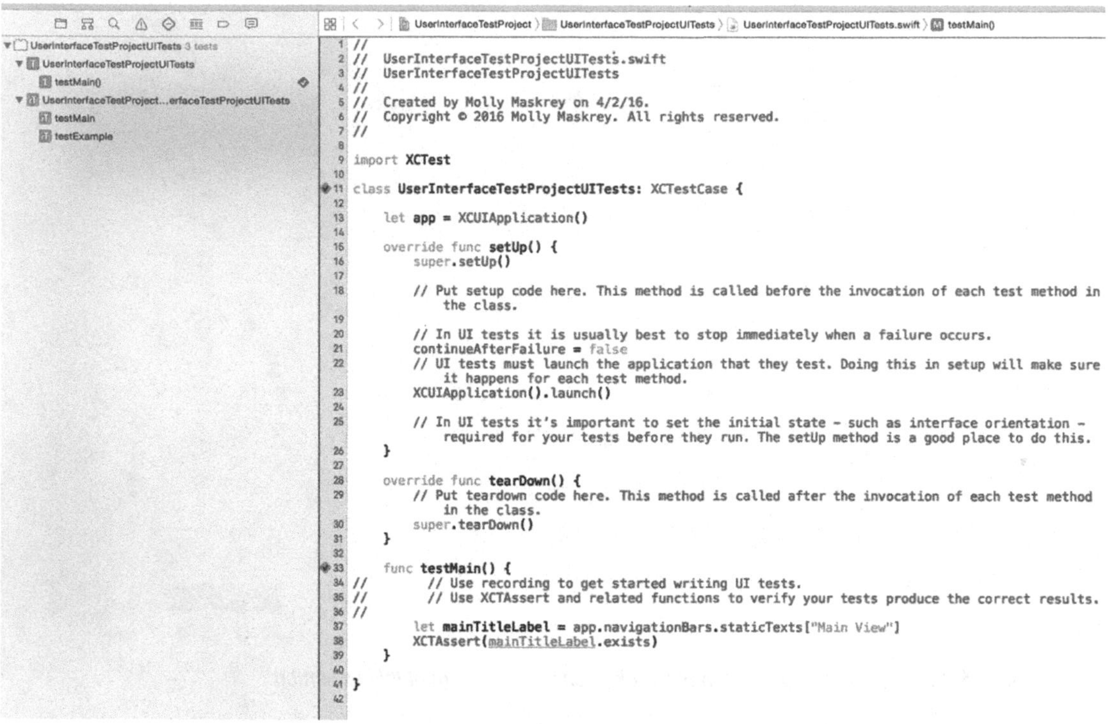

Figure 12-27. *Our test should now complete successfully, validating that when our app loads we do see the view controller that we expect*

Now, let's test things out. Change the testMain function in the UserInterfaceTestProjectUITests.swift file to that shown in Listing 12-11. We will first verify that we're on the main controller, then drop down into the first secondary view controller, make sure the label is correct, press the button, make sure the label changes, and return to the main view controller, where we'll repeat this for the second secondary view controller.

Listing 12-11. *Test All the Functions of Our App*

```swift
    func testMain() {
//        // Use recording to get started writing UI tests.
//        // Use XCTAssert and related functions to verify your tests produce the correct results.
//
        XCTAssert(app.navigationBars.staticTexts["Main View"].exists)

        // Test SecondaryView1 View Controller
        app.buttons["Secondary View 1"].tap()
        XCTAssert(app.navigationBars.staticTexts["Secondary View 1"].exists)
        XCTAssert(app.staticTexts["Secondary View 1"].exists)
        app.buttons["Display Text"].tap()
        XCTAssert(app.staticTexts["ALPHA"].exists)
        app.navigationBars.buttons["Back"].tap()
```

```
        // Test SecondaryView2 View Controller
        app.buttons["Secondary View 2"].tap()
        XCTAssert(app.navigationBars.staticTexts["Secondary View 2"].exists)
        XCTAssert(app.staticTexts["Secondary View 2"].exists)
        app.buttons["Display Text"].tap()
        XCTAssert(app.staticTexts["BETA"].exists)
        app.navigationBars.buttons["Back"].tap()
}
```

When we execute this, we should see the successful completion as in Figure 12-28.

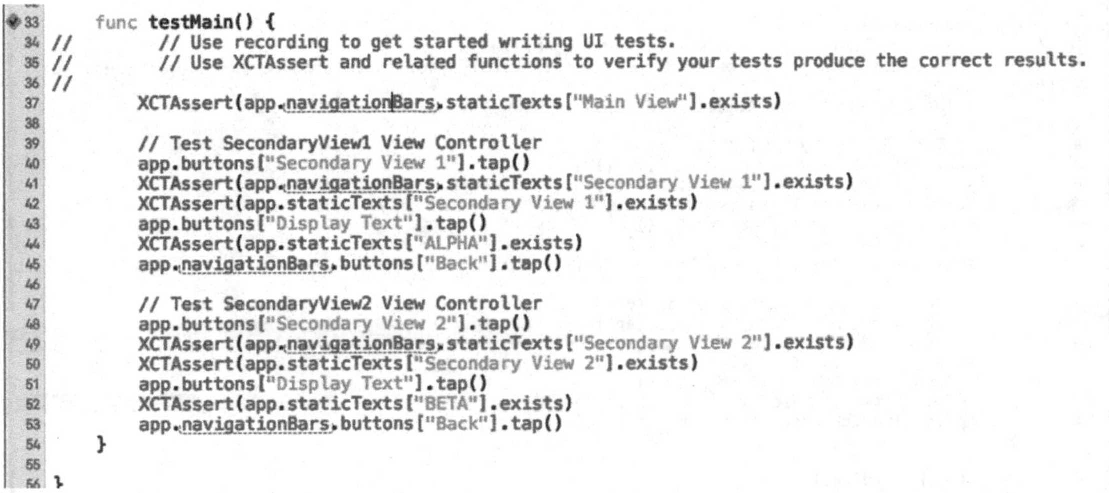

Figure 12-28. We can test all the way down into our app

So far, everything has worked. To verify we can detect a failure, change the last XCTAssert to look for ALPHA instead of BETA. You should get a test failure, as we see in Figure 12-29.

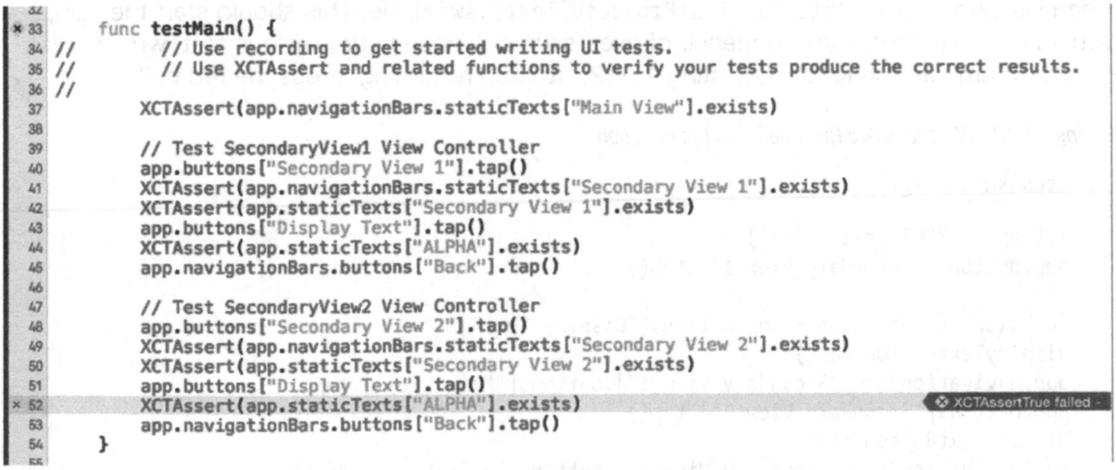

Figure 12-29. You should verify that your tests will also correctly detect errors

Recording

We've covered enough of the basics of UI Testing for you to have the tools you need to get started. One last aspect I want to touch on is recording. Basically, recording lets us go through the steps interactively on our simulator, recording the actions so that we don't have to manually enter them from scratch as we did in the last section.

To quickly see how it works, create a new test function called `testRecording()` in the `UserInterfaceTestProjectUITests.swift` file (Figure 12-30). Note that we've left off where we were last time with our error on the second view controller.

```
32
33    func testMain() {
34 //        // Use recording to get started writing UI tests.
35 //        // Use XCTAssert and related functions to verify your tests produce the correct results.
36 //
37        XCTAssert(app.navigationBars.staticTexts["Main View"].exists)
38
39        // Test SecondaryView1 View Controller
40        app.buttons["Secondary View 1"].tap()
41        XCTAssert(app.navigationBars.staticTexts["Secondary View 1"].exists)
42        XCTAssert(app.staticTexts["Secondary View 1"].exists)
43        app.buttons["Display Text"].tap()
44        XCTAssert(app.staticTexts["ALPHA"].exists)
45        app.navigationBars.buttons["Back"].tap()
46
47        // Test SecondaryView2 View Controller
48        app.buttons["Secondary View 2"].tap()
49        XCTAssert(app.navigationBars.staticTexts["Secondary View 2"].exists)
50        XCTAssert(app.staticTexts["Secondary View 2"].exists)
51        app.buttons["Display Text"].tap()
52        XCTAssert(app.staticTexts["ALPHA"].exists)                    ⊗ XCTAssertTrue failed -
53        app.navigationBars.buttons["Back"].tap()
54    }
55
56    func testRecording() {
57
58    }
59
60    }
```

Figure 12-30. Add the testRecording method, which is where we will store our UI recording

Place the cursor in the function and then press the round red record button at the bottom when viewing the `UserInterfaceTestProjectUITests.swift` file. This should start the app. You should then follow the sequence of events we outlined in our previous test, which records them into the function (Listing 12-12). To stop recording, press the red ball icon.

Listing 12-12. UI Actions Are Recorded into the Function

```
func testRecording() {

    let app = XCUIApplication()
    app.buttons["Secondary View 1"].tap()

    let displayTextButton = app.buttons["Display Text"]
    displayTextButton.tap()
    app.navigationBars["Secondary View 1"].buttons["Main View"].tap()
    app.buttons["Secondary View 2"].tap()
    displayTextButton.tap()
    app.navigationBars["Secondary View 2"].buttons["Main View"].tap()

}
```

There are some differences, notably the different way to get back to the main view from the secondary view, but the key thing you should notice is that there are no assertions. Fix that by copying the assertions from the testMain() function into similar locations in the testRecording() function, replacing the second forced failure ALPHA to BETA, as shown in Listing 12-13.

Listing 12-13. Our New Recorded UI Trace with Assertions

```
func testRecording() {

    let app = XCUIApplication()

    XCTAssert(app.navigationBars.staticTexts["Main View"].exists)
    app.buttons["Secondary View 1"].tap()
    XCTAssert(app.navigationBars.staticTexts["Secondary View 1"].exists)
    XCTAssert(app.staticTexts["Secondary View 1"].exists)

    let displayTextButton = app.buttons["Display Text"]
    displayTextButton.tap()
    XCTAssert(app.staticTexts["ALPHA"].exists)

    app.navigationBars["Secondary View 1"].buttons["Main View"].tap()
    app.buttons["Secondary View 2"].tap()
    XCTAssert(app.navigationBars.staticTexts["Secondary View 2"].exists)
    XCTAssert(app.staticTexts["Secondary View 2"].exists)

    displayTextButton.tap()
    XCTAssert(app.staticTexts["BETA"].exists)
    app.navigationBars["Secondary View 2"].buttons["Main View"].tap()

}
```

Comment out the testMain() function and run the test. The same UI actions should occur as we saw previously, and our test should complete successfully (Figure 12-31).

```
55
56    func testRecording() {
57
58        let app = XCUIApplication()
59
60        XCTAssert(app.navigationBars.staticTexts["Main View"].exists)
61        app.buttons["Secondary View 1"].tap()
62        XCTAssert(app.navigationBars.staticTexts["Secondary View 1"].exists)
63        XCTAssert(app.staticTexts["Secondary View 1"].exists)
64
65        let displayTextButton = app.buttons["Display Text"]
66        displayTextButton.tap()
67        XCTAssert(app.staticTexts["ALPHA"].exists)
68
69        app.navigationBars["Secondary View 1"].buttons["Main View"].tap()
70        app.buttons["Secondary View 2"].tap()
71        XCTAssert(app.navigationBars.staticTexts["Secondary View 2"].exists)
72        XCTAssert(app.staticTexts["Secondary View 2"].exists)
73
74        displayTextButton.tap()
75        XCTAssert(app.staticTexts["BETA"].exists)
76        app.navigationBars["Secondary View 2"].buttons["Main View"].tap()
77
78    }
```

Figure 12-31. Our recorded test should complete successfully just as we saw earlier

User Interface Testing Summary

Very similar to the way we worked with Unit Tests, UI Testing allows us to navigate the view path in our app to look for various elements to verify their existence as well as to activate controls such as buttons. We used static values for locating our UI elements, such as looking for the text in a button or label. As our skill and experience grows, we'll find ourselves leaving these simple static checks behind in favor of using XCUIElementQuery to locate various XCUIElements such as table views, cells, buttons, or any other element.

Using recording, we can interactively log our transition through the app's UI path, just as the intended user might, pressing buttons, moving sliders, entering text, and do on. The actions are recorded into a method of our choosing, thus allowing us to go back, add assertions, and verify system functionality.

Beta Testing

In Chapter 10 we followed all the steps needed to submit our project archive to the App Store. One of the last things we saw was the email confirmation from Apple (Figure 12-32). We won't go over those steps again here; rather, we'll start from the point we left off at in Chapter 10, but instead of an actual submission to the App Store, we'll figure out how to test using TestFlight.

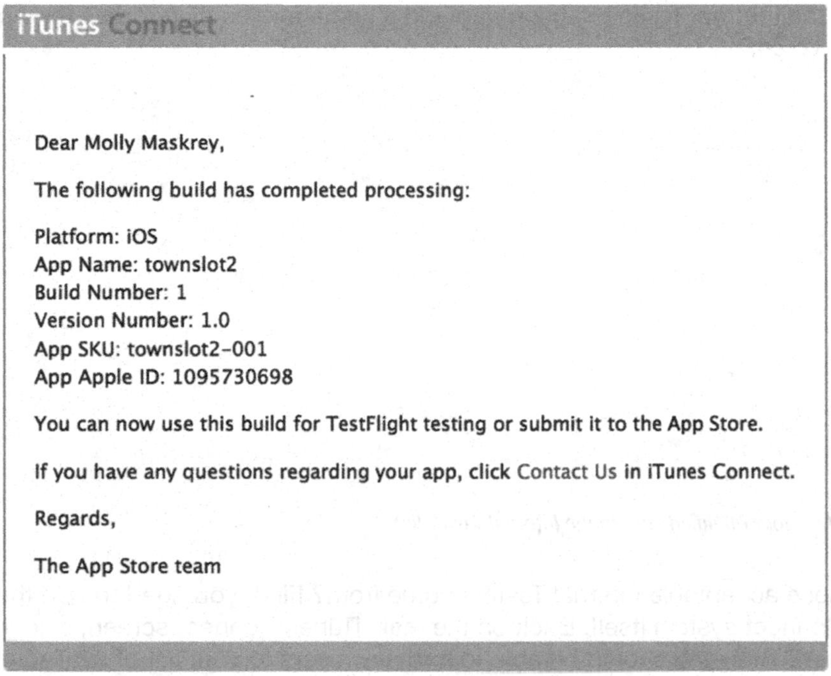

Dear Molly Maskrey,

The following build has completed processing:

Platform: iOS
App Name: townslot2
Build Number: 1
Version Number: 1.0
App SKU: townslot2-001
App Apple ID: 1095730698

You can now use this build for TestFlight testing or submit it to the App Store.

If you have any questions regarding your app, click Contact Us in iTunes Connect.

Regards,

The App Store team

Figure 12-32. For our exercise in Beta Testing with TestFlight, we will begin where we left off in Chapter 10

Internal Testers

An Internal Tester is someone who is part of your team and has either Admin, Technical, or Legal access to your app through iTunes Connect. To add an Internal Tester, log in to the iTunes Connect portal, go to My Apps, choose the TestFlight pane, and then select "Test Information" on the left (Figure 12-33). At a minimum, complete the "Feedback Email" and "Marketing URL" fields.

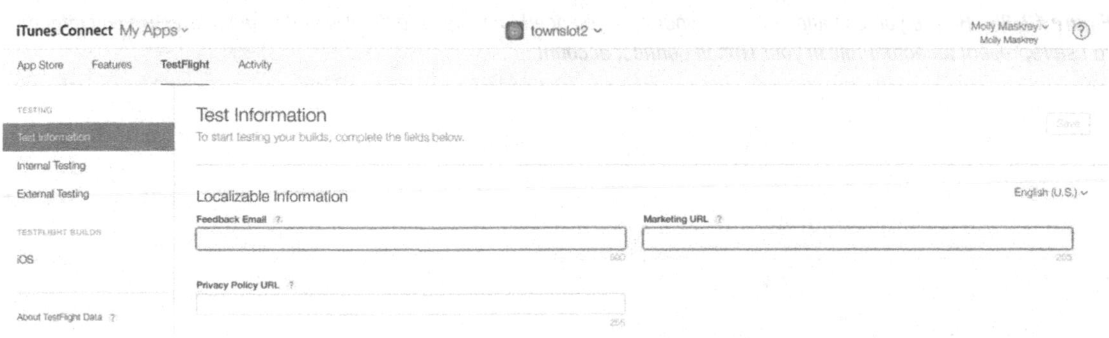

Figure 12-33. Begin setting up TestFlight by entering basic information about feedback and marketing

Go down to the Internal Testing section and add a name and email address for a qualified user (Figure 12-34).

***Figure 12-34.** Add your qualified user to the Internal Tester list*

Where do these acceptable Internal Testers come from? First, you need to add them into the iTunes Connect system itself. Back on the main iTunes Connect screen, select the Users and Roles icon. Then you should be able to add new users to your list of available testers (Figure 12-35). I always select "Technical" as the role for my testers. Because I manage my own email domains, I generally add an identifiable email address that I've created so the account can be added. If you try to add invalid accounts, the iTunes Connect process will usually detect this and will not allow the addition.

Users (2) ⊕		Q Search		
Apple ID	Name ^		Role	Apps
mollymaskrey@gmail.com	Molly **Maskrey** ⓘ		Admin, Legal	All Apps
iostest1@globalteklabs.com			Technical	All Apps

***Figure 12-35.** Before you can add testers to your app, you need to make sure the IDs and email addresses you intend to use represent an actual role in your iTunes Connect account*

Under TestFlight Builds, select "iOS"; you can see that our app (townslot2) from Chapter 10 is ready for internal testing (Figure 12-36).

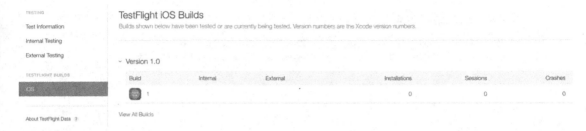

Figure 12-36. Verify that your app is ready for TestFlight internal testing

Go back to the "Internal Testing" section and select which iOS version you wish to test (Figure 12-37), then click Next to enter compliance data.

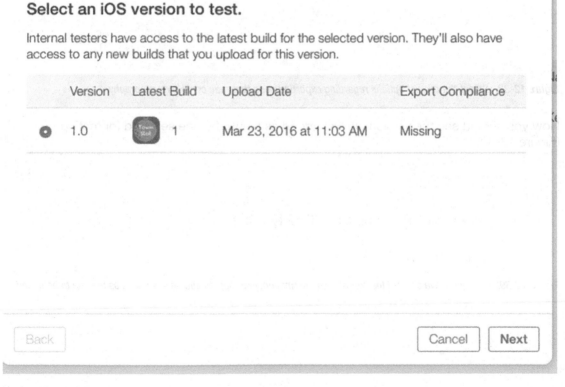

Figure 12-37. Select which app you plan on testing internally

As you can see in Figure 12-38, I've said we have no export compliance issues.

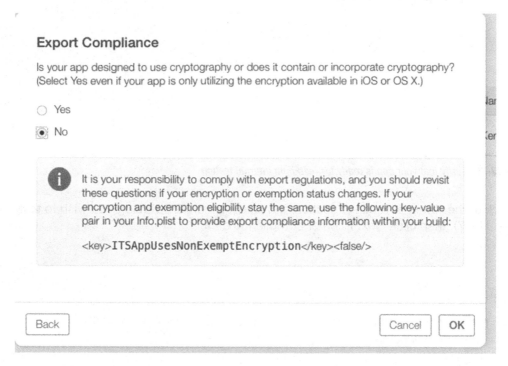

Export Compliance

Is your app designed to use cryptography or does it contain or incorporate cryptography?
(Select Yes even if your app is only utilizing the encryption available in iOS or OS X.)

○ Yes

◉ No

ⓘ It is your responsibility to comply with export regulations, and you should revisit
these questions if your encryption or exemption status changes. If your
encryption and exemption eligibility stay the same, use the following key-value
pair in your Info.plist to provide export compliance information within your build:

`<key>ITSAppUsesNonExemptEncryption</key><false/>`

Back   Cancel   OK

***Figure 12-38.** Select the correct options regarding exporting apps that may contain cryptography*

Now you should see the version we just added as being the one selected for testing
(Figure 12-39).

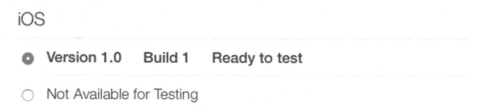

iOS

◉ **Version 1.0   Build 1   Ready to test**

○ Not Available for Testing

***Figure 12-39.** Once you have entered the compliance information, your app should be selectable as the one to be tested*

The last thing is to click the Start Testing button, which will send invitations to your Internal Tester list (Figure 12-40).

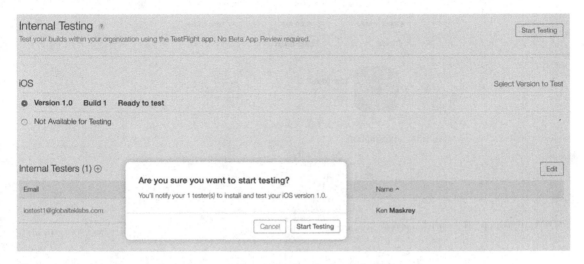

Figure 12-40. Select Start Testing to have your Internal Testers begin playing with your app

Your tester will get an invitation email inviting them to install and use the app (Figure 12-41).

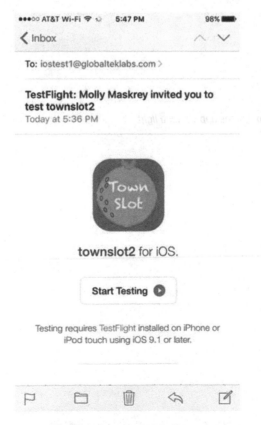

Figure 12-41. Your testers receive an email inviting them to start testing your app

After clicking on Start Testing, the user will be invited to install the app and be provided with detailed information about the build (Figure 12-42).

Figure 12-42. Your tester can install the app via TestFlight

They can open and run the app immediately after the download has completed (Figure 12-43).

Figure 12-43. *As soon as the app download has completed, your users may begin testing the app*

External Testers

The external beta test process follows pretty much the same steps as we took with internal testers, with a few differences. One important distinction between internal and external testing is that external testers do not have to be part of your team; that is, they don't have to be entered as members of your organization in iTunes Connect. However, this means that your app—the unproven, beta version of it—is going out into the "real world." Apple has some say in this and will not allow this distribution without first examining the app themselves for serious issues. Much like when an app is reviewed before placing it on the App Store, they need to make sure it's not filled with bugs and, more importantly, that it is free of viruses and malware. The level of examination is at less detail than with an official release, but don't expect it to be significantly so.

Just like before, add your external testers, either from an existing list or by adding new testers (Figure 12-44).

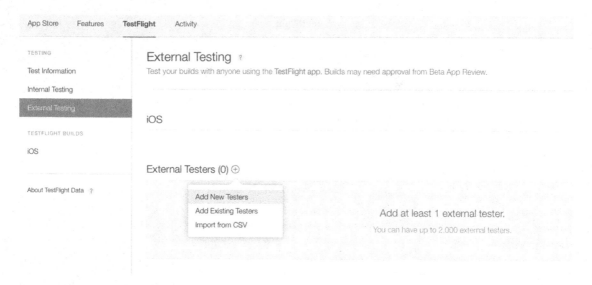

Figure 12-44. *You'll need to first add external testers to your beta program; they do not have to be part of your team*

You may add existing testers from other groups. In Figure 12-45 you can see I've added one of my CoinToss game app's testers.

Figure 12-45. *You can add existing external testers of other apps you may have already beta tested*

You can also add new testers, making sure that their email address is valid and reachable (Figure 12-46).

Figure 12-46. *Most likely, unless the beta version of your app is for an existing client or a new version, you'll want to add new testers specifically for this project*

And, just as with internal testing, you'll add a build to distribute (Figure 12-47).

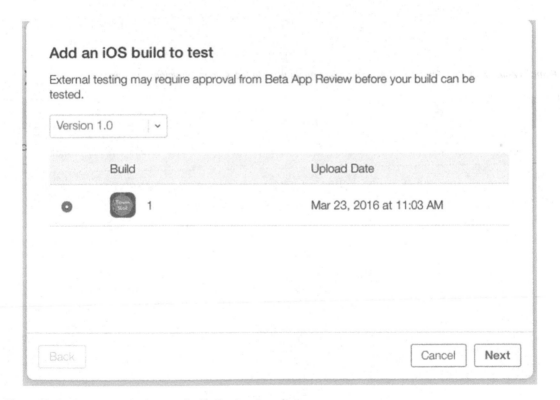

Figure 12-47. *Add your build for test distribution to external users*

In the case of external beta testing, you'll be entering a bit more information so that your testers can get a sense of what you're looking for; Apple's will look at this information also during the pre-test before your app can actually be distributed to users (Figure 12-48).

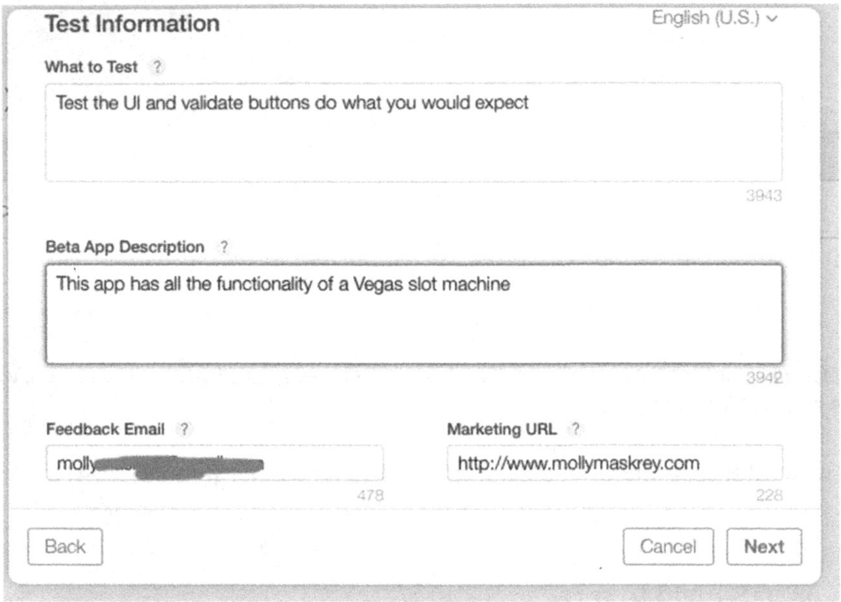

Figure 12-48. Add the information that your testers might want to focus on when using your app

Add your contact information (Figure 12-49).

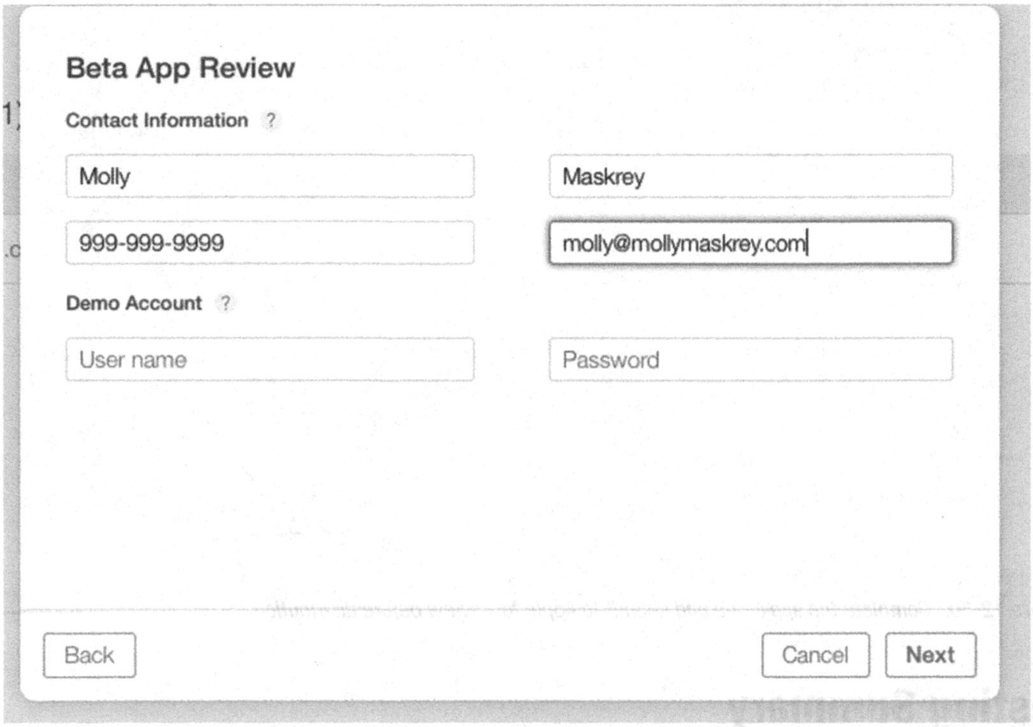

Beta App Review

Contact Information   ?

| Molly | | Maskrey |

| 999-999-9999 | | molly@mollymaskrey.com| |

Demo Account   ?

| User name | | Password |

| Back | | Cancel | Next |

Figure 12-49. Add the correct contact information so your testers can reach you

Finish up with any notes you might want to include, such as test accounts needed by Apple or the users (Figure 12-50). Press the Submit button, and the build, along with the information we just entered, will be passed to Apple for review. I've personally found that this step takes about a day or two as the process may be a bit streamlined, though no one knows for sure, and Apple isn't telling. I've had apps be approved for beta testing within a couple hours, and some have taken as long as three days. My suspicion is that it depends on the workload Apple is dealing with at the time of submission.

Beta App Review

Review Notes ?

no notes at this time|

3979

Back   Cancel   Submit

Figure 12-50. Complete the app setup and submit to Apple for review before distribution

Testing Summary

As with pretty much every other chapter and section in this book, there's far more material that can be covered on the subject of testing than is covered here. If you look around you'll find books and online courses on test-driven development, many specific to iOS and Mac OS X.

What I hope to have accomplished in this chapter is to have given you the basics to get started and to get past the fear that testing and designing for test is something all powerful and mysterious. Basically, it's really nothing more than taking a lot of your specifications and implementing them as tests; unit tests more so, but UI testing as well. By creating your tests first, set against your system requirements, as you write your Swift code you can immediately see if you are meeting those requirements. What's more, you're doing it empirically, not just thinking about it, but specifically measuring your results against preset criteria.

We talked about Unit Testing and User Interface Testing, which are now, with the release of Xcode 7, integral parts of the IDE and far easier to use than in times past. UI Recording offers you the ability to create much of your test functions by simply going through the UI as a user might do. All your app interactive transitions are recorded, and all you need do is to add the proper assertions to verify successful completion.

Finally, we talked about the two types of beta testing in which you can have actual users play with your project and give you valuable feedback. Internal Testers, part of your development team and entered into your iTunes Connect portal, can test your app without significant review from Apple. Your bundle is checked upon upload by an automated process for correctness, but functional issues and even crashes are not covered. There is no human in the loop checking it for internal testing—not at this time, anyway.

External beta testing follows pretty much the same path as internal testing with some additional information being required, as well as having Apple review the app before it can be distributed to your testers. This ensures, to the extent that it can, that many of the common issues that Apple sees every day, such as crashes, are addressed before being released.

iOS Accessories

What Is an Accessory?

What do we mean by *accessory*? I define an accessory as any external hardware device that connects to the iPhone via the Lightning connector at the bottom of the phone or via Bluetooth 2.1+EDR wireless signal, i.e., standard Bluetooth. Connecting electronic equipment to an iOS device by either of these means requires the developer to be part of Apple's MFi program. You can, of course, connect other accessories to your iPhone through Wi-Fi, Bluetooth 4.0 Low Energy (BTLE), and, with a little work, the headphone jack.

> **Note** The Apple MFi (Made for iPod/iPhone/iPad) program allows developers access to components, tools, documentation, technical support, and logos to create sophisticated accessories that connect to iOS devices.

I know what you're thinking. The iPhone is a portable, self-contained device that got us away from all the cables associated with keyboards, mice, game controllers, tablets, and the like. Why would we want to bring all that junk back onto our desk?

The answer is simple: Functionality. Connecting an accessory to the iPhone adds new features that can greatly expand its use into as yet unidentified realms. The addition of functionality increases the usefulness of the iPhone and makes it even more valuable than ever. Many people who previously thought the iPhone was just a fancy calling device (why would they ever need one?) can now see real potential in the problems that this combination (iOS device + accessory) may help to solve.

© Molly K. Maskrey 2016

M.K. Maskrey, *App Development Recipes for iOS and watchOS*, DOI 10.1007/978-1-4842-1820-4_13

Uses of Accessories

Years ago in my book, *Building iPhone OS Accessories* (2010), I described several potential uses of accessories that could be coupled with an iOS device. I included mobile point-of-sale terminals, electronic wallets, in-store purchasing, glucose and blood pressure monitoring, in-home diagnostics and monitoring, and game controllers. Those and hundreds of other more interesting devices are bought and sold every day as all aspects of our lives become interconnected through the use of mobile devices and connected accessory equipment. Let's take a brief survey of some of the areas where these unique creations make our lives easier and better before diving into just exactly what we mean by an accessory.

Point-of-Sale (PoS)

Merchants can attend craft fairs and sell their products using a credit card accessory to accept cashless payments. This market has skyrocketed with systems from Square, VeriFone, PayPal, IDTech, and so many others. At the end of 2009 I actually had my first MFi accessory, the AirePoint point-of-sale terminal, approved by Apple. It was a small credit card reader that attached through the 30-pin dock connector (Figure 13-1). By offering a more "blocky"—some called it ugly—device, no modifications to either the hardware or the app were needed when the iPad first came out to immediately have an iPad point-of-sale system. Merchants began duct taping the AirePoint to iPad devices mounted on stands, thus creating early versions of self-service kiosks.

Figure 13-1. The author designed, manufactured, and sold one of the first commercially available credit card swipe accessories for the iPhone in late 2009

By designing a very simple system of electronics and firmware (Figures 13-2 and 13-3), I kept costs significantly lower than first anticipated and increased profits during early sale years.

Figure 13-2. With a few pieces of plastic, a low-cost reader head, a dock-connector, and a circuit board, merchants could now accept credit card payments anywhere they had a WiFi or cellular signal

Figure 13-3. Using only a small 8-bit microcontroller and minimal support circuitry, the essence of a complete point-of-sale system was born

With the introduction of the iPad and its larger screen size, self-service point-of-sale terminals rapidly started taking brick-and-mortar establishments by storm. In 2011 Jennifer and I helped start a company that designs and manufactures production and custom tablet kiosk systems. Customers at restaurants, retail shops, museums, and even churches can order or purchase products, view information interactively, and even make donations at their own pace.

With the EMV mandate that occurred October 2015, simple magnetic stripe cards are quickly being replaced by smart cards with built-in electronics, including a computing engine, to address security concerns and fraudulent charges. EMV systems for Apple devices have already started hitting the market, with products such as VeriFone's e333 payment solution, which includes chip-and-pin, NFC (Near Feld Communications), swipe, and a 2D optical scanner. More devices are likely just around the corner.

> **Note** The EMV (EuroPay/MasterCard/Visa) mandate shifts the liability for fraudulent credit card transactions to the weakest link in the processing chain. EMV describes it this way: The party, either the issuer or merchant, that does not support EMV assumes liability for counterfeit card transactions.

> **Note** Near Field Communications (NFC) technology provides a short-range (typically 10cm or less) communications set of protocols that allow devices to communicate when placed close together. This provides security measures to help prevent other forms of wireless sniffers from reading personal data such as credit card information.

Apple Pay, introduced in September 2014, takes payments a step further and eliminates the need to use separate accessories. With the recent integration of Apple Watch, making payments for purchases using this wireless feature will surely offer some serious competition for point-of-sale accessories. By using NFC technology, the customer no longer needs to insert a physical card or even carry her actual card with her. Information about the account is securely stored in her iOS device, allowing fast and secure transactions.

While payments became a huge market for iOS accessories, other exciting markets also sprang up that offered new and interesting ways to connect to people.

Sports and Games

From an app-enabled robot-like sphero (Figure 13-4) to smart soccer balls such as the adidas miCoach SMART BALL to the LiveRowing Connect, accessories are taking over the sports and game market, allowing for creativity, performance monitoring, and friendly competition with your online friends. It seemed to begin with small robot vehicles, cars, trucks, and even drones that came to market in the early days of the MFi program. To be able to control something that moved independently and without wires really extended the reach of your iPhone beyond texting or browsing the Web. Engineers, including myself, scooped up these early products with all their imperfections and expanded our concept of what could be accomplished. We imagined, made improvements, and created altogether new ideas that still surprise me when they first show up. It's either, "I need that!" or "Why didn't I think of that?" New ideas, even if not my own, spur my imagination and drive my passion to keep doing this type of work.

Figure 13-4. Games like sphero turn your living room into a video game with augmented reality apps, or upgrade family game night with multiplayer games. Sphero is also pet-proof, swims, and is ready to roll wherever you go

As mentioned earlier, LiveRowing (Figure 13-5) offers a rowing-machine-to-iPhone cable permitting the monitoring and tracking of your workouts. The cable connects the USB port of a Concept2 Performance Monitor (PM) (Figure 13-6) with an Apple Lightning connector, allowing for complete data collection of your exercise session. The USB connection on the PM can often be difficult to find; it sits underneath the PM head unit and is a standard Type B port.

Figure 13-5. Concept2 rowing machines found in many gyms and health clubs across the world offer a USB port on the bottom of the Performance Monitor head unit allowing use of the LiveRowing Connect cable accessory with your iPhone

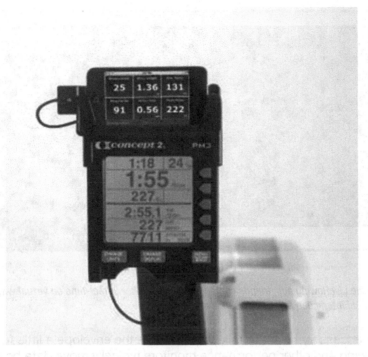

Figure 13-6. A predecessor to LiveRowing Connect, the Concept2 iPhone Connection Kit, tracked and monitored workouts using your 30-pin Apple device

In April of 2014 we contracted with LiveRowing to help bring this unique product to the marketplace. The design essentially expands on the original Concept2 iPhone Connection kit, which used a 30-pin dock connector that allowed the attachment of the original iPhone through to the iPhone 4 series. The ErgData app permitted basic collection and monitoring of your workout. LiveRowing extended this to a fully interactive system (Figure 13-7) that allows you to race your connected friends on various waterways and courses.

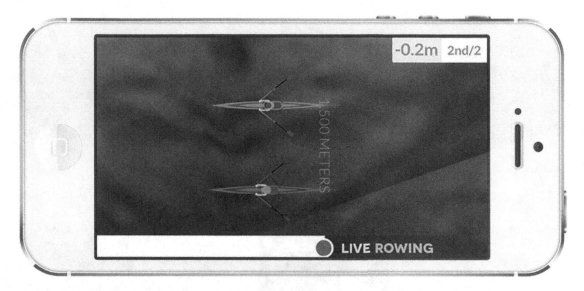

Figure 13-7. *Using the LiveRowing app, friends compete with each other in real-time on virtual waterways and race courses, allowing social interaction across thousands of miles*

The next sports accessory I want to talk about pushes the envelope a little further. Systems such as LiveRowing and other performance monitors typically move data between a piece of equipment and your iOS device to allow for monitoring, tracking, goal setting, and even competition. Over the past year I have developed a sensor system that wirelessly tracks the orientation and movement of itself. That is, if the sensor is moved in a direction, that spend and direction is measured and sent out wirelessly. Similarly, if the sensor's orientation in the X, Y and Z axes is changed, that data also gets sent out over the air. The astute reader will, of course, tell me this is what the iPhone already does. But what if I specifically and independently wanted to measure the movement and orientation of my feet?

As I've no doubt beat into the ground, my passion of dance drives many aspects of my life, especially my occupation and choice of research. Dance is by nature a nearly pure artistic form of expression. You move to an outside stimulus, the music, but are driven by your own internal interpretation of that music combined with the syllabus of the style of dance. The student follows a syllabus on the journey to becoming more skilled and determining if they should compete or simply practice more until they get it right.

> **Note**   A syllabus in dance refers to the written framework denoting the proper movements for each level of achievement a student attempts as they try to improve. It also defines proficiency levels during competitions. If, for example, you compete at a certain level, but do not stay within the syllabus for that level, you might have points deducted or even be disqualified. Essentially, a syllabus offers the rules of dance.

The question becomes, "How do I get it right?" As a dancer, I don't want to concern myself with the rules as much as I want to express myself artistically. But my engineering brain continually and objectively analyzes each and every movement; are my feet in the proper position, did I make that last step correctly, how's my frame looking, is my rear sticking out? Other than having a skilled and observant instructor constantly watching my every (mis)step, there's really no way for me to know. I decided that I had to change things, because this inability to quantify basic body movement seemed ludicrous.

The first step was to determine how the measurement would be performed. This was pretty easy, as the parts have been readily available for some time. I used a small micro-electrical mechanical system (MEMS) integrated circuit (Figure 13-8) with several built-in functions and a standard serial peripheral interconnect (SPI) bus interface port.

Figure 13-8. Readily available devices can measure movement and orientation in each of three axes and provide that information over standardized communications ports

Step two connected the I/O port of the MEMS part to an off-the-shelf Bluetooth module, using a small, four-layer printed circuit board (PCB) (Figure 13-9). Although the complete circuit could have been put together on a breadboard for testing, using a PCB with soldered components permitted the prototypes to be used in actual testing attached to each of the dancer's feet. The sensors can be placed into an orthotic underneath the dancer's foot, or be externally mounted to the top or bottom of the shoe (Figure 13-10). As the measurement data and analysis results combine to change our perceptions and reshape our actions, we move toward the concept of a connected self. The connected self enhances our senses and perceptions of our movements and reactions to stimuli. Rather than diminishing, we improve and reach for our goals using empirical information and objective methodology as opposed to just wishing and hoping we improve as we practice.

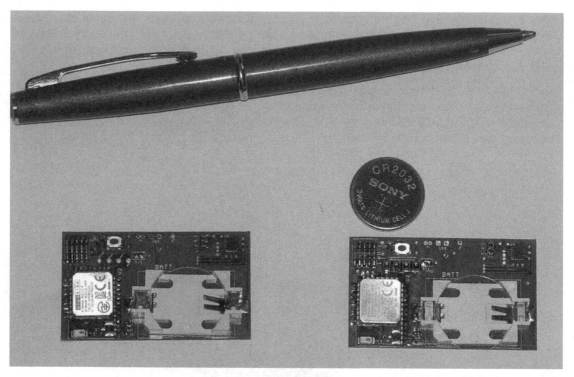

Figure 13-9. Two small PCBs, one for each foot, allow continuous wireless monitoring of the dancer's movements during training, or even during a performance, and takes us toward the connected self

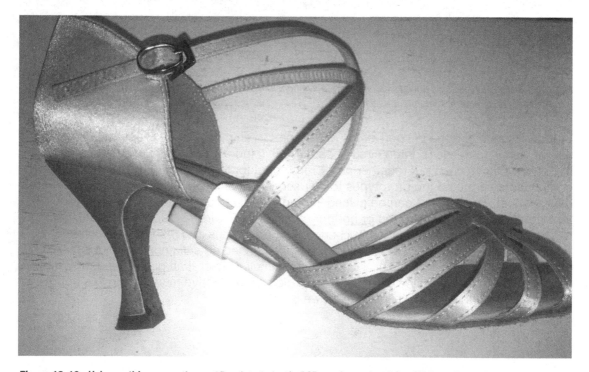

Figure 13-10. Using nothing more than a 3D-printed plastic PCB carrier and a strip of Velcro, the author was able to test the sensor system on an actual dance floor

After fitting the prototype sensor module to the bottom of my shoe, I was able to move about the dance floor as the sensor recorded my foot position at a rate of 20 samples per second. Initially limiting testing to one foot at a time, I was able to not only monitor the pitch and roll of my foot, but also determine whether that position was correct or incorrect for the dance style I attempted. Using an Apple Watch, the information was presented visually, audibly, and haptically. The latter was achieved by generating a vibration of the watch through the use of the Apple Watch's taptic engine when an incorrect movement was detected.

I'll go into much more detail in Chapter 17, where I present a complete walkthrough of the project. My hope is to show, through examples, how you too can find a problem that you might have been mulling over for some time and use the innovation inside yourself along with the techniques and skills presented throughout this book to discover innovative solutions that push your abilities toward their limits.

Home Automation and the Internet of Things

A couple of months ago I was asked to give a talk on IoT technology as the keynote speaker to a good-sized crowd of people, the vast majority of whom I had never met. IoT is one of those areas that has become such a buzzword and pretty much everything out there is becoming IoT'd. Whether or not this is a good thing is pretty much irrelevant; it's happening whether anyone likes it or not. The question becomes, will we use it, and if so, how will we use it?

My main experience with IoT comes from those annoying tire pressure sensors hidden somewhere on my car. Since I live in Colorado at about 6,200 feet, the weather changes are significant, and transitions of 50 degrees or more can happen in a single day. For some reason this sets off my car's pressure gauges. Checking manually, there's no difference in pressure. They were 24 lbs. yesterday and they're 24 lbs. today, so why is that stupid alarm going off?

Like any new use of technology, IoT will have its good and bad points. Every few days a news article surfaces about how someone's baby monitor was hacked or how a car was taken over remotely. These are of definite concern and are being addressed by the whole IoT community. Although IoT encompasses a vast landscape of devices, from industrial systems management to tracking your pet's whereabouts through a smart tag on their collar, we're going to focus on the area of home automation in this section (Figure 13-11).

Figure 13-11. *Just about any electronic device in your home can be monitored and controlled though IoT and home automation technology*

Apple announced HomeKit in 2014 at the Worldwide Developer's Conference as an iOS feature that provides rationality and consistency in the home automation space. The key features of HomeKit include a common database for the devices or accessories that are part of the HomeKit environment, encrypted data and protocol links, a hierarchical structure for defining your home, higher-level constructs such as zones, and Siri control of your devices, which lets you speak commands to manage your home.

The top-down structure begins with the home as the master container. You can have multiple homes, of course, but everything is contained in a home. Each home has rooms, and accessories are found inside rooms. So far this is all fairly logical and follows the natural organization of the physical nature of most everyone's setup.

Just below accessory is the service layer. By this we mean that every accessory contains one or more services. Some services are mandatory, such as the information about the service, whereas others are optional and depend on the accessory. For example, a lamp might have a light bulb service, while a garage door opener would also have a light bulb service, but a motor service and maybe a sensor service as well. Services are controlled and monitored through the bottom layer of the hierarchy—characteristics. A light bulb service could have a status characteristic that showed it as on or off, or it might have a brightness characteristic that ranges from 0.0 (off) to 1.0 (fully on). It could have a hue characteristic that lets you change the color of the light. Characteristics can be read or write. You might only read a sensor characteristic on a garage door, but you would read and write to the motor characteristic.

In Chapter 16 we'll work our way through a simple home automation project using the HomeKit framework to see how it is used from a software perspective. Obviously, to see the true effects of our work, we'd want to have actual devices to control. For our project I found a relatively inexpensive HomeKit-enabled power plug from iHome (Figure 13-12). Because it manages a standard AC outlet, you can plug in pretty much anything that doesn't draw too much current. As I kind of like to show off, my appliance of choice happens to be a small disco ball. I mean, don't we all have a disco ball somewhere in our homes? But a lamp works just as well.

Figure 13-12.   The SmartPlug from iHome offers a low-cost, easy way to get started with HomeKit and IoT home automation software projects

In the early days after WWDC 2014 and the HomeKit announcement, there were very few—a.k.a. zero—HK accessories in the marketplace. In fact, it wasn't until late in the summer of 2015 that I personally started seeing more and more HK accessories arriving on sites like Amazon. Apple helped developers by also releasing the HomeKit Accessory Simulator OS X application (Figure 13-13), which allows you to create a basic accessory database on your Mac to emulate different types of accessories. Using a BTLE-enabled Mac, you can even control these simulated accessories from your iOS device and use Siri for voice commands.

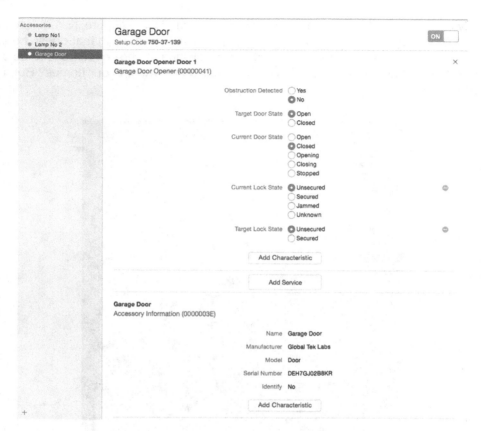

Figure 13-13. The HomeKit Accessory Simulator OS X application provides a way to create simulated accessories that you can control and monitor from your iOS HK app

Usage Summary

In the past few sections we have covered some of the basic areas of iOS accessories that have sprung up since their introduction over five years ago. From fun and games to serious medical applications to home automation, accessories span the full range of what can be done fairly easily using iOS. But how do we work with accessories within iOS and Xcode? How we access and use an accessory depends on what kind of accessory we are working with. We won't discuss WiFi accessories here, as those would use normal Unix-like transport protocols. Accessories using the headphone jack are a little more specialized, though not that hard, and in that case we typically work with the audio frameworks to convert audio signals so they have the ability to carry data. These techniques are used for PoS and other accessories like the Square credit card reader.

If an accessory uses Bluetooth 4.0 Low Energy, then we work with the iOS Core Bluetooth framework; we'll get more experience with this in our project chapters. The remaining category of accessories is for those created under Apple's MFi program. For those, you will need to use Apple's EAAccessory framework. Because we're going to be focusing our interconnection discussions around BTLE in order to keep things simple and not requiring an MFi license, we'll only briefly address using the EAAccessory framework.

EAAccessory Framework

iPhone OS 3.0, released in June 2009, included the External Accessory framework, which allowed an iPhone application to communicate with a user-defined piece of hardware for the first time. As of today we're running iOS 9.1, and, with a few small differences, the framework hasn't changed all that much.

When I first started programming in Mac OS X, for a long time the term *framework* confused me. Even though it was made clear that a framework was basically a library, I couldn't seem to get around the difference in terminology. Why did they call it framework and not just library?

The main thing to remember is that a framework is more than a library. A framework is actually a directory—a hierarchical directory that contains shared resources such as a library. In addition to a library, a framework may contain xib/nib files, images, strings, header files, and even documentation. Think of it as the all-encompassing package one level above a library.

A framework, by means of its included libraries, provides a set of routines that can be used by the application to perform specific tasks. For example, UIKit provides the mechanisms needed for your application to communicate with the user via the iPhone's touchscreen. The Audio Toolbox framework provides the tools needed to allow the application to use sound. Figure 13-14 illustrates the general structure of a framework. Note that a framework includes much more than the shared library that we tend to think of as being the framework itself.

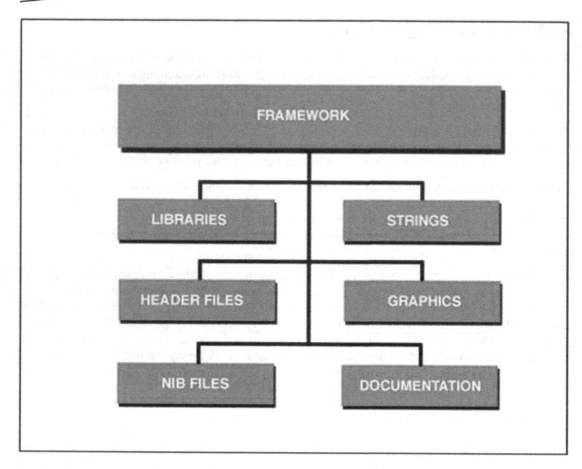

Figure 13-14. A framework contains much more than the precompiled libraries used for a specific functionality such as audio or accessories

> **Note**   For legacy reasons, in this chapter we use xib and nib interchangeably, although they differ slightly. Nibs were the original UI files we created using Interface Builder (IB), which was, in the early days, separate from the IDE part of Xcode. Xib files, Xml nIB, are essentially human-readable versions of nibs. This allows for hand tweaking of nibs by direct editing of the XML.

Apple's External Accessory framework provides the iPhone software developer with necessary support for communicating with external hardware. Support is provided for both the wired (30-pin or Lightning) dock connector and the wireless Bluetooth 2.1+EDR (standard Bluetooth). The framework actually implements an agnostic interface; that is, the code looks the same whether you're using a 30-pin connector, a Lightning connector, or standard Bluetooth. While changing an accessory from one protocol to another would require MFi requirements changes, and in effect it would become a different accessory, the software would likely function the same without modification.

An iOS application communicates with an MFi accessory and the EAAccessory framework using streams—specifically, NSInputStream and NSOutputStream. Prior to communications, both the hardware and the app agree on how they will communicate and specify one or more protocols. The term *protocol* as used here significantly differs from our normal Xcode usage of the term. In this context a protocol is really nothing more than a name for the data path between the external hardware and the iOS device.

When you create a hardware accessory, you define what data gets sent back and forth across the communications channel. You might have long strings of ASCII data, such as names scanned by a barcode reader, or you could be dealing with binary data from a remote sensor. You could send individual messages for each signal, or you might package them all in one message and deconstruct them on the other side. It's up to you to decide. Much of the time you would use a single protocol, and thus a single protocol name, for communication. In some more complex accessories you could have several protocols, such as a setup protocol, an operational protocol, or a diagnostic protocol. Again, these are names and definitions you choose. Personally, other than pseudo-bookkeeping, I've found no reason to create more than a single protocol for an accessory.

A protocol name is specified in reverse-DNS notation. A typical name format I often use is com.<company>.protocol1 or com.<company>.p1 for simplicity. The protocol name is specified in both the Xcode project and the accessory firmware. Upon connecting an accessory to a device, the accessory goes through a series of initiation steps to identify itself to the device and iOS. Part of that sequence is telling iOS the name of the accessory protocol. In Xcode, specifically in the Info.plist, you specify the protocol name.

> **Note**   Apple distinguishes between devices and accessories. An accessory is a piece of hardware created by an MFi developer. A device is an Apple device, such as an iPod, iPhone, iPad, or Apple Watch.

After an accessory has been connected and verified, the app will create an EASession object to manage the continued communications between the two pieces of hardware. This is where you specify the protocol you wish to use to communicate with the accessory. After the session instance is created, you set up the input and output streams for communications. You have complete responsibility for configuring and managing the selected protocol. Neither the session object nor the EASession class has any knowledge of specific accessory protocols and makes no attempt to format the data in any way before or after transferring it.

Here's an example of how to create a session object using Objective-C:

```
EASession *session = [[EASession alloc] initWithAccessory:accessory
                  forProtocol:protocolString];
```

Streams

Streams are basically what their name implies: a sequence of data that goes from one point to another. Like its watery namesake, our streams travel in one direction: downstream. Therefore, in order to support bi-directional traffic, we require both an input and an output stream.

From within our frame of reference inside the iPhone application, we create an input stream to handle data coming from the accessory and an output stream to handle the data we send to the accessory. We use the Cocoa classes NSInputStream and NSOutputStream, both of which are derived from NSStream.

Stream objects also have properties associated with them. Most properties have to do with network security and configuration, and as such will not be discussed here. Most important, a stream object has a delegate associated with it. The delegate object, which in our case will be the accessory controller object, must support the stream:handleEvent: method. Apple has provided a prototype implementation for dealing with events from streams, which we will discuss shortly.

What happens is this: whenever something happens in regards to a stream, the stream:handleEvent: method is called. Depending on what eventCode was received, we take one of several actions. First, we need to create the streams, and that is done in three steps for each (input and output) stream.

Listing 13-1 provides an Objective-C example of setting up our input/output streams to communicate with an MFi accessory.

Listing 13-1. Setting Up NSStreams

```
if (session)
    {
        [[session inputStream] setDelegate:self];
        [[session inputStream] scheduleInRunLoop:[NSRunLoop currentRunLoop]
                        forMode:NSDefaultRunLoopMode];
        [[session inputStream] open];

        [[session outputStream] setDelegate:self];
        [[session outputStream] scheduleInRunLoop:[NSRunLoop currentRunLoop]
                        forMode:NSDefaultRunLoopMode];
        [[session outputStream] open];
    }
    else
    {
        NSLog(@"creating session failed");
    }
```

Note In order to maintain the best compatibility with Apple's Xcode documentation, I've continued to use Objective-C when discussing the EAAccessory framework and accessory communications in general.

As you can see in the preceding code example, we have three things we need to do:

1. Set the stream delegate (usually to self).

2. Schedule the stream to execute within a run loop.

3. Open the stream.

Once the streams have been opened, the stream:handleEvent: method will handle events from both the input and output streams. Why does this statement handle both input and output streams? It does so because we set the delegate to be self for both the input and output streams in the previous code snippet.

When any event of interest happens in either stream, this method gets called. Note the NSStreamEventOpenCompleted, NSStreamEventErrorOccurred, and NSStreamEventEndOccurred cases; these would occur for both the input and output streams and should be handled accordingly.

The event codes of most interest to us, NSStreamEventHasBytesAvailable and NSStreamEventHasSpaceAvailable, refer to the input and output streams, respectively. As is mostly obvious, the first code means that the accessory has sent data to the iPhone and it is ready to be read. The second code means that there is space available in the stream to send data to the accessory.

To deal with these two instances, either the _writeData or _readData method gets called. These obviously handle the outgoing or incoming data transmissions.

Listing 13-2 provides an Objective-C example of using NSStreams for accessories.

Listing 13-2. Handling Events for an NSStream

```
- (void)stream:(NSStream *)aStream handleEvent:(NSStreamEvent)eventCode
{
    switch (eventCode) {
        case NSStreamEventNone:
            NSLog(@"stream %@ event none", aStream);
            break;
        case NSStreamEventOpenCompleted:
            //  Do something for Open Completed event
                    break;
        case NSStreamEventHasBytesAvailable:
            NSLog(@"stream %@ event bytes available", aStream);
            [self _readData];
            break;
        case NSStreamEventHasSpaceAvailable:
            NSLog(@"stream %@ event space available", aStream);
            [self _writeData];
            break;
        case NSStreamEventErrorOccurred:
            //  Do something for Error event
            break;
```

```
        case NSStreamEventEndEncountered:
                    //  Do something for End event
            break;
        default:
            break;
    }
}
```

EAAccessory Framework Summary

In this section I gave you a basic overview of using the EAAccessory framework to communicate with an MFi accessory. Although a few terms might be new and some are very infrequently used, trust me that working with an accessory is no different than working with any other iOS framework. In fact, compared to the complexities of audio or location services, using the EAAccessory framework is much simpler. You're only doing a couple of things, such as creating a session and moving data. You'll also respond to other events, such as connecting or disconnecting a piece of hardware, but those use simple delegate methods you're likely already familiar with.

To actually work with iOS MFi accessories, refer to the external accessory references in the Xcode documentation. Next, we'll spend some time talking about a more widely used way to connect an accessory to your iPhone—BTLE and the CoreBluetooth framework.

Bluetooth Low Energy

To work with Apple's Core Bluetooth framework, we first need to understand the differences between standard Bluetooth and Bluetooth LE (BTLE). When we talk about standard Bluetooth, we most often refer to Bluetooth 2.1+EDR (enhanced data rate). This mechanism provides us with a data transfer rate somewhere around 2 million bits per second. depending, of course, on any number of different conditions.

Because of its implementation across many different usage scenarios, Bluetooth offers a number of different standard profiles so as to use specific services in particular scenarios. A profile is a specification of aspects related to the wireless communications between devices. Rather than get deeper and deeper into terminology, think of it like this: If you use a wireless headset to talk while driving, the Headset profile (HSP) would be used. Keyboards, mice, and other such devices would use the Human Interface Device (HID) profile. Many other standard profiles exist and are used depending on the specific application.

For communicating between devices where general data transfer occurs, the Serial Port Profile (SPP) and Radio Frequency Communications (RFCOMM) protocols would be in use. Specifically, SPP defines how the ports between two Bluetooth-enabled devices get connected. RFCOMM defines the serial communications protocols, which essentially emulate RS-232 ports. Basically, you can think of using standard Bluetooth as being the wireless replacement for a wired connection between two pieces of equipment. For our purposes, the two things that really matter are: 1) standard Bluetooth should be used when connecting an accessory to an Apple device where a high data rate is required and 2) the hardware accessory must be an MFi-qualified product. For lower data rates—somewhere below 700,000 bits per second—we would use BTLE. Again, by using BTLE we don't have to work with MFi accessories, nor do we need to use the EAAccessory framework.

Figure 13-15 depicts the hierarchical structure of Bluetooth LE. At the top is the actual BTLE device. The device contains one or more services, and each service may contain one or more characteristics. Note the similarity to the HomeKit hierarchy described earlier in this chapter.

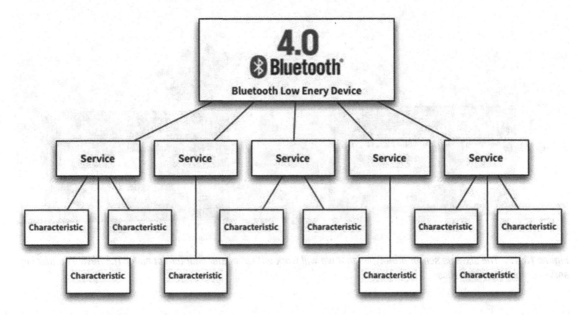

Figure 13-15. *The hierarchy of a BTLE device matches closely with the architecture of a HomeKit accessory*

In the "Sports and Games" section of this chapter I described a six-axis orientation sensor (Figure 13-16) that I developed a while back as part of an effort to quantify ballroom dance moves. Within the BTLE hierarchy, the PCB that contains the sensor functionality would be considered to be at the top of the tree; that is, it is the actual BTLE device. Although the accessory contains more than the actual Bluetooth radio, we generally refer to this as the BTLE device.

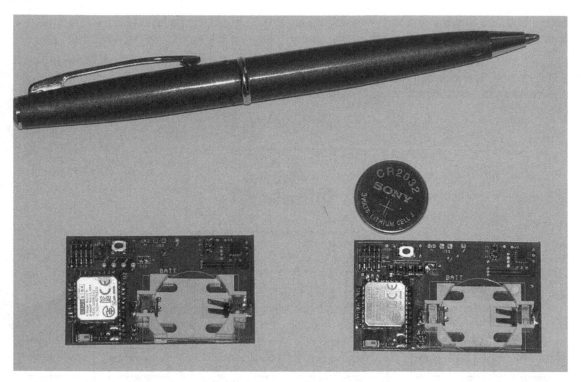

Figure 13-16. *The six-axis sensor prototypes that we will work with in a later chapter act as a BTLE device containing services and characteristics*

Note   Apple and the Bluetooth SIG (special interest group) use *device* differently. While Apple uses the term *device* to exclusively refer to an iPod, iPhone, iPad, or Apple Watch, common vernacular is to refer to something that functions as a Bluetooth accessory as a device. It's a bit confusing, but if you just pay attention to the context of the reference, you should be okay. To try and make things more clear, I'll try to use the combined terms *BTLE device* or *Apple device* as appropriate.

Just as in standard Bluetooth, BTLE contains several profile types that are common across BTLE devices. We generally only use the Generic Attribute (GATT) profile, which I like to think of as defining the memory areas for the storage of information that we will transmit across the wireless link. For the six-axis sensor, this information is described in an XML file (Figures 13-17 and 13-18).

```
1    <?xml version="1.0" encoding="UTF-8" ?>
2    <configuration>
3
4        <service uuid="1800">
5          <description>Generic Access Profile</description>
6
7          <characteristic uuid="2a00">
8            <properties read="true" const="true" />
9            <value>iThotics Sensor</value>
10         </characteristic>
11
12         <characteristic uuid="2a01">
13           <properties read="true" const="true" />
14           <value type="hex">4142</value>
15         </characteristic>
16       </service>
17
18       <service uuid="180A">
19           <characteristic uuid="2A29">
20               <properties read="true" const="true" />
21               <value>Global Tek Labs</value>
22           </characteristic>
23           <characteristic uuid="2A24">
24               <properties read="true" const="true" />
25               <value>BLE112</value>
26           </characteristic>
27           <characteristic uuid="2A25" id="xgatt_dis_2a25">
28               <properties read="true"/>
29               <value type="hex" length="6"/>
30           </characteristic>
31       </service>
```

Figure 13-17. *GATT profile (first part) for the six-axis sensor containing the standard Generic Access and Device Information services*

```
44
45    <service uuid="6d480f49-91d3-4a18-be29-0d27f4109c23">
46        <description>Sensor Attitude Data</description>
47        <!-- WHOAMI REG VALUE -->
48        <characteristic uuid="00dbf8d7-1481-43a0-a27a-62c8f56d0361" id="gatt_whoami">
49            <properties notify="true" />
50            <value length="1" type="user">0</value>
51        </characteristic>
52        <!-- status data -->
53        <characteristic uuid="e33fb4fc-8423-4124-91ba-3f933274759f" id="sensor_status">
54            <properties notify="true" />
55            <value length="1" type="user">0</value>
56        </characteristic>
57        <characteristic uuid="35c93ef0-5517-440a-ad32-222a596eafc1" id="gatt_x_motion">
58            <properties notify="true" />
59            <value length="2" type="user">0</value>
60        </characteristic>
61        <characteristic uuid="192773e5-b433-4dfe-93ae-17b713172145" id="gatt_y_motion">
62            <properties notify="true" />
63            <value length="2" type="user">0</value>
64        </characteristic>
65        <characteristic uuid="ca3c7cc5-29b9-42ad-bf78-6c73b747cd9a" id="gatt_z_motion">
66            <properties notify="true" />
67            <value length="2" type="user">0</value>
68        </characteristic>
69        <characteristic uuid="11c3876c-9bda-42cc-a30b-1be83c8059d3" id="gatt_pitch_data">
70            <properties notify="true" />
71            <value length="2" type="user">0</value>
72        </characteristic>
73        <characteristic uuid="7c55527b-4027-42ae-ae6d-6d1309e5d97e" id="gatt_roll_data">
74            <properties notify="true" />
75            <value length="2" type="user">0</value>
76        </characteristic>
77        <characteristic uuid="f1fa1ce8-cbcc-4401-8428-ae947bd512ae" id="gatt_yaw_data">
78            <properties notify="true" />
79            <value length="2" type="user">0</value>
80        </characteristic>
81
82
83    </service>
84
85 </configuration>
```

Figure 13-18. GATT profile (second part) for the six-axis sensor contains the Sensor Attitude Data Service and specific characteristics defined by the design of the circuitry and PCB

Below the device level in the BTLE hierarchy, as well as contained in the six-axis sensor PCB, are services, which then in turn contain characteristics. So, what do a service and a characteristic really look like?

Within a BTLE, we first define services, which can be seen in both Figures 13-17 and 13-18. In the first figure, two services are defined—the Generic Access Service and the Device Information Service—with UUIDs (universally unique identifier) of 1800 and 180a (hexadecimal), respectively. Note that these UUIDs are each four characters long. In the second figure, you should be able to see that only one service, the Sensor Attitude Data Service, has been defined, and with a much longer UUID. This is because the latter service is unique and specific to this piece of hardware. That is, you're not likely to find too many BTLE accessories out there with this service. Because I designed this PCB and circuitry essentially from scratch, I got to define what I want to call the service. The UUID is the unique key that I will use in the software in order to find and connect with this service when using the CoreBluetooth frameworks. The Sensor Attitude Data Service is what contains the specific sensor information, such as that regarding movement and orientation.

Again, I want to point out the difference in the lengths of the UUIDs. The first two services are common across BTLE devices. All BTLE devices should have Generic Access and Device Information services. The Generic Access Service is where you would specify the name of the BTLE device using the characteristic UUID 2a00. Because all BTLE devices should have a name, the shorter and more common four-digit UUID is used. Similarly, the Device Information Service provides placeholders for information such as the manufacturer name (Global Tek Labs, UUID: 2a29) and the model number (BLE112, UUID:2a24).

Finally, let's talk about characteristics, which are the data items that will be passed across the BTLE wireless link. To be a bit more specific, the characteristics are actually the data areas within the memory of the BTLE portion of the sensor circuitry where those values are stored. It's just like defining and naming a variable in a computer program. Looking at the first part of the GATT profile XML listing, we have already talked about the BTLE device name, manufacturer, and model number and how, because they are common, they use a four-digit UUID.

But if we look at the second part of the GATT profile, within my own defined Sensor Attitude Data Service, you'll see a number of unnamed characteristics with the much longer, 128-bit UUID structure and an ID used to name the characteristic. In our Swift code, we only use the 128-bit UUID to determine the characteristic we intend to access. In fact, we can, using the Let statement, define our UUIDs as any constant name we so choose.

> **Note**   128-bit UUIDs are used to minimize the chances of overlapping definitions of either services or characteristics in BTLE devices. Because of the long word length, the chances of two identical UUIDs being discovered with BTLE are minimal. Many online generators can be found to create UUIDs for use in BTLE devices. As an iOS developer, you should never have to be concerned with UUID generation.

Just to make sure we're on the same page, in the second part of the GATT profile you should be able to locate eight unique characteristics under the Sensor Attitude Data Service:

1. gatt_whoami

2. sensor_status

3. gatt_x_motion

4. gatt_y_motion

5. gatt_z_motion

6. gatt_pitch_data

7. gatt_roll_data

8. gatt_yaw_data

We'll discuss the relevant characteristics in greater depth as we work through the External Sensor Interface Project in Chapter 17. At this point, I just want to make sure you have a basic understanding of the information we will be accessing via the BTLE interface.

For each characteristic, regardless the service, you'll see that there is a properties line. In the first half of the GATT profile you should see a few lines that are similar to the following:

```
<properties read="true" const="true" />
```

This defines that characteristic. You can also think of it as being sort of like a property—as being read only and constant. This is because things like the name, manufacturer, model number, and so on won't change though the course of using the accessory. The read property means this characteristic gets read when initiated by the app on the other side of the Bluetooth link. If you look at the second part of the profile, you'll find lines that look like this:

```
<properties notify="true" />
```

This property line is used by the characteristic that holds changing values from the sensor electronics. Remember, the PCB (electronics circuitry) consists of two parts: the sensor and the Bluetooth module. In this section we're talking specifically about the Bluetooth communications. The sensor is really just a source of bits that get stuffed into the characteristics. These properties, in turn, define how the communications section of the Bluetooth circuitry, what we typically refer to as the Bluetooth radio, uses that data. By specifying notify="true", the radio knows to transmit this information over the Bluetooth wireless link whenever the value changes.

Although you don't see the firmware that is also part of this circuitry, it is in that code where we read the sensor values and place them into the characteristic at a rate of 10 to 20 times a second. Remember, we have six axes of data, which multiplies out to 60 to 120 data values captured and stored per second. If the sensor is still, the value may not change, and thus we don't want to reduce battery life by transmitting a value we already have. This is the essence of the notify parameter. The radio only sends a value when it changes, thus keeping the power usage as low as possible and extending battery life to the fullest.

One thing I haven't mentioned yet that is key to this whole discussion of BTLE is the roles assumed by the different sides of the communications link. The reason for this delay isn't necessarily my ineptitude as a writer, but that, as with so many other terms, Apple uses a different naming convention, and I wanted to wait until we were ready before adding much confusion to the mix.

As with most distributed systems, BTLE operates with two sides: the client and the server. The server creates or, more specifically, sources the data. It may gather the data from elsewhere, but the Bluetooth radio that sends the data is called the server. Conversely, the side that consumes or uses the data is what we refer to as the client. And while in some cases both sides may assume either role, in our remote sensor example the sensor is the server and the app running on our Apple device is the client. Got it? Now, let's make it confusing.

Core Bluetooth

In Core Bluetooth, Apple defines two different terms for the roles used in BTLE configurations. The producer of the data stream is referred to as the *peripheral* while the consumer of the data goes by the term *central*. When viewed from a software aspect, as is the role of the Core Bluetooth frameworks anyway, this sort of makes sense. Because we're writing an app, that's where all our effort tends to be focused. Our coding tends to be centralized in the iOS device we're using, and that's where we concentrate our work. In this situation, to us, the producer of the data is just a peripheral.

So, just to reiterate:

Common Bluetooth Vernacular	Apple Terminology
SERVER	PERIPHERAL
CLIENT	CENTRAL

Processing Flow

Because Apple uses their own specific terms for the two roles in a BTLE link, the use of the Core Bluetooth (CB) framework references those roles throughout the documentation. To start to become familiar with Apple terminology, I'm going to now talk a little bit about how the flow of processing would work in your iOS app. In describing the flow and code setup using Swift, I'll only use references from our project in Chapter 17 to help with consistency. The basic operational flow, when reading data from a server-only BTLE device, consists of the following steps:

1. Instantiate a central manager object.

2. Discover peripherals within range.

3. Connect to the desired peripheral(s).

4. Determine what services the peripheral has to offer.

5. For those services of interest, determine which characteristics are available.

6. Retrieve the characteristic data of interest.

Instantiate Central Manager Object

The first thing that needs to be done when using the Core Bluetooth framework is to import the framework and create a CBCentralManager, as shown below. The queue parameter sets to where we dispatch the central role events. If the value is nil, the central manager dispatches central role events using the main queue. As you see, I've simply retrieved the main queue using the dispatch_get_main_queue() method for documentation clarity, for which I could just have easily set to nil.

```
import CoreBluetooth
var manager:CBCentralManager!

manager = CBCentralManager(delegate: self, queue: dispatch_get_main_queue())
```

Note also that the delegate is set to `self`, which means that we need to subscribe to the appropriate delegate protocol. Since this happens in my `ViewController.swift` file for the sample project, the `ViewController` declaration will look like the following:

```
class ViewController: UIViewController, CBCentralManagerDelegate, CBPeripheralDelegate {}
```

You can see that we subscribe to both the `CBCentralManagerDelegate` and `CBPeripheralDelegate` protocols. We'll use the `CBCentralManagerDelegate` protocol methods immediately and the `CBPeripheralDelegate` methods once we connect to a peripheral of interest. As you will recall from our earlier discussion, in a BTLE connection we have both, in Apple terminology, a central and a peripheral. Each has its own set of protocols that we will need to follow.

After we create the central manager object, we wait to see if the object posts any changes of its state. Specifically, we are looking to see if we get an indication that the central manager is powered on. Otherwise, we may need to let the user know to turn on Bluetooth in Settings. To do this, we use the `CBCentralManager` delegate method, `centralManagerDidUpdateState`, as shown here:

```
func centralManagerDidUpdateState(central: CBCentralManager) {
    // see if our BT is powered on first
    if central.state == CBCentralManagerState.PoweredOn  { ...}
...}
```

If we determine that we are in a powered-on state, meaning Bluetooth is up and functional, we want to see what's out there. We scan for any peripherals within the range of the Bluetooth radio using the `scanForPeripheralsWithServices` method call.

Note   Bluetooth Low Energy was designed to maintain a range (distance between the Central and Peripheral) similar to standard Bluetooth, or roughly 100 meters.

Discover Peripherals

After we start the scanning process, we wait for the BTLE processor and iOS to discover and report back any BTLE devices found within range. These are identified using the Central Manager delegate method `didDiscoverPeripheral` as shown here:

```
func centralManager(central: CBCentralManager, didDiscoverPeripheral peripheral:
CBPeripheral, advertisementData: [String : AnyObject], RSSI: NSNumber) { ... }
```

This method returns an array of `CBPeripheral` objects over which we can iterate to find the specific peripheral (BTLE server) in which we are interested and to which we desire to be connected. In our example project this will be the sensor logic board.

> **Caution**   The `didDiscoverPeripheral` delegate method returns all BTLE objects in range. This could be a keyboard, a fitness monitor, a game controller, and so on. If you're at home and have an electromagnetically benign environment, then things tend to work well. Once you get out into the real, noisy, world, you'll see a lot more devices. You need to be careful as to how you look for a specific peripheral. In Swift, the `CBPeripheral` object, depending on current versus future changes in the language, could be a Swift optional. As such, you need to be careful and not force unwrap the object in case it turns out to be nil. This would crash your app.

Connect Peripheral

After iterating over the `CBPeripheral` array returned to us by the `didDiscoverPeripheral` method, we connect to that peripheral using the `connectPeripheral` method call of our Central Manager object as shown:

```
manager.connectPeripheral(peripheral, options: nil)
manager.stopScan()
```

We also may want to stop the scanning for peripherals in order to conserve the battery on our Apple device using the `stopScan` method. However, if we are looking for multiple peripherals, such as would happen if we were looking to connect to two sensors—one for each foot, for example—we'd only stop scanning once we knew that all peripherals of interest had been successfully connected.

When a successful connection is made, we are notified by the Central Manager delegate method `didConnectPeripheral` as shown here:

```
func centralManager(central: CBCentralManager, didConnectPeripheral peripheral:
CBPeripheral) { ...}
```

It is in this method where we will start to discover services using the `CBPeripheral` delegate methods. We also have other Central Manager methods we will be using, such as when we disconnect or fail to connect to a peripheral, that we'll cover more completely in Chapter 17. Just as a reminder, each peripheral (BTLE server) contains one or more services that will contain characteristics (the data) that we want to use in our iOS application.

To start the service discovery process, we use the `discoverServices` of the peripheral object of interest, first setting the delegate for our peripheral object:

```
peripheral.delegate = self
peripheral.discoverServices(nil)
```

> **Caution**   Remember, if you are connecting to multiple peripherals in the application you want to make sure you do this for each one; for example, a sensor for both the left and right feet.

Because we now have one or more connected peripherals, we'll start using peripheral methods and CBPeripheral delegate callback methods. Sometimes, when first working with the CoreBluetooth framework, it can be a little confusing as to which protocol and methods to use. Just remember that until we have a connected peripheral we don't have any CBPeripheral objects with which to work, so we use the CBCentralManager object and delegate methods.

Determine Services

After we set the peripheral delegate and call the discoverServices method, and upon receiving a set of services, the CBPeripheral delegate callback method didDiscoverServices gets activated and returns a CBService object, which represents a peripheral's service—the collection of data and associated behaviors for accomplishing a function or feature of the peripheral—as shown here:

```
func peripheral(peripheral: CBPeripheral, didDiscoverServices error: NSError?) { ..}
```

Within this method we will iterate over all the characteristics in the collection to find those of interest in our application. In our sample sensor project (Chapter 17) three services exist within the GATT profile: General Access, Device Information, and Sensor Attitude Data. We're most concerned with the characteristics in the Sensor Attitude Data Service, as that will be where information about the sensor's movement and orientation exists. Our app needs that data in order to provide a visual representation of the sensor's position and movement. The next step in the sequence would be to, for each service of interest, discover its associated characteristics using the discoverCharacteristics method:

```
sensor.discoverCharacteristics(nil , forService: aService)
```

Discover Characteristics

Once characteristics are found, the didDiscoverCharacteristicsForService CBPeripheral delegate method (Listing 13-3) callback returns a list of characteristics for each service of the connected peripheral of interest. As we iterate over the collection of characteristics for a particular service in which we are interested, we set the notify value of the characteristic to true using the setNotifyValue method. This will allow our app to process the data only when the value of a characteristic changes, thus saving power and extending the battery life.

Listing 13-3. Discovering Characteristics

```
func peripheral(peripheral: CBPeripheral, didDiscoverCharacteristicsForService service:
            CBService, error: NSError?) {
    for aCharacteristic in service.characteristics! {
        if aCharacteristic.UUID.description.uppercaseString ==
                ROLL_CHARACTERISTIC.uppercaseString
        {
                sensor.setNotifyValue(true, forCharacteristic: aCharacteristic)
        }
        if aCharacteristic.UUID.description.uppercaseString ==
                PITCH_CHARACTERISTIC.uppercaseString
```

```
        {
            sensor.setNotifyValue(true, forCharacteristic: aCharacteristic)
        }
    }
}
```

You'll see in the previous code snippet that we're only interested in two characteristics for our service—the roll and pitch. As you'll see later when we discuss the project, we put the sensor on the foot to monitor two angles along the same plane as the floor. The pitch refers to how much the toe is angled up or down relative to the floor. In other words, it's the angle of the foot to the floor. Roll refers to how much the inside or outside edge of the foot is angled to the floor, or how much you roll your foot in or out. If you've played any active sports such as tennis, volleyball, and so on, you're probably familiar with the tremendous pain when you roll your foot, resulting in a twisted ankle.

What we've done up to this point is set everything up. We still have not retrieved any actual sensor information other than the names of everything. That happens next.

> **Note** We discover characteristics of a service and not of a peripheral. The peripheral does come back to us in the delegate callback method, though in the sample project we don't make any use of it.

Retrieve Data

After we've discovered the characteristics of interest to us and set the notify value as appropriate (in our case this is true), all we need do is to fill in the didUpdateValueForCharacteristic delegate method (Listing 13-4), including whatever functionality we need to properly use characteristics, such as pitch and roll of the foot.

Listing 13-4. To Get Data from the Sensor, Use the didUpdateValueForCharacteristic Function

```
func peripheral(peripheral: CBPeripheral, didUpdateValueForCharacteristic
            characteristic: CBCharacteristic, error: NSError?) {
//
// X AXIS === FOOT ROLL
//
   if characteristic.UUID.description.uppercaseString ==
            ROLL_CHARACTERISTIC.uppercaseString { ...}


//
// Y AXIS === FOOT PITCH
//
   if characteristic.UUID.description.uppercaseString ==
            PITCH_CHARACTERISTIC.uppercaseString {...}
}
```

Core Bluetooth Summary

We've covered a lot of ground in our discussion of BTLE and the CoreBluetooth framework, which we'll be using later on to work with our sensor accessory. BTLE (Bluetooth 4.0 Low Energy) is a subset of the Bluetooth 4.0 specification and provides a way to conserve battery power in accessories. Initially intended for use where an accessory gets power from a coin cell battery such as the common CR2032 (Figure 13-19), BTLE provides a simpler, easier-to-implement solution for circuitry that does not need continuous data transmission. Most often BTLE provides a solution for BTLE servers that need to send small amounts of information from time to time. BTLE works extremely well for fitness products such as heart rate monitors. In fact, several standard BTLE profiles are available for these common types of accessories.

Figure 13-19. *Designed to work with standard coin cell batteries, BTLE provides a low-power solution for circuitry that needs to only transmit small amounts of information infrequently*

Core Bluetooth and the CoreBluetooth framework are Apple's implementation of the software tools necessary to create an iOS app that works with BTLE accessories. From Apple's perspective and the CB framework, you have a central that consumes the data provided by the peripheral. This tracks a bit differently from the more common use of *client* and *server* to represent the consumer of data and producer of data, respectively. With Core Bluetooth you set up a CBCentralManager and then use either the CBCentralManager or the CBPeripheral delegate methods to do all the work by filling in the methods with the proper logic as required.

iBeacons

One last topic I would like to address is beacons or, more specifically, iBeacons (Figure 13-20), as Apple chooses to call them. An iBeacon can be thought of as the simplest BTLE device imaginable. In fact, an iBeacon is nothing but a BTLE transmitter that sends out three pieces of information: the UUID, which we already talked about, a major number, and a minor number. There's nothing magic about major and minor; they are nothing more than a 16-bit unsigned integer and can range between 1 and 65,535; zero is not used.

iBeacon

Figure 13-20. Apple's iBeacon technology based on BTLE provides a very easy method for providing targeted information to potential customers

Note   Beacons and iBeacons are often used interchangeably, as beacon technology is also used with Android devices. To make things simpler, I'm just going to use the term iBeacon, since we're focused on Apple iOS applications in this text.

From what you've read so far, I'm sure you've discovered that I really enjoy working with hardware that connects with Apple devices. iBeacons are no exception. I love all the ideas and applications yet to be discovered that can be addressed with technology so simple. Interestingly, although I've known of iBeacons since around the release of iOS 7, they just didn't show up on my radar for a long while. Then, a few months prior to writing this chapter, I was giving the keynote speech to an IoT group about HomeKit technology. After my talk I was approached by several people wanting to know about iBeacons. I met representatives from a company called PlaceGlobal and immediately became fascinated with this technology.

From a personal perspective, I'm on a task force that is looking at how we might make our small town of Parker, Colorado (Figure 13-21) become a "connected" community for the betterment of all residents. We've designed a series of incremental pilot programs where we try something out, evaluate the results, then adjust our strategy for the next, slightly larger experiment.

Figure 13-21. The author's committee is evaluating the use of iBeacon technology to make her hometown into a better place to live while preserving its old town charm

Using iBeacon technology, we're looking at establishing relationships with a few small businesses in the main part of town. Near to each storefront will be placed an iBeacon piece of hardware (Figure 13-22) that broadcasts the three small pieces of data—UUID, major number, and minor number. Using the PlaceApp (Figures 13-22 and 13-23), information about the nearest business will be displayed on the user's mobile device. The PlaceBMS (Beacon Management System) provides customization of what the user sees and experiences as they go into and out of iBeacon hardware range.

Figure 13-22. iBeacon devices such as these are being used to create connected communities, including the author's own hometown

Figure 13-23. The PlaceApp from PlaceGlobal begins searching for any iBeacons within the area

Because the PlaceApp is customized to the specific user during setup with properties such as gender, age, and other preferences, information, like directed advertising, can be tailored to the desired needs of the user. Another very cool feature is the ability to dynamically send emergency information to PlaceApp users. If, for example, you were walking through a museum using iBeacons to navigate your way and an emergency happened, directed evacuation paths could appear on your device, taking you to the nearest exit.

We expect, over the coming months, to work with this technology to find many new and exciting scenarios to make the lives of users easier and more efficient. iBeacons won't replace the casual walk through a small town's business district, and you can always turn off your phone, but it will provide added value to the experience by highlighting those experiences you might otherwise miss. If you're a big fan of frozen yogurt and the local shop just got that new flavor you've been craving, you can instantly know about it.

Before ending this section on iBeacon technology, I want to clarify a common misperception. Many people who are casually familiar with beacons and iBeacons think that the beacon sends information to the user via BTLE and that's it. As stated previously, only three pieces of information are transmitted by the iBeacon hardware: the UUID and the major and minor numbers. That's it—nothing else is sent over BTLE.

There is one other piece of data that the receiver, the user's mobile device, has access to, and that is the signal strength of the beacon. You may recall from our discussion of Core Bluetooth that one of the parameters that came back on some of our delegate methods was RSSI, or, Received Signal Strength Indicator. This is a number that depicts how strong a signal is that we are receiving from a BTLE device. Since an iBeacon is a BTLE device, the RSSI can be used to determine the closest beacon, and we then know to which iBeacon-enabled business we are closest.

But this still does not tell us any information about the business. So, how do we get information about the business itself? We use the UUID and major and minor numbers to download information from the Internet that is then translated to what we want to know or, actually, what the business wants us to know.

Using a beacon management system such as PlaceBMS, we set up each UUID of each iBeacon with a set of records that tell the app what to do when that beacon is prominent. So, the app detects an iBeacon and sends the data to the server. The server's back-end matches the UUID, major, and minor to what has been set up, such as a specific business website. The URL for that site is then sent back to the mobile device and displayed within the window on the app.

Apps could also be customized based on both local and Internet-facilitated data, such as a walking map or even a giant arrow on the display pointing you to the storefront (Figure 13-24). For that matter, directions could be audibly provided for those people with visual impairments, or there could even be haptic feedback to distinguish between heading in the right or wrong direction. The possibilities are limited more by one's imagination than by technology.

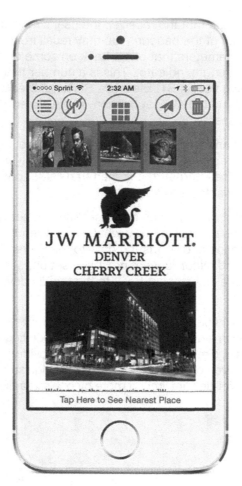

Figure 13-24.   Once iBeacon hardware has been discovered, information about the business, such as the company website, appears within the app window. The user can then interact with the site just as she would using any mobile browser.

Summary

In this last non-project chapter of our journey down the road of becoming better iOS developers, I've taken a step away from showing you *how* to do something in order to show you *what can be done*. Working with Swift and Xcode and creating this or that project will be fraught with problems, frustrations, and eventual fixes every month, week, and maybe every day for periods of time. You'll almost certainly hit, from time to time, what appears to be your breaking point and want to give up. I've been there. I've been there many times, in fact.

I'd like to be able to give you the answer, but I really don't think one exists, at least not a single answer for all situations. What I've hoped to do in this last chapter, and really throughout our journey, is to inspire you to the greatness we both know is inside us all. By working through the various steps and anticipated pitfalls, I hope I've shown to you that problems are solvable. Other people have done it for half a decade, so you can too. By showing you the fun and interesting things that are possible and being done each and every day, I hope to inspire you to continue and persevere in your own journey. Whatever you decide, I hope you have fun and can bring passion to your career to make each and every day better than the last.

Chapter 14

Swift Conversion Project

In this chapter we're going to start with an existing, very old iOS project I wrote around 2009. It's a very simple slot machine app that came out for the second-generation iPhone, the iPhone 3G. In fact, at that time there was no iOS. Apple called the operating system iPhone OS, even though it worked on the iPod Touch device as well. There was no iPad released yet.

Problem

You're asked to add features to an existing Objective-C project that would be better served using the Swift language because of its modern features, or to simply update the project.

Solution

You need to go through each of the Objective-C files and make the conversion yourself in order to ensure that things work properly.

Let's Work Through the Project

By the time this book is released I expect there will be at least a few Objective-C-to-Swift conversion programs. Today there is one called Swiftify that can be easily found on the Internet. It actually seemed to work for some simple code segments, and at the time of this writing it had a subscription-based pricing. That is, you need to pay to convert code of more than 10 KB in size. So, just for fun, I'll show you what it can do.

Listing 14-1 shows a code snippet in Objective-C that implements the ubiquitous `cellForRowAtIndexPath`, which anyone who's ever coded more than the simplest Hello, World app has written.

© Molly K. Maskrey 2016

M.K. Maskrey, *App Development Recipes for iOS and watchOS*, DOI 10.1007/978-1-4842-1820-4_14

Listing 14-1. Objective-C Showing How to Fill a Table View

```
- (UITableViewCell *)tableView:(UITableView *)tableView
        cellForRowAtIndexPath:(NSIndexPath *)indexPath
{
    static NSString *simpleTableIdentifier = @"ItemID";

    UITableViewCell *cell = [tableView dequeueReusableCellWithIdentifier:simpleTable
    Identifier];

    if (cell == nil) {
        cell = [[UITableViewCell alloc] initWithStyle:UITableViewCellStyleDefault
                reuseIdentifier:simpleTableIdentifier];
    }

    cell.textLabel.text = [tableData objectAtIndex:indexPath.row];
    return cell;
}
```

Listing 14-2 shows the result of the code in Listing 14-1 using the free version of the program.

Listing 14-2. Using the Code from Earlier

```
func tableView(tableView: UITableView, cellForRowAtIndexPath indexPath: NSIndexPath) ->
UITableViewCell {
    static var simpleTableIdentifier: String = "ItemID"
    var cell: UITableViewCell =
                tableView.dequeueReusableCellWithIdentifier(simpleTableIdentifier)
    if cell == nil {
        cell = UITableViewCell(style: UITableViewCellStyleDefault,
                reuseIdentifier: simpleTableIdentifier)
    }
    cell.textLabel.text = tableData.objectAtIndex(indexPath.row)
    return cell
}
```

I might be inclined to use this for segments of code here and there to see how well it works. For now, though, I'm going to work through our project by essentially taking it line by line or in sections where appropriate. Why, you ask? I've come up with at least three reasons. First, if I rely on a conversion program and just do quick inspections of the result, by the time I get to the point where all the conversions are completed, if the app doesn't work, I'll just have to go through it anyway to find the problem or problems. The truth is that I'm not doing much more than what this type of conversion program accomplishes, except that I'm looking at each line as I do the conversion. Because I wrote the original program, I should know every detail about the program, and they should be in the comments to make sure any details are not overlooked. Second, this app was written in a very early version of Objective-C, and the conversion tools may not be designed to work with a code base that old. Finally, the app is heavily graphics oriented. It's not a consuming game with animation or stuff like that, it's just that during this period of iPhone OS, the rudimentary graphics manipulations, such as stacking images to mask other graphics out, had to be done for even this simple game app. It was really hard back then! And yes, it was my very first "real" app, and there wasn't much around in the way of technical support.

About the App

First, I want to give a brief description about the parts of the app itself.

Naming Conventions

There are three different names that we want to be aware of. First, the original app was called TownSlot and was written to work on the iPhone 3G. For purposes of this project, I converted that project to the latest version of Objective-C and Xcode and called it SlotMachine for simplicity and to avoid confusion. The Swift-converted version of the app is called TownSlot2, again to differentiate it from the original. To speed things along, we'll use the same graphics files as were included in the original version; that is, we won't be changing the graphics to reflect the new name; it will still show on the UI as just The Town Slot.

- TownSlot = original iPhone OS app written for iPhone 3G in Objective-C

- SlotMachine = Updated version in Objective-C that will be our starting point for the conversion

- TownSlot2 = Converted Swift version, i.e., the result of this project.

Appearance

SlotMachine, our starting point, presents a single view to the user of a three-wheel Las Vegas–style slot machine, as shown in Figure 14-1. At the very top are three lights that blink after the player taps the Spin button until the "wheels" stop spinning. Each wheel is actually a long, narrow strip of images that repeats to help give the illusion of a wheel turning. The long strip contains four smaller, 9-element segments connected at the top and bottom to create a 36-element column. Figure 14-2 shows the long strip broken down into the four repeating segments. Note that the two center, 9-element strips are blurred to help give the illusion of the wheel spinning.

Figure 14-1. *Our app project presents a simple, three-wheel slot machine to the user*

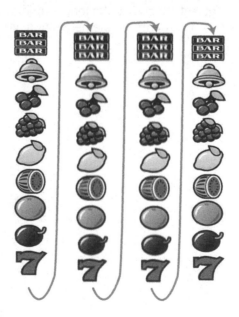

Figure 14-2. *Each "wheel" consists of a 4 x 9 (36) item strip of images. The center 18 items have been blurred to help the illusion of fast spinning*

Below the wheels are three text fields that indicate, from left to right, the amount of credits owned by the user, the amount of the current bet, and the winnings paid on the last spin. If a player loses a turn, the amount of the bet is deducted from the credits. Similarly, if she wins, the bet amount is added to the total credits. The winning or losing criteria is set inside the logic and is written in Objective-C. It varies depending on what the final spin looks like. You don't have to have three-of-a-kind necessarily to win back your bet.

Finally, at the bottom are three buttons. The Bet Max button provides the user an easy way to bet the max on a spin. The code is set to allow a maximum bet of 10 credits. The Bet+1 button adds one to the bet amount. If the current bet is 10 credits, tapping the Bet+1 button will roll over the bet to 1 credit. The Spin button starts the animation, essentially acting like the pull-arm of a traditional one-armed-bandit.

There are several sound animations. When the player presses any of the three buttons, a click is played. When the wheels are spinning, a Vegas-like little snippet of music plays. If the player loses, a sad sounding horn plays, but if she wins, a much happier bit of music is heard.

Architecture

The app consists of an AppDelegate and ViewController, each with both a header (.h) and implementation (.m) file. Because of the timeframe of when the app was initially created, storyboards are not used. Instead, the view is built programmatically in the viewDidLoad method of the ViewController.m file. The images are stacked on top of one another, with the topmost graphics being the "closest" visually to the player. At the bottom, furthest away, would be the wheels shown in Figure 14-2. Next would be the slot machine front-facing panel with any accoutrements (Figure 14-3).

Figure 14-3. The slot machine's front panel graphics are placed atop the wheels. The holes in the panel allow the current position of the wheel to be seen by the player

Labels, buttons, and flashing lights are then placed on top of the front face to allow for player interaction.

The application delegate exists as generated during the initial creation of the project and is shown in Listing 14-3.

Listing 14-3. The App Delegate Initializes the View Controller to Make It Visible to the User

```
//
//  AppDelegate.m
//  SlotMachine
//
//  Created by Molly Maskrey on 9/23/15.
//  Copyright © 2015 Global Tek Labs. All rights reserved.
//

#import "AppDelegate.h"
#import "ViewController.h"

@implementation AppDelegate

@synthesize window;
@synthesize viewController;
```

```
- (void)applicationDidFinishLaunching:(UIApplication *)application {

    [window addSubview:viewController.view];
    [window makeKeyAndVisible];
}

@end
```

The complete functionality of the app resides in the ViewController files and consists of two primary methods, viewDidLoad() and spin(). The viewDidLoad() method sets up everything for the app to function: the view hierarchy as we described earlier, the user defaults persistent storage, sounds, labels, size determination based on which device is being used, and a few others. The spin() function does all of the work when the user presses the Spin button, calling any number of subordinate methods.

To begin the conversions from Objective-C to Swift, the path I chose was to implement a top-down translation. This allowed the basics of the app to begin functioning very early in the conversion to Swift. As each method was translated to Swift, more and more operational functionality was added until eventually things worked exactly the same in both versions.

In Figure 14-4 you can see the first step of the conversion process, which shows a collapsed visualization of the ViewController.Swift file. We'll discuss the initial project creation momentarily, but since this section is concerned with the project architecture, this hierarchy of methods represents a good overview. The viewDidLoad method does all the setup; we'll show much more detail on this shortly. The didReceiveMemoryWarning method is a standard method included with any project creation to allow us to handle any cleanup when iOS may be running short of resources and thinking about shutting our app down. Because this is just a game, we're not too concerned with what happens in this example. Here, we focus more on converting between languages.

```
☐  ⊠  Q  ⚠  ⊙  ☰  ▭  ▣        ⊞  ⟨   ⟩  ⧉ townslot2 ⟩ ▥ townslot2 ⟩ ▤ ViewController.swift ⟩ ⓒ ViewController
▼ ⬚ townslot2                        7  //
  ▼ ⬚ townslot2                      8
      ▤ AppDelegate.swift            9  import UIKit
      ▤ ViewController.swift        10
      ▤ Main.storyboard             11  class ViewController: UIViewController {
      ▦ Assets.xcassets             12
      ▤ LaunchScreen.storyboard     13      override func viewDidLoad() {
      ▤ Info.plist                  14          super.viewDidLoad()
  ▶ ⬚ Products                      15          // Do any additional setup after loading the view, typically from a nib.
                                     16      }
                                     17
                                     18      override func didReceiveMemoryWarning() {
                                     19          super.didReceiveMemoryWarning()
                                     20          // Dispose of any resources that can be recreated.
                                     21      }
                                     22
                                     23
                                     24      //
                                     25      // PORTED OBJ-C METHODS to FUNCS
                                     26      //
                                     27      override func prefersStatusBarHidden() -> Bool {
                                     28          return true
                                     29      }
                                     30      func addToBet() -> () {  // Null return OPTIONAL
                                     31      }
                                     32      func addMaxToBet() {
                                     33      }
                                     34      func spin() {
                                     35      }
                                     36      func firstWheelReverse(animationID: String) {
                                     37      }
                                     38      func secondWheelReverse(animationID: String) {
                                     39      }
                                     40      func thirdWheelReverse(animationID: String) {
                                     41      }
                                     42      func spinningHasStopped(animationID: String) {
                                     43      }
                                     44      func resetGame() {
                                     45      }
                                     46      func updateLabels() {
                                     47      }
                                     48      func calculateWinnings() -> Int {
                                     49          return 1    // ****PLACEHOLDER****
                                     50      }
                                     51      func youLost() {
                                     52      }
                                     53      func setupGreenLightSequence() {
                                     54      }
                                     55      func startGreenLightAnimation() {
                                     56      }
                                     57      func stopGreenLightAnimation() {
                                     58      }
                                     59      func setupRedLightSequence() {
                                     60      }
                                     61      func startRedLightAnimation() {
                                     62      }
                                     63      func stopRedLightAnimation() {
                                     64      }
                                     65      func makeButtonClick() {
                                     66      }
                                     67      func saveGameState() {
                                     68      }
                                     69      func restoreUserSettings() {
                                     70      }
                                     71
                                     72  //
                                     73  // END VIEW CONTROLLER CLASS
                                     74  //
                                     75
                                     76  }
                                     77
```

Figure 14-4. *All the methods making up the content of the ViewController implementation file*

The prefersStatusHidden method tells iOS if we want the iPhone's status bar to be seen at the time the app is loaded. Since this is a full-screen game, we do not, so we return true. The operating system essentially calls this method in each app and, depending on the response, either hides or shows the status bar.

The addToBet and addMaxToBet methods either increment the amount the user bets on the spin by one credit or set it to the default maximum of ten credits. The spin method is called when the player taps the Spin button, simulating a pull of the arm on the one-arm-bandit. As with the viewDidLoad method, we'll also cover this in great detail shortly.

The next three routines—firstWheelReverse, secondWheelReverse, thirdWheelReverse—create a change of direction on the animation of each of the wheel image strips. Because we don't really have wheels, and because the strips are of a finite length, the spinning is simulated by moving the strip using animation one way and then the other. This creates a longer wheel-spinning effect without needing an unnecessarily long image strip. The initial animation is started in the spin method with these three being called once the animation ends; that is, when the last image on each strip is reached. Along with blurring, this provides a fairly satisfactory appearance of a spinning wheel. In a similar category, the spinningHasStopped method performs everything to determine whether the player as won or lost after the last wheel has stopped moving. The lights stop flashing, the music terminates, either a happy win sound or a sad lose sound plays, and the score is updated.

Either at the beginning of a new game or when a player has lost everything, the resetGame method clears out all the variables and starts everything at the beginning with the initial set of credits. Whenever a player wins or loses, the updateLabels method adds or subtracts the proper values from the score and shows the value on the face of the slot machine. The values are derived from the calculateWinnings method, which evaluates the quantity of credits to be added depending on the values of the wheels. This is where you might change things up; for example, maybe you want the "bar" icon to be the default scoring value rather than the cherries as I've set it. It's all up to you. If the calculateWinnings method determines the player is completely out of credits, then the youLost method gets called and the player can restart everything.

Six methods control the flashing of the red and green lights atop the image of the slot machine: setupGreenLightSequence, startGreenLightSequence, stopGreenLightSequence, setupRedLightSequence, startRedLightSequence, and stopRedLightSequence. Setup methods position the various colors depending on what size of device screen the player uses. Stop and start methods do exactly what you would expect.

The makeButtonClick method plays the audio file that simulates the clicking noise when the button is pressed. An ideal replacement might be to swap that audio file for one that sounds like an arm being pulled on an actual machine.

Finally, saveGameState and restoreUserSettings put and get critical information to persistent storage with NSUserDefaults.

These methods exist in both the Objective-C and Swift versions, though Figure 14-4 reflects the Swift file because of the ability in Xcode to easily collapse all the method implementations.

Objective-C Code

Because all of the functionality for this app resides in the ViewController files, we'll only be looking at these in our analysis. Listing 14-4 shows the ViewController.h header file, while Listing 14-5 depicts the implementation.

Listing 14-4. Objective-C ViewController Header (.h) File

```
//
//  ViewController.h
//  SlotMachine
//
//  Created by Molly Maskrey on 9/23/15.
//  Copyright © 2015 Global Tek Labs. All rights reserved.
//
```

```objc
#import <UIKit/UIKit.h>
#include <AudioToolbox/AudioToolbox.h>

#import "AppDelegate.h"

#define  numberOfIcons  9

#define  kInitialCredits 100

@class  SetupViewController;

@interface ViewController : UIViewController  {

    UIImageView  *greenLightSequenceImageView;
    UIImageView  *redLightSequenceImageView;

    SetupViewController  *setupViewController;
    BOOL        allowSpin;
    BOOL        isSpinning;
    BOOL        gameOver;
    UIView      *contentView;
    CGRect      slotStripViewWheel1PosStart;
    CGRect      slotStripViewWheel1PosEnd;
    CGRect      slotStripViewWheel2PosStart;
    CGRect      slotStripViewWheel2PosEnd;
    CGRect      slotStripViewWheel3PosStart;
    CGRect      slotStripViewWheel3PosEnd;
    CGRect      slotStripViewWheel1PosComplete;
    CGRect      slotStripViewWheel2PosComplete;
    CGRect      slotStripViewWheel3PosComplete;

    // These are the three buttons, two used for betting and one to start the spin
    UIButton    *spinButton;
    UIButton    *betButton;
    UIButton    *betMaxButton;

    // These are the three numbers shown in red at about the center of the display
    UILabel            *creditsLabel;
    UILabel            *betLabel;
    UILabel            *winLabel;

    // These three image views hold the slot icons on a long strip that we
    // move underneath the main Slot machine frame to give a sense of spinning.
    UIImageView *slotStripViewWheel1;
    UIImageView *slotStripViewWheel2;
    UIImageView *slotStripViewWheel3;

    // These are used to hold the random values for each virtual wheel
    // and the adjusted value of all three.
    NSUInteger  spin1;
    NSUInteger  spin2;
    NSUInteger  spin3;
    NSUInteger  spinValue;
```

```
    // properties that hold the credit, bet, and winnings values
    Int                winThisSpin;
    int                thisBet;
    int                totalCredits;

    // URL reference and sound object IDs for spinning, button click, winning, and losing
    CFURLRef           spinFileURLRef;
    SystemSoundID      spinSoundObject;
    CFURLRef           clickFileURLRef;
    SystemSoundID      clickSoundObject;
    CFURLRef           winFileURLRef;
    SystemSoundID      winSoundObject;
    CFURLRef           loseFileURLRef;
    SystemSoundID      loseSoundObject;

    Float       stoppingPoints[9];
}

@property         (nonatomic,retain) UIImageView  *greenLightSequenceImageView;
@property         (nonatomic,retain) UIImageView  *redLightSequenceImageView;

@property         (nonatomic,retain) SetupViewController  *setupViewController;

@property         (nonatomic, retain) UILabel     *creditsLabel;
@property         (nonatomic, retain) UILabel     *betLabel;
@property         (nonatomic, retain) UILabel     *winLabel;

@property         (nonatomic,retain) UIButton *spinButton;
@property         (nonatomic,retain) UIButton *betButton;
@property         (nonatomic,retain) UIButton *betMaxButton;

@property         (nonatomic)     BOOL    allowSpin;
@property         (nonatomic)     BOOL    gameOver;
@property         (nonatomic)     BOOL    isSpinning;

@property (readwrite)    CFURLRef           spinFileURLRef;
@property (readonly)     SystemSoundID      spinSoundObject;
@property (readwrite)    CFURLRef           clickFileURLRef;
@property (readonly)     SystemSoundID      clickSoundObject;
@property (readwrite)    CFURLRef           winFileURLRef;
@property (readonly)     SystemSoundID      winSoundObject;
@property (readwrite)    CFURLRef           loseFileURLRef;
@property (readonly)     SystemSoundID      loseSoundObject;

@property (nonatomic)  int              winThisSpin;
@property (nonatomic)  int              thisBet;
@property (nonatomic)  int              totalCredits;

@property (nonatomic, retain) UIView  *contentView;
@property (nonatomic) CGRect    slotStripViewWheel1PosStart;
@property (nonatomic) CGRect    slotStripViewWheel1PosEnd;
@property (nonatomic) CGRect    slotStripViewWheel2PosStart;
```

```objc
@property (nonatomic) CGRect      slotStripViewWheel2PosEnd;
@property (nonatomic) CGRect      slotStripViewWheel3PosStart;
@property (nonatomic) CGRect      slotStripViewWheel3PosEnd;
@property (nonatomic) CGRect      slotStripViewWheel1PosComplete;
@property (nonatomic) CGRect      slotStripViewWheel2PosComplete;
@property (nonatomic) CGRect      slotStripViewWheel3PosComplete;

@property (nonatomic, retain)     UIImageView    *slotStripViewWheel1;
@property (nonatomic, retain)     UIImageView    *slotStripViewWheel2;
@property (nonatomic, retain)     UIImageView    *slotStripViewWheel3;

@property (nonatomic, retain)     UIImageView    *topMostView;

typedef enum {
    kiPhone4S,
    kiPhone5,
    kiPhone6,
    kiPhone6Plus
} iPhoneType;

@property (nonatomic)    iPhoneType iphoneType;

-(void)spin;
-(void)makeButtonClick;
-(void)saveGameState;
-(void)restoreUserSettings;
-(int)calculateWinnings;
-(void)updateLabels;
-(void)youLost;
-(void)resetGame;

// Animations of the lights on top of the machine
-(void)setupGreenLightSequence;
-(void)startGreenLightAnimation;
-(void)stopGreenLightAnimation;
-(void)setupRedLightSequence;
-(void)startRedLightAnimation;
-(void)stopRedLightAnimation;

@end
```

Listing 14-5. Objective-C ViewController Implementation (.m) file

```objc
//
//  ViewController.m
//  SlotMachine
//
//  Created by Molly Maskrey on 9/23/15.
//  Copyright © 2015 Global Tek Labs. All rights reserved.
//
```

```
#import    <AudioToolbox/AudioToolbox.h>

#import "ViewController.h"

@implementation ViewController

@synthesize    setupViewController;
@synthesize    greenLightSequenceImageView;
@synthesize    redLightSequenceImageView;

@synthesize    gameOver;
@synthesize allowSpin;
@synthesize    isSpinning;
@synthesize spinButton;

@synthesize    betButton;
@synthesize betMaxButton;

@synthesize winThisSpin;
@synthesize thisBet;
@synthesize    totalCredits;

@synthesize    creditsLabel;
@synthesize    betLabel;
@synthesize    winLabel;

@synthesize    contentView;
@synthesize    slotStripViewWheel1PosStart;
@synthesize    slotStripViewWheel1PosEnd;
@synthesize    slotStripViewWheel2PosStart;
@synthesize    slotStripViewWheel2PosEnd;
@synthesize    slotStripViewWheel3PosStart;
@synthesize    slotStripViewWheel3PosEnd;
@synthesize slotStripViewWheel1PosComplete;
@synthesize slotStripViewWheel2PosComplete;
@synthesize slotStripViewWheel3PosComplete;

@synthesize    slotStripViewWheel1;
@synthesize    slotStripViewWheel2;
@synthesize    slotStripViewWheel3;
@synthesize topMostView;

@synthesize spinFileURLRef;
@synthesize spinSoundObject;
@synthesize clickFileURLRef;
@synthesize clickSoundObject;
@synthesize winFileURLRef;
@synthesize winSoundObject;
@synthesize loseFileURLRef;
@synthesize loseSoundObject;

@synthesize iphoneType;
```

```
//NSNotificationCenter messages
NSString * const userResetGame = @"resetGame";

// delta value used to move over the wheels
float shiftOverValue = 0.0;

// By setting this the return value of this method to YES, the
// UIViewController will hide the small status bar at the top
// allowing more usable space for the slot graphics.
-(BOOL)prefersStatusBarHidden{
    return YES;
}

// Used to set the amount of credits that we bet on the next spin
-(void)addToBet
{
    if (thisBet < totalCredits) {
        if (self.thisBet < 10)
        {
            self.thisBet++;         // bump bet
        } else
            self.thisBet = 1;
        [self updateLabels];
        self.allowSpin = YES;
    }else { // can't bet more than what you have left
        NSLog(@"Can't bet more than you have left");
        self.thisBet = 0;
        [self updateLabels];
        self.allowSpin = NO;
    }

}

// Default to the max bet, which is 10 credits
-(void)addMaxToBet
{
    if (totalCredits == 0) return;     // can't bet
    if (totalCredits < 10) {
        self.thisBet = totalCredits;
    }
    else {
        self.thisBet = 10;
    }

    [self updateLabels];

}

//
// The primary method called when the device loads the view.
// Here, we set up pretty much everything to begin playing the game.
// NSLog statements are used to show information to the console periodiclly
```

```objc
// as things happen (as the program runs) to let us know what's going on.
//
- (void)viewDidLoad {
    [super viewDidLoad];
    // Do any additional setup after loading the view, typically from a nib
    NSLog(@"viewDidLoad");

    isSpinning    = NO;          // initially not spinning;

    stoppingPoints[0] = 95.0;
    stoppingPoints[1] = 35.0;
    stoppingPoints[2] = -25.0;
    stoppingPoints[3] = -85.0;
    stoppingPoints[4] = -145.0;
    stoppingPoints[5] = -210.0;
    stoppingPoints[6] = -270.0;
    stoppingPoints[7] = -330.0;
    stoppingPoints[8] = -395.0;

    //SETUP NOTIFICATION CENTER
    NSNotificationCenter *nc = [NSNotificationCenter defaultCenter];
    [nc addObserver:self selector:@selector(resetGame) name:userResetGame object:nil];
    NSLog(@"Registered with notification center");

    // *** Create the MAIN WINDOW
    CGSize     appSize      = [UIScreen mainScreen].bounds.size;
    CGRect  appRect = CGRectMake(0.0, 0.0, appSize.width, appSize.height);

    NSLog(@"screen size: Width: %f, Height: %f",appSize.width,appSize.height);

    //
    // Determine iPhone type (4,5,6,6P) from screen size so we can
    // us that to correctly position
    if ((appSize.width == 320.0) && (appSize.height == 480.0)) {
        iphoneType = kiPhone4S;
        NSLog(@"iPhone4S");
    } else if ((appSize.width == 320.0) && (appSize.height == 568.0)) {
        iphoneType = kiPhone5;
        NSLog(@"iPhone5");
    } else if ((appSize.width == 375.0) && (appSize.height == 667.0)) {
        iphoneType = kiPhone6;
        NSLog(@"iPhone6");
    } else if ((appSize.width == 414.0) && (appSize.height == 736.0)) {
        iphoneType = kiPhone6Plus;
        NSLog(@"iPhone6 Plus");
    }

    contentView = [[UIView alloc]    initWithFrame:appRect];
    contentView.backgroundColor = [UIColor blackColor];
    [self.view  addSubview:contentView];
```

```objc
// Pick Slot Face Image based on screen size
switch (iphoneType) {
    case kiPhone4S:
        topMostView = [[UIImageView alloc] initWithFrame:CGRectMake(0.0f,0.0f,320.0f,480.0f)];
        [topMostView        setImage:[UIImage        imageNamed:@"SlotFaceiPhoneBasic.png"]];
        break;
    case kiPhone5:
        topMostView = [[UIImageView alloc] initWithFrame:CGRectMake(0.0f,0.0f,320.0f,568.0f)];
        [topMostView        setImage:[UIImage        imageNamed:@"SlotFaceiPhone5.png"]];
        break;
    case kiPhone6:
        topMostView = [[UIImageView alloc] initWithFrame:CGRectMake(0.0f,0.0f,375.0f,66
        7.0f)];
        [topMostView        setImage:[UIImage        imageNamed:@"SlotFaceiPhone6.png"]];
        break;
    case kiPhone6Plus:
        topMostView = [[UIImageView alloc] initWithFrame:CGRectMake(0.0f,0.0f,414.0f,736.0f)];
        [topMostView        setImage:[UIImage        imageNamed:@"SlotFaceiPhone6Plus.png"]];
        break;

    default:
        break;
}

// See if the user has played before and pull up last wheel positions

NSMutableArray        *userData;
userData = [[NSUserDefaults standardUserDefaults] objectForKey:@"gameState"];

// Slide the wheels over to the right (value) depending on screen size
switch (iphoneType) {
    case kiPhone4S:
    case kiPhone5:
        break;
    case kiPhone6:
        shiftOverValue = 30.0;
        break;
    case kiPhone6Plus:
        shiftOverValue = 50.0;
        break;

    default:
        break;
}

if ([userData count] == 6)  // if data is present, then the game state was saved previously
{

    slotStripViewWheel1PosStart  = CGRectMake(33.0f + shiftOverValue,
stoppingPoints[[[userData objectAtIndex:0]  intValue]], 90.0f, 2900.0f);
    slotStripViewWheel2PosStart  = CGRectMake(116.0f + shiftOverValue,
stoppingPoints[[[userData objectAtIndex:1]  intValue]], 90.0f, 2900.0f);
```

```
        slotStripViewWheel3PosStart  = CGRectMake(199.0f + shiftOverValue,
stoppingPoints[[[userData objectAtIndex:2]   intValue]], 90.0f, 2900.0f);

        self.winThisSpin = [[userData  objectAtIndex:3] intValue];
        self.thisBet     = [[userData  objectAtIndex:4] intValue];
        self.totalCredits = [[userData objectAtIndex:5] intValue];

    } else {  // if not any data, then restart game state

        NSLog(@"initializing game - no data was stored");

        slotStripViewWheel1PosStart    = CGRectMake(33.0f + shiftOverValue, 95.0f, 90.0f, 2900.0f);
        slotStripViewWheel2PosStart    = CGRectMake(116.0f + shiftOverValue, 95.0f, 90.0f, 2900.0f);
        slotStripViewWheel3PosStart    = CGRectMake(199.0f + shiftOverValue, 95.0f, 90.0f, 2900.0f);

        [self resetGame];
    }
    // set up the slot wheel positions that are not saved...i.e., the end position where we
    reverse the wheel
    // to make it look like a long spin

    slotStripViewWheel1PosEnd    = CGRectMake(33.0f + shiftOverValue, -2600.0f, 90.0f, 2900.0f);
    slotStripViewWheel2PosEnd    = CGRectMake(116.0f + shiftOverValue, -2600.0f, 90.0f, 2900.0f);
    slotStripViewWheel3PosEnd    = CGRectMake(199.0f + shiftOverValue, -2600.0f, 90.0f, 2900.0f);

    slotStripViewWheel1  = [[UIImageView alloc] initWithFrame:slotStripViewWheel1PosStart];
    [slotStripViewWheel1    setImage:[UIImage    imageNamed:@"SlotStripLong.png"]];

    slotStripViewWheel2  = [[UIImageView alloc] initWithFrame:slotStripViewWheel2PosStart];
    [slotStripViewWheel2    setImage:[UIImage imageNamed:@"SlotStripLong.png"]];

    slotStripViewWheel3  = [[UIImageView alloc] initWithFrame:slotStripViewWheel3PosStart];
    [slotStripViewWheel3      setImage:[UIImage        imageNamed:@"SlotStripLong.png"]];

    // SET UP SCORING LABELS
    // CREDITS

    creditsLabel = [[UILabel alloc] initWithFrame:CGRectMake(0.0f, 0.0f, 75.0f, 20.0f)];
    self.creditsLabel.textAlignment = NSTextAlignmentRight;
    self.creditsLabel.backgroundColor = [UIColor blackColor];
    self.creditsLabel.textColor = [UIColor redColor];
    self.creditsLabel.font = [UIFont boldSystemFontOfSize:20];
    NSString *totString = [[NSString alloc] initWithFormat:@"%d",totalCredits];

    // THIS BET
    betLabel = [[UILabel alloc] initWithFrame:CGRectMake(0.0f, 0.0f, 25.0f, 20.0f)];
    self.betLabel.textAlignment = NSTextAlignmentRight;
    self.betLabel.backgroundColor = [UIColor blackColor];
    self.betLabel.textColor = [UIColor redColor];
    self.betLabel.font = [UIFont boldSystemFontOfSize:20];
    NSString *betString = [[NSString alloc] initWithFormat:@"%d",thisBet];
```

```objc
// THIS SPIN'S WIN VALUE
winLabel = [[UILabel alloc] initWithFrame:CGRectMake(0.0f, 0.0f, 35.0f, 20.0f)];
self.winLabel.textAlignment = NSTextAlignmentRight;
self.winLabel.backgroundColor = [UIColor blackColor];
self.winLabel.textColor = [UIColor redColor];
self.winLabel.font = [UIFont boldSystemFontOfSize:20];
NSString *winString = [[NSString alloc] initWithFormat:@"%d",winThisSpin];

// SET UP BUTTONS
// SPIN BUTTON
spinButton = [[UIButton    alloc] initWithFrame:CGRectMake(0.0f, 0.0f, 65.0f, 65.0f)];
[spinButton    setBackgroundImage:[UIImage        imageNamed:@"spinButton.
png"]         forState:UIControlStateNormal];
[spinButton  setBackgroundImage:[UIImage            imageNamed:@"spinButtonPressed.
png"]     forState:UIControlStateHighlighted];
[spinButton  addTarget:self action:@selector(spin) forControlEvents:UIControlEventTouch
UpInside];
[spinButton  addTarget:self action:@selector(makeButtonClick) forControlEvents:UIContro
lEventTouchDown];

//BET BUTTON
betButton = [[UIButton    alloc] initWithFrame:CGRectMake(0.0f, 0.0f, 65.0f, 65.0f)];
[betButton  setBackgroundImage:[UIImage        imageNamed:@"betButton.png"]      forState:
UIControlStateNormal];
[betButton  addTarget:self action:@selector(addToBet) forControlEvents:UIControlEvent
TouchUpInside];
[betButton  addTarget:self action:@selector(makeButtonClick) forControlEvents:UIControl
EventTouchDown];

//BET MAX BUTTON
betMaxButton = [[UIButton  alloc] initWithFrame:CGRectMake(0.0f, 0.0f, 65.0f, 65.0f)];
[betMaxButton      setBackgroundImage:[UIImage          imageNamed:@"betMaxButton.png"]
forState:UIControlStateNormal];
[betMaxButton        addTarget:self action:@selector(addMaxToBet) forControlEvents:
UIControlEventTouchUpInside];
[betMaxButton        addTarget:self action:@selector(makeButtonClick) forControlEvents:
UIControlEventTouchDown];

// Pick based on screen size
switch (iphoneType) {
    case kiPhone4S:
    case kiPhone5:
        [creditsLabel    setCenter:CGPointMake(93.0f,213.0f)];
        [betLabel  setCenter:CGPointMake(160.0f,213.0f)];
        [winLabel  setCenter:CGPointMake(220.0f,213.0f)];
        [spinButton  setCenter:CGPointMake(260.0f,300.0f)];
        [betButton  setCenter:CGPointMake(150.0f,300.0f)];
        [betMaxButton      setCenter:CGPointMake(65.0f,300.0f)];
        break;
```

```
        case kiPhone6:
            [creditsLabel      setCenter:CGPointMake(120.0f,216.0f)];
            [betLabel  setCenter:CGPointMake(190.0f,216.0f)];
            [winLabel  setCenter:CGPointMake(255.0f,216.0f)];
            [spinButton  setCenter:CGPointMake(290.0f,302.0f)];
            [betButton  setCenter:CGPointMake(190.0f,302.0f)];
            [betMaxButton  setCenter:CGPointMake(100.0f,302.0f)];
            break;
        case kiPhone6Plus:
            [creditsLabel  setCenter:CGPointMake(140.0f,212.0f)];
            [betLabel  setCenter:CGPointMake(212.0f,212.0f)];
            [winLabel  setCenter:CGPointMake(280.0f,212.0f)];
            [spinButton  setCenter:CGPointMake(320.0f,300.0f)];
            [betButton  setCenter:CGPointMake(220.0f,300.0f)];
            [betMaxButton  setCenter:CGPointMake(120.0f,300.0f)];
            break;

        default:
            break;
    }
    self.creditsLabel.text = totString;
    self.betLabel.text = betString;
    self.winLabel.text = winString;

    [contentView        addSubview:slotStripViewWheel1];
    [contentView        addSubview:slotStripViewWheel2];
    [contentView        addSubview:slotStripViewWheel3];
    [contentView        addSubview:topMostView];

    [contentView        addSubview:spinButton];
    [contentView        addSubview:betButton];
    [contentView        addSubview:betMaxButton];
    [contentView        addSubview:creditsLabel];
    [contentView        addSubview:betLabel];
    [contentView        addSubview:winLabel];

    // restore user setting
//    [self restoreUserSettings];                     // things like spin, score, etc

    // SET UP SOUNDS
    CFBundleRef mainBundle;
    mainBundle = CFBundleGetMainBundle ();

    // Get the URL to the sound file to play
    spinFileURLRef =     CFBundleCopyResourceURL (
                                        mainBundle,
                                        CFSTR ("spinSound1"),
                                        CFSTR ("wav"),
                                        NULL
                                        );
```

```
  clickFileURLRef  =     CFBundleCopyResourceURL (
                                        mainBundle,
                                        CFSTR ("click1"),
                                        CFSTR ("wav"),
                                        NULL
                                        );
  winFileURLRef  =     CFBundleCopyResourceURL (
                                        mainBundle,
                                        CFSTR ("win"),
                                        CFSTR ("wav"),
                                        NULL
                                        );
  loseFileURLRef  =     CFBundleCopyResourceURL (
                                        mainBundle,
                                        CFSTR ("youLose"),
                                        CFSTR ("wav"),
                                        NULL
                                        );
  // Create a system sound object representing the sound file
  AudioServicesCreateSystemSoundID (
                                    spinFileURLRef,
                                    &spinSoundObject
                                    );
  AudioServicesCreateSystemSoundID (
                                    clickFileURLRef,
                                    &clickSoundObject
                                    );
  AudioServicesCreateSystemSoundID (
                                    winFileURLRef,
                                    &winSoundObject
                                    );
  AudioServicesCreateSystemSoundID (
                                    loseFileURLRef,
                                    &loseSoundObject
                                    );

  //SETUP LIGHTS
  [self setupGreenLightSequence];
  [self setupRedLightSequence];

}

- (void)didReceiveMemoryWarning {
    [super didReceiveMemoryWarning];
    // Dispose of any resources that can be recreated.
}
```

```
// GAME PLAY METHODS

// Spin, of course, does the most of the work when the player clicks on the 'spin' button.
// in the viewDidLoad method above, you can see that when we create the spin button, we set
// the "selector" to 'spin,' which is this function. This is the example of event-driven
programming;
// when the spin button event occurs, iOS (the operating system) calls this function to be
executed.
-(void)spin
{

    // start flashing the red and green lights at the top of
    // the slot machine image on the device.
    [self startGreenLightAnimation];
    [self startRedLightAnimation];

    // If we're spinning, disable the buttons so the player can't cause
    // problems much like a real slot machine

    isSpinning = YES;
    spinButton.enabled = NO;
    betButton.enabled = NO;
    betMaxButton.enabled = NO;

    //  THE THREE SPINS - generate a random place to stop on our simulated 'wheel'

    spin1 = arc4random() % numberOfIcons;                        // large number
modulo the # of icons
    spin2 = arc4random() % numberOfIcons;                        // large number
modulo the # of icons
    spin3 = arc4random() % numberOfIcons;                        // large number
modulo the # of icons

    // Create a single number that tells us what the spin is
    // using a decimal scheme...one wheel is the hundreds position, one the tens, and
    // the right-most is the ones position.

    spinValue = (spin1 * 100) + (spin2 * 10) + spin3;

    NSLog(@"The three wheel spins are: %lu, %lu, %lu",(unsigned long)spin1,(unsigned long)
spin2,(unsigned long)spin3);
    NSLog(@"Spin Value = %lu", (unsigned long)spinValue);

    slotStripViewWheel1PosComplete       = CGRectMake(33.0f + shiftOverValue,
stoppingPoints[spin1], 90.0f, 2900.0f);
    slotStripViewWheel2PosComplete       = CGRectMake(116.0f + shiftOverValue,
stoppingPoints[spin2], 90.0f, 2900.0f);
    slotStripViewWheel3PosComplete       = CGRectMake(199.0f + shiftOverValue,
stoppingPoints[spin3], 90.0f, 2900.0f);
```

```
    // These three chunks of code set up the animation of each of the three 'wheels'
    // essentially, all were doing is moving the strips of fruit images up and down
    // to give the appearance of the three wheels spinning.
    //
    [UIView      beginAnimations:@"wheel1" context:nil];
    [UIView      setAnimationDelegate:self];
    [UIView      setAnimationDidStopSelector:@selector(firstWheelReverse:)];
    [UIView      setAnimationCurve: UIViewAnimationCurveEaseIn];
    [UIView      setAnimationDuration:2.0];
    [slotStripViewWheel1      setFrame:slotStripViewWheel1PosEnd];
    [UIView      commitAnimations];

    [UIView      beginAnimations:@"wheel2" context:nil];
    [UIView      setAnimationDelegate:self];
    [UIView      setAnimationDidStopSelector:@selector(secondWheelReverse:)];
    [UIView      setAnimationCurve: UIViewAnimationCurveEaseIn];
    [UIView      setAnimationDuration:2.0];
    [slotStripViewWheel2      setFrame:slotStripViewWheel2PosEnd];
    [UIView      commitAnimations];

    [UIView      beginAnimations:@"wheel3" context:nil];
    [UIView      setAnimationDelegate:self];
    [UIView      setAnimationDidStopSelector:@selector(thirdWheelReverse:)];
    [UIView      setAnimationCurve: UIViewAnimationCurveEaseIn];
    [UIView      setAnimationDuration:2.0];
    [slotStripViewWheel3      setFrame:slotStripViewWheel3PosEnd];
    [UIView      commitAnimations];

    // SOUNDS
    AudioServicesPlaySystemSound (self.spinSoundObject);

} // end SPIN method

//
// Because we are using finite-length strips of images to simulate a continuous
// 'wheel' to get that sense of spinning, when we reach the end of a strip, we
// just reverse it and move it the other way, hoping the details of what we're doing
// aren't visible on the screen to the player.

- (void)firstWheelReverse:(NSString *)animationID {
    [UIView      beginAnimations:@"reverseWheel1" context:nil];
    [UIView      setAnimationCurve: UIViewAnimationCurveEaseOut];
    [UIView      setAnimationDuration:1.0];
    [slotStripViewWheel1      setFrame:slotStripViewWheel1PosComplete];
    [UIView      commitAnimations];
}
- (void)secondWheelReverse:(NSString *)animationID {
    [UIView      beginAnimations:@"reverseWheel2" context:nil];
    [UIView      setAnimationCurve: UIViewAnimationCurveEaseOut];
    [UIView      setAnimationDuration:1.4];
    [slotStripViewWheel2      setFrame:slotStripViewWheel2PosComplete];
    [UIView      commitAnimations];
}
```

```
- (void)thirdWheelReverse:(NSString *)animationID  {          // Assume third wheel is the
last to stop
    NSLog(@"Spinning Has Stopped");
    [UIView     beginAnimations:@"reverseWheel3" context:nil];
    [UIView     setAnimationDelegate:self];
    [UIView     setAnimationDidStopSelector:@selector(spinningHasStopped:)];

    [UIView     setAnimationCurve: UIViewAnimationCurveEaseOut];
    [UIView     setAnimationDuration:1.8];
    [slotStripViewWheel3     setFrame:slotStripViewWheel3PosComplete];
    [UIView     commitAnimations];
}


//
// When the animation has completed, this method executes.
// We enable the buttons again so the player can continue,
// play sounds, stop flashing the lights, etc.
//
-(void)spinningHasStopped:(NSString *)animationID
{

    int     winMultiplier;
    NSLog(@"spinningHasStopped CALLED");
    isSpinning = NO;
    spinButton.enabled = YES;
    betButton.enabled = YES;
    betMaxButton.enabled = YES;

    //STOP LIGHTS
    [self stopGreenLightAnimation];
    [self stopRedLightAnimation];

    // CHECK FOR WIN

    winMultiplier = [self calculateWinnings];
    // Lose
    if (winMultiplier == 0) {
        self.totalCredits -= self.thisBet;
        AudioServicesPlaySystemSound (self.loseSoundObject);
    } else { // Win
        self.totalCredits += (self.thisBet * winMultiplier);
        AudioServicesPlaySystemSound (self.winSoundObject);
    }

    [self updateLabels];
    // save state
    [self saveGameState ];
}
```

```objc
-(void)resetGame
{
    NSLog(@"RESET GAME");
    [self makeButtonClick];
    self.winThisSpin = 0;
    self.thisBet = 1;
    self.totalCredits = kInitialCredits;
    self.allowSpin = YES;
    self.gameOver = NO;
    [self updateLabels];
    // save state - in case user exits immediately after a reset either from alert or info panel
    [self saveGameState];

}


//
// This method posts the values for bet, total credits, and win amount to the
// display on the slot machine front panel image.
//
-(void)updateLabels;
{
    //TOTAL
    NSString *totString = [[NSString alloc] initWithFormat:@"%d", totalCredits];
    [creditsLabel    setText:totString];
    //BET
    NSString *betString = [[NSString alloc] initWithFormat:@"%d", thisBet];
    [betLabel       setText:betString];
    //WIN AMMOUNT
    NSString *winString = [[NSString alloc] initWithFormat:@"%d", winThisSpin];
    [winLabel       setText:winString];
}


//
// Here is where you can change how you want to pay out to the
// player depending on the spin
//
-(int)calculateWinnings
{
    int     winMultiplier;

    // Any single cherry
    if ((spin1  == 2) && (spin2 != 2) && (spin3 != 2)) return 1;
    if ((spin1  != 2) && (spin2 == 2) && (spin3 != 2)) return 1;
    if ((spin1  != 2) && (spin2 != 2) && (spin3 == 2)) return 1;

    // Any DOUBLE cherry
    if ((spin1  == 2) && (spin2 == 2) && (spin3 != 2)) return 3;
    if ((spin1  != 2) && (spin2 == 2) && (spin3 == 2)) return 3;
    if ((spin1  == 2) && (spin2 != 2) && (spin3 == 2)) return 3;
```

```objc
    // Three CHERRIES
    if ((spin1 == 2) && (spin2 == 2) && (spin3 == 2)) return 150;

    switch (spinValue) {
        case 000:
            winMultiplier = 100;     // 3 Bars
            break;
        case 888:
            winMultiplier = 100;     // 3 sevens
            break;
        case 111:
        case 222:
        case 333:
        case 444:
        case 555:
        case 666:
        case 777:
            winMultiplier = 3;          // 3 anything else --> 3X bet
            break;

        default:
            winMultiplier = 0;          // anything else --> lose
            break;
    }
    return     winMultiplier;
}

// Pop up an alert to let user reset the game
-(void) youLost
{
    UIAlertController   *alert = [UIAlertController      alertControllerWithTitle:@"You Lose"
message:@"Lost it all huh? Way to go champ!" preferredStyle:UIAlertControllerStyleAlert];
    [self presentViewController:alert animated:YES completion:nil];
}

// LIGHT ANIMATIONS
-(void)setupGreenLightSequence
{
    UIImage* img1;
    UIImage* img2;
    UIImage* img3;
    UIImage* img4;
    UIImage* img5;

    greenLightSequenceImageView = [[UIImageView alloc] init];
    if (iphoneType == kiPhone6Plus) {
        img1 = [UIImage imageNamed:@"100greenTop6P.png"];
        img2 = [UIImage imageNamed:@"110greenTop6P.png"];
        img3 = [UIImage imageNamed:@"111greenTop6P.png"];
        img4 = [UIImage imageNamed:@"011greenTop6P.png"];
```

```objc
    } else { //smaller screen size
        img1 = [UIImage imageNamed:@"100greenTop.png"];
        img2 = [UIImage imageNamed:@"110greenTop.png"];
        img3 = [UIImage imageNamed:@"111greenTop.png"];
        img4 = [UIImage imageNamed:@"011greenTop.png"];

    }
    NSArray *images = [NSArray arrayWithObjects:img1, img2,img3,img4,img5, nil];

    [greenLightSequenceImageView setAnimationImages:images];
    [greenLightSequenceImageView setAnimationRepeatCount:0];
    [greenLightSequenceImageView setAnimationDuration:0.5];

    switch (iphoneType) {
        case kiPhone4S:
            greenLightSequenceImageView.frame = CGRectMake(71,1, 200, 20);
            break;
        case kiPhone5:
            greenLightSequenceImageView.frame = CGRectMake(71,1, 200, 20);
            break;
        case kiPhone6:
            greenLightSequenceImageView.frame = CGRectMake(100,1, 200, 20);
            break;
        case kiPhone6Plus:
            greenLightSequenceImageView.frame = CGRectMake(114,1, 200, 20);
            break;

        default:
            break;
    }

}

-(void)startGreenLightAnimation
{
    [greenLightSequenceImageView startAnimating];
    [self.view addSubview:greenLightSequenceImageView];
}
-(void)stopGreenLightAnimation
{
    [greenLightSequenceImageView stopAnimating];
    [greenLightSequenceImageView       removeFromSuperview];
}
-(void)setupRedLightSequence
{
    UIImage* img1;
    UIImage* img2;
    UIImage* img3;
    UIImage* img4;
    UIImage* img5;
```

```objc
    redLightSequenceImageView = [[UIImageView alloc] init];
    if (iphoneType == kiPhone6Plus) {
        img1 = [UIImage imageNamed:@"001redBottom6P.png"];
        img2 = [UIImage imageNamed:@"011redBottom6P.png"];
        img3 = [UIImage imageNamed:@"111redBottom6P.png"];
        img4 = [UIImage imageNamed:@"110redBottom6P.png"];
        img5 = [UIImage imageNamed:@"100redBottom6P.png"];
    } else { //smaller screen size
        img1 = [UIImage imageNamed:@"001redBottom.png"];
        img2 = [UIImage imageNamed:@"011redBottom.png"];
        img3 = [UIImage imageNamed:@"111redBottom.png"];
        img4 = [UIImage imageNamed:@"110redBottom.png"];
        img5 = [UIImage imageNamed:@"100redBottom.png"];

    }
    NSArray *images = [NSArray arrayWithObjects:img1, img2,img3,img4,img5, nil];

    [redLightSequenceImageView setAnimationImages:images];
    [redLightSequenceImageView setAnimationRepeatCount:0];
    [redLightSequenceImageView setAnimationDuration:0.5];
    switch (iphoneType) {
        case kiPhone4S:
            redLightSequenceImageView.frame = CGRectMake(71,5, 200, 15);
            break;
        case kiPhone5:
            redLightSequenceImageView.frame = CGRectMake(71,5, 200, 15);
            break;
        case kiPhone6:
            redLightSequenceImageView.frame = CGRectMake(100,5, 200, 15);
            break;
        case kiPhone6Plus:
            redLightSequenceImageView.frame = CGRectMake(114,5, 200, 15);
            break;

        default:
            break;
    }
}

-(void)startRedLightAnimation
{
    NSLog(@"Start Animating RED");
    [redLightSequenceImageView startAnimating];
    [self.view addSubview:redLightSequenceImageView];
}
-(void)stopRedLightAnimation
{
    [redLightSequenceImageView stopAnimating];
    [redLightSequenceImageView     removeFromSuperview];
}
```

```objc
// SOUND ANIMATIONS
-(void)makeButtonClick
{
    AudioServicesPlaySystemSound (self.clickSoundObject);
}


// PERSISTANCE - this saves the player's game state.
// Because we greatly simplified this game for newer versions of
// iOS, we don't actually do that much here. We're more concerned
// in this exercise about the process of converting, so while we
// do care about game state items such as score and last spin, we
// are not concerned about switch settings for whether to play sounds
// or not.
//
-(void)saveGameState
{
    NSLog(@"Calling Save Game State");
    NSMutableArray *userData = [[NSMutableArray    alloc] init];
    [userData    addObject:[NSNumber numberWithInt:(int)spin1]];
    [userData    addObject:[NSNumber numberWithInt:(int)spin2]];
    [userData    addObject:[NSNumber numberWithInt:(int)spin3]];
    [userData    addObject:[NSNumber    numberWithInt:self.winThisSpin]];
    [userData    addObject:[NSNumber    numberWithInt:self.thisBet]];
    [userData    addObject:[NSNumber    numberWithInt:self.totalCredits]];

    [[NSUserDefaults    standardUserDefaults] setObject: userData forKey:@"gameState"];
    [[NSUserDefaults    standardUserDefaults] synchronize];
}

-(void)restoreUserSettings
{

    NSLog(@"Called restore user settings");
    // CHECK USER SETTINGS

}

@end
```

We won't be going through the conversion line by line, as that would take up far too much space, and, frankly, it would be pretty boring. Instead, I want to walk through a few examples of where we convert Objective-C to Swift. Simple assignments, conditionals, operations and so forth work nearly the same across the languages. Other specific features of Swift as it differs from Objective-C are well known, such as not needing semicolons, or that all potential conditions in a switch need to be explicitly handled.

I'll focus instead on the issues you're likely to come up against that you probably didn't think about. Also, we'll cover some of the differences in how you use certain frameworks when porting our slot machine app.

Project Setup

Problem

You're given the Objective-C project, but you can't just convert it as it is. You want to use it as a reference and make sure things work as expected.

Solution

We want to set up a completely new project and work with them side by side until everything functions exactly as we would expect. First, create a new iOS single view application project, as shown in Figure 14-5.

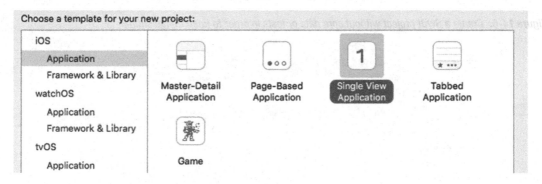

Figure 14-5. Create a single view project to begin the conversion

I chose to call this project townslot2 (Figure 14-6) in order to differentiate it from the original app name, but at the same time keep it similar. If we decide to publish it in the App Store we'll have a usable name, since Apple's database would recognize the original townslot app and reject our reuse of the name. Note that I'm not including any Unit or UI Testing in order to focus on just the conversion process. While we could use Core Data for persistent storage, that would be a bit of overkill for our needs of simply storing six values; it would also deviate from the original app's design. Finally, as seen in Figure 14-7, don't select "Create a Git repository," as we will address source control in a different section of this book.

Product Name: townslot2

Organization Name: Global Tek Labs

Organization Identifier: ▆▆▆▆▆▆▆▆▆

Bundle Identifier: ▆▆▆▆▆▆▆▆.townslot2

Language ✓ Swift

Objective-C

Devices: iPhone

☐ Use Core Data
☐ Include Unit Tests
☐ Include UI Tests

Figure 14-6. Create a Swift project without core data or tests in order to keep things simple

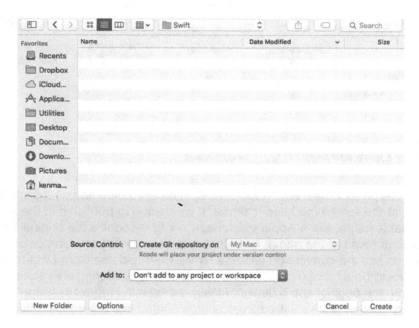

Figure 14-7. We won't be worried about source code control in this example

That gets us to where we need to be, with a new, blank Swift project in which we can place our newly converted Swift code.

Problem

After creating the project, our build settings show that we have no project team assigned.

Solution

In the project navigator on the left side of Xcode, select the top-level folder, i.e., the name of the project, which in our case is townslot2. To the left select "General" and look for the Identity section. If you see beside Team anything other than "None" (Figure 14-8), verify that it is either your individual team, which should show as your name, or a team that you created for your company info. If it shows the word "None," use the drop-down menu to select the desired team. If you don't see any options, you may want to review Chapter 3 on how to set up Xcode for this operation.

Figure 14-8. Unless you've previously set up your certificates, app IDs, devices, provisioning, and teams, you may see no team selected under Identity in project settings

Problem

You need to set up your code-signing identities.

Solution

From where we just were, select "Build Settings" and look for the Code Signing section. You'll probably see something that looks like Figure 14-9 and shows the generic term "iOS Developer," which usually represents the team and works for localized testing. However, once you're ready to distribute to beta testers you'll need to set this to a specific identity, as shown in Figure 14-10.

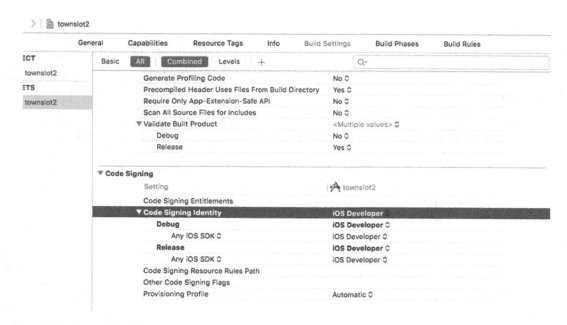

Figure 14-9. *In the Code Signing section of Build Settings, make sure you select a valid identity for debug builds. It's also a good idea to verify that Release is also set properly*

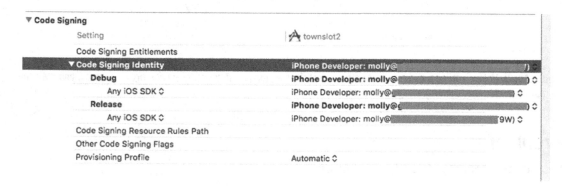

Figure 14-10. *Set up specific identities when building for beta testing or App Store release*

Problem

Xcode shows you have no provisioning profiles set up, as seen in Figure 14-11.

Figure 14-11. After setting up identities for what you need to accomplish, you may find that Xcode now gives you a missing provisioning profile error

Solution

Sometimes simply pressing the Fix Issue button will handle the problem. This usually works if you have a single Apple developer account, as Xcode can easily figure out what needs to happen. There are two situations in which Xcode sometimes won't be able to correct things. The first situation is if you haven't yet set up any profiles in the developer portal, although at the time you're reading this, that feature may have already been added to Xcode. If that is the situation you're facing and Xcode doesn't do it for you, refer to Chapter 3 and set up your provisioning profiles with the steps I've outlined there.

The second situation wherein Xcode may not automatically handle things for you is when you have a company account or multiple accounts, either individual, company, or mixed. In this situation, what I usually do is to force the issue, or rather, force the fix to the issue. Simply put, with multiple developer IDs, signing credentials, and so on, Xcode can get a little confused. So, if I've created a provisioning profile for my app, I download it from the portal to my computer and then drag the downloaded file icon right on top of the Xcode app icon. This is the way we used to do things a couple years ago, and as of the time of writing, it still works consistently. You'll likely only need this if you have a more confusing developer account setup, but it's a good trick to know when you have to use it.

Conversions

Problem

You start converting your program to Swift from Objective-C and you immediately see the error shown in Figure 14-12. The error "Class ViewController has no initializers" means that there are variables that have either not been initialized or should be treated as optionals.

```
14
15  class ViewController: UIViewController {                          Class 'ViewController' has no initializers
16
17      //
18      // PROPERTIES from OBJ-c to Swift
19      //
20
21      var thisBet : Int
22      var totalCredits : Int
23      var allowSpin: Bool
24
```

Figure 14-12. No Initializer error

Solution

In Objective-C we declared our properties in one place, the header (.h) file; synthesized the accessors at the top of the implementation (.m) file; and usually allocated and initialized them later in the implementation. In Swift we just call them variables using the var keyword, but, unless we declare it as an optional, it has to be initialized when declared. This is part of the safety features built in to the language that, while annoying at first, will save us time down the road, preventing a crash when our backs are against the wall. So, as shown in Figure 14-13, we initialize the variables when they are declared, and the problem goes away.

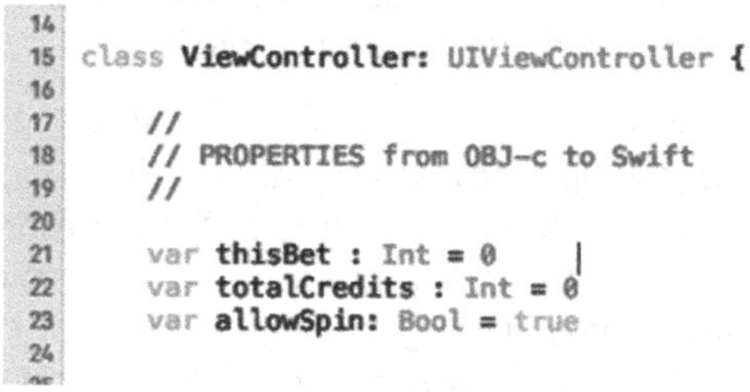

```
14
15  class ViewController: UIViewController {
16
17      //
18      // PROPERTIES from OBJ-c to Swift
19      //
20
21      var thisBet : Int = 0
22      var totalCredits : Int = 0
23      var allowSpin: Bool = true
24
```

Figure 14-13. By initializing the variables when created, our class error goes away

We obviously can't go through everything line by line, so I want to cover a few functions so you get the basic idea before we move on. We'll start by looking at some of the simpler supporting functions.

Problem

When converting the function to save the state of the game into persistent storage, you get a lot of errors, as shown in Figure 14-14. The error "NSMutableArray is not implicitly convertible to [AnyObject]" tells us that there is no automatic conversion between the types from Objective-C to Swift.

```
24   func saveGameState() {
25       NSLog("Calling Save Game State")
26       var userData: [AnyObject] = NSMutableArray()  ● NSMutableArray' is not implicitly convertible to '[AnyObject]'; did you mean to use 'as' to explicitly convert?
27       userData.addObject(Int.numberWithInt(spin1))
28       userData.addObject(Int.numberWithInt(spin2))
29       userData.addObject(Int.numberWithInt(spin3))
30       userData.addObject(Int.numberWithInt(self.winThisSpin))
31       userData.addObject(Int.numberWithInt(self.thisBet))
32       userData.addObject(Int.numberWithInt(self.totalCredits))
33       NSUserDefaults.standardUserDefaults()["gameState"] = userData
34       NSUserDefaults.standardUserDefaults().synchronize()
35   }
```

Figure 14-14. Use of AnyObject causing conversion errors

Solution

Although it worked in earlier versions, Swift now does not convert between
NSArray/NSMutableArray and Swift's native array type. While we could cast this to make
it work in much the same manner, a better approach would be to explicitly set the values
we want to save into the standard user defaults, because there are only six items that we
need to track. Simply create a constant defaults object. Since we're not actually changing
the object, but only calling the methods on that object, we can use the safer, Swift let
statement as shown in Figure 14-15. Note that we also change to the Swift print to let us
know we're in this function as well. Then, all we need do is use the setInteger method to
save each of our six items with an explicit key for each.

```
646   func saveGameState() {
647       print("Calling Save Game State")
648       {
649       let defaults = NSUserDefaults.standardUserDefaults()
650       defaults.setInteger(spin1, forKey: "spin1")
651       defaults.setInteger(spin2, forKey: "spin2")
652       defaults.setInteger(spin3, forKey: "spin3")
653       defaults.setInteger(winThisSpin, forKey: "winthisspin")
654       defaults.setInteger(thisBet, forKey: "thisbet")
655       defaults.setInteger(totalCredits, forKey: "totalcredits")
656       defaults.synchronize()
657   }
```

Figure 14-15. Rather than directly converting from Objective-C to Swift, in many cases it's easier to change the way the code functions. Here, we've added explicit keys to store each item individually, making the code easier to read

Then, it becomes a simple matter of making similar explicit calls to get and restore the
defaults when needed, as shown in Figure 14-16. However, you do have to be careful here.
Since it's possible to call the restoreUserSettings function before any items have been
saved, if you just try to use a value, it could be nil, which would cause the app to crash.
So, what I've done is to create a check to see if the first value we want to return, spin1, is nil
or not. If it is NOT nil, then we know we've saved our values and can reasonably expect to
be able to retrieve and use the remaining five items successfully. If the value is nil, then we
haven't yet saved any defaults and want to start by initializing the game. It would actually
be even safer—and you should do this in a true production application—to check each and
every value before attempting to access it. As always, there are many ways to execute the
same functionality, and each case would be slightly different in how it should be addressed.

```
659   func restoreUserSettings() {
660       let defaults = NSUserDefaults.standardUserDefaults()
661       // Determine if values have been previously saved and if so,
662       // load them in. Otherwise, initialize the game
663       if (defaults.objectForKey("spin1") != nil) {
664           spin1 = defaults.objectForKey("spin1") as! Int
665           slotStripViewWheel1PosStart = CGRectMake(33.0 + CGFloat(shiftOverValue), CGFloat(spin1), 90.0, 2900.0)
666           slotStripViewWheel2PosStart = CGRectMake(116.0 + CGFloat(shiftOverValue), CGFloat(defaults.objectForKey("spin2") as! Int),
                   90.0, 2900.0)
667           slotStripViewWheel3PosStart = CGRectMake(199.0 + CGFloat(shiftOverValue), CGFloat(defaults.objectForKey("spin3") as! Int),
                   90.0, 2900.0)
668           winThisSpin = defaults.objectForKey("winthisspin") as! Int
669           thisBet = defaults.objectForKey("thisbet") as! Int
670           totalCredits = defaults.objectForKey("totalcredits") as! Int
671       } else {
672           print("initializing game - no data was stored")
673           slotStripViewWheel1PosStart = CGRectMake(33.0 + CGFloat(shiftOverValue), 95.0, 90.0, 2900.0)
674           slotStripViewWheel2PosStart = CGRectMake(116.0 + CGFloat(shiftOverValue), 95.0, 90.0, 2900.0)
675           slotStripViewWheel3PosStart = CGRectMake(199.0 + CGFloat(shiftOverValue), 95.0, 90.0, 2900.0)
676           self.resetGame()
677       }
678   }
```

Figure 14-16. Make sure to check that a value is present before attempting to use it

Problem

After converting your Objective-C to Swift, the app crashes on an iPhone 4S or iPhone 5, but works fine otherwise. The crash occurs as soon as you hit Spin in the area shown in Figure 14-17. Because arc4random returns a 32-bit unsigned integer, on a 32-bit device like the iPhone 4S and iPhone 5, if the returned value is large enough, it could overflow and cause the app to crash. The "EXEC_BAD_INSTRUCTION" error is an indication that the calls used on Objective-C likely don't match what we need to implement here in the Swift code.

```
367
368       // THE THREE SPINS - generate a random place to stop on our simulated 'wheel'
369       spin1 = Int(arc4random())         % numberOfIcons    // large number modulo the # of icons
370       spin2 = Int(arc4random())         % numberOfIcons    // large number modulo the # of icons   Thread 1: EXC_BAD_INSTRUCTION (code=EXC_I386_INVOP,
371       spin3 = Int(arc4random())         % numberOfIcons    // large number modulo the # of icons
372
```

Figure 14-17. Although this run crashed at spin2, it may occur at any of these three statements

Solution

By using arc4random_uniform and passing an upper bound to the possible return value (Figure 14-18), you prevent the operation from overflowing. This works fine on all four devices of interest in this app: iPhone 4S, iPhone 5, iPhone 6, and iPhone 6 Plus.

```
373       spin1 = Int(arc4random_uniform(10000)) % numberOfIcons
374       spin2 = Int(arc4random_uniform(10000)) % numberOfIcons
375       spin3 = Int(arc4random_uniform(10000)) % numberOfIcons
376
```

Figure 14-18. Use arc4random_uniform and pass in an upper limit to prevent overflows on 32-bit devices such as iPhone 4S and iPhone 5

Problem

You work through the rest of the conversions, but once you load the app onto a real device, no app icon is displayed, as in Figure 14-19.

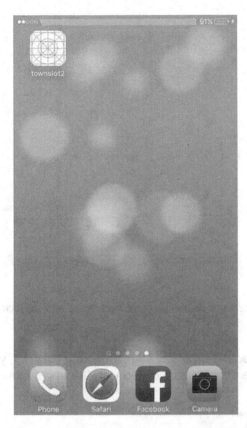

Figure 14-19. Once you install the app onto a device, only the default app icon is displayed

Solution

To make the icon display, we need to associate the image files we intend to use with the app in the AppIcon set. If you look in the project at the AppIcon, you see no images, as shown in Figure 14-20.

Figure 14-20. *Because we created a new project, we haven't yet moved over any icon images, so the AppIcon xcassets will be empty*

If we look back at the Objective-C project's AppIcon xcassets set, you see that all the images we need to use are properly associated with the app (Figure 14-21).

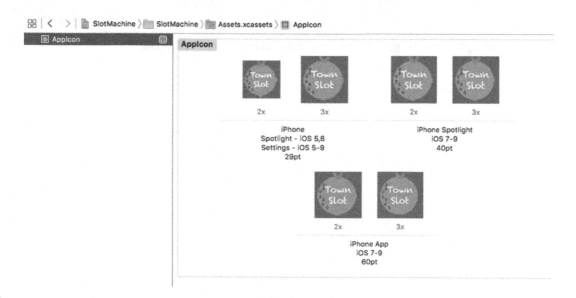

Figure 14-21. *The Objective-C version of the project shows the proper AppIcon images*

If you right-click on any of the images seen in Figure 14-21, you can select "Show In Finder" to see where the actual image files are located (Figure 14-22). Then simply copy them to the same relative place, the `AppIcon.appiconset` sub-folder of the `Assets.appiconset` folder in the Swift version and you're almost there. You will need to go back into the Xcode project and move the icons in the AppIcon set to the proper position, but they should be in the proper order already. If not, verify the size as shown in the Xcode window. Rebuild the app and load it onto your device. You may discover that you need to do a clean project first, but this has not been necessary in the most recent version of Xcode. You should then see the icon properly displayed on the home screen, as in Figure 14-23.

Name	^	Date Modified	Size	Kind
AppDelegate.swift		Nov 10, 2015, 4:15 AM	2 KB	Swift S
▼ Assets.xcassets		Today, 4:11 PM	--	Folder
▼ AppIcon.appiconset		Today, 4:11 PM	--	Folder
appicon58-1.png		Sep 25, 2015, 9:41 AM	4 KB	PNG im
appicon80.png		Sep 25, 2015, 9:41 AM	6 KB	PNG im
appicon87.png		Sep 25, 2015, 9:41 AM	7 KB	PNG im
appicon120-2.png		Sep 25, 2015, 9:41 AM	10 KB	PNG im
appicon120.png		Sep 25, 2015, 9:41 AM	10 KB	PNG im
appicon180.png		Sep 25, 2015, 9:41 AM	15 KB	PNG im

Figure 14-22. The appropriate image files most likely will be found in a sub-directory of the original project. Simply copy them to the same relative place in the new project hierarchy, then move them to the proper place in Xcode

Figure 14-23. *Finally, clean (if necessary) and rebuild the project, loading it to your device, and the icon should be properly displayed*

Swift Code

As I mentioned earlier, we could cover every detail of every conversion issue in this project. But, even with this simple app, that would likely take much more time and space than either of us have to devote at this stage of our journey. Listing 14-6 shows our final conversion of the Objective-C project.

Listing 14-6. *ViewController.swift File*

```
//
//  ViewController.swift
//  townslot2
//
//  Created by Molly Maskrey on 11/10/15.
//  Copyright © 2015 Global Tek Labs. All rights reserved.
//
```

```swift
import UIKit
import AudioToolbox

let userResetGame: String = "resetGame"
let kInitialCredits : Int = 100

class ViewController: UIViewController {

    //
    // PROPERTIES from OBJ-c to Swift
    //

    var thisBet : Int = 0
    var totalCredits : Int = 0
    var allowSpin: Bool = true
    var isSpinning: Bool = false
    var gameOver: Bool = false
    var stoppingPoints : [Double] = [95.0,35.0,-25.0,-85.0,-145.0,-210.0,-270.0,-330.0,-395.0]

    enum iPhoneType {
        case knotSelectedYet
        case kiPhone4S
        case kiPhone5
        case kiPhone6
        case kiPhone6Plus
    }
    var iphoneType : iPhoneType = .knotSelectedYet

    var topMostView : UIView?

    var shiftOverValue = 0.0

    var slotStripViewWheel1PosStart: CGRect?
    var slotStripViewWheel1PosEnd: CGRect?
    var slotStripViewWheel2PosStart: CGRect?
    var slotStripViewWheel2PosEnd: CGRect?
    var slotStripViewWheel3PosStart: CGRect?
    var slotStripViewWheel3PosEnd: CGRect?
    var slotStripViewWheel1PosComplete: CGRect?
    var slotStripViewWheel2PosComplete: CGRect?
    var slotStripViewWheel3PosComplete: CGRect?

    var winThisSpin : Int = 0

    var slotStripViewWheel1 : UIImageView?
    var slotStripViewWheel2 : UIImageView?
    var slotStripViewWheel3 : UIImageView?

    var greenLightSequenceImageView : UIImageView = UIImageView()
    var redLightSequenceImageView : UIImageView = UIImageView()
```

```swift
var creditsLabel : UILabel?
var betLabel : UILabel?
var winLabel : UILabel?

let spinButton = UIButton(frame: CGRectMake(0.0, 0.0, 65.0, 65.0))
let betButton = UIButton(frame: CGRectMake(0.0, 0.0, 65.0, 65.0))
let betMaxButton = UIButton(frame: CGRectMake(0.0, 0.0, 65.0, 65.0))

var spinFileURLRef: CFURLRef?
var spinSoundObject: SystemSoundID = 0
var clickFileURLRef: CFURLRef?
var clickSoundObject: SystemSoundID = 0
var winFileURLRef: CFURLRef?
var winSoundObject: SystemSoundID = 0
var loseFileURLRef: CFURLRef?
var loseSoundObject: SystemSoundID = 0

var spin1: Int = 0
var spin2: Int = 0
var spin3: Int = 0
var spinValue : Int = 0
let numberOfIcons : Int = 9

override func viewDidLoad() {
    super.viewDidLoad()
    // Do any additional setup after loading the view, typically from a nib.
    print("viewDidLoad")

    isSpinning      = false          // initially not spinning - NOTE this is not needed
                                     // because it was set as an initializer...

    let nc: NSNotificationCenter = NSNotificationCenter.defaultCenter()
    nc.addObserver(self, selector: "resetGame", name: userResetGame, object: nil)
    print("Registered with notification center")

    let appSize: CGSize = UIScreen.mainScreen().bounds.size
    let appRect: CGRect = CGRectMake(0.0, 0.0, appSize.width, appSize.height)
    print("screen size: Width:  \(appRect.width), Height: \(appRect.height)")

    let contentView = UIView(frame: appRect)
    contentView.backgroundColor = UIColor.blackColor()
    self.view.addSubview(contentView)

    //
    // Determine iPhone type (4,5,6,6P) from screen size so we can
    // us that to correctly position
    if (appSize.width == 320.0) && (appSize.height == 480.0) {
        iphoneType = .kiPhone4S
        print("iPhone4S")
    }
```

```swift
        else {
            if (appSize.width == 320.0) && (appSize.height == 568.0) {
                iphoneType = .kiPhone5
                print("iPhone5")
            }
            else {
                if (appSize.width == 375.0) && (appSize.height == 667.0) {
                    iphoneType = .kiPhone6
                    print("iPhone6")
                }
                else {
                    if (appSize.width == 414.0) && (appSize.height == 736.0) {
                        iphoneType = .kiPhone6Plus
                        print("iPhone6 Plus")
                    }
                }
            }
        }
    }

    switch iphoneType {
    case .kiPhone4S:
        topMostView = UIImageView(frame: CGRectMake(0.0, 0.0, 320.0, 480.0))
        topMostView?.backgroundColor = UIColor(patternImage: UIImage(named:
"SlotFaceiPhoneBasic.png")!)
        print("iPhone 4S")
    case .kiPhone5:
        topMostView = UIImageView(frame: CGRectMake(0.0, 0.0, 320.0, 568.0))
        topMostView?.backgroundColor = UIColor(patternImage: UIImage(named:
"SlotFaceiPhone5.png")!)
        print("iPhone 5")
    case .kiPhone6:
        topMostView = UIImageView(frame: CGRectMake(0.0, 0.0, 375.0, 667.0))
        topMostView?.backgroundColor = UIColor(patternImage: UIImage(named:
"SlotFaceiPhone6.png")!)
        print("iPhone 6")
    case .kiPhone6Plus:
        topMostView = UIImageView(frame: CGRectMake(0.0, 0.0, 414.0, 736.0))
        topMostView?.backgroundColor = UIColor(patternImage: UIImage(named:
"SlotFaceiPhone6Plus.png")!)
        print("iPhone 6 Plus")
    default:
        print("entered iphoneType set topMostView DEFAULT case")
    }

    // Slide the wheels over to the right (value) depending on screen size
    switch iphoneType {

        case .kiPhone4S:
            shiftOverValue = 0.0
        case .kiPhone5:
            shiftOverValue = 0.0
```

```
        case .kiPhone6:
            shiftOverValue = 30.0
        case .kiPhone6Plus:
            shiftOverValue = 50.0
        default:
            break
    }

    // SET UP SCORING LABELS
    creditsLabel = UILabel(frame: CGRectMake(0.0, 0.0, 75.0, 20.0))
    self.creditsLabel!.textAlignment = .Right
    self.creditsLabel!.backgroundColor = UIColor.blackColor()
    self.creditsLabel!.textColor = UIColor.redColor()
    self.creditsLabel!.font = UIFont.boldSystemFontOfSize(20)
    let totString: String = String(format: "%d", totalCredits)
    self.creditsLabel!.text = totString;

    betLabel = UILabel(frame: CGRectMake(0.0, 0.0, 25.0, 20.0))
    self.betLabel!.textAlignment = .Right
    self.betLabel!.backgroundColor = UIColor.blackColor()
    self.betLabel!.textColor = UIColor.redColor()
    self.betLabel!.font = UIFont.boldSystemFontOfSize(20)
    let betString: String = String(format: "%2d", totalCredits)
    self.betLabel!.text = betString;

    winLabel = UILabel(frame: CGRectMake(0.0, 0.0, 35.0, 20.0))
    self.winLabel!.textAlignment = .Right
    self.winLabel!.backgroundColor = UIColor.blackColor()
    self.winLabel!.textColor = UIColor.redColor()
    self.winLabel!.font = UIFont.boldSystemFontOfSize(20)
    let winString: String = String(format: "%d", totalCredits)
    self.winLabel!.text = winString;

    restoreUserSettings()

    slotStripViewWheel1PosEnd     = CGRectMake(33.0 + CGFloat(shiftOverValue), -2600.0,
    90.0, 2900.0);
    slotStripViewWheel2PosEnd     = CGRectMake(116.0 + CGFloat(shiftOverValue), -2600.0,
    90.0, 2900.0);
    slotStripViewWheel3PosEnd     = CGRectMake(199.0 + CGFloat(shiftOverValue), -2600.0,
    90.0, 2900.0);

    slotStripViewWheel1 = UIImageView(frame: slotStripViewWheel1PosStart!)
    slotStripViewWheel1?.image = UIImage(named: "SlotStripLong.png")
    slotStripViewWheel2 = UIImageView(frame: slotStripViewWheel2PosStart!)
    slotStripViewWheel2?.image = UIImage(named: "SlotStripLong.png")
    slotStripViewWheel3 = UIImageView(frame: slotStripViewWheel3PosStart!)
    slotStripViewWheel3?.image = UIImage(named: "SlotStripLong.png")

    spinButton.setImage(UIImage(named: "spinButton.png"), forState: .Normal)
    spinButton.setImage(UIImage(named: "spinButtonPressed.png"), forState: .Highlighted)
    spinButton.addTarget(self, action: "spin", forControlEvents: .TouchUpInside)
    spinButton.addTarget(self, action: "makeButtonClick", forControlEvents: .TouchUpInside)
```

```
betButton.setImage(UIImage(named: "betButton.png"), forState: .Normal)
betButton.addTarget(self, action: "addToBet", forControlEvents: .TouchUpInside)
betButton.addTarget(self, action: "makeButtonClick", forControlEvents: .TouchUpInside)

betMaxButton.setImage(UIImage(named: "betMaxButton.png"), forState: .Normal)
betMaxButton.addTarget(self, action: "addMaxToBet", forControlEvents: .TouchUpInside)
betMaxButton.addTarget(self, action: "makeButtonClick", forControlEvents: .TouchUpInside)

switch iphoneType {
case .kiPhone4S, .kiPhone5:
    creditsLabel!.center = CGPointMake(93.0, 213.0)
    betLabel!.center = CGPointMake(160.0, 213.0)
    winLabel!.center = CGPointMake(220.0, 213.0)
    spinButton.center = CGPointMake(260.0, 300.0)
    betButton.center = CGPointMake(150.0, 300.0)
    betMaxButton.center = CGPointMake(65.0, 300.0)

case .kiPhone6:
    creditsLabel!.center = CGPointMake(120.0, 216.0)
    betLabel!.center = CGPointMake(190.0, 216.0)
    winLabel!.center = CGPointMake(255.0, 216.0)
    spinButton.center = CGPointMake(290.0, 302.0)
    betButton.center = CGPointMake(190.0, 302.0)
    betMaxButton.center = CGPointMake(100.0, 302.0)

case .kiPhone6Plus:
    creditsLabel!.center = CGPointMake(140.0, 212.0)
    betLabel!.center = CGPointMake(212.0, 212.0)
    winLabel!.center = CGPointMake(280.0, 212.0)
    spinButton.center = CGPointMake(320.0, 300.0)
    betButton.center = CGPointMake(220.0, 300.0)
    betMaxButton.center = CGPointMake(120.0, 300.0)

default:
    break
}

contentView.addSubview(slotStripViewWheel1!)
contentView.addSubview(slotStripViewWheel2!)
contentView.addSubview(slotStripViewWheel3!)
contentView.addSubview(topMostView!)
// Note Order of buttons and labels ON TOP of TOPMOST VIEW
contentView.addSubview(creditsLabel!)
contentView.addSubview(betLabel!)
contentView.addSubview(winLabel!)
contentView.addSubview(spinButton)
contentView.addSubview(betButton)
contentView.addSubview(betMaxButton)
```

```
        // SET UP SOUNDS
        var mainBundle: CFBundleRef
        mainBundle = CFBundleGetMainBundle()

        // Get the URL to the sound file to play
        spinFileURLRef = CFBundleCopyResourceURL(mainBundle, "spinSound1" as CFString ,
"wav" as CFString , nil)
        AudioServicesCreateSystemSoundID(spinFileURLRef!, &spinSoundObject)

        clickFileURLRef = CFBundleCopyResourceURL(mainBundle, "click1" as CFString , "wav"
as CFString , nil)
        AudioServicesCreateSystemSoundID(clickFileURLRef!, &clickSoundObject)

        winFileURLRef = CFBundleCopyResourceURL(mainBundle, "win" as CFString , "wav" as
CFString , nil)
        AudioServicesCreateSystemSoundID(winFileURLRef!, &winSoundObject)

        loseFileURLRef = CFBundleCopyResourceURL(mainBundle, "youLose" as CFString , "wav"
as CFString , nil)
        AudioServicesCreateSystemSoundID(loseFileURLRef!, &loseSoundObject)

        setupGreenLightSequence()
        setupRedLightSequence()

        updateLabels()

    }  // END VIEW_DID_LOAD *******

    override func didReceiveMemoryWarning() {
        super.didReceiveMemoryWarning()
        // Dispose of any resources that can be recreated.
    }

    //
    // PORTED OBJ-C METHODS to FUNCS
    //
    override func prefersStatusBarHidden() -> Bool {
        return true
    }
    func addToBet() -> () {  // Null return OPTIONAL
        if thisBet < totalCredits {
            if self.thisBet < 10 {
                self.thisBet++
            }
            else {
                self.thisBet = 1
            }
            self.updateLabels()
            self.allowSpin = true
        }
```

```swift
        else {
            print("Can't bet more than you have left")
            self.thisBet = 0
            self.updateLabels()
            self.allowSpin = false
        }
    }
    func addMaxToBet() {
        if totalCredits == 0 {
            return
        }
        if totalCredits < 10 {
            self.thisBet = totalCredits
        }
        else {
            self.thisBet = 10
        }
        self.updateLabels()
    }


//
//   SPIN FUNCTION - This is where most of the activity takes place
//

    func spin() {

        print("SPIN called")
        // start flashing the red and green lights at the top of
        // the slot machine image on the device.
        startGreenLightAnimation()
        startRedLightAnimation()

        // If we're spinning, disable the buttons so the player can't cause
        // problems, much like a real slot machine
        isSpinning = true
        spinButton.enabled = false
        betButton.enabled = false
        betMaxButton.enabled = false

        //   THE THREE SPINS - generate a random place to stop on our simulated 'wheel'
//      spin1 = Int(arc4random()) % numberOfIcons         // large number modulo the # of icons
//      spin2 = Int(arc4random()) % numberOfIcons         // large number modulo the # of icons
//      spin3 = Int(arc4random()) % numberOfIcons         // large number modulo the # of icons

        spin1 =  Int(arc4random_uniform(10000)) % numberOfIcons
        spin2 =  Int(arc4random_uniform(10000)) % numberOfIcons
        spin3 =  Int(arc4random_uniform(10000)) % numberOfIcons

        // Create a single number that tells us what the spin is
        // using a decimal scheme. One wheel is the hundreds position, one the tens, and
        // the right-most is the ones position.
```

```
    spinValue = (spin1 * 100) + (spin2 * 10) + spin3;

    print("The three wheel spins are: \(spin1) , \(spin2), \(spin3) ")
    print("SpinValue = \(spinValue)")

    slotStripViewWheel1PosComplete = CGRectMake(33.0 + CGFloat(shiftOverValue), CGFloat(
    stoppingPoints[Int(spin1)]), 90.0, 2900.0)
    slotStripViewWheel2PosComplete = CGRectMake(116.0 + CGFloat(shiftOverValue), CGFloat
    (stoppingPoints[Int(spin2)]), 90.0, 2900.0)
    slotStripViewWheel3PosComplete = CGRectMake(199.0 + CGFloat(shiftOverValue), CGFloat
    (stoppingPoints[Int(spin3)]), 90.0, 2900.0)

    // These three chunks of code set up the animation of each of the three 'wheels.'
    // Essentially, all we're doing is moving the strips of fruit images up and down
    // to give the appearance of the three wheels spinning.
    //

    UIView.beginAnimations("wheel1", context: nil)
    UIView.setAnimationDelegate(self)
    UIView.setAnimationDidStopSelector("firstWheelReverse:")
    UIView.setAnimationCurve(.EaseIn)
    UIView.setAnimationDuration(2.0)
    slotStripViewWheel1!.frame = slotStripViewWheel1PosEnd!
    UIView.commitAnimations()

    UIView.beginAnimations("wheel2", context: nil)
    UIView.setAnimationDelegate(self)
    UIView.setAnimationDidStopSelector("secondWheelReverse:")
    UIView.setAnimationCurve(.EaseIn)
    UIView.setAnimationDuration(2.0)
    slotStripViewWheel2!.frame = slotStripViewWheel2PosEnd!
    UIView.commitAnimations()

    UIView.beginAnimations("wheel3", context: nil)
    UIView.setAnimationDelegate(self)
    UIView.setAnimationDidStopSelector("thirdWheelReverse:")
    UIView.setAnimationCurve(.EaseIn)
    UIView.setAnimationDuration(2.0)
    slotStripViewWheel3!.frame = slotStripViewWheel3PosEnd!
    UIView.commitAnimations()

    // SOUNDS
    AudioServicesPlaySystemSound(spinSoundObject)
}

func firstWheelReverse(animationID: String) {
    UIView.beginAnimations("reverseWheel1", context: nil)
    UIView.setAnimationCurve(.EaseOut)
    UIView.setAnimationDuration(1.0)
    slotStripViewWheel1!.frame = slotStripViewWheel1PosComplete!
    UIView.commitAnimations()
}
```

```swift
func secondWheelReverse(animationID: String) {
    UIView.beginAnimations("reverseWheel2", context: nil)
    UIView.setAnimationCurve(.EaseOut)
    UIView.setAnimationDuration(1.4)
    slotStripViewWheel2!.frame = slotStripViewWheel2PosComplete!
    UIView.commitAnimations()
}

func thirdWheelReverse(animationID: String) {
    UIView.beginAnimations("reverseWheel3", context: nil)
    UIView.setAnimationDelegate(self)
    UIView.setAnimationDidStopSelector("spinningHasStopped:")
    UIView.setAnimationCurve(.EaseOut)
    UIView.setAnimationDuration(1.8)
    slotStripViewWheel3!.frame = slotStripViewWheel3PosComplete!
    UIView.commitAnimations()
}

func spinningHasStopped(animationID: String) {
    print("Spinning Has Stopped")
    var allCreditsGone: Bool = false
    var winMultiplier: Int = 0
    isSpinning = false
    spinButton.enabled = true
    betButton.enabled = true
    betMaxButton.enabled = true

    //STOP LIGHTS
    stopGreenLightAnimation()
    stopRedLightAnimation()

    winMultiplier = calculateWinnings()
    // Lose
    if winMultiplier == 0 {
        self.totalCredits -= self.thisBet
        if self.totalCredits <= 0 {
            allCreditsGone = true
        }
        AudioServicesPlaySystemSound(self.loseSoundObject)
    }
    else {
        // Win
        self.totalCredits += (self.thisBet * winMultiplier)
        AudioServicesPlaySystemSound(self.winSoundObject)
    }

    updateLabels()
    if allCreditsGone {
        youLost()
    }
```

```swift
        saveGameState()

    }

    func resetGame() {
        print("ResetGame")
        makeButtonClick()
        winThisSpin = 0
        thisBet = 1
        totalCredits = kInitialCredits
        allowSpin = true
        gameOver = false
        updateLabels()
        saveGameState()
    }
    func updateLabels() {
        // TOTAL
        let totString: String = String(format: "%d", totalCredits)
        creditsLabel!.text = totString
        //BET
        let betString: String = String(format: "%d", thisBet)
        betLabel!.text = betString
        //WIN AMMOUNT
        let winString: String = String(format: "%d", winThisSpin)
        winLabel!.text = winString

    }
    func calculateWinnings() -> Int {
        var winMultiplier: Int = 1

        // Any single cherry
        if (spin1 == 2) && (spin2 != 2) && (spin3 != 2) {
            return 1
        }
        if (spin1 != 2) && (spin2 == 2) && (spin3 != 2) {
            return 1
        }
        if (spin1 != 2) && (spin2 != 2) && (spin3 == 2) {
            return 1
        }

        // Any DOUBLE cherry
        if (spin1 == 2) && (spin2 == 2) && (spin3 != 2) {
            return 3
        }
        if (spin1 != 2) && (spin2 == 2) && (spin3 == 2) {
            return 3
        }
        if (spin1 == 2) && (spin2 != 2) && (spin3 == 2) {
            return 3
        }
```

```swift
    // Three CHERRIES
    if (spin1 == 2) && (spin2 == 2) && (spin3 == 2) {
        return 150
    }

    switch spinValue {
    case 000:
        winMultiplier = 100
        // 3 Bars

    case 888:
        winMultiplier = 100
        // 3 sevens

    case 111, 222, 333, 444, 555, 666, 777:
        winMultiplier = 3      // 3 anything else --> 3X bet

    default:
        winMultiplier = 0      // anything else --> lose
    }
    return winMultiplier
}

func youLost()  {
    let alertController = UIAlertController(title: "Lost it All", message: "APress OK to
    play again.", preferredStyle: .Alert)
    let OKAction = UIAlertAction(title: "OK", style: .Default) { (action:UIAlertAction!) in
        self.resetGame()
    }
    alertController.addAction(OKAction)

    self.presentViewController(alertController, animated: true, completion:nil)
}

func setupGreenLightSequence() {
    var img1: UIImage
    var img2: UIImage
    var img3: UIImage
    var img4: UIImage

    if iphoneType == .kiPhone6Plus {
        img1 = UIImage(named: "100greenTop6P.png")!
        img2 = UIImage(named: "110greenTop6P.png")!
        img3 = UIImage(named: "111greenTop6P.png")!
        img4 = UIImage(named: "011greenTop6P.png")!
    }
    else {
        //smaller screen size
        img1 = UIImage(named: "100greenTop.png")!
        img2 = UIImage(named: "110greenTop.png")!
        img3 = UIImage(named: "111greenTop.png")!
        img4 = UIImage(named: "011greenTop.png")!
    }
```

```swift
        var images: [UIImage] = []
        images.append(img1)
        images.append(img2)
        images.append(img3)
        images.append(img4)

        greenLightSequenceImageView.animationImages = images
        greenLightSequenceImageView.animationRepeatCount = 0
        greenLightSequenceImageView.animationDuration = 0.5

        switch iphoneType {
        case .kiPhone4S:
            greenLightSequenceImageView.frame = CGRectMake(71, 1, 200, 20)
        case .kiPhone5:
            greenLightSequenceImageView.frame = CGRectMake(71, 1, 200, 20)
        case .kiPhone6:
            greenLightSequenceImageView.frame = CGRectMake(100, 1, 200, 20)
        case .kiPhone6Plus:
            greenLightSequenceImageView.frame = CGRectMake(114, 1, 200, 20)
        default: break
        }

    }

    func startGreenLightAnimation() {
        greenLightSequenceImageView.startAnimating()
        view.addSubview(greenLightSequenceImageView)
    }

    func stopGreenLightAnimation() {
        greenLightSequenceImageView.stopAnimating()
        greenLightSequenceImageView.removeFromSuperview()
    }

    func setupRedLightSequence() {
        var img1: UIImage
        var img2: UIImage
        var img3: UIImage
        var img4: UIImage
        var img5: UIImage

        if iphoneType == .kiPhone6Plus {
            img1 = UIImage(named: "001redBottom6P.png")!
            img2 = UIImage(named: "011redBottom6P.png")!
            img3 = UIImage(named: "111redBottom6P.png")!
            img4 = UIImage(named: "110redBottom6P.png")!
            img5 = UIImage(named: "100redBottom6P.png")!
        }
        else {
            //smaller screen size
            img1 = UIImage(named: "001redBottom.png")!
            img2 = UIImage(named: "011redBottom.png")!
```

```swift
        img3 = UIImage(named: "111redBottom.png")!
        img4 = UIImage(named: "110redBottom.png")!
        img5 = UIImage(named: "100redBottom.png")!
    }
    var images: [UIImage] = []
    images.append(img1)
    images.append(img2)
    images.append(img3)
    images.append(img4)
    images.append(img5)

    redLightSequenceImageView.animationImages = images
    redLightSequenceImageView.animationRepeatCount = 0
    redLightSequenceImageView.animationDuration = 0.5

    switch iphoneType {
    case .kiPhone4S:
        redLightSequenceImageView.frame = CGRectMake(71, 1, 200, 20)
    case .kiPhone5:
        redLightSequenceImageView.frame = CGRectMake(71, 1, 200, 20)
    case .kiPhone6:
        redLightSequenceImageView.frame = CGRectMake(100, 1, 200, 20)
    case .kiPhone6Plus:
        redLightSequenceImageView.frame = CGRectMake(114, 1, 200, 20)
    default: break
    }

}
func startRedLightAnimation() {
    redLightSequenceImageView.startAnimating()
    view.addSubview(redLightSequenceImageView)
}

func stopRedLightAnimation() {
    redLightSequenceImageView.stopAnimating()
    redLightSequenceImageView.removeFromSuperview()
}

func makeButtonClick() {
    AudioServicesPlaySystemSound(clickSoundObject)
}
func saveGameState() {
    print("Calling Save Game State")

    let defaults = NSUserDefaults.standardUserDefaults()
    defaults.setInteger(spin1, forKey: "spin1")
    defaults.setInteger(spin2, forKey: "spin2")
    defaults.setInteger(spin3, forKey: "spin3")
    defaults.setInteger(winThisSpin, forKey: "winthisspin")
    defaults.setInteger(thisBet, forKey: "thisbet")
    defaults.setInteger(totalCredits, forKey: "totalcredits")
    defaults.synchronize()
}
```

```swift
func restoreUserSettings() {
    let defaults = NSUserDefaults.standardUserDefaults()
    // Determine if values have been previously saved and, if so,
    // load them in. Otherwise, initialize the game.
    if (defaults.objectForKey("spin1") != nil) {
        spin1 = defaults.objectForKey("spin1") as! Int
        slotStripViewWheel1PosStart = CGRectMake(33.0 + CGFloat(shiftOverValue),
        CGFloat(spin1), 90.0, 2900.0)
        slotStripViewWheel2PosStart = CGRectMake(116.0 + CGFloat(shiftOverValue),
        CGFloat(defaults.objectForKey("spin2") as! Int), 90.0, 2900.0)
        sslotStripViewWheel3PosStart = CGRectMake(199.0 + CGFloat(shiftOverValue),
        CGFloat(defaults.objectForKey("spin3") as! Int), 90.0, 2900.0)
        winThisSpin = defaults.objectForKey("winthisspin") as! Int
        thisBet = defaults.objectForKey("thisbet") as! Int
        totalCredits = defaults.objectForKey("totalcredits") as! Int
    } else {
        print("initializing game - no data was stored")
        slotStripViewWheel1PosStart = CGRectMake(33.0 + CGFloat(shiftOverValue), 95.0,
        90.0, 2900.0)
        slotStripViewWheel2PosStart = CGRectMake(116.0 + CGFloat(shiftOverValue), 95.0,
        90.0, 2900.0)
        slotStripViewWheel3PosStart = CGRectMake(199.0 + CGFloat(shiftOverValue), 95.0,
        90.0, 2900.0)
        self.resetGame()
    }
}

//
// END VIEW CONTROLLER CLASS
//

}
```

Summary

In this chapter we have addressed the basics of what it would be like to convert from an existing Objective-C program to Swift. As a new employee at an iOS development organization, it's quite likely that you could be given these kind of assignments to prove your worth to the organization.

By the time of publication, there will likely exist several methods of conversion between existing Objective-C code and Swift to make your life easier. Most likely your company will have standards in place to address these, along with guidelines you'll be required to follow.

As the Swift compiler and Xcode progress and new features are added to the language, some of the syntax requirements may cause warnings or errors, especially with tricky conversions from much older projects. The best answer is to research the literature, message boards, and Apple documentation to stay on top of things.

Chapter 15

Coin Toss Project

In this chapter we'll move into developing a more up-to-the-minute kind of application. We'll work with Swift and the Apple Watch to create a very simple game of flipping a coin. I've actually used this on occasion, out in the world, to choose a path when I'm confronted with a couple of different, seemingly equal choices. I often wonder why I make so many wrong decisions.

Problem

We want to get started in Swift, but make it a fun experience.

Solution

We'll build a simple, easy-to-implement app for the Apple Watch.

Let's Work Through the Project

This time, we will take a different approach in our development, and I'll endeavor to do the same in the upcoming projects as well. We would normally create the project (which we will always start with) then dive into the logic of the algorithms, finishing up with embellishments such as the app icons. Because Xcode gives us complete functioning templates in an architectural sense—functionally they do nothing—we can generally build and run our apps right from the start, without adding much code at all.

What we'll do here is to create the project in Xcode, build the project to ensure that it works to the extent of loading onto our devices, work through getting our app icons in place and displayed properly, then add the other necessary code and objects to provide the coin-flipping functionality.

© Molly K. Maskrey 2016
M.K. Maskrey, *App Development Recipes for iOS and watchOS*, DOI 10.1007/978-1-4842-1820-4_15

Create the Project

Start by creating the project, as shown in Figure 15-1. At this point, you should be familiar with creating any type of project in Xcode. Here, the easiest solution is to go to File ➤ New ➤ Project... in Xcode, then select under "WatchOS" the "iOS App with WatchKit" option. By default, for me anyway, Xcode chose a universal build—that is, for both iPhone and iPad. Since we're working toward an Apple Watch app, and at the time of this writing this would only work through an iPhone, you should probably change the "Devices" drop-down to "iPhone."

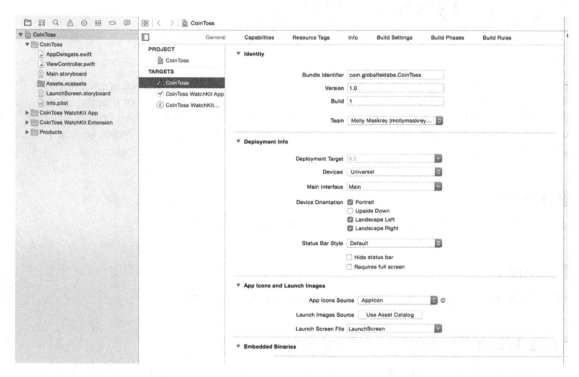

Figure 15-1. Create the project in Xcode, but instead of "Universal," you may want to change this to "iPhone only" since that will be our focus

Note that there are three targets: the Coin Toss app that executes on the phone, the Watch app itself, and the Watch App extension. As we are at the early stages of development on Apple Watch, projects using Watch are set up so that an iPhone app is required in addition to two Watch targets. The iPhone-only (currently) app allows connection with and the proper setup of the Watch. The two Watch targets provide the UI (the Watch App itself) and the logic (the Watch App extension). The splitting of the two parts of Watch is derived from the original WatchOS 1 release. The Watch app represents the UI that the user sees on the face, whereas the extension contains most of the logic. Previously, in WatchOS (aka version 1) ·
the extension ran on the iPhone and communicated with the Watch app—the UI—that ran on the Watch device. With the release of WatchOS 2, the extension now runs on the Watch device, permitting native Watch apps to be built.

You can, of course, choose to either work with the simulator at this point or build directly onto your devices. I'm taking the latter approach, building directly to my device to give you an idea of how things work with this more complicated approach. Once you've set up and verified that all your credentials in the project settings are correct, go ahead and build the project. You won't get anything very useful except a blank screen on the simulator or actual iPhone device. What we want to do now is to press the Home button, either on the phone or virtually in the simulator, to get to the splash screen. Look for the app icon, and you should see something that looks like Figure 15-2.

Figure 15-2. Initially building the app to your device will show the default icon

Fix the App's Icons

I'll certainly detail how we're going to make the app work, but for a little bit of fun let's fix the icon right away. In fact, because we're building for the Watch and the iPhone, let's get them both in shape before proceeding. First, locate the image files in the additional source code for the AppIcon, as shown in Figure 15-3, and the Watch, Figure 15-4. The quickest way to locate the actual image files, or any project file for that matter, is to, from within Xcode, right-click on the file name you're interested in—for the image files that would be the Assets. xcassets icon in the Project Navigator—then select "Show in Finder." From there, open the enclosing folder to see the actual image files.

Figure 15-3. Either use the provided files or create your own images for icons used on the iPhone

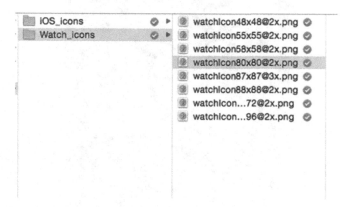

Figure 15-4. While you're at it, get the Watch icons ready as well

Locate the AppIcon in the xcassets section of the iPhone target files in the Xcode organizer, as shown in Figure 15-5. Drag the appropriate size file from its location in the Finder onto the blank place for it in Xcode. You should be able to verify that the correct size is properly associated with the appropriate icon slot. You should know immediately if an incorrectly sized file has been placed. A yellow triangle with an '!' mark will show at the top. In the organizer on the left, click on the Issue Navigator to get more information on the incorrect file placement.

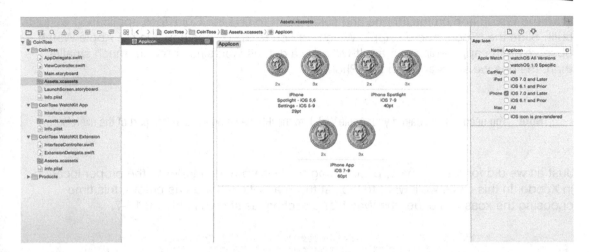

Figure 15-5. *Place the image file onto its correct spot in the xcassets, AppIcon section in Xcode. Errors should be shown instantly in the Issue Navigator*

Build and install the app onto your device, and the proper app icon should now show up on the iPhone splash screen, as in Figure 15-6.

Figure 15-6. *Now the iPhone app icon is properly displayed*

Start the Watch app on the iPhone and scroll down to find the Coin Toss application we just built. Slide the "Show App on Apple Watch" option to the ON position. On the Apple Watch, observe as the app begins to load. It will have a default icon similar to, but much smaller than, the one we saw earlier on the iPhone.

> **Note**   You need to have paired your Apple Watch to the iPhone being used in this part of the exercise.

Just as we did for the iPhone app icon, drag the files from the Finder to the proper location in Xcode. In this case, we'll want to look at the xcassets in Xcode as before, this time choosing the xcassets under the Watch app section, as shown in Figure 15-7.

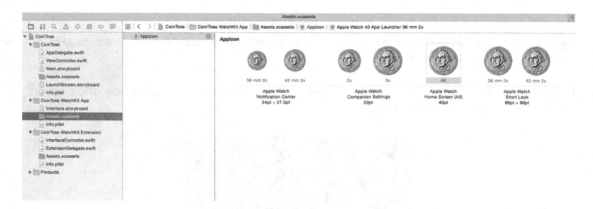

Figure 15-7. *Similar to the iPhone, we want to properly install the images for the Watch*

From the project pull-down, select "Clean" and then rebuild your app for your device or simulator. If using an actual device, go to the Watch app and slide the "Show App on Apple Watch" option to the ON position. You should now see the app begin to load on your Watch as before, but with the proper icon, as shown in Figures 15-8 and 15-9.

Figure 15-8. The app will begin to load using the proper icon on your Watch

Figure 15-9. When loading completes, the app icon will properly appear and function on the Watch face

Set Up the Remaining Icons

Now that we have the iPhone and Watch icons set correctly, let's finish off the rest of the graphics. First, we need an image of the heads and tails sides of a coin, and, because we want to simulate the flipping of the coin in the air, we'll also add a side shot.

In the xcassets section where we added the Watch app, create a new, blank imageset as shown in Figures 15-10 and 15-11. The new imageset will be named something generic, such as image. Click on the name and change it to heads, as shown in Figure 15-12.

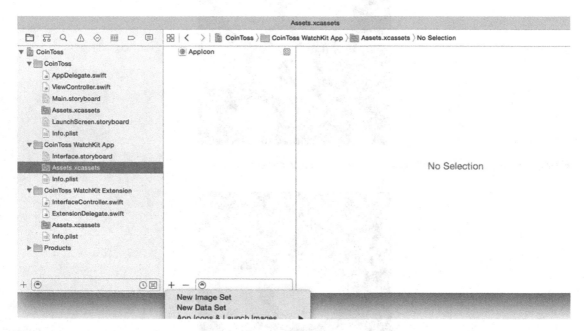

Figure 15-10. Click the '+' button at the bottom of the Assets.xcassets center window and choose "New Image Set"

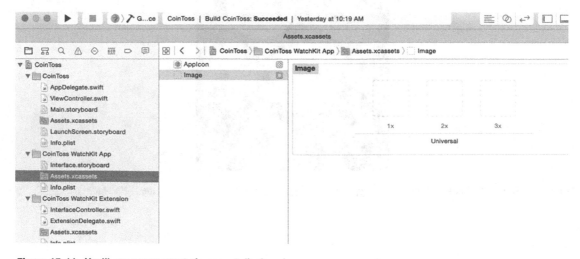

Figure 15-11. You'll see a new empty imageset displayed

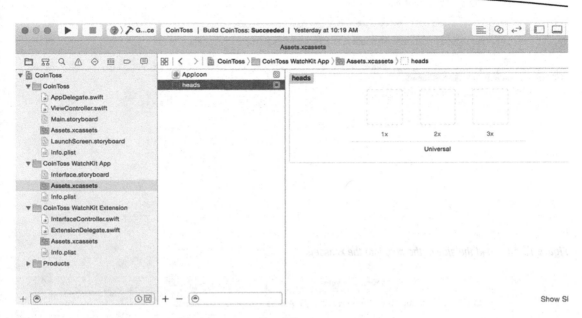

Figure 15-12. Change the name of the imageset to "heads"

Repeat the previous steps for the tails and side of the coin images. Locate the three files using Finder, as shown in Figure 15-13. Drag the appropriate images to the correct spots in the xcassets section, as shown in Figures 15-14, 15-15, and 15-16. Note that, because we're working with the Watch, I'm only loading the 1X images into the assets folder. Using the technique we described earlier, you'll find these images in the source code.

Figure 15-13. Locate either the provided set or your own images of the heads, tails, and side of the coin

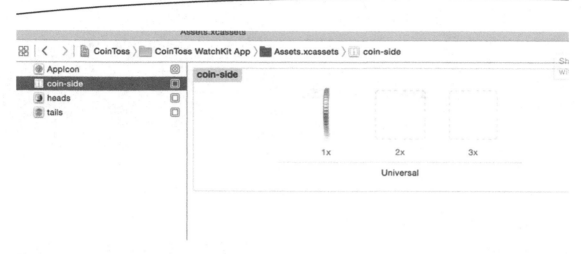

Figure 15-14. *Load the side of the coin into the xcassets*

Figure 15-15. *Load the heads side of the coin into the xcassets*

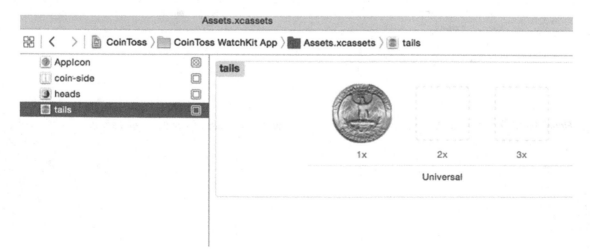

Figure 15-16. *Load the tails side of the coin into the xcassets*

The last thing we need to do is create a sequence of images that we can use to simulate a coin flip. Create a series of images named flip1 through flip10. In the code, we'll use the image set name "flip" and 10-image sequence that will automatically append the increment number to the sequence and pull the images from the xcassets, i.e., flip1, flip2, flip3, through flip10. This way, we have all our graphics files managed by Xcode through the xcassets mechanism and simplify our functional code a great deal. While it looks like we have a lot more images, as shown in Figure 15-17, in actuality, outside of the iPhone and Watch icons, we still only have the three additional files for heads, tails, and the side of the coin.

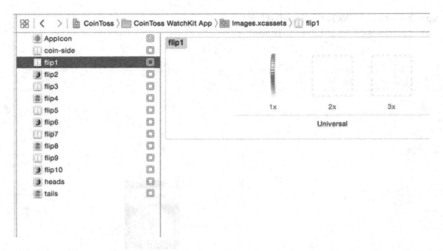

Figure 15-17. Add the sequence of ten image assets and set to the correct graphic as described previously

One important note: the image selected for each of the image assets must be in a specific order to work in our code. For example, if we landed on heads, our next flip sequence would be side, tails, side, heads, side, etc. But if we landed on tails, we'd want our sequence to be side, heads, side, tails, etc. Where we start is in the Swift code, which we'll get to shortly, but for now, order the sequence of image assets as follows:

1. flip1 = side

2. flip2 = heads

3. flip3 = side

4. flip4 = tails

5. flip5 = side

6. flip6 = heads

7. flip7 = side

8. flip8 = tails

9. flip9 = side

10. flip10 = heads

Create the Storyboards

Select the Project Navigator in the organizer on the left of the Xcode screen and go to the CoinToss WatchKit App, not the extension, and select `interface.storyboard`.

Add three objects from the library, in this order: button, separator, image. Then set the image in the attributes inspector to be flip2 (Figure 15-8). Add `IBOutlets` to the WatchKit extension `InterfaceController.swift` file by bringing up the assistant editor and control-dragging from the button and image in the usual manner:

```
@IBOutlet var button:    WKInterfaceButton!
@IBOutlet var coinImage: WKInterfaceImage!
```

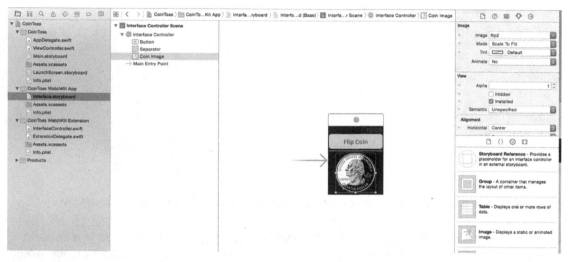

Figure 15-18. *Add three objects to the Watch interface storyboard Interface Controller: a button, a separator, and an image that we will default to flip2*

Also, add an `IBAction` for the button, called `buttonPressed`:

```
@IBAction func buttonPressed() {
}
```

You now have completed the UI setup and added the skeleton code for the action and outlets for our app. Next, we'll complete the app by adding just a little bit of code.

Write the Code

Listing 15-1 shows the code for the `ViewController.swift` file. It should be apparent that this is the Swift generated by Xcode when we created the project. Confused? You needn't be. This simply means that we do not write any additional code to execute on the iPhone. We could if, say, we wanted to do a coin flip on the phone itself, but then it'd be just as simple to pull a coin from our purse.

Listing 15-1. No Code Needs to Be Added to the ViewController.swift File

```
//
//  ViewController.swift
//  CoinToss
//
//  Created by Molly Maskrey on 12/14/15.
//  Copyright © 2015 Global Tek Labs. All rights reserved.
//

import UIKit

class ViewController: UIViewController {

    override func viewDidLoad() {
        super.viewDidLoad()
        // Do any additional setup after loading the view, typically from a nib.
    }

    override func didReceiveMemoryWarning() {
        super.didReceiveMemoryWarning()
        // Dispose of any resources that can be recreated.
    }

}
```

In the awakeFromContext method, in the WatchKit extension file, we want to first make sure that the image is not animating in case something happened, such as a hang from a previous execution of the app. This puts us in a known state when the app awakes on our Watch.

The only other thing we need do is to add the logic to simulate the flip inside the buttonPressed() method we added when creating the storyboard. All the additional needed code is shown in Listing 15-2. First, we set the coinImage outlet to the image named flip. There is no actual image so named, but we're using this as our sequence for the animation. Next, we generate a random number between 0 and 1—that is, one of two options, like a heads or a tails. Finally, depending on the random number generated, we start animating and either stop on a heads or tails depending on the random number. The animation is pretty crude and has a staccato appearance. This is intentional for this exercise so you can get a better sense of what is happening as the app executes.

Listing 15-2. Add the Following Code to the InterfaceController.swift File

```
@IBAction func buttonPressed() {
    self.coinImage.setImageNamed("flip")
    let randomNumber = arc4random_uniform(2)   // random # between 0 and 1
    if randomNumber == 0 {
        self.coinImage.startAnimatingWithImagesInRange(NSRange(location: 1, length: 10),
        duration: 1, repeatCount: 2)
    } else  {
        self.coinImage.startAnimatingWithImagesInRange(NSRange(location: 1, length: 7),
        duration: 1, repeatCount: 2)
    }
}
```

```
override func awakeWithContext(context: AnyObject?) {
    super.awakeWithContext(context)

    // Configure interface objects here.
    self.coinImage.stopAnimating()
}
```

That completes the Coin Toss application. Build the app onto your iPhone and Apple Watch, and you should now have a virtual coin on your wrist whenever you need it.

Problem

The app won't install onto your Apple Watch. This is usually a problem centered on build settings.

Solution

This problem generally appears as a Watch app that installs most of the way then disappears. Typically, the Watch icon will load to about three-fourths of the way, then disappear as shown in Figure 15-19. Most often this is the result of a couple of things. At the time of this writing, many developers reported a similar issue that was solved by adding a specific, user-defined setting for the Watch App and extension, or at the project level so it is distributed to all targets. In the project's build settings, click the '+' and select "Add User-Defined Setting," as shown in Figure 15-20.

Figure 15-19. *A common install issue in early Watch development is that the app partially installs, but then disappears*

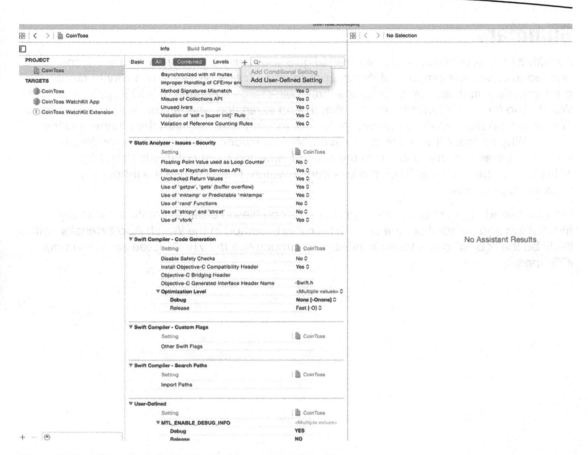

Figure 15-20. Add a user-defined setting to the project's build settings

Add the value STRIP_BITCODE_FROM_COPIED_FILES and set the value to NO. Clean and rebuild the project, and this should fix the problem.

Finally, if this does *not* fix the problem, make sure the deployment target for your Watch in the build settings, for both the Watch App and the extension, is set correctly. Often, when creating a new Xcode Watch project, the settings will default to the latest values. For example, in my case, WatchOS 2.1 was the default deployment target, but the development Apple Watch I used for this exercise was at WatchOS 2.0.

It's always a good idea to quickly look through all the build settings for each of the three targets—iPhone, Watch App, and extension—when you're working on a new project and have strange problems.

Summary

As with all projects in this book, I wanted to give you a very brief overview of the steps needed to create the simplest of Watch applications. Xcode provides us a way to create our template Watch app by creating the three blank targets needed: the iOS app, the actual Watch App (or user interface), and the Watch App extension wherein the actual logic resides. The extension also provides the mechanism for moving data between the iPhone and the Watch. Why do that? If you look at the available frameworks Apple provides for Watch, you'll see several are missing. From my point of view, the most notable is Core Bluetooth. This means I can't access BTLE devices from a Watch. I need to use the iPhone as a pass-through device.

We also talked about dealing with graphics and icon files in order to create a minimally functioning app. In addition, the awakeWithContext method in the Watch App extension will likely be the "go-to" place for your initialization, much like the viewDidLoad services in our iOS apps.

Chapter 16

Home Automation Project

With the Internet of Things (IoT) space surging and new products being added daily, it seemed fitting to explore how to use Apple's version of home automation. HomeKit can be thought of as many things: a label on products to assure consumers of compatibility, a set of software frameworks to create HomeKit apps, and even a hardware set of specifications if you're developing hardware under the MFi program. For this section, we'll start by using the HomeKit framework to create a simple, on-off toggle of an AC outlet to control a disco ball (Figure 16-1). Why a disco ball? Well, why not? Seriously, though, you can use any AC-powered device; a desk or table lamp, for example, works just as well.

Figure 16-1. *To make things more fun, we'll control a disco ball in order to get our home automation party started*

© Molly K. Maskrey 2016

M.K. Maskrey, *App Development Recipes for iOS and watchOS*, DOI 10.1007/978-1-4842-1820-4_16

Problem

We want to get started with home automation using Apple's HomeKit iOS features, but current tutorials are far more complicated than we'd like to tackle as our first attempt. Apple offers a HomeKitCatalog sample app that contains pretty much everything you'd need to know to work with HomeKit. However, we just want to control a switch and, for now, nothing else.

Solution

We'll build the simplest app imaginable in order to control our disco ball. Our app's UI contains one control: a button that turns the power on or off from the HomeKit accessory device. For our accessory device, I chose the iHome Control SmartPlug, which is, as you can see in Figure 16-2, certified to work with Apple HomeKit.

Figure 16-2. To manage power to our disco ball, we're using the iHome Control SmartPlug Certified HomeKit accessory

Let's Work Through the Project

As you may recall from the earliest chapters of this book, my goal was not so much to teach you programming as to help you overcome the typical issues that arise while creating and building iOS apps. In the last project, our coin-flipping app, we addressed making sure that the icons for both the iPhone and Watch devices were correct. Normally, we might want to do that in this project or in any other project. Or, we might save that kind of issue until the very end of the development cycle. It really depends on your style and your organization's guidance. It certainly seems like something superfluous to be concerned about before the code is written, but if we're planning on demoing this to a client, we want our first impressions to be at the top of the game. Delivering or even just showing something that looks incomplete at first glance can give the wrong impression. While we may have 50 percent or more of the logic and functionality ready to show, a crappy looking icon or screen can set the wrong mood at the start.

Having said all that, for the sake of brevity, since we addressed icon issues in the last project, we're going to skip them in this chapter and try to address other common issues certain that may arise in your career.

Create the Project

Create a new project using the single view template and call it whatever you wish. I've chosen to call mine DiscoBall, as that is the target device that we'll control. Initialize the project without using core data or setting any test targets in order to keep it simple for now, as shown in Figure 16-3. I also chose to build it for the iPhone, but that's up to you. When finishing up project creation, do not choose to create a Git repository (Figure 16-4).

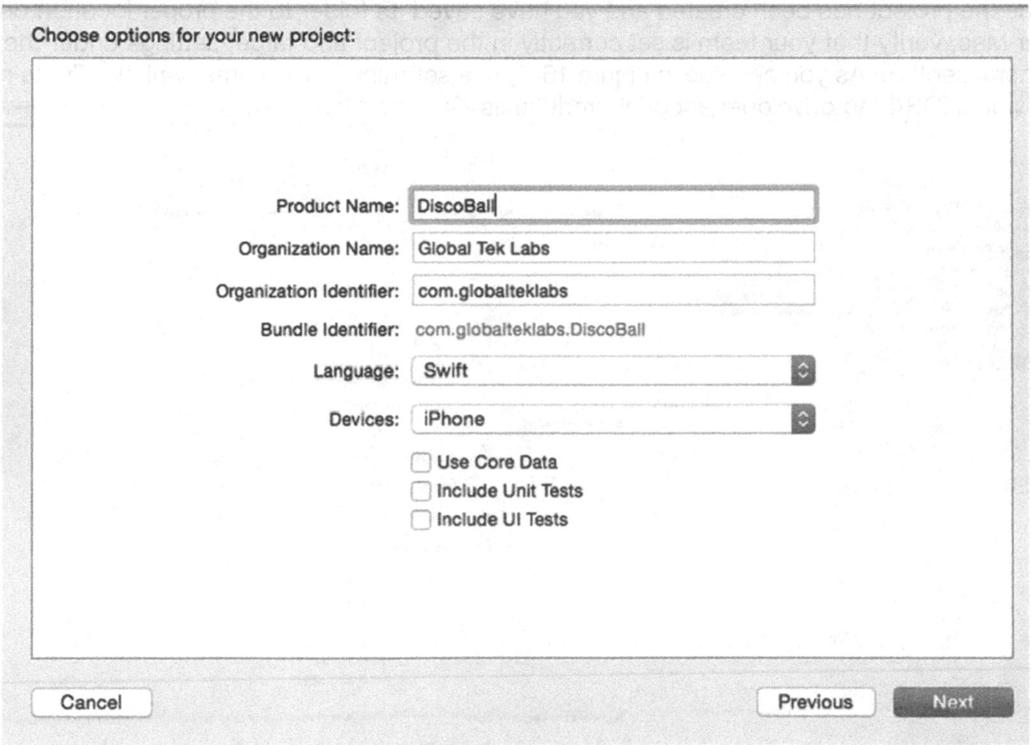

Figure 16-3. *Create our disco ball project without core data or testing capability*

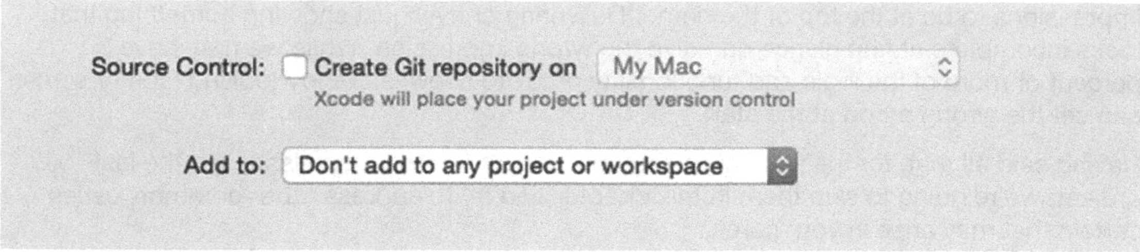

Figure 16-4. *Don't use source control for this project. We will address that in a different chapter*

> **Note**   While using core data would not make any sense for this small app, setting up testing as well as creating a Git repository would, in most cases, be the way to do things. I've left them off intentionally to show how they would be handled separately in other chapters.

Once the project has been created and you have saved its folder to the proper location on your Mac, verify that your team is set correctly in the project and target settings under the General section. As you can see in Figure 16-5, I've set mine to my name, which reflects my individual iOS/Mac developer account credentials.

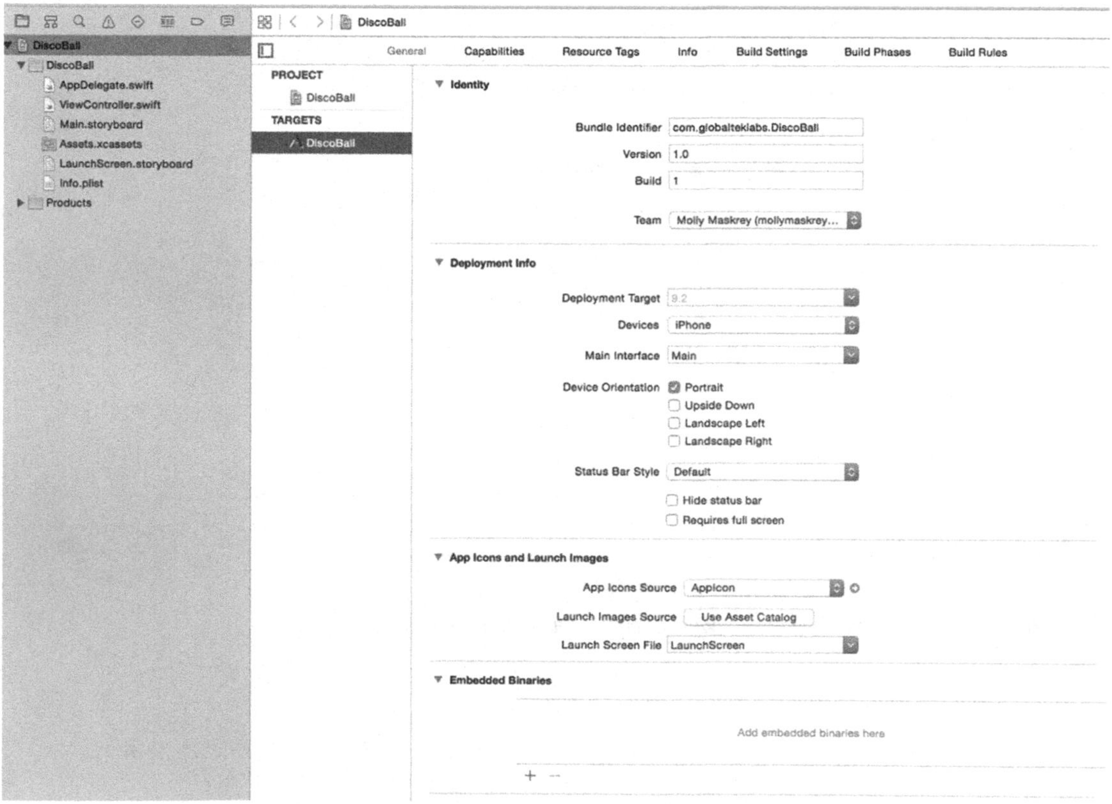

Figure 16-5. *Set the project to the team account you are using to create this app*

Verify the Build Process

Similar to how we wanted to make sure the iPhone and Watch icons were properly displayed in the Coin Toss project, before we go any further into developing the logic, let's make sure we can build this project to our device.

First, let's make a simple change to our `LaunchScreen.storyboard` so we can see if everything works. We could add something to our `Main.storyboard` as well, but we'll get to that shortly. For now, I just put a label at the center of the launch screen so we'll see something happen when and if the app builds and loads correctly (Figure 16-6).

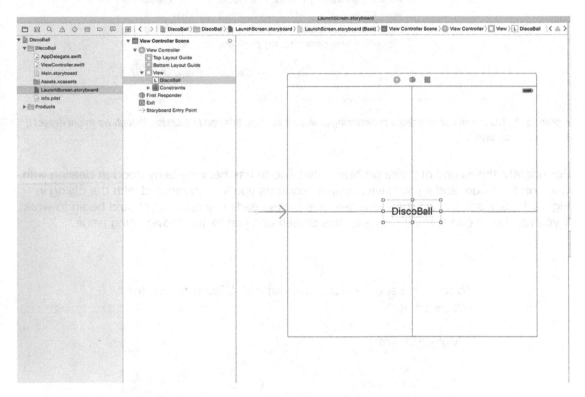

Figure 16-6. Add a simple label in the center of the launch screen to see if the app at least tries to start properly

You should now expect, because we've set up everything and made one very simple change to one storyboard, that the app should build okay, load, and start running on your connected device. Trying this, however, likely yields results similar to those shown in Figure 16-7.

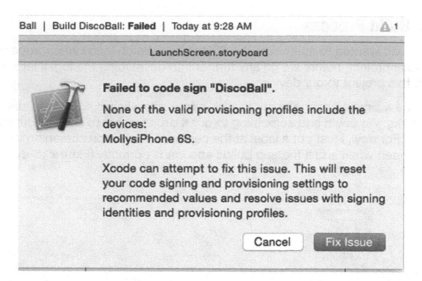

Figure 16-7. *You haven't yet created a provisioning profile for building this app to a device, though we might expect it to use our team profile*

Fortunately, this is one of those problems that Xcode has become fairly good at dealing with. Click on Fix Issue, and if you have multiple accounts you'll be presented with the dialog in Figure 16-8. If so, choose the same team we picked earlier, and things should begin to work. If you have only one team, it may skip this screen and just fix the provisioning issue.

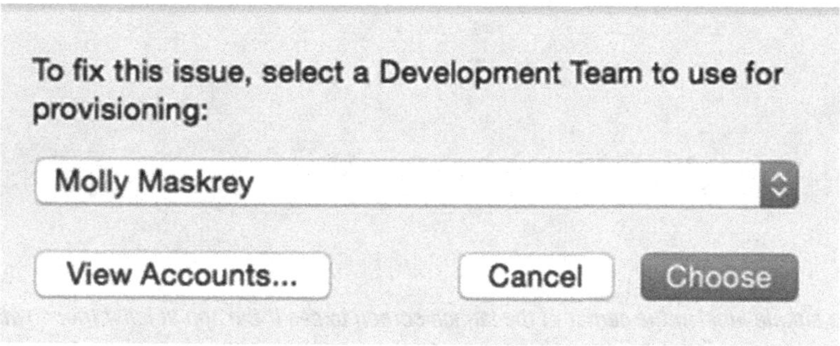

To fix this issue, select a Development Team to use for provisioning:

Molly Maskrey

View Accounts...   Cancel   Choose

Figure 16-8. *If presented with a choice, select the same team we did earlier in the General project settings*

Test your work by building, downloading, and executing the project onto your device. You should quickly see the launch screen we modified followed by a completely blank screen.

Create the User Interface

Because all we're looking to do in this project is control a simple AC-powered device, our disco ball, rather than spend time developing hierarchical table view screens, I'm going to go with a few simple controls and indicators as shown in Figure 16-9. Starting from the top:

- Add a label to indicate the status of the device, either on or off

- Add a button to turn the device on or off.

- Add a label that we'll use to show the user when we found an accessory and what the accessory is called.

- Add a label to show if the accessory is connected to our app.

- Add another button to attach the accessory when the app finds it.

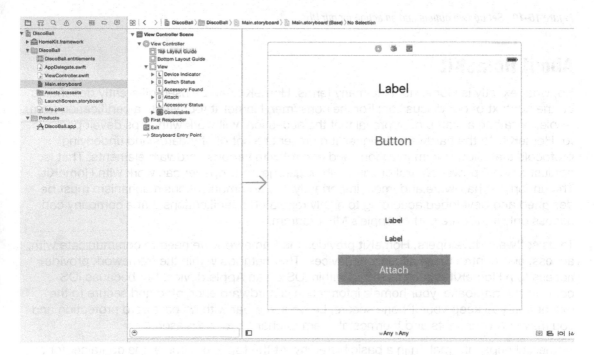

Figure 16-9. For this project, because we're more concerned about using HomeKit, our UI will consist of very simple buttons and simple labels as indicators

Add the actions and outlets for the UI objects to the ViewController.swift file as shown in Figure 16-10. The deviceIndicator label shows whether the disco ball is turned on or not. The switchStatus UIButton outlet allows us to change the label on the ON/OFF button as appropriate. The activateDevice action turns the disco ball on or off—this is the main power switch. The accessoryFound label shows the name of the accessory that the app has located, and accessoryStatus tells us if that accessory is connected to the app or not. Finally, the attachAccessory action will try to connect an accessory that has been found to the app so it can be operated upon.

```
27
28    @IBOutlet weak var deviceIndicator: UILabel!
29    @IBOutlet weak var switchStatus: UIButton!
30
31    @IBAction func activateDevice(sender: AnyObject) {
32
33    }
34
35    @IBOutlet weak var accessoryFound: UILabel!|
36    @IBOutlet weak var accessoryStatus: UILabel!
37
38    @IBAction func attachAccessory(sender: AnyObject) {
39         self.addMyAccessory()
40    }
41     .
42
```

Figure 16-10. Set up two outlets and an action for our UI

About HomeKit

So, what exactly is HomeKit? Like many terms, HomeKit can be used differently depending on the context of our discussion. For the consumer, HomeKit represents a certification from Apple, or rather, a stamp of approval that the accessory will work with apps developed for HomeKit. To the hardware designer, it represents a set of standards and underlying protocols that allow communications and control with various hardware elements. That is, not just any AC power control or light bulb or garage door opener can work with HomeKit. The underlying hardware and, most importantly, the communications mechanism must be designed and developed according to highly regulated specifications that a company can access only if they are part of Apple's MFi program.

To us software developers, HomeKit provides the framework we need to communicate with, access, and control these accessory devices. The methods within the framework provide access to a HomeKit database stored within iOS on an Apple device. So, because iOS controls the database, your home's information is hardware encrypted and secure to the extent that you keep your iPhone secure. Leave it in a bar with no password protection and you may find your lights and thermostat seem to change for no reason.

HomeKit keeps information in a basic hierarchy. At the top is the home, the container for all your devices. Actually, you can have as many homes as you need, e.g., a vacation home, a rental property, etc. Underneath are rooms that contain the third layer, the accessories. Just as a home can contain multiple rooms, a room can contain multiple accessories.

Continuing, each accessory can contain one or more services. This is where things may seem to get a little more complicated, but if you've looked at the Bluetooth network standard, it will seem very familiar. A service is pretty much as it sounds—something that the accessory does. A desk lamp accessory would have a lamp service to provide illumination. A garage door would have a motor or door service, but could also have a lamp service and maybe an alarm service.

Each service contains one or more characteristics. These are the various data elements, essentially the leaves of our hierarchy tree. For the garage door, the door service would have an open characteristic indicating whether the door is closed or not. This would be a characteristic that we read; that is, through our HomeKit framework methods, we read whether the door is open or closed. But, this characteristic might also allow write access. We would write to the characteristic whether we want to open or close the door. Characteristics can be read only, write only (less common), or read/write.

To delve deep into HomeKit would require nearly an entire book to itself. What we've covered in this section are the very basic elements, but it is enough to begin designing our app around our AC power control for the disco ball.

Our Configuration

I plan to keep things extremely simple in order to get the most out of the HomeKit explanations, so we'll have a very simple hierarchy. At the top is MyHome. We will use only one home and won't worry about changes, deletions, additions, and so on. Below that, our home will have one room. Imagine a cabin in the mountains. For our work we'll simply call it MainRoom. In that room we'll have our DiscoBall accessory and LightBulb service, as that is a standard option when using the HomeKit Accessory Simulator. Our characteristics for the LightBulb service will be on and outlet in use. We write to the on characteristic in order to control the outlet to which the disco ball is connected. Outlet in Use serves as a status indicating whether the outlet is actually powered on or not.

MyHome ➤ MainRoom ➤ DiscoBall ➤ LightBulb ➤ (on and outlet_in_use)

Problem

We have our iHome Control AC Power switch, as shown earlier in Figure 16-2, but how do we work with it? Moreover, upon opening the box we find the contents include nothing more than the product itself and a simple card telling us to download the associated app. But what we want to do is work with this product.

Solution

Let's work through building our HomeKit app and see what happens. For early testing, use the Xcode simulator, as this gives you better control over resets, which we'll need shortly.

First, we have to instantiate an HMHomeManager object to manage our home. Because our app should be extremely simple, we'll do everything inside the ViewController class viewDidLoad method in the ViewController.swift file.

You need to do four things:

- Import the HomeKit framework.
- Make sure the class conforms to the HMHomeManagerDelegate protocol.
- Instantiate an HMHomeManager object.
- Set the manager's delegate.

All this can be seen clearly in Listing 16-1.

Listing 16-1. Adding an HMHomeManager to Our ViewController

```swift
//
//  ViewController.swift
//  DiscoBall
//
//  Created by Molly Maskrey on 12/17/15.
//  Copyright © 2015 Global Tek Labs. All rights reserved.
//

import UIKit
import HomeKit

class ViewController: UIViewController, HMHomeManagerDelegate{

    @IBOutlet weak var deviceIndicator: UILabel!
    @IBOutlet weak var switchStatus: UIButton!

    @IBAction func activateDevice(sender: AnyObject) {

    }

    override func viewDidLoad() {
        super.viewDidLoad()
        // Do any additional setup after loading the view, typically from a nib.

        //
        // Create a home manager
        //
        let manager = HMHomeManager()
        manager.delegate = self

    }

    override func didReceiveMemoryWarning() {
        super.didReceiveMemoryWarning()
        // Dispose of any resources that can be recreated.
    }

}
```

Let's build this to the simulator and see what happens. You should see the alert shown in Figure 16-11 asking you, the user, to allow your app to access accessory data. For this you would click OK, as we want to move on from here. However, a common situation happens when you select Don't Allow because you want to make a few more changes or maybe just by accident. What you will find, in many cases, is that restarting the app does not show this dialog. That is, you've selected the option to preclude this app from accessing your home or accessory data and iOS will remember this. Deleting the app, cleaning the project, and even rebooting your iPhone won't usually fix this. So, what do you do?

Figure 16-11. *On initial launch iOS will confirm with you as to whether you want to allow the app to access your home database*

Go to the Settings app and scroll down to find the DiscoBall app and select it. You will, of course, need to have the app built and on your device in case you just deleted it. You should see something similar to Figure 16-12 with the switch set to off. Simply set the switch to on (Figure 16-13), and now your app will have access to your home accessory data. Let's move on to the next step.

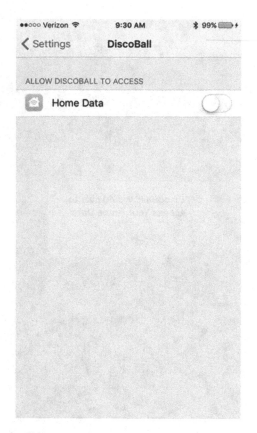

Figure 16-12. *Home data access is off for your app*

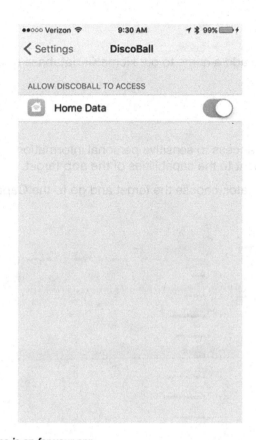

Figure 16-13. Home data access is on for your app

Add a Home

Now that we have our manager instantiated, let's try adding our home. To do so we use the addHomeWithName method as shown in Listing 16-2. However, running this will return the message:

```
Error happened.. message: Missing entitlement for API
```

Listing 16-2. Simple Call to addHomeWithName in Our viewDidLoad Method

```
//
// Add our Home
//
manager.addHomeWithName("MyHome", completionHandler: {(home, error) in

    print("Trying to add MyHome")
    if error != nil{
        print("Error happened.. message: \(error!.localizedDescription)")
    }
})
```

Problem

Trying the simplest way to add a home to our HomeKit database returned a Missing Entitlement error.

Solution

Because HomeKit allows access to sensitive personal information, you need to specifically add the HomeKit entitlement to the capabilities of the app target.

In the Xcode Project Navigator, choose the target and go to the Capabilities section (Figure 16-14).

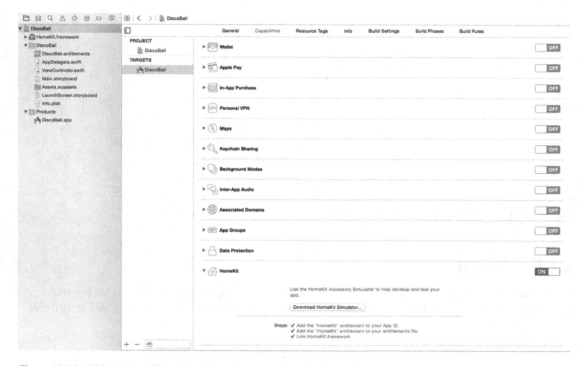

Figure 16-14. Add the HomeKit entitlements to your app in the Capabilities section

Scroll down to HomeKit and flip the switch to ON.

Rebuilding and testing the app now should eliminate the entitlements error. One of the things you might want to be aware of when early testing your app is that after adding a home to the database, trying to add it a second time will return an error.

Problem

After making some corrections to your app, you can no longer add your home to the database. You see the localized error description: "Home with similar name exists."

Solution

In the short-term while testing, the easiest thing would be to use the "Reset Content and Settings. . ." option of the simulator, as shown in Figure 16-15.

Figure 16-15. "Reset Content and Settings..." provides an easy way to reset everything on your simulator so as to test adding a new home. However, this will require you to reallow the app to access home data as shown earlier

The better solution, of course, is to handle the error condition in the app. And while it is an error in the sense that the call did not add our home because it was already there, it's not going to crash our app or mess up what we're trying to do. Remember, all we want to do is to add our home.

That said, let's take things a couple steps further in our code. We'll not only add our home, but also add a room to the home MainRoom and make our home the primary. And, of course, we'll add checks as to what is returned by our attempts to add a home and a room. Listing 16-3 shows the code handling these three simple functions. Note that error code 32 reflects the condition returned by the addHomeWithName method and indicates the home provided is already in the database. Similarly, error code 13 means that the room specified is already in the home. I've added numerous print() statements so that you can see what happens in the console as the code executes.

Listing 16-3. Our Complete Code to Add a Room and Our Home, and Make It the Primary

```
//
// Add our Home
//
func addMyHome() {
    manager.addHomeWithName(kmyHome, completionHandler: {(home, error) -> Void in
        print("Trying to add MyHome")
        if error == nil || error?.code == 32 { // error code 32 means the home is already in
        the database

            if error == nil {
                print("MyHome added to database")
                self.primaryHome = home
            } else {
                print("MyHome already in database")
            }

            print("…either way, we can add a room to the home now")
            //
            // We've stored the house we added as our primary so we'll
            // now add a room to it
            //
            if self.primaryHome != nil {
                self.primaryHome!.addRoomWithName(self.kmainRoom, completionHandler: {
                (room, error) -> Void in
                    if error == nil || error?.code == 13  { // error code 13 means room
                    already in home
                        if error == nil {
                            print("Room added to Home")
                        } else {
                            print("Room ALREADY there")
                        }
                    //
                    // This might seem tricky, but we have to tell HomeKit to make
                    this
                    // our primary home as well. Previously, we just essentially
                    called it that
                    // but we have to do it in code so the database is "correct"
                    //
                    self.manager.updatePrimaryHome(self.primaryHome!,
                    completionHandler: {(error) -> Void in
                    if error == nil {
                            print("\(self.primaryHome!.name) now defined as the
                            primary home")
                        } else {
                            print("ERROR: setting primary home: \(error)")
                        }
                    })
```

```
                        } else {
                            print("ERROR: attempting to add room. \(error!.
                            localizedDescription)")
                        }

                    })
                } else {
                        print("ERROR: For some reason our global primary home was not
                        set")
                }
            } else {
                print("ERROR: attempting to add home: \(error)")
            }

        })
}
//
//  End of setting up our simple one room home
//  Note that we didn't do anything with accessories. We will deal with those separately.
//
```

Hierarchical Differences

Earlier I showed our top-down hierarchy, starting with homes. In our case, the primary home is at the top and lower levels contain with each of the characteristics for a service within our accessory. This structure is pretty straightforward, and we fairly easily grasp the concept. Implementation tells a different story. At first pass, when confronted with a problem like this, we construct this intricate series of if-then-else statements, which works fine for a couple levels, but with a five-tier problem it's just too unwieldy.

The trick is to logically break it down. Think of it this way: there might be five levels in the hierarchy, but you could classify them into two categories. The "holders of the object" are the top layers: the room and the home. The "objects being held", i.e., the accessories, comprise the bottom layers: the accessory, the services, and the characteristics. Work on each of these subsections and things will seem a lot clearer.

I wish there were a logical way to deconstruct a HomeKit application that made it clear and simple. Unfortunately, I haven't found any, and I don't profess to be brilliant enough to do so. What I've tried to do is minimize all the superfluous "stuff," the noise, if you will, and focus on the key elements. In the previous sections you saw the basics of the top sub-hierarchy, the containers. We'll dive into the accessory code shortly, but first I want to quickly cover our key delegation issues.

HomeKit Delegation

Listing 16-4 shows the definition line of our ViewController class indicating that it should conform to three different delegate protocols: HomeManager, AccessoryBrowser, and Accessory.

Listing 16-4. Our View Controller Conforms to Three Delegate Protocols

```
class ViewController: UIViewController, HMHomeManagerDelegate, HMAccessoryBrowserDelegate,
HMAccessoryDelegate{
```

HMHomeManagerDelegate

The HMHomeManagerDelegate protocol allows you to track changes to your collection of homes with four methods:

1. homeManager(_:didAddHome:)

2. homeManager(_:didRemoveHome:)

3. homeManagerDidUpdateHomes(_:)

4. homeManagerDidUpdatePrimaryHome(_:)

In our code, I've implemented three of these and excluded didRemoveHome since we're not going that far with our example. If you get the first three, the fourth one should be obvious. Listing 16-5 shows two of the methods where all we do is to print to the log when the method is called. This is always a good idea in your early stages of development so you can keep track of what's going on in case anything funky seems to be happening. Listing 16-6 shows how we handle things when a change to our homes database occurs through our implementation of the homeManagerDidUpdateHomes method. This is a very important method because, after starting your app, until this method is called the homes database shouldn't be considered as valid.

Listing 16-5. Adding Simple print() Calls to Track What's Happening with Our Delegate Methods

```
func homeManagerDidUpdatePrimaryHome(manager: HMHomeManager) {
    print("homeManagerDidUpdatePrimaryHome called")
}

func homeManager( manager: HMHomeManager,
            didAddHome home: HMHome) {
    print("Home Manager added a home")
}
```

Listing 16-6. Handling Notification of Changes to Our Home Database

```
func homeManagerDidUpdateHomes(manager: HMHomeManager) {

    print("Home Manager updated the homes database")
    for home in manager.homes as [HMHome] {
        if home.name == kmyHome {
            self.primaryHome = home
            print("Setting primaryHome to MyHome")
        }
    }
}
```

HMAccessoryBrowserDelegate

Similar to how the HMHomeManagerDelegate protocol allows you to track changes in your collection of homes, the HMAccessoryBrowserDelegate protocol permits tracking of when accessories become available or go missing. This could be when you power on an accessory, initialize a new accessory, remove an accessory, and so on. The protocol offers two methods that should be pretty obvious as to their intent:

1. accessoryBrowser(_:didFindNewAccessory:)

2. accessoryBrowser(_:didRemoveNewAccessory:)

Listing 16-7 shows how we implement the :didFindNewAccessory method in our code. We talk more about this in the section on managing our accessories.

Listing 16-7. Method Called When the Accessory Manager Locates a New Accessory

```
func accessoryBrowser(browser: HMAccessoryBrowser,
  didFindNewAccessory accessory: HMAccessory) {

    print("Found a new accessory: \(accessory)")
    if accessory.name == kdiscoball {
        self.discoballAccessory = accessory
        self.accessoryFound.text = "Found \(accessory.name)"
        }
}
```

HMAccessoryDelegate

While this sounds similar to the last protocol, the HMAccessoryDelegate protocol provides methods associated with monitoring any changes to specific accessories. Once we have an accessory object that we wish to monitor, we set its delegate and use the following methods for monitoring:

1. accessoryDidUpdateName(_:)

2. accessoryDidUpdateReachability(_:)

3. accessoryDidUpdateServices(_:)

4. accessory(_:didUpdateNameForService:)

5. accessory(_:service:didUpdateValueForCharacteristic:)

6. accessory(_:didUpdateAssociatedServiceTypeForService:)

The key method we're concerned with is the :didUpdateValueForCharacteristic method. So, for a particular characteristic of a particular service in a specific accessory, we get this method call. The provided parameters include enough information to tell us where this change was applied. Listing 16-8 shows how we implemented this method. One important note about this is that if we change the state of the power to the disco ball remotely, as we'll see in the complete code later, this method may not get called, since the hardware may not supply the status information about the local control interaction actuated remotely. Some devices will do this properly, but the fact is, HomeKit accessories are in the early stages of deployment, so don't expect perfection in every case. In fact, for me, I never saw it called unless I changed the power on the accessory directly, either through the accessory simulator or on an actual device.

Listing 16-8. Detecting Changes to the Power Supplied to Our Disco Ball

```
func accessory(accessory: HMAccessory, service: HMService, didUpdateValueForCharacteristic
characteristic: HMCharacteristic) {
    print("\(accessory.name): \(characteristic.metadata!.manufacturerDescription!) has
    changed to \(characteristic.value!)")
    if accessory.name == "DiscoBall" && characteristic.metadata!.manufacturerDescription ==
    "Power State" {
        //
        // NOTE: in Apple's documentation, this value is shown in the list as a string, but
        //        in the details as a Bool. It works as a Bool as you see here...
        //
        if characteristic.value as! Bool == true {
            self.isDiscoBallPowerOn = true
            self.deviceIndicator.text = "Disco Ball ON"
            self.switchStatus.setTitle("Stop Party", forState: UIControlState.Normal)
            self.switchStatus.titleLabel?.textAlignment = NSTextAlignment.Center
        } else {
            self.isDiscoBallPowerOn = false
            self.deviceIndicator.text = "Disco Ball OFF"
            self.switchStatus.setTitle("Start Party", forState: UIControlState.Normal)
            self.switchStatus.titleLabel?.textAlignment = NSTextAlignment.Center
        }
    }
}
```

Accessory Management

Working with any remote hardware device, we'll need to be able to find the right piece of equipment, get access to it, see what services it offers and figure out what information we can read from and write to the device. We'll want to be able to securely connect, disconnect, and determine if some interruption occurred while we plan to use the device. This is all part of managing the accessories that we'll be using.

Problem

How do we find accessories in the first place?

Solution

We use the HMAccessoryBrowser to start and stop our search and the HMAccessoryBrowserDelegate protocol methods to handle changes in the accessory landscape.

As we're interested in just our disco ball power controller, the first thing we need to do is to find it. So, step one, after making sure we conform to the HMAccessoryBrowserDelegate protocol, is to create an HMAccessoryBrowser:

```
let browser = HMAccessoryBrowser()
```

This creates the object that will search for all accessories within our network, but only after we tell it to do so. For that, we tell our browser to start searching for accessories:

```
browser.startSearchingForNewAccessories()
```

Because searching with our device's radio can be a power-hungry operation, we need to limit the amount of time we do this by stopping the search when we're done, i.e., after we've found the accessory we're looking for. Listing 16-9 shows the helper method I created to stop the accessory search and to conserve power in our mobile device.

Listing 16-9. Stop Searching for Accessories Helper Method

```
func stopSearching() {
    print("stopSearching")
    browser.stopSearchingForNewAccessories()
}
```

But how do we know when to call this method? There are two reasonable answers. The first one is that we call it whenever we've found what we're looking for. In our case, as soon as we locate the disco ball power controller we can stop searching. But what if we don't find it, or, a more likely scenario, what if we're looking for all available accessories? We don't want to stop after the first one. We also don't want to have to tell our app what or how many to look for. It needs to be dynamic. This is where you have to make a decision and choose a timeout:

```
NSTimer.scheduledTimerWithTimeInterval(20.0, target: self, selector: "stopSearching",
userInfo: nil, repeats: false)
```

This instruction will start a timer for 20 seconds, and at the end of that will execute the stopSearching() method contained within this code file (target: self). How do you know how long is long enough? You don't. Trial and error, my friends. I've found that 20 seconds works, but many other sections of code that I've looked over use a shorter time, about 10 seconds. Again, it's up to you.

What about if you have a large number of accessories? Setting a few up could run past whatever time you set. The trick I use is to restart the timer after you locate and handle each accessory. One way to do this would be to stop then restart the timer in the didFindNewAccessory delegate method. That way, after the actual last accessory is set up, you give it one more 20 second (or whatever time you choose) try to make sure you've exhausted the search.

What about if things change, like an accessory is dropped or removed? Similarly, you may want to create a periodic startSearching() helper method as well that gets called periodically, maybe every few minutes or so. In that case, within that periodic search method, you might only search for 5 seconds to keep radio usage contained in order to prolong battery life.

Problem

We need an accessory to work with. What do we do?

Solution

There are, of course, two options: use a real accessory or use the HomeKit Accessory Simulator. We'll do both.

HomeKit Accessory Simulator

First, you must download the latest version of the simulator. I've found when using older versions of the simulator that the created accessories will not connect with the app, even if they're both running on your Mac. To get the latest version, go to the capabilities section of your project, as shown in Figure 16-16, scroll down to where we enabled the HomeKit entitlement earlier, and click on the Download HomeKit Simulator… button. Place it in a convenient spot in your filesystem—I put mine in Applications, but then made a shortcut for the desktop.

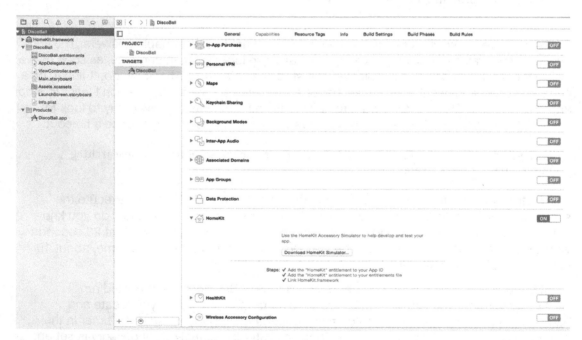

Figure 16-16. To avoid problems, make sure to download the latest version of the HomeKit Accessory Simulator from the project capabilities section of Xcode

Start the HomeKit Accessory Simulator, click the '+' at the bottom left, and select "New Accessory…" (Figure 16-17). Then configure the accessory, adding the name as DiscoBall (Figure 16-18). For manufacturer and model you can put in anything you want. The serial number will likely be autofilled by the simulator. When complete, it should look something like Figure 16-19. You should see at the top a setup code you'll need to use when attaching the accessory during execution of your app. iOS will automatically pop up a dialog for you to enter this code at the appropriate time during execution.

Figure 16-17. Add a new accessory to the HomeKit Accessory Simulator

Figure 16-18. Configure the name of the accessory as DiscoBall so we'll know what to look for in the code

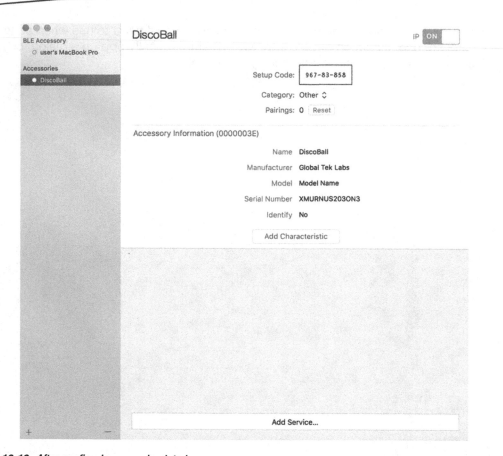

Figure 16-19. After configuring your simulated accessory

Next, we need to add our LightBulb service to the accessory, so click on the Add Service.
. . button (Figure 16-20), then go to the drop-down and select "Outlet" since our service
will be to allow power to our disco ball or not. Selecting "Outlet" will give us the default
characteristics we need in our code. This last step will complete our simulator accessory
setup, and you should see something that looks like Figure 16-21. Make sure that the IP
slide switch in the upper right-hand side is on, otherwise the accessory won't be able to be
seen on the network.

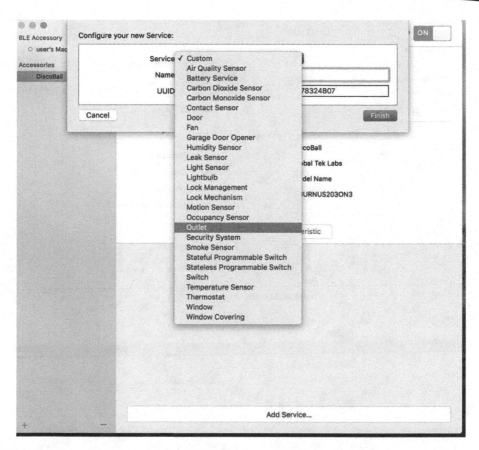

Figure 16-20. Configure an outlet service named LightBulb for our disco ball accessory

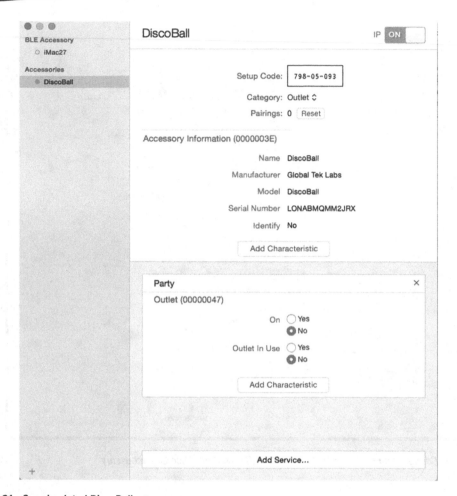

Figure 16-21. Our simulated DiscoBall accessory

> **Note**   An important point to note here is that the simulator allows us to completely configure our accessory from scratch. When using an actual hardware accessory such as the iHome accessory described in the next section, we'll need to locate and identify all the information that the manufacturer set up in the hardware and firmware of the device. We'll see how to access that information shortly.

iHome Control SmartPlug

Working with real HomeKit accessories, especially those produced early in the program, can sometimes be a challenge. Many of the accessory features built into the firmware of the device will not work as expected or may be intermittent in their operation. Such was the case with the iHome Control SmartPlug, one of the early HomeKit devices available at the time of this writing. While there were firmware updates available, for my work at least, none of them corrected the issue with that first device. Later, using a second-generation iHome device, I had no such issues. But, with a little effort, I was able to get it to function with minimal changes to the code from what we wrote to work with the HomeKit Accessory Simulator. In fact, I only changed two lines of code and added one, with only one change being absolutely required to get the accessory to function.

Verify Accessory Functions Properly

First, using the supplied instructions and the iHome app, which can be found on the Apple App Store, I verified that the device worked properly. In Figure 16-22 you can see the plug and app in the OFF position. In Figure 16-23 the indicator on the app is darker, indicating that the button was pressed to turn on the device. You can also see that the *H* indicator on the actual device—in the lower-left bottom—is illuminated, showing that power is flowing.

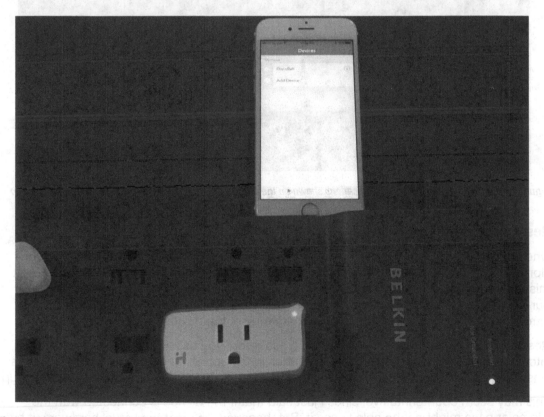

Figure 16-22. Switch power off using iHome-supplied app

Figure 16-23. Switch power on, with indications shown on the actual device and the button on the iHome native app

Reset Accessory for HomeKit

One of the early issues I discovered was that an actual hardware accessory designed for HomeKit may not be seen by other apps if it has been paired up with a different app. What this meant was that, when I tested the device using the iHome native app, then tried to run our disco ball app without doing anything except for resetting the iPhone simulator, the hardware accessory was never seen. So I had to reset the device.

Resetting the device will be different for each accessory you use. Plug the iHome SmartPlug into an AC outlet, then press and hold the button in the upper right (near the green LED) for at least 12 seconds. The LED will flash, and then you use the iHome app to continue setting it up.

This may seem counterintuitive, since I just said that if the device is connected with the iHome app we might not be able to see it. But, because we reset the actual hardware, it has no wireless connection. So what we do is use the iHome app to set it up, without actually completing the setup. In other words, we exit the iHome app before everything is complete. We just want to get far enough along in the process so the hardware accessory sees our WiFi network. So, after resetting the device and starting the iHome app, you'll select "Add a New Device," as shown in Figure 16-24. At this point you may want to go through the 12-second reset again just to be sure. Tapping Next in the upper right corner of the app starts the search for any compatible accessories (Figure 16-25).

Figure 16-24. *After verifying that the accessory works properly with the native app, use the manufacturer's instructions to reset the device to work with our disco ball HomeKit project*

Figure 16-25. The app uses the iPhone hardware to search for compatible accessories within range

Once the HomeKit app finds available devices, it will allow you to select them and set them up, as shown in Figure 16-26. Here's where things really begin to deviate enough to affect our Swift project code. Note that the accessory is named iHome SmartPlug-XXXXXX, where XXXXXX will be unique to the specific unit, i.e., its serial number. What we've done to this point is use the iHome app on our iPhone to locate the hardware accessory. Right now, it's not connected to any WiFi network, so it can't know how it's being configured, much less know about any network password protection. So, we tap Continue and move on with our setup (Figure 16-27).

Figure 16-26. Select the appropriate accessory and tap Continue to proceed

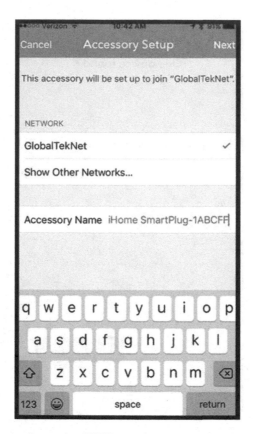

Figure 16-27. Connect the accessory to your local WiFi network

As you can see, I've set up a temporary company network called GlobalTekNet to which my Mac is connected and thus, my iPhone simulator is too. Here, of course, we're working with WiFi networks, but HomeKit also works from your iOS device directly to accessories via Bluetooth Low Energy. This, in fact, was how we began the setup of the accessory.

Note in the middle of the screen in Figure 16-27 you can see the default name of the device. Here is where you would expect to be able to change the name—for example, to DiscoBall—and have it work with our existing code. But, for some reason, this did not work with this version of the iHome app or the latest accessory firmware. We will have to change the code so that the constant that previously pointed to DiscoBall now points to this default name. In a real-life scenario we'd actually just read the name of the accessory returned by the accessory browser and use that from the start, but for now I wanted to keep things as simple as I could, knowing full well that it might seem a little complicated. What I've shown is kind of the "tip of the iceberg" when dealing with HomeKit accessories and to thoroughly work with just a few devices, exploring their differences and handling exceptions, would take a complete book of its own.

Normally, this process goes pretty smoothly, and you should be presented with the screen seen in Figure 16-28. You are asked to enter the accessory code, which is usually printed on the actual device (accessory). The code can be entered manually, as we do in our project, or by holding the camera in front of the printed code so the software will automatically translate it to enter the information. HOWEVER, DO NOT ENTER OR SCAN A CODE AT THIS TIME. This is where you actually want to terminate the app. If you were planning to use the iHome app, you would go ahead and enter the code, add the accessory to a home, assign it to a room, and proceed with operation.

Figure 16-28. Screen showing that you need to enter the code, which is usually printed on the actual hardware accessory

At this point, the accessory, the iHome SmartPlug, is set up for us to use with our project and the iPhone simulator.

Problem

How do we access the accessory's services and characteristics? Similarly, how do we know what services and characteristics the accessory offers?

Solution

The manufacturer may include, either in the packaging material or in online instructions, the information needed to access the device's services and characteristics. It's pretty simple if using the HomeKit Accessory Simulator, since we completely defined services and characteristics, including what they were called.

Earlier, in Listing 16-8, I showed how you can see when a characteristic has changed and then take the necessary action. This, as we discussed, applies mainly to changes that are made manually at the accessory device and not changes we perform in our code. Because we were discussing the various delegation aspects of HomeKit, we had not yet gotten to how we found the names of the services and characteristics. We kind of left a "hole" in our knowledge that I will address now.

The way I address this in our project is to create functions that list the services and characteristics of our accessory. In those functions I use a simple print() statement to show me the names of those items. In Listing 16-9 you can see in the addMyAccessory() function the call to the first of these methods. The call, self.listServices(self. discoballAccessory!), begins the process of getting the information we need. Listing 16-10 shows the implementation of that function.

Listing 16-9. Function to List the Services Provided by a Discovered Accessory

```
func addMyAccessory() {
    if self.discoballAccessory != nil {
        print("addMyAccessory: discoball: \(self.discoballAccessory)")
        self.primaryHome?.addAccessory(self.discoballAccessory!, completionHandler: {(error) in
            if error != nil {
                print("Could not add \(self.discoballAccessory!.name) to \(self.primaryHome!.name)")
                print("error: \(error)")
            } else {
                print("Successfully added \(self.discoballAccessory!.name) to \(self.
                primaryHome!.name)")
                //
                // Set the delegate for the accessory so we can see updates to it
                //
                self.discoballAccessory!.delegate = self

                self.accessoryStatus.text = "\(self.discoballAccessory!.name) CONNECTED"
                //
                // CALL THE FUNCTION TO LIST THE SERVICES FOR THIS ACCESSORY
                //
                print("Services offerred...")
                self.listServices(self.discoballAccessory!)
                //
                // No need to continue searching
                //
                self.stopSearching()
            }

        })
    } else {
        self.accessoryStatus.text = "No accessory identified to attach"
    }
}
```

Listing 16-10. This Function Lists the Available Services for an Accessory

```
func listServices(accessory : HMAccessory) {
    for service in accessory.services {
        //
        // Go through any available services, find the Outlet service, which
        // is just a HomeKit standard name that we've called our party service,
        // and list all the characteristics for our "Party" service.
        //
```

```
        if service.serviceType == HMServiceTypeOutlet {
        self.services.append(service as HMService)
            print("found \(service.name) of type HMServiceTypeOutlet service for \(accessory.name)")
            self.partyService = service
            listCharacteristics(service)
        }
    }
}
```

Without showing the large `listCharacteristics` function, Listing 16-11 shows the key part of the code where we iterate over each characteristic in a service and display its name.

Listing 16-11. Critical Portion of the listCharacteristics Function

```
func listCharacteristics(service: HMService) {
    for characteristic_item in service.characteristics {
        characteristics.append(characteristic_item as HMCharacteristic)
        print("value \(characteristic_item.value!) : \(characteristic_item.metadata!.
        manufacturerDescription!)")
        //
        // Notification of changes in characteristics are NOT automatically enabled, you
        have to do this yourself
        //
        if characteristic_item.properties.contains(HMCharacteristicPropertySupportsEvent
        Notification) {
            characteristic_item .enableNotification(true, completionHandler: {(error) in
            if error != nil {
                print("Error while enabling notification for \(characteristic_item.
                metadata?.manufacturerDescription)")
            }
            else    {
                print("\(characteristic_item.metadata?.manufacturerDescription) Notification
                enabled")
                }
            })
        }
}
```

> **Note**   The function shown in Listing 16-11 is incomplete for brevity.

Summary

In this somewhat lengthy chapter, we have discussed key elements of using Apple HomeKit with both simulated and actual hardware accessories. We've touched on just enough aspects of HomeKit to get you up and running; for example, controlling your own disco ball or anything else. Our focus was on a power control switch, specifically the iHome Smart Plug, but the methods and functions we've discussed work with any other type of accessory you might come across in the near future.

Figure 16-29 show the user interface screen our project presents, allowing us to turn our disco party ball on or off, starting or stopping the party.

Figure 16-29. *The user interface for turning on or off our accessory. Tapping the "Start Party" button turns on our disco ball while "Stop Party" turns it off.*

Listing 16-12 shows the complete code for the ViewController.swift file where we discover and attach our accessory, list our services and methods, and control our actual HomeKit accessory.

Listing 16-12. Complete ViewController.swift Class File

```
//
//  ViewController.swift
//  DiscoBall
//
//  Created by Molly Maskrey on 12/17/15.
//  Copyright © 2015 Global Tek Labs. All rights reserved.
//

import UIKit
import HomeKit
```

```
class ViewController: UIViewController, HMHomeManagerDelegate, HMAccessoryBrowserDelegate,
HMAccessoryDelegate{

    // convenience constants
    let kmyHome = "MyHome"
    let kmainRoom = "MainRoom"
    // If using the simulator...
//    let kdiscoball = "DiscoBall"

    // If using the actual iHome SmartPlug
    // Note that the serial # will likely be different
    // on a device that you may use
    let kdiscoball = "iHome SmartPlug-1ABCFF"
    let kdiscoballDisplayName = "DiscoBall"

    // "Global" variables
    let manager = HMHomeManager()
    let browser = HMAccessoryBrowser()
    var accessories = [HMAccessory]()
    var services = [HMService]()
    var characteristics = [HMCharacteristic]()
    var discoBallPowerSwitch: HMCharacteristic?
    var isDiscoBallPowerOn : Bool = false

    // Some local "testing" variables
    var primaryHome : HMHome?
    var discoballAccessory : HMAccessory?
    var partyService : HMService?

    // OUTLET: Indicates if ball is on or off
    // if using the HKAccessory Similator this will
    // be the "Outlet in Use" characteristic
    @IBOutlet weak var deviceIndicator: UILabel!

    // OUTLET: Used to change the name on the top
    // UI button...the one that controls our disco ball
    // e.g., when the ball is on, we want the switch to
    // read "OFF" and vice versa
    @IBOutlet weak var switchStatus: UIButton!

    // ACTION: This method is called when the top button
    // is activated, used to turn the disco ball (accessory
    // outlet) ON or OFF
    @IBAction func activateDevice(sender: AnyObject) {
        self.activateDiscoBall()
    }

    // OUTLET: A simple, mostly diagnostic label we use
    // to display information about the located accessory.
    // It lets the user know the app has found our disco ball
    @IBOutlet weak var accessoryFound: UILabel!
```

```
    // OUTLET: A simple, mostly diagnostic label used
    // to indicate whether or not the accessory is connected
    // to the app.
    @IBOutlet weak var accessoryStatus: UILabel!

    // ACTION: This method is called when the bottom button "ATTACH"
    // is pressed to make an attempt to connect the located accessory
    // to the app
    @IBAction func attachAccessory(sender: AnyObject) {
        self.addMyAccessory()
    }

    override func viewDidLoad() {
        super.viewDidLoad()
        // Do any additional setup after loading the view, typically from a nib.

        manager.delegate = self
        print("Home Manager created and delegate set to self")

        browser.delegate = self
        print("Accessory Browser created and delegate set to self")

        // Go see if there are any accessories in the area
        browser.startSearchingForNewAccessories()

        // Only do it for a short period as it will drain the battery
        NSTimer.scheduledTimerWithTimeInterval(20.0, target: self, selector:
        "stopSearching", userInfo: nil, repeats: false)

        for home in self.manager.homes as [HMHome] {

            if home.name == kmyHome {
                print("Found MyHome")
                }
        }

        self.switchStatus.enabled = false
        self.switchStatus.titleLabel!.text = "Disabled"

        // call the addMyHome convenience method
        self.addMyHome()

    }

// Our Helper Methods
    func stopSearching() {
        print("stopSearching")
        browser.stopSearchingForNewAccessories()
    }
```

```
//
// Add our Home
//
func addMyHome() {
    manager.addHomeWithName(kmyHome, completionHandler: {(home, error) -> Void in
        print("Trying to add MyHome")
        if error == nil || error?.code == 32 { // error code 32 means the home is
        already in the database

            if error == nil {
                print("MyHome added to database")
                self.primaryHome = home
            } else {
                print("MyHome already in database")
            }

            print("…either way, we can add a room to the home now")
            //
            // We've stored the house we added as our primary so we'll
            // now add a room to it
            //
            if self.primaryHome != nil {
                self.primaryHome!.addRoomWithName(self.kmainRoom, completionHandler:
                { (room, error) -> Void in
                    if error == nil || error?.code == 13  { // error code 13 means
                    room already in home
                        if error == nil {
                            print("Room added to Home")
                        } else {
                            print("Room ALREADY there")
                        }
                    //
                    // This might seem tricky, but we have to tell HomeKit to
                    make this
                    // our primary home as well. Previously, we just essentially
                    called it that
                    // but we have to do it in code so the database is
                    "correct."
                    //
                    self.manager.updatePrimaryHome(self.primaryHome!,
                    completionHandler: {(error) -> Void in
                    if error == nil {
                        print("\(self.primaryHome!.name) now defined as the
                        primary home")
                    } else {
                        print("ERROR: setting primary home: \(error)")
                        }
                    })
```

```
                            } else {
                                print("ERROR: attempting to add room. \(error!.
                                    localizedDescription)")
                            }

                        })
                    } else {
                        print("ERROR: For some reason our global primary home was not set")
                    }
                } else {
                    print("ERROR: attempting to add home: \(error)")
                }

            })
    }
    //
    // End of setting up our simple one room home
    // Note that we didn't do anything with accessories. We will deal with those separately.
    //


    //
    // Stock method - no changes
    override func didReceiveMemoryWarning() {
        super.didReceiveMemoryWarning()
        // Dispose of any resources that can be recreated.
    }

func homeManagerDidUpdateHomes(manager: HMHomeManager) {

    print("Home Manager updated the homes database")
    for home in manager.homes as [HMHome] {
        if home.name == kmyHome {
            self.primaryHome = home
            print("Setting primaryHome to MyHome")
        }
    }
}

func homeManagerDidUpdatePrimaryHome(manager: HMHomeManager) {
    print("homeManagerDidUpdatePrimaryHome called")
}

func homeManager( manager: HMHomeManager,
            didAddHome home: HMHome) {
    print("Home Manager added a home")
}

func accessoryBrowser(browser: HMAccessoryBrowser,
    didFindNewAccessory accessory: HMAccessory) {
```

```
        print("Found a new accessory: \(accessory)")
        if accessory.name == kdiscoball {
            self.discoballAccessory = accessory
            self.accessoryFound.text = "Found \(self.kdiscoballDisplayName)"
            }
}

func listServices(accessory : HMAccessory) {
    for service in accessory.services {
        //
        // Go through any available services, find the Outlet service, which
        // is just a HomeKit standard name that we've called our party service,
        // and list all the characteristics for our "Party" service.
        //
        if service.serviceType == HMServiceTypeOutlet {
        self.services.append(service as HMService)
            print("found \(service.name) of type HMServiceTypeOutlet service for \(accessory.name)")
            self.partyService = service
            listCharacteristics(service)
        }
    }
}

func listCharacteristics(service: HMService) {
    for characteristic_item in service.characteristics {
        characteristics.append(characteristic_item as HMCharacteristic)
        print("value \(characteristic_item.value!) : \(characteristic_item.metadata!.
        manufacturerDescription!)")
        //
        // Notification of changes in characteristics are NOT automatically enabled; you
        have to do this yourself
        //
        if characteristic_item.properties.contains(HMCharacteristicPropertySupportsEventNot
        ification) {
            characteristic_item .enableNotification(true, completionHandler: {(error) in
            if error != nil {
                print("Error while enabling notification for \(characteristic_item.
                metadata?.manufacturerDescription)")
            }
            else    {
                print("\(characteristic_item.metadata?.manufacturerDescription) Notification
                enabled")
                }
            })
        }
        //
        // let's also set our main power switch to a global for access by our UI button
        //
        if characteristic_item.metadata!.manufacturerDescription == "Power State" {
            print("Setting up our global discoBallPowerSwitch")
            self.discoBallPowerSwitch = characteristic_item
```

```
            //
            // Read the switch to determine if it is on or not and set the
            // power switch and button indicators appropriately, then
            // enable the power button
            //

            // First make sure the characteristic is readable
        if self.discoBallPowerSwitch!.properties.contains(HMCharacteristicPropertyReadable) {
            // Then prepare the value for reading
            self.discoBallPowerSwitch?.readValueWithCompletionHandler({(error) in
                if (error) != nil {
                    print("Error occured reading the value of the Power Switch")
                    } else {
                        // Read the value
                      self.isDiscoBallPowerOn = self.discoBallPowerSwitch!.value as! Bool
                      print("Power On readback = \(self.discoBallPowerSwitch!.value
                      as! Bool)")
                      print(self.isDiscoBallPowerOn)
                      }
                })

            } else {
                // Just as an example of the alternative
                print("NO HMCharacteristicPropertyReadable PROPERTY")
                }
            // enable the button
            self.switchStatus.enabled = true

            // Set the state of the label and power button depending on what we read back
            if self.isDiscoBallPowerOn  == true {
                print("Turning indicator to ON")
                self.deviceIndicator.text = "Disco Ball ON"
                self.switchStatus.setTitle("Stop Party", forState: UIControlState.Normal)
                self.switchStatus.titleLabel?.textAlignment = NSTextAlignment.Center
            } else {
                print("Turning indicator to OFF")
                self.deviceIndicator.text = "Disco Ball OFF"
                self.switchStatus.setTitle("Start Party", forState: UIControlState.Normal)
                self.switchStatus.titleLabel?.textAlignment = NSTextAlignment.Center
                }
            }
        }
}

func accessoryBrowser(browser: HMAccessoryBrowser,
        didRemoveNewAccessory accessory: HMAccessory) {
      print("didRemoveNewAccessory: \(accessory.name)")
}
```

```
// ACCESSORY DELEGATE METHODS
    func accessory(accessory: HMAccessory, service: HMService,
didUpdateValueForCharacteristic characteristic: HMCharacteristic) {
        print("\(accessory.name): \(characteristic.metadata!.manufacturerDescription!) has
changed to \(characteristic.value!)")
        if accessory.name == kdiscoball && characteristic.metadata!.manufacturerDescription
== "Power State" {
            //
            // NOTE: in Apple's documentation, this value is shown in the list as a string, but
            //        in the details as a Bool. It works as a Bool as you see here.
            //
            if characteristic.value as! Bool == true {
                self.isDiscoBallPowerOn = true
                self.deviceIndicator.text = "Disco Ball ON"
                self.switchStatus.setTitle("Stop Party", forState: UIControlState.Normal)
                self.switchStatus.titleLabel?.textAlignment = NSTextAlignment.Center
            } else {
                self.isDiscoBallPowerOn = false
                self.deviceIndicator.text = "Disco Ball OFF"
                self.switchStatus.setTitle("Start Party", forState: UIControlState.Normal)
                self.switchStatus.titleLabel?.textAlignment = NSTextAlignment.Center
            }
        }
    }

// CONVENIENCE METHODS SUPPORTING BUTTON ACTIONS

func addMyAccessory() {
    if self.discoballAccessory != nil {
        print("addMyAccessory: discoball: \(self.discoballAccessory)")
        self.primaryHome?.addAccessory(self.discoballAccessory!, completionHandler: {(error) in
        if error != nil {
            print("Could not add \(self.discoballAccessory!.name) to \(self.primaryHome!.name)")
            print("error: \(error)")
        } else {
            print("Successfully added \(self.discoballAccessory!.name) to \(self.
            primaryHome!.name)")
            //
            // Set the delegate for the accessory so we can see updates to it
            //
            self.discoballAccessory!.delegate = self

            self.accessoryStatus.text = "\(self.discoballAccessory!.name) CONNECTED"
            //
            // CALL THE FUNCTION TO LIST THE SERVICES FOR THIS ACCESSORY
            //
            print("Services offerred...")
            self.listServices(self.discoballAccessory!)
            //
```

```
                    // No need to continue searching
                    //
                    self.stopSearching()
                    }


            })
        } else {
            self.accessoryStatus.text = "No accessory identified to attach"
        }
}


// Bottom Button
func activateDiscoBall() {
//    print("User pressed \(self.switchStatus.titleLabel!.text) button")
    if self.discoBallPowerSwitch != nil {
        if isDiscoBallPowerOn == false {
            self.discoBallPowerSwitch?.writeValue(true, completionHandler: { (error)  in
                if error != nil {
                    print("Error setting power to Disco Ball: \(error)")
                } else {
//                    print("Power to Disco Ball Set Successfully")
                    self.isDiscoBallPowerOn = true
                    self.deviceIndicator.text = "Disco Ball ON"
                   self.switchStatus.setTitle("Stop Party", forState: UIControlState.Normal)
                    self.switchStatus.titleLabel!.textAlignment = NSTextAlignment.Center
                }
            })
        } else {
            self.discoBallPowerSwitch?.writeValue(false, completionHandler: { (error)  in
                if error != nil {
                    print("Error turning power OFF to Disco Ball: \(error)")
                } else {
//                    print("Power to Disco Ball now OFF")
                    self.isDiscoBallPowerOn  = false
                    self.deviceIndicator.text = "Disco Ball OFF"
                   self.switchStatus.setTitle("Start Party", forState: UIControlState.Normal)
                    self.switchStatus.titleLabel!.textAlignment = NSTextAlignment.Center
                }
            })
        }
    }
}

}
```

Chapter 17

External Sensor Interface Project

In this chapter we examine two of the ways to connect external hardware to iOS devices. We saw in the previous project how we could use Apple's HomeKit framework to do pretty much the same thing. However, while many of the same types of hardware devices can be controlled by various means, HomeKit projects are restricted to HomeKit-certified accessories. Some electronics, such as sensors, drones, medical devices, and so on, use a more generalized mechanism for moving data to and from an iPhone, for example.

Outside of HomeKit, there are two different categories of accessories that we've talked about in previous chapters. An accessory can either be an MFi-certified device or not be one. An MFi-certified accessory means that it was developed and manufactured by an Apple MFi-certified company. It has undergone rigorous development and testing in order to provide assurances to the consumer that it will work with Apple devices that run iOS. MFi accessories communicate either via the dock connector (Lighting, or previously the 30-pin) or using standard Bluetooth (2.1+EDR). Non-MFi accessories would use WiFi, Bluetooth Low Energy (BTLE), or, such as the case with the Square credit card reader, the headphone jack.

For this discussion, we'll exclude WiFi accessories, as they operate using standard data transfer protocols—really no different than any desktop application. So, why choose one option over another? That is, when would you want to use an MFi accessory as compared with a non-MFi device?

© Molly K. Maskrey 2016
M.K. Maskrey, *App Development Recipes for iOS and watchOS*, DOI 10.1007/978-1-4842-1820-4_17

Problem

How do you choose which type of accessory, MFi certified or not, you need for your project?

Solution

MFi accessories in general provide a higher-speed and more reliable connection. A BTLE accessory is limited by the small packet size and thus is restricted to a much lower data rate. A headphone jack–connected accessory uses a special encoding scheme to convert the audio input (mic) and output (headphone) signals to a low-rate data stream. Also, because the audio codecs and frameworks were never intended for this purpose, communications can be less reliable.

Most of the time, you won't have a choice at all. You simply use what your client or employer provides. If you do wind up having input, consider selecting an MFi-validated accessory if you need a secure, high-speed, and/or continuous connection. For intermittent connections such as you might have with a fitness monitor, many IoT devices, or even the sensor we talk about in this chapter, Bluetooth Low Energy provides the lower cost, easier to manage options.

Problem

You want to work with an MFi-certified accessory and saw the EADemo code at Apple, but it's old and written in Objective-C. You need a Swift baseline.

Solution

After the announcement of Swift as the language of choice, many iOS developers working with MFi accessories found themselves in the same situation. And although our project focus in this chapter will be a BTLE-enabled sensor, it's worth the time to see how working with MFi accessories is handled.

Swift External Accessory Demo

In this section we'll walk through an example of connecting to an external device, in Apple terms, an accessory. But first, we'll talk about the different types of accessories to which you can connect.

MFi Accessory Types

As mentioned previously, MFi accessories connect and communicate data with an iPhone in two ways. First, an MFi accessory can use the dock connector at the bottom of the device. Figure 17-1 shows a typical wired MFi accessory that uses the Lightning connector to mate with the iPhone. This accessory connects a rowing machine to your Apple device, thus enabling competitive and simultaneous workouts across time and space.

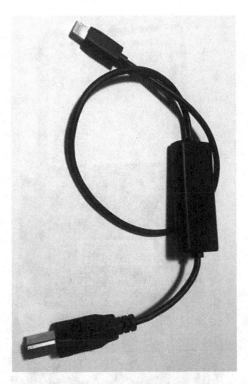

Figure 17-1. *This sports accessory that connects a rowing machine to your iPhone uses the Lightning connector to make a physical high-speed connection*

The second type of communication that an MFi accessory might use is wireless Bluetooth 2.1+EDR, typically referred to as standard Bluetooth. The proximity card detector, shown in Figure 17-2, is such a device. At the top of the figure, you see the loop antenna that is used to detect a card. Typically found on secure doors in offices and other locations, this wireless version can be used for many different setups where portability is an issue. One example might be to use this accessory to track inventory of scripts at an on-location movie set.

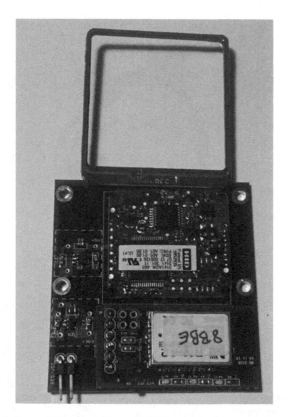

Figure 17-2. A wireless proximity card detector such as this MFi accessory uses standard Bluetooth for communications with the iOS device

MFi Accessory Demo App

How It Works

Our demo code uses Apple's MFi frameworks to manage the accessory device. The app consists of a simple table view and detail screen inside a navigation controller (Figure 17-3). The table view will display the connected accessory, whether it is a wired device (Figure 17-4), or a Bluetooth device (Figures 17-5 and 17-6). Here, we've used the two accessories just shown for demo purposes.

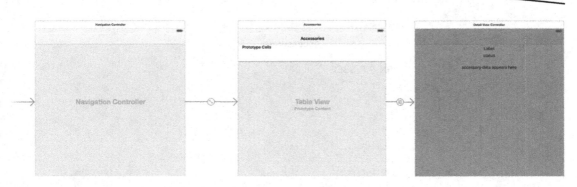

Figure 17-3. Our Swift accessory demo code consists of a navigation controller with a table view and detail view

●●○○○ AT&T Wi-Fi 📶   7:32 AM   ⚡ 🗼 89% ⬛⬛⬛▶

Accessories

Live Rowing

Figure 17-4. The main table view showing a Lightning connector–attached accessory by name

●●○○○ AT&T 📶   7:43 AM   ✈ ✳ 89% ▭ ⚡

Accessories

RN-IAP-8BBE

Figure 17-5. The same app can be used for Bluetooth-connected devices without any modification

Figure 17-6. *On the detail screen, when a prox card is tapped against the antenna of the accessory, you can see the data displayed*

The Code

Before we deviate too far from our intended project, let's see what the Swift code looks like to perform basic MFi accessory management. The first thing we need to do is to include the EAAccessory framework by importing External Accessory and having our `TableViewController` subscribe to the proper protocol (Listing 17-1).

> **Note**   Because we've inherited from the `UITableViewController` class we do not have to explicitly include `tableView` delegate and/or datasource protocols.

Listing 17-1. Include the External Accessory Framework and Subscribe to the Protocol for the Delegate Methods

```
//  ViewController.swift
//  EADemoS
//

import UIKit
import ExternalAccessory

class ViewController: UITableViewController,  EAAccessoryDelegate {
```

Here in the table view we need to know when an accessory is connected and when it is disconnected so we can populate the table correctly. To manage things, we will use two variables and a constant:

```
let accessoryManager: EAAccessoryManager = EAAccessoryManager.sharedAccessoryManager()
var accessoryList:[EAAccessory]?              // our list of accessories, most likely just one
var connectedAccessory: EAAccessory?
```

Because we can have multiple accessories connected to an iOS device, though we do not normally do so, we use a list of EAAccessory types. We also use a single connectedAccessory variable to manage the current accessory of interest, and the accessoryManager is the controlling singleton that handles accessories in the background for us.

The next thing to be aware of is that the accessory delegate methods use notifications to activate the proper method. Since we're concerned with the connecting and disconnecting accessory conditions, we need to observe those notifications and react accordingly. We set this up in the ViewDidLoad method as shown in Listing 17-2. First, we register with our accessoryManager to receive notifications, then we add observers for the EAAccessoryDidConnectNotification and EAAccessoryDidDisconnectNotification notifications, pointing them to the connectedAccessory and disconnectedAccessory methods, respectively (Listings 17-3 and 17-4).

Listing 17-2. Set Up to Receive Notifications from the Accessory Manager to Handle Connect and Disconnect Events

```
    override func viewDidLoad() {
        super.viewDidLoad()
        // Do any additional setup after loading the view, typically from a nib.

        print("EADEMO_S: registering for notifications")
        accessoryManager.registerForLocalNotifications()

        print("EADEMO_S: Adding notification observation")
        NSNotificationCenter.defaultCenter().addObserver(self, selector:
"connectedAccessory:", name: EAAccessoryDidConnectNotification, object: nil)
        NSNotificationCenter.defaultCenter().addObserver(self, selector:
"disconnectedAccessory:", name: EAAccessoryDidDisconnectNotification, object: nil) ·
    }
```

Listing 17-3. Method Called When an Accessory Is Connected Either to the Physical Dock Connector or via Standard Bluetooth

```
func connectedAccessory(notification:NSNotification) {
    print("Accessory was found")
    let dict : [NSObject : AnyObject] = notification.userInfo!
    self.connectedAccessory = dict[EAAccessoryKey] as? EAAccessory
    sampleAccessoryArray[0] = connectedAccessory!.name
    let ip: [NSIndexPath] = [NSIndexPath(forRow:0, inSection: 0)]
    self.tableView.reloadRowsAtIndexPaths(ip, withRowAnimation: UITableViewRowAnimation.None)

}
```

Listing 17-4. Method Called When an Accessory Is Disconnected

```
func disconnectedAccessory(notification:NSNotification) {
    print("Accessory gone, possibly removed")
    sampleAccessoryArray[0] = ""
    let ip: [NSIndexPath] = [NSIndexPath(forRow:0, inSection: 0)]
    self.tableView.reloadRowsAtIndexPaths(ip, withRowAnimation: UITableViewRowAnimation.None)
}
```

Without going into too much detail, since MFi accessories are not part of this chapter's project, these methods basically handle the tableView population and accessory variables. Listing 17-5 shows the complete ViewController class Swift file.

Listing 17-5. Main Table View Controller Swift Code

```
//
//  ViewController.swift
//  EADemoS
//
//  Created by Molly Maskrey on 1/18/16.
//  Copyright © 2016 Global Tek Labs. All rights reserved.
//

import UIKit
import ExternalAccessory

class ViewController: UITableViewController, EAAccessoryDelegate {

@IBOutlet weak var infoLabel: UILabel!

// SAMPLE DATA FOR TABLE VIEW
//var sampleAccessoryArray:[String] = ["see no accessory", "hear no accessory", "speak no
accesory"]
var sampleAccessoryArray: [String] = [""]

// External Accessory Stuff
```

```swift
var accessoryList:[EAAccessory]?                // our list of accessories, most likely there
will only be one
let accessoryManager: EAAccessoryManager = EAAccessoryManager.sharedAccessoryManager()
var connectedAccessory: EAAccessory?

    override func viewDidLoad() {
        super.viewDidLoad()
        // Do any additional setup after loading the view, typically from a nib.

        print("EADEMO_S: registering for notifications")
        accessoryManager.registerForLocalNotifications()

        print("EADEMO_S: Adding notification observation")
        NSNotificationCenter.defaultCenter().addObserver(self, selector:
"connectedAccessory:", name: EAAccessoryDidConnectNotification, object: nil)
        NSNotificationCenter.defaultCenter().addObserver(self, selector:
"disconnectedAccessory:", name: EAAccessoryDidDisconnectNotification, object: nil)
    }

    //
    // Not really used
    override func didReceiveMemoryWarning() {
        super.didReceiveMemoryWarning()
        // Dispose of any resources that can be recreated.
    }

    deinit {
        NSNotificationCenter.defaultCenter().removeObserver(self)
        accessoryManager.unregisterForLocalNotifications()
    }

//
// This method gets notified via the accessory manager and notifcations when an accessory is connected
// via the dock connector or using Standard Bluetooth—NOT BT low energy
//
func connectedAccessory(notification:NSNotification) {
    print("Accessory was found")
    let dict : [NSObject : AnyObject] = notification.userInfo!
    self.connectedAccessory = dict[EAAccessoryKey] as? EAAccessory
    sampleAccessoryArray[0] = connectedAccessory!.name
    let ip: [NSIndexPath] = [NSIndexPath(forRow:0, inSection: 0)]
    self.tableView.reloadRowsAtIndexPaths(ip, withRowAnimation: UITableViewRowAnimation.None)

}

//
// This method gets notified via the accessory manager and notifcations when an accessory is
DISCONNECTED
// via the dock connector or using Standard Bluetooth—NOT BT low energy
// All we do is erase the item in the table view cell...note that there is still a cell
there, but it's blank
// so it might be that if you tap the blank cell things will not work properly.
```

```
// ***NOTE*** There is an issue when you've gone into the detail view, come back to here,
and then
// disconnect the accessory. It doesn't seem to work properly. But that's probably not important
// to spend a lot of effort on as this is just for demo and baseline testing.

func disconnectedAccessory(notification:NSNotification) {
    print("Accessory gone, possibly removed")
    sampleAccessoryArray[0] = ""
    let ip: [NSIndexPath] = [NSIndexPath(forRow:0, inSection: 0)]
    self.tableView.reloadRowsAtIndexPaths(ip, withRowAnimation: UITableViewRowAnimation.None)
}

//
//  This is how we pass the accessory to the detail view controller via the segue
//  as shown in the storyboards. Note that the name of the segue must be the same here
//  and as shown in the storyboard.
//
override func prepareForSegue(segue: UIStoryboardSegue, sender: AnyObject?) {
    if segue.identifier == "accessorySegue" {
        let accessoryScene = segue.destinationViewController as! DetailViewController
        accessoryScene.connectedAccessory  = self.connectedAccessory
    }
}

//
// Table View Data Source Methods
// Basic Xcode table view routines
//
override func numberOfSectionsInTableView(tableView: UITableView) -> Int {
//
    return 1
}
override func tableView(tableView: UITableView, numberOfRowsInSection section: Int) -> Int {
//
    return self.sampleAccessoryArray.count
}

override func tableView(tableView: UITableView, cellForRowAtIndexPath indexPath:
NSIndexPath) -> UITableViewCell {

    // NOTE: because this will be a small table view, I'm not worrying about
    //       reusing cells. It's just not needed here.
    //
    let cell = tableView.dequeueReusableCellWithIdentifier("accessorycell", forIndexPath:
indexPath) as UITableViewCell

    cell.textLabel?.text = self.sampleAccessoryArray[indexPath.row]
    return cell
}

}
```

Once we're ready to use an accessory shown in the table view, tapping that accessory takes us to the detail view where we will make the actual "connection" to the accessory. By connection, I mean that we establish what is known as an EASession between our app and the accessory in order to move data back and forth. As such, the detail view code will need to have External Accessory framework support as well as NSStreams support. An NSStream is used to move data in a standard, familiar manner. For accessories, we use two streams: one for input and one for output. This means we have to subscribe to both protocols:

```
class DetailViewController: UIViewController, EAAccessoryDelegate, NSStreamDelegate {
```

Another concept you want to be familiar with is that of External Accessory protocol. The name is kind of a misnomer. It's not really a protocol, but more a unique name or identifier for the accessory. While that does gloss over a number of details, for what we need with simple accessory communications, that definition works fine. Here's our protocol definition:

```
// CHANGE THIS TO YOUR PROTOCOL STRING
// *NOTE* make sure to change the Supported External Accessory item in the "info.plist"
let myProtocolString = "com.RovingNetworks.btdemo"
```

The protocol is defined by the accessory manufacturer and is built into their product's firmware. It usually takes on a reverse-DNS notational prefix. Since we're using a Bluetooth module from a company called Roving Networks, our protocol string is com.RovingNetworks.btdemo.

> **Note** Roving Networks was acquired by Microchip, and newer modules may have a different protocol string.

The protocol string also must be defined in your Info.plist file, as shown in Figure 17-7. This provides metadata about the app to iOS so that when an accessory is connected, if the app is not already installed on the device, iOS will try to take you to the App Store to locate the proper app for use with the connected accessory. It goes without saying that both the plist and code protocol strings must match exactly.

Key	Type	Value
▼ Information Property List	Dictionary	(15 items)
Localization native development r... ⬍	String	en
Executable file ⬍	String	$(EXECUTABLE_NAME)
Bundle identifier ⬍	String	$(PRODUCT_BUNDLE_IDENTIFIER)
InfoDictionary version ⬍	String	6.0
Bundle name ⬍	String	$(PRODUCT_NAME)
Bundle OS Type code ⬍	String	APPL
Bundle versions string, short ⬍	String	1.0
Bundle creator OS Type code ⬍	String	????
Bundle version ⬍	String	1
Application requires iPhone envir... ⬍	Boolean	YES
Launch screen interface file base... ⬍	String	LaunchScreen
Main storyboard file base name ⬍	String	Main
▼ Supported external accessor... ⬍ ⊕⊖	Array	⌄ (1 item)
Item 0	String	com.RovingNetworks.btdemo
▶ Required device capabilities ⬍ ⊕⊖	Array	(1 item)
▶ Supported interface orientations ⬍	Array	(3 items)

Figure 17-7. The protocol string must be defined in the project's Info.plist file

In the detail controller's `viewDidLoad` method we set up our labels, register for notifications like before (this time only interested in the disconnect notification), and try to open a session with the accessory (Listing 17-6).

Listing 17-6. Our Detail View's Initial Method Attempts to Open a Session with the Accessory Using the openSession Convenience Function

```
override func viewDidLoad() {
//
    super.viewDidLoad()
    self.accessoryTitleLabel.text = connectedAccessory!.name
    self.statusLabel.text = "accessory connected"
    self.connectedAccessory?.delegate = self

    accessoryManager.registerForLocalNotifications()
    NSNotificationCenter.defaultCenter().addObserver(self, selector:
"disconnectedAccessory:", name: EAAccessoryDidDisconnectNotification, object: nil)
    self.openSession()
}
```

In our `openSession` function (Listing 17-7), we use the protocol string to establish contact with the accessory and set up our input and output NSStreams.

Listing 17-7. The openSession Method in the ViewController.swift File Establishes the Connection and Two-way Data Path with Our Accessory

```
func openSession() {
    self.statusLabel.text = "opening session"
    session = EASession.init(accessory: self.connectedAccessory!, forProtocol: myProtocolString)
    if session != nil {
            self.statusLabel.text = "opened session to accessory"

            session?.inputStream?.delegate = self
            session?.inputStream?.scheduleInRunLoop(NSRunLoop.currentRunLoop(), forMode:
            NSDefaultRunLoopMode)
            session?.inputStream?.open()

            session?.outputStream?.delegate = self
            session?.outputStream?.scheduleInRunLoop(NSRunLoop.currentRunLoop(), forMode:
            NSDefaultRunLoopMode)
            session?.outputStream?.open()

    } else {
            self.statusLabel.text = "could not open session"
    }
}
```

That's the basics you'll need to know in order to begin working with MFi accessories. The complete `DetailViewContoller.swift` file is shown in Listing 17-8. Next, we'll start on our sensor interface project that uses Bluetooth 4.0 Low Energy and the Core Bluetooth framework.

Listing 17-8. DetailViewController.swift File

```
//
//  DetailViewController.swift
//  EADemoS
//
//  Created by Molly Maskrey on 1/22/16.
//  Copyright © 2016 Global Tek Labs. All rights reserved.
//

import UIKit
import ExternalAccessory

// CHANGE THIS TO YOUR PROTOCOL STRING
// *NOTE* make sure to change the Supported External Accessory item in the "info.plist"
let myProtocolString = "com.RovingNetworks.btdemo"

//
// Because this class deals with the accessory, it needs to conform to the EAAccessory
Delegate protocol.
// And, since this is where we handle the actual data I/O across the channel, it must also conform
// to the NSStream Delegate protocol.
//
class DetailViewController: UIViewController, EAAccessoryDelegate, NSStreamDelegate {
```

```
@IBOutlet weak var accessoryTitleLabel: UILabel!

@IBOutlet weak var statusLabel: UILabel!
@IBOutlet weak var outputDataLabel: UILabel!

//
// References to the accessory and the session
var connectedAccessory: EAAccessory?
var session: EASession?

// get access to the shared accessory manager
let accessoryManager: EAAccessoryManager = EAAccessoryManager.sharedAccessoryManager()

override func viewDidLoad() {
//
    super.viewDidLoad()
    self.accessoryTitleLabel.text = connectedAccessory!.name
    self.statusLabel.text = "accessory connected"
    self.connectedAccessory?.delegate = self

    accessoryManager.registerForLocalNotifications()
    NSNotificationCenter.defaultCenter().addObserver(self, selector:
"disconnectedAccessory:", name: EAAccessoryDidDisconnectNotification, object: nil)
    self.openSession()
}

override func viewDidDisappear(animated: Bool) {
//
    print("DetailView Did Disappear")
    self.closeSession()
    NSNotificationCenter.defaultCenter().removeObserver(self)
    accessoryManager.unregisterForLocalNotifications()
}

// DATA MOVEMENT

//
// This is the event handler for any of the NSStream activity.
// In this demo, we're only concerned with reading data from the device.
// I've included the writeData call and method, but they're
// just placeholders, as the example BT device I'm using doesn't get
// written to.
func stream(aStream: NSStream, handleEvent eventCode: NSStreamEvent) {
    switch (eventCode) {
        case NSStreamEvent.None:
            print("NSStream Event None")
        case NSStreamEvent.OpenCompleted:
            print("NSStream Open Completed")
        case NSStreamEvent.HasBytesAvailable:
            print("NSStream Has Bytes Available")
            self.readData()
```

```
            case NSStreamEvent.HasSpaceAvailable:
                self.writeData()
            case NSStreamEvent.ErrorOccurred:
                print("NSStream Error Occured")
            case NSStreamEvent.EndEncountered:
                print("NSStream End Encountered")
            default:
                break;
        }

}


//
// KEY DATA I/O Method *** This is where the data from the accessory is brought into this
app
// via the NSStreams, mostly managed by iOS and converted for display in a UILabel.
//

func readData() {
    let maxReadLength = 20
    var inputDataArray = [UInt8](count: maxReadLength, repeatedValue: 0)

    var outputDataString : String = ""
//    print("array: \(inputDataArray)")
    while ((session?.inputStream?.hasBytesAvailable) == true) {
        let len = session?.inputStream?.read(&inputDataArray, maxLength: maxReadLength)
        if len > 0 {

//              print("\(len!) Read\n")
//              print("inputArray: \(inputDataArray)")

            // Conversion for display of some data
            // this is just for the demo app and only displays
            // some of the info from the BT board/card scanner
            // YOU'LL NEED TO CUSTOMIZE THIS AS APPROPRIATE FOR THE APPLICATION
            for value in inputDataArray {
                outputDataString += String(value, radix: 16)
            }

//              print("outputArray: \(outputDataString)")
            dispatch_async(dispatch_get_main_queue()) {
                self.statusLabel.text = "New Data Available:"
                self.outputDataLabel.text = outputDataString as String
                }

        }
    }
}
```

```
func    writeData() {
// This example does not write any data

}

func disconnectedAccessory(notification:NSNotification) {
    print("Accessory gone, possibly removed")
    self.statusLabel.text = "accessory disconnected"
    self.accessoryTitleLabel.text = "none"
    self.closeSession()
    NSNotificationCenter.defaultCenter().removeObserver(self)
    //
    //  Go back to table view controller
    //
    self.navigationController?.popToRootViewControllerAnimated(true)
}

//
func openSession() {
    self.statusLabel.text = "opening session"
    session = EASession.init(accessory: self.connectedAccessory!, forProtocol: myProtocolString)
    if session != nil {
            self.statusLabel.text = "opened session to accessory"

            session?.inputStream?.delegate = self
            session?.inputStream?.scheduleInRunLoop(NSRunLoop.currentRunLoop(), forMode:
            NSDefaultRunLoopMode)
            session?.inputStream?.open()

            session?.outputStream?.delegate = self
            session?.outputStream?.scheduleInRunLoop(NSRunLoop.currentRunLoop(), forMode:
            NSDefaultRunLoopMode)
            session?.outputStream?.open()

        } else {
            self.statusLabel.text = "could not open session"
        }
}

func closeSession() {
    session?.inputStream?.close()
    session?.inputStream?.removeFromRunLoop(NSRunLoop.currentRunLoop(), forMode:
    NSDefaultRunLoopMode)
    session?.inputStream?.delegate = nil

    session?.outputStream?.close()
    session?.outputStream?.removeFromRunLoop(NSRunLoop.currentRunLoop(), forMode:
    NSDefaultRunLoopMode)
    session?.outputStream?.delegate = nil

}

}
```

BTLE Sensor Interface

Problem

You need to work with iOS and a custom Bluetooth Low Energy (BTLE) accessory and don't know how to get started.

Solution

In this project we'll work with a hardware accessory, a six-axis sensor that we connect to using BTLE and Apple's Core Bluetooth framework.

Ballroom Dancing

In this last project, we're going to focus on my favorite interest—ballroom dancing. While considered more of a social activity than a highly competitive sport, ballroom actually requires highly developed muscle control, a sense of spatial awareness, musicality, and the ability to perform while in pain and managing every other aspect required to compete and win.

Let's focus on the feet. At its most rudimentary foundations, ballroom requires the dancers to move in specific ways or patterns while staying together (Figure 17-8). Patterns are a very simple sequence of steps, mostly mirrored between the leader and follower. Several of these patterns, when performed in an encompassing sequence, make up the routine.

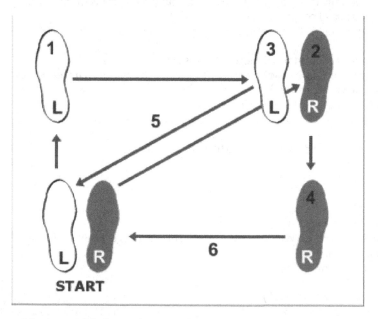

Figure 17-8. At its most fundamental, ballroom dance consists of making a series of steps, or patterns, that are woven together to create a routine

We could create a complex sensor system to track each foot and its motion over the course of a pattern as well as the overall routine. Using that system, we could record a perfect performance and then store it in a database so that when we, as amateurs, want to duplicate the performance of our favorite dance pro, we have a detailed reference to use as our guideline. This, in fact, is the goal of sports performance quantification, an area of study in which I am highly engaged.

For now, though, to keep it simple, we'll focus on one single aspect of dance and use only one sensor to track one foot. In ballroom, there are two ways to move your foot across the floor in a pattern. You either move your foot keeping the toe touching the ground, or you move your foot so that your heel stays (or mostly stays) in contact with the floor. The first is called a toe lead because you're leading your foot with your toe. For converse reasons, we call the latter a heel lead. In this project we'll track, in real-time, the pitch angle of the foot—it doesn't matter whether it's the left foot or the right. To do so, we'll use an integrated circuit called a microelectromechanical system (MEMS) device. This part, or a version of it, is used in all mobile devices. It detects when you change the angle of the device so it can rotate the screen automatically. While there are many such devices from different manufacturers that measure a variety of angles, rotation, movement, and direction from a North–South pole perspective (Figure 17-9), for our project we'll only deal with the accelerometer portion of the device.

Figure 17-9. *For this project we'll get information from the accelerometer portion of the MEMS device to quickly determine the foot's deviation from parallel to the plane of the floor so we can see if the wearer is performing a heel lead or a toe lead*

One last aspect of this I want to cover before we get into the technical details is exactly when we would want to differentiate between a toe lead and a heel lead. In ballroom, there are essentially four styles of dance: American Smooth, Standard, American Rhythm, or Latin (also known as International). In the first two styles, Smooth and Standard, moving the foot is done primarily using heel leads, much like a normal walking gait, while in the latter two styles, the goal is to keep the toe pressed to the floor and lead with the toe.

User Interface

As with some of our other projects, we're going to use Apple Watch as our interface. Two good reasons exist for doing it this way. First, we only need to convey a very small bit of information to the user; our dancer is trying to know if she's doing the proper move of her foot. If she's dancing Latin and needs to lead with her toe, but her toe is off the ground, we need to let her know.

Second, because she's on the floor dancing with a partner and can't carry around a tablet or phone as the user interface (Figure 17-10), Watch, with its taptic engine and the ability to provide haptic feedback, i.e., vibration, can let her know when her steps are not in keeping with the intent of the performance.

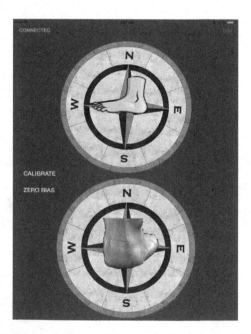

Figure 17-10. The typical user interface on an iPad or iPhone displaying characteristics about foot position do not accommodate the needs of a dancer during her performance. She needs a more subtle, less obtrusive means to know when she's doing a movement incorrectly.

Let's say our dancer is practicing her Rumba routine, one of the primary Latin dances. As such, she needs to focus on her foot movements and keep her toes to the floor. Imagine a piece of tissue paper between the toes of your shoes and the floor. You need to move your foot so the tissue is always between your foot and the floor. Using the interface on the Apple Watch, the screen as shown in Figures 17-11 and 17-12 in conjunction with the taptic engine, our dancer can know when she's performing her toe lead correctly through the lack of any vibration or when she's mistakenly leading with her heel though the vibration on her wrist.

Figure 17-11. By selecting the dance style of interest, the code will determine, based on the angle of the sensor, if the foot movement is being performed correctly

Figure 17-12. If the angle of the sensor on the shoe is not correct for the dance style selected, in addition to an audio-visual indication, the Watch vibrates to let the dancer know of her error

We saw the sensor we'll be using (Figure 17-13) in a previous chapter and how to quickly attach it to a dance shoe (Figure 17-14) for testing out our project. Of course, in a production environment, the method of attaching the device to the shoe would be slightly different in an effort to create a more physically secure connection. Note that in Figure 17-14 the sensor does not rest on the same plane as the floor due to the angle of the sole of our dancer's shoe. This creates a bias in our measurement data. Because we're converting raw sensor output into an angle relative to the plane of the floor on our iPhone, we'll take out that bias in the code.

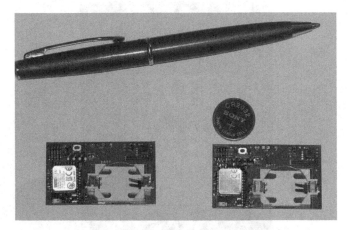

Figure 17-13. *The prototype sensor board we'll use to detect the pitch of our dancer's foot as compared with the plane of the floor*

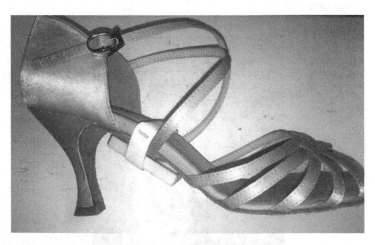

Figure 17-14. *A simple, but efficient way to attach the sensor to a dancer's heel*

The Code

We discussed BTLE in Chapter 13 and won't spend time covering it again in this project description. So, if you need to review the BT 4.0 or BTLE hierarchy, please refer to that chapter.

In Listing 17-9 you can see some of the key elements needed for the iPhone side of our project. We need to include the Core Bluetooth framework, of course, so we can connect to our sensor wirelessly. The Watch Connectivity framework provides the resources for passing data between the iPhone and the Apple Watch. This feature was made available at the launch of WatchOS 2. Prior to that, it was not possible to create native Watch applications. In WatchOS 1, the actual logic that resides in the WatchKit extension executed on the iPhone and communicated with the UI elements on the watch. While the Watch logic still resides in the WatchKit extension, that code now executes on the Watch itself.

Listing 17-9. Key Elements of Our iPhone View Controller

```
//
//  ViewController.swift
//  Sensor Interface
//
//  Created by Molly Maskrey on 8/14/15.
//  Copyright (c) 2015 Global Tek Labs. All rights reserved.
//

import UIKit
import CoreBluetooth
import WatchConnectivity

// Services
let GAP_SERVICE = "1800"
let DEV_INFO_SERVICE = "180a"
let DEVBD_SERVICE = "53239E8E-4EC5-4869-8773-52018C93CA3D"
let SENSOR_DATA_SERVICE =   "6D480F49-91D3-4A18-BE29-0D27F4109C23"

//
// Characteristics - we only care about two for this demo
//
let ROLL_CHARACTERISTIC = "35c93ef0-5517-440a-ad32-222a596eafc1"
let PITCH_CHARACTERISTIC = "192773e5-b433-4dfe-93ae-17b713172145"

// Helper Extension to Float type
extension Float {
    var degreesToRadians : CGFloat {
        return CGFloat(self) * CGFloat(M_PI) / 180.0
    }
}
```

However, not all frameworks are available for the Watch hardware. Of specific interest to us is the Core Bluetooth framework needed to communicate with the sensor. The sensor can, because of current development system limitations, only communicate with the iPhone (as well as an iPad or iPod Touch). Thus, we require use of the Watch Connectivity framework to move data from the sensor through the iPhone to the Apple Watch. You can also see the 128-bit Universally Unique Identifiers (UUIDs) for the board services and characteristics. Though we do include them, for the actual functionality of this project we only need to be concerned with the sensor data service and the pitch characteristic. You can also see I included a simple extension to the Float type that converts degrees to radians.

For this project I created three Watch Connectivity convenience functions, shown in Listing 17-10. The function openSession checks to see if Watch Connectivity is supported and, if so, opens the session. The function sendConnectionStatus passes a Boolean to the Watch via the previously open session to indicate whether or not there is a connection between the iPhone and the Watch. Finally, sendLeadType also passes a Boolean to the Watch to indicate whether the sensor is at a positive or negative angle, indicating either a toe or heel lead.

Listing 17-10. Watch Connectivity Convenience Functions

```
// WKSession convenience functions


    func openSession () -> () {
        if(WCSession.isSupported()) {
            session = WCSession.defaultSession()
            session?.delegate = self
            session?.activateSession()
            print("WC Session is SUPPORTED")
        } else {
            print("WC Session is NOT SUPPORTED")
        }
    }

    func sendConnectionStatus (status:Bool) -> (){
        if let session = session where session.reachable {
            print("WCSession with Watch is REACHABLE")
            session.sendMessage(["CONNECT":status], replyHandler: nil, errorHandler: {
            (error ) -> Void in
                print("Error in sendConnectionStatus: \(error)")
            })
        } else {
            print("WCSession with Watch is NOT REACHABLE")
        }
    }

    func sendLeadType (leadType:Bool) -> (){
        if let session = session where session.reachable {
            print("WCSession with Watch is REACHABLE")
            session.sendMessage(["LEAD_TYPE":leadType], replyHandler: nil, errorHandler: {
            (error ) -> Void in
                print("Error in sendLeadType: \(error)")
            })
        } else {
            print("WCSession with Watch is NOT REACHABLE")
        }
    }
```

Recalling that the Core Bluetooth framework uses the terms *central* and *peripheral* to represent the iPhone and sensor board respectively, Listing 17-11 shows the key functionality used to traverse the BTLE hierarchy to get to the characteristic we use that represents the pitch angle of the dancer's foot. I've only shown the major functions used to get to the characteristic of interest and not the ancillary functionally, such as disconnecting a BLTE device or when it fails to connect, such as might happen if requiring a pairing key.

Listing 17-11. Core Bluetooth Functions in the ViewController.swift File to Locate the Foot's Pitch Characteristic from the Sensor Board

```
// create a Core Bluetooth central manager (client) object with ourselves as the delegate
manager = CBCentralManager(delegate: self, queue: dispatch_get_main_queue())

// CORE BLUETOOTH CENTRAL MANAGER DELEGATE METHODS

// THIS METHOD IS REQUIRED to find any Bluetooth devices
// First make sure BT is available and turned on
// Then, start scanning for BT peripherals
func centralManagerDidUpdateState(central: CBCentralManager) {
    // see if our BT is powered on first
    if central.state == CBCentralManagerState.PoweredOn  {
        print("Bluetooth is on, scanning for peripherals")
        manager.scanForPeripheralsWithServices(nil, options: nil)
    }
}
//
// DISCOVERED A PERIPHERAL
// A Bluetooth device is within range, try connecting to it
//
func centralManager(central: CBCentralManager, didDiscoverPeripheral peripheral:
CBPeripheral, advertisementData: [String : AnyObject], RSSI: NSNumber) {

    if let _ = peripheral.name {
        if peripheral.name == "iThotics Sensor" {
            // set our sensor in case we need it later
            sensor = peripheral
            print("Found \(peripheral.name), stop scanning and connect it")
            manager.connectPeripheral(peripheral, options: nil)
            manager.stopScan()
        }
    }
}
//
// CONNECTED PERIPHERAL
// We connected to the Bluetooth device, let's see what services it has
//
func centralManager(central: CBCentralManager, didConnectPeripheral peripheral:
CBPeripheral) {
    //
    print("Connected to the MovementTek Sensor")
    statusLabel.text = "CONNECTED"
    statusLabel.textColor = UIColor.greenColor()
```

```
    // Let the Watch know we're connected
    sendConnectionStatus(true)
    peripheral.delegate = self
    peripheral.discoverServices(nil)
}

//  PERIPHERAL DELAGATE METHODS
//  SERVICES
//
func peripheral(peripheral: CBPeripheral, didDiscoverServices error: NSError?) {
//
    print("Did discover \(peripheral.services!.count) services for \(sensor.name)")
    for aService in peripheral.services! {

        print("Service = \(aService.UUID.description)")
        if aService.UUID.description.uppercaseString == DEVBD_SERVICE.uppercaseString {
            print("Go discover Characteristics for \(aService.UUID.description)")
            sensor.discoverCharacteristics(nil , forService: aService )
        }
        print("Looking for \(SENSOR_DATA_SERVICE.uppercaseString)")
        if aService.UUID.description.uppercaseString == SENSOR_DATA_SERVICE.
uppercaseString {
            print("Go discover Characteristics for Sensor Data")
            sensor.discoverCharacteristics(nil , forService: aService )
        }
    }
}


//
//  CHARACTERISTICS
//
func peripheral(peripheral: CBPeripheral, didDiscoverCharacteristicsForService service:
CBService, error: NSError?) {
//
    for aCharacteristic in service.characteristics! {
        if aCharacteristic.UUID.description.uppercaseString == ROLL_CHARACTERISTIC.
        uppercaseString  {
            print("Found Foot Roll Characteristic")
            sensor.setNotifyValue(true, forCharacteristic: aCharacteristic )
        }
        if aCharacteristic.UUID.description.uppercaseString == PITCH_CHARACTERISTIC.
uppercaseString  {
            print("Found Foot Pitch Characteristic")
            sensor.setNotifyValue(true, forCharacteristic: aCharacteristic  )
        }
    }
}
```

The first thing we do is create the Core Bluetooth central manager object in the ViewController.swift file using the CBCentralManager function, which allows us to interface all necessary functionality of our device. Because we set its delegate to self, we'll have all the appropriate delegate methods in this file.

Then we check using the `centralManagerDidUpdateState` to see if a state change occurred in the central manager to indicate that the Bluetooth is available and activated on our device. A typical error condition would happen if the user had not turned on the Bluetooth radio on their device. If we see that the central manager returns a `PoweredOn` state, then we know the radio is active and we can start scanning to locate all peripherals in range using the `manager.scanForPeripheralsWithServices` function call.

The central manager delegate method `didDiscoverPeripheral` will be called for each peripheral found within range of the Bluetooth radio's reception. This will of course depend on the transmitting power of the device and other factors, such as distance and interference between the iPhone and the transmitters. Because we're only interested in one particular sensor, we use the code in Listing 17-12 in the `ViewController.swift` file to connect only to our device of interest.

Listing 17-12. Discovering a Peripheral

```
if let _ = peripheral.name {
  if peripheral.name == "iThotics Sensor" {
      // set our sensor in case we need it later
      sensor = peripheral
      print("Found \(peripheral.name), stop scanning and connect it")
      manager.connectPeripheral(peripheral, options: nil)
      manager.stopScan()
  }
}
```

The peripheral name, iThotics Sensor, is the name found in the sensor's firmware, specifically the device's Generic Attributes Profile (GATT profile), and was set by the manufacturer. In our case, this was the original name I chose to call this particular version of the sensor.

> **Note** We're using the "if let" Swift construct to make sure we only try to use the peripheral name if the name exists; that is, it's not nil. Because we have to examine every BTLE device in range, it's often the case that some lower quality devices may not have populated the peripheral name, and trying to use a nil value will result in the app crashing.

If our connection attempt is successful, we'll get the delegate call `didConnectPeripheral` that returns a peripheral object for us to use in the code. As you may recall from earlier, there are two sides when working with Core Bluetooth, the central and the peripheral. Just as we did with the central, or specifically the central manager object, we have to set our delegate for the returned peripheral object, which we set to `self` so we can access the peripheral delegate methods. And, of course, we want to search for services offered by this peripheral:

```
peripheral.delegate = self
peripheral.discoverServices(nil)
```

As with the central manager, I'm leaving out the ancillary functions for this discussion so we can focus on getting to the information we need for our project. The delegate method didDiscoverServices returns the list of services provided by the BTLE device; in this case, our iThotics Sensor board. In the following code snippet, you can see that I'm only interested in two services, the device board service, which tells me some metadata about the board itself, and the sensor data service, which has our pitch and roll information for our foot (Listing 17-13).

Listing 17-13. Discovering Services in the ViewController.swift File

```
print("Service = \(aService.UUID.description)")
if aService.UUID.description.uppercaseString == DEVBD_SERVICE.uppercaseString {
    print("Go discover Characteristics for \(aService.UUID.description)")
    sensor.discoverCharacteristics(nil , forService: aService )
}
print("Looking for \(SENSOR_DATA_SERVICE.uppercaseString)")
if aService.UUID.description.uppercaseString == SENSOR_DATA_SERVICE.uppercaseString  {
    print("Go discover Characteristics for Sensor Data")
    sensor.discoverCharacteristics(nil , forService: aService )
}
```

Once we've found the service of particular interest to us—in this case it's the sensor data service—we use the discoverCharacteristics method call on the sensor object to get all the available characteristics of that service. In the delegate method didDiscoverCharacteristicsForService we iterate over all the characteristics of that service looking for the one of particular interest to us (Listing 17-14).

Listing 17-14. Discovering Characteristics in the ViewController.swift File

```
for aCharacteristic in service.characteristics! {
    if aCharacteristic.UUID.description.uppercaseString == ROLL_CHARACTERISTIC.
    uppercaseString  {
        print("Found Foot Roll Characteristic")
        sensor.setNotifyValue(true, forCharacteristic: aCharacteristic )
    }
    if aCharacteristic.UUID.description.uppercaseString == PITCH_CHARACTERISTIC.
    uppercaseString  {
        print("Found Foot Pitch Characteristic")
        sensor.setNotifyValue(true, forCharacteristic: aCharacteristic )
    }
}
```

You can see that we've identified both the pitch and roll characteristics of the foot. For reference, the roll of the foot would indicate how much the dancer's ankle is rolled in or out. Think of when you twist your ankle playing a sport such as basketball or tennis. For a production system, this would very important, as another key element of footwork in ballroom dance is actually trying to maintain foot pressure near your big toe. An outside roll would therefore indicate an incorrect weight distribution of the foot, and therefore incorrect form.

Now that we have all the information we need to measure the pitch angle of the foot, how do we use it? Again, delegate methods come to our rescue, specifically the didUpdateValueForCharacteristic method, which gets called when a characteristic that we are monitoring changes. In the preceding code snippet, notice the line where we call the setNotifyValue method on the sensor to true for the specific characteristic. This call is what allows us to use the didUpdateValueForCharacteristic method, as shown in Listing 17-15.

Listing 17-15. Handling Updates from Our Sensor's Characteristics in the ViewController.swift File

```
// WHEN THE CHARACTERISTICS UPDATE (new data)
// This is where we get the new data from the sensor and do something with it
//
func peripheral(peripheral: CBPeripheral, didUpdateValueForCharacteristic characteristic:
CBCharacteristic, error: NSError?) {
//
// X AXIS === FOOT ROLL
//
    if characteristic.UUID.description.uppercaseString == ROLL_CHARACTERISTIC.uppercaseString  {

        let dataBytes = characteristic.value
        let dataLength = dataBytes!.length
        var dataArray = [UInt8](count: dataLength, repeatedValue: 0)
        dataBytes!.getBytes(&dataArray, length: dataLength * sizeof(UInt8))
        var sensorValue : Int16 = Int16(dataArray[0]) << 8 + Int16(dataArray[1])
        sensorValue /= 4
        xMotionAverage = ( (xMotionAverage * xAveragingFactor) + Float(sensorValue) ) / 40
        xMotionAverage += rollBias

        rollValue = xMotionAverage
        rollView.transform = CGAffineTransformMakeRotation(xMotionAverage.degreesToRadians)
    }

//
// Y AXIS === FOOT PITCH
//
    if characteristic.UUID.description.uppercaseString == PITCH_CHARACTERISTIC.
    uppercaseString {

        let dataBytes = characteristic.value
        let dataLength = dataBytes!.length
        var dataArray = [UInt8](count: dataLength, repeatedValue: 0)
        dataBytes!.getBytes(&dataArray, length: dataLength * sizeof(UInt8))
        var sensorValue : Int16 = Int16(dataArray[0]) << 8 + Int16(dataArray[1])
        sensorValue /= 4
        yMotionAverage = ( (yMotionAverage * yAveragingFactor) + Float(sensorValue) ) / 20
        yMotionAverage += pitchBias

        pitchValue = yMotionAverage
        pitchView.transform = CGAffineTransformMakeRotation(-yMotionAverage.degreesToRadians)
```

```
        //
        // FOR FOOT PITCH, PASS THE DATA TO WATCH via WATCH CONNECTIVITY
        //
        if pitchValue >= 0 {
            sendLeadType(true)    // TOE LEAD
        } else {
            sendLeadType(false)   // HEEL LEAD
        }
    }
}
```

For now, do not be too concerned about the numeric calculations in the two if statements. They are primarily used to provide a visual indication of rotation to the graphics displayed on the iPhone. Because we're focusing on a non-intrusive mechanism to let the dancer know when her steps are incorrect, the important part is shown in Listing 17-16.

Listing 17-16. Sending Messages to the Watch App Extension from the ViewController.swift File

```
if pitchValue >= 0 {
    sendLeadType(true)    // TOE LEAD
} else {
    sendLeadType(false)   // HEEL LEAD
}
```

This bit of code checks the pitch value, and if it is greater than or equal to zero, it sends a Boolean to the Watch using the sendLeadType convenience method to let the Watch indicate that the dancer is leading with her toe. Otherwise, a false indicates that she is leading with her heel. Note that there is no quantification of whether the toe versus heel lead is correct for the dance, only that the dancer's foot is either tilted up or tilted down. The reason is that the iPhone does not know what dance the dancer is performing, and certainly not the proper foot movement.

iPhone User Interface

As we mentioned earlier, since Apple's current (at the time of this writing) version of WatchKit does not support Core Bluetooth, we must use an iPhone as an intermediary. To help with isolating issues and debugging the code, I created a simple iPhone UI, shown in Figure 17-15.

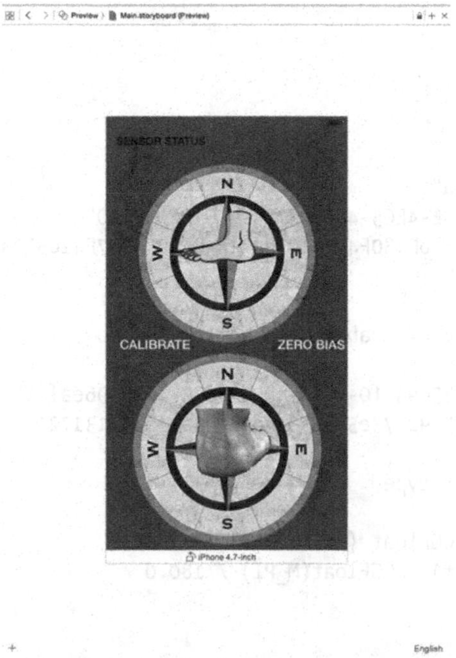

Figure 17-15. A very simple iPhone UI, using very ugly graphics, allows us to quickly see issues in our project

At the top of the interface is a simple status label so as to see what's happening as we try to connect to a sensor. The two large image displays depict the rotation of the foot in either pitch or roll (side to side). We do this by calling an affine transform inside the didUpdateValueForCharacteristic method call to change the angle of the foot image. Near the middle on either side are two buttons. The Calibrate button is use to take out the bias of the sensor, in pitch, when it is attached to a shoe. For a lady's Latin heel, the attachment might be at an angle of approximately forty-five degrees. Placing the shoe on a level surface and pressing Calibrate adjusts the angle used to rotate the pitch foot image so that it is normalized to that angle, essentially removing the bias. Pressing Zero Bias removes any calibration adjustment that has been place into the app.

Listing 17-17 depicts the complete ViewController.swift code that deals with connecting and monitoring the sensor, displaying graphical information to the user, and interfacing with the Apple Watch.

Listing 17-17. ViewController.swift Code That Executes on the iPhone

```
//
//  ViewController.swift
//  Sensor Interface
//
//  Created by Molly Maskrey on 8/14/15.
//  Copyright (c) 2015 Global Tek Labs. All rights reserved.
//
```

```
import UIKit
import CoreBluetooth
import WatchConnectivity

// Services
let GAP_SERVICE = "1800"
let DEV_INFO_SERVICE = "180a"
let DEVBD_SERVICE = "53239E8E-4EC5-4869-8773-52018C93CA3D"
let SENSOR_DATA_SERVICE =   "6D480F49-91D3-4A18-BE29-0D27F4109C23"

//
// Characteristics - we only care about two for this demo
//
let ROLL_CHARACTERISTIC = "35c93ef0-5517-440a-ad32-222a596eafc1"
let PITCH_CHARACTERISTIC = "192773e5-b433-4dfe-93ae-17b713172145"

// Helper Extension to Float type
extension Float {
    var degreesToRadians : CGFloat {
        return CGFloat(self) * CGFloat(M_PI) / 180.0
    }
}

//
// The CBCentralManagerDelegate protocol allows us to find Bluetooth Peripherals to connect with
//
// The CBPeripheralDelegate protocol allows us to locate services and characteristics of
BTLE Peripherals
//
// And...add delegate for Watch Connectivity framework
//
class ViewController: UIViewController, CBCentralManagerDelegate,CBPeripheralDelegate,
WCSessionDelegate {

    @IBOutlet weak var statusLabel: UILabel!

    // Session Object for using Watch Connectivity
    var session :WCSession?

    var pitchValue : Float = 0
    var pitchBias : Float = 0
    var rollValue : Float = 0
    var rollBias : Float = 0

    // WKSession convenience functions
    func openSession () -> () {
        if(WCSession.isSupported()) {
            session = WCSession.defaultSession()
            session?.delegate = self
            session?.activateSession()
            print("WC Session is SUPPORTED")
```

```swift
    } else {
        print("WC Session is NOT SUPPORTED")
    }
}

func sendConnectionStatus (status:Bool) -> (){
    if let session = session where session.reachable {
        print("WCSession with Watch is REACHABLE")
        session.sendMessage(["CONNECT":status], replyHandler: nil, errorHandler: {
        (error ) -> Void in
            print("Error in sendConnectionStatus: \(error)")
        })
    } else {
        print("WCSession with Watch is NOT REACHABLE")
    }
}

func sendLeadType (leadType:Bool) -> (){
    if let session = session where session.reachable {
        print("WCSession with Watch is REACHABLE")
        session.sendMessage(["LEAD_TYPE":leadType], replyHandler: nil, errorHandler: {
        (error ) -> Void in
            print("Error in sendLeadType: \(error)")
        })
    } else {
        print("WCSession with Watch is NOT REACHABLE")
    }
}

@IBAction func calibrateSensor(sender: AnyObject) {
    pitchBias = -pitchValue
    rollBias = rollValue
    print("roll bias = \(rollBias); pitch bias = \(pitchBias)")

}

@IBAction func zeroBias(sender: AnyObject) {
    pitchBias = 0
    rollBias = 0

    print("Ext: Setting sensorStatus = false")

}

@IBOutlet weak var pitchView: UIImageView!
@IBOutlet weak var rollView: UIImageView!

var manager:CBCentralManager!
var sensor:CBPeripheral!                  // our MovementTek sensor
var peripheralArray : [CBPeripheral] = []
```

```swift
    var xMotionAverage : Float = 0
    var yMotionAverage : Float = 0
    var xAveragingFactor : Float = 0.9
    var yAveragingFactor : Float = 0.9

    var managerState : Bool = false

//***********************************************************
//**************   THE BORING STUFF    ********************
//***********************************************************

    override func viewDidLoad() {
        super.viewDidLoad()
    // create a Core Bluetooth central manager (client) object with ourselves as the
delegate
//******************INTERESTING***************************
    manager = CBCentralManager(delegate: self, queue: dispatch_get_main_queue())

    // Open session with Watch
    openSession()

    // Assume we're not connected at start
    sendConnectionStatus(false)

//***********************************************************
    // Set up Labels
    statusLabel.text = "NOT CONNECTED"
    statusLabel.textColor = UIColor.redColor()
    }

    override func viewDidAppear(animated: Bool) {
    // debug
        print("VIEW DID APPEAR")

    // Pass data to Watch through WATCH CONNECTIVITY
    }

    override func didReceiveMemoryWarning() {
        super.didReceiveMemoryWarning()
        // Dispose of any resources that can be recreated.
    }

//***********************************************************
//**************   THE INTERESTING STUFF    *****************
//***********************************************************

    // CORE BLUETOOTH CENTRAL MANAGER DELEGATE METHODS

    // THIS METHOD IS REQUIRED to find any Bluetooth devices
    // First make sure BT is available and turned on
    // Then, start scanning for BT peripherals
    func centralManagerDidUpdateState(central: CBCentralManager) {
```

```swift
        // see if our BT is powered on first
        if central.state == CBCentralManagerState.PoweredOn  {
            print("Bluetooth is on, scanning for peripherals")
            manager.scanForPeripheralsWithServices(nil, options: nil)
        }
    }


    //
    // DISCOVERED A PERIPHERAL
    // A Bluetooth device is within range, try connecting to it
    //
    func centralManager(central: CBCentralManager, didDiscoverPeripheral peripheral:
CBPeripheral, advertisementData: [String : AnyObject], RSSI: NSNumber) {

        if let _ = peripheral.name {
            if peripheral.name == "iThotics Sensor" {
                // set our sensor in case we need it later
                sensor = peripheral
                print("Found \(peripheral.name), stop scanning and connect it")
                manager.connectPeripheral(peripheral, options: nil)
                manager.stopScan()
            }
        }
    }


    //
    // CONNECTED PERIPHERAL
    // We connected to the Bluetooth device, let's see what services it has
    //
    func centralManager(central: CBCentralManager, didConnectPeripheral peripheral:
CBPeripheral) {
        //
        print("Connected to the MovementTek Sensor")
        statusLabel.text = "CONNECTED"
        statusLabel.textColor = UIColor.greenColor()
        // Let the Watch know we're connected
        sendConnectionStatus(true)
        peripheral.delegate = self
        peripheral.discoverServices(nil)
    }


    //
    // DIS-CONNECTED PERIPHERAL
    // The peripheral disconnected, let's try reconnecting
    //
    func centralManager(central: CBCentralManager, didDisconnectPeripheral peripheral:
CBPeripheral, error: NSError?) {
        //
        print("Disconnected from the MovementTek Sensor - let's try reconnecting")
        statusLabel.text = "NOT CONNECTED"
        statusLabel.textColor = UIColor.redColor()
```

```
        // Let the Watch know we're disconnected
        sendConnectionStatus(false)

        // try to reconnect
        manager.connectPeripheral(peripheral, options: nil)

        // reset graphics
        rollView.transform = CGAffineTransformMakeRotation(0)
        pitchView.transform = CGAffineTransformMakeRotation(0)
    }

    //
    // FAILED TO CONNECT TO PERIPHERAL
    // When, for some reason, we can't connect to the peripheral, this method is executed
    //
    func centralManager(central: CBCentralManager, didFailToConnectPeripheral peripheral:
CBPeripheral, error: NSError?) {
        print("Error: Couldn't connect to a peripheral - let's try again")
        // try to reconnect
        manager.connectPeripheral(peripheral, options: nil)
    }

    //
    // PERIPHERAL DELAGATE METHODS
    //
    //*********************************************************************************
    //
    // SERVICES
    //

    func peripheral(peripheral: CBPeripheral, didDiscoverServices error: NSError?) {
        //
        print("Did discover \(peripheral.services!.count) services for \(sensor.name)")
        for aService in peripheral.services! {

            print("Service = \(aService.UUID.description)")
            if aService.UUID.description.uppercaseString == DEVBD_SERVICE.uppercaseString {
                print("Go discover Characteristics for \(aService.UUID.description)")
                sensor.discoverCharacteristics(nil , forService: aService )
            }
            print("Looking for \(SENSOR_DATA_SERVICE.uppercaseString)")
            if aService.UUID.description.uppercaseString == SENSOR_DATA_SERVICE.
            uppercaseString {
                print("Go discover Characteristics for Sensor Data")
                sensor.discoverCharacteristics(nil , forService: aService )
            }
        }
    }
```

```
//
//  CHARACTERISTICS
//
func peripheral(peripheral: CBPeripheral, didDiscoverCharacteristicsForService service:
CBService, error: NSError?) {
    //
    for aCharacteristic in service.characteristics! {
        if aCharacteristic.UUID.description.uppercaseString == ROLL_CHARACTERISTIC.
        uppercaseString {
            print("Found Foot Roll Characteristic")
            sensor.setNotifyValue(true, forCharacteristic: aCharacteristic )
        }
        if aCharacteristic.UUID.description.uppercaseString == PITCH_CHARACTERISTIC.
        uppercaseString {
            print("Found Foot Pitch Characteristic")
            sensor.setNotifyValue(true, forCharacteristic: aCharacteristic  )
        }
    }
}


//
// WHEN THE CHARACTERISTICS UPDATE (new data)
// This is where we get the new data from the sensor and do something with it
//
func peripheral(peripheral: CBPeripheral, didUpdateValueForCharacteristic
characteristic: CBCharacteristic, error: NSError?) {
    //
    // X AXIS === FOOT ROLL
    //
    if characteristic.UUID.description.uppercaseString == ROLL_CHARACTERISTIC.
uppercaseString  {

        let dataBytes = characteristic.value
        let dataLength = dataBytes!.length
        var dataArray = [UInt8](count: dataLength, repeatedValue: 0)
        dataBytes!.getBytes(&dataArray, length: dataLength * sizeof(UInt8))
        var sensorValue : Int16 = Int16(dataArray[0]) << 8 + Int16(dataArray[1])
        sensorValue /= 4
        xMotionAverage = ( (xMotionAverage * xAveragingFactor) + Float(sensorValue) ) / 40
        xMotionAverage += rollBias

        rollValue = xMotionAverage
        rollView.transform = CGAffineTransformMakeRotation(xMotionAverage.degreesToRadians)
    }

    //
    // Y AXIS === FOOT PITCH
    //
    if characteristic.UUID.description.uppercaseString == PITCH_CHARACTERISTIC.
uppercaseString  {
```

```
        let dataBytes = characteristic.value
        let dataLength = dataBytes!.length
        var dataArray = [UInt8](count: dataLength, repeatedValue: 0)
        dataBytes!.getBytes(&dataArray, length: dataLength * sizeof(UInt8))
        var sensorValue : Int16 = Int16(dataArray[0]) << 8 + Int16(dataArray[1])
        sensorValue /= 4
        yMotionAverage = ( (yMotionAverage * yAveragingFactor) + Float(sensorValue) ) / 20
        yMotionAverage += pitchBias

        pitchValue = yMotionAverage
        pitchView.transform = CGAffineTransformMakeRotation(-yMotionAverage.degreesToRadians)

        //
        // FOR FOOT PITCH, PASS THE DATA TO WATCH via WATCH CONNECTIVITY
        //
        if pitchValue >= 0 {
            sendLeadType(true)    // TOE LEAD
        } else {
            sendLeadType(false)   // HEEL LEAD
        }
    }
  }
}   // END of the viewController CLASS
```

Apple Watch Interface

We want to give our dancer the simplest, most unobtrusive indication of when she's doing something incorrectly as we can. To that end, though we will have a visual Watch UI, the key feedback mechanism will be haptic; that is, a vibration on her wrist will indicate that she is doing the wrong type of foot lead. We'll also focus on only two dance styles: waltz and rumba. In waltz, she needs to move her feet much like normal walking—that is, she needs to do heel leads (Figure 17-16) and not move through her toes (Figure 17-17). Conversely, in rumba we want to keep our toes connected to the floor—toe leads (Figures 17-18 and 17-19).

Figure 17-16. *In the waltz, our dancer must move her feet much like normal walking, using heel leads as she travels the floor*

Figure 17-17. *If our dancer moves through her toes during the waltz, in addition to a visual indication on the Watch face, she will also receive haptic feedback, a vibration, to make her aware of the mistake*

Figure 17-18. *In rumba our dancer must keep her toes connected with the floor. This is a much more difficult movement than heel leads in waltz, as it puts her ankle at an unnatural angle.*

Figure 17-19. *And, as in waltz, when our dancer performs rumba incorrectly, both visual and haptic feedback is provided to her in order to make the correction*

We create this interface in the SensorInterface WatchKit App section of the project, not the extension section. From the `mainController` scene create two additional scenes, one for rumba and one for waltz (Figure 17-20). When the user selects one of the dance styles, that interface screen is displayed.

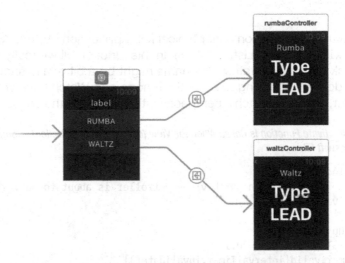

Figure 17-20. *Setting up the interface storyboard on the WatchKit app (not the extension)*

Note that, like our more general iOS devices where we have view controllers, we need code to back them up, and we need that code to match our Watch interface controllers: `interfaceController.swift`, `rumbaInterfaceController.swift`, and `waltzInterfaceController.swift`, (Figure 17-21). These will be placed in the WatchKit extension.

Figure 17-21. *For each of the three Watch interface controllers we saw earlier, we need code to do the actual work. The functional code is placed into the WatchKit extension*

> **Note**   The reason for the Watch code and storyboard being separate has to do with the original
> version of WatchOS, where Watch code actually executed on the iPhone and not on the Watch itself.
> This changed with the release of WatchOS 2 in late 2015.

Much like the `viewDidLoad` function in our typical iOS application, for the Watch the related
function is called `willActivate` (Listing 17-18). In this function all we really want to do is set
up a timer to check the sensor status. This name might be a bit of a misnomer, because
what we're really doing is checking to see if the iPhone and Watch have connectivity
(Listing 17-19). But, from the Watch's perspective, the iPhone *is* the sensor.

*Listing 17-18. The willActivate Function Is Called When the View (or Interface) Controller Becomes Visible to the User in
the InterfaceController.swift File*

```
override func willActivate() {
    // This method is called when watch view controller is about to be visible to user
    super.willActivate()

    // Let's set up a timer
    let interval:NSTimeInterval = 0.1
    if intervalTimer.valid{intervalTimer.invalidate()}
    intervalTimer = NSTimer.scheduledTimerWithTimeInterval(interval, target: self, selector:
    "checkSensorStatus", userInfo: nil, repeats: true)
}
```

*Listing 17-19. The checkSensorStatus Convenience Function Makes Sure That Communications Between the iPhone
and the Watch Exist in the InterfaceControler.swift File*

```
// This is our custom function that gets called whenever the timer fires
// We check the sensorStatus and set the label as appropriate
//
func checkSensorStatus () -> () {
    // Get Data from phone using Watch Connectivity

    // First, always try and open session if not already opened
    if let session = session where session.reachable {
        print("watch:WCSession with Watch is REACHABLE")
    } else {
        openSession()
    }
}
```

The complete `InterfaceController.swift` file is shown in Listing 17-20. Because this is the
primary view that the dancer sees on her Watch, all we need do here is to first make sure the
connection is present through the iPhone to the sensor, and then offer her a choice of dance
style to which her foot movements will be quantified.

Listing 17-20. The Watch InterfaceController.swift File

```
//
//  InterfaceController.swift
//  Sensor Interface WatchKit Extension
//
//  Created by Molly Maskrey on 8/30/15.
//  Copyright (c) 2015 Global Tek Labs. All rights reserved.
//

import WatchKit
import Foundation
import WatchConnectivity

class InterfaceController: WKInterfaceController, WCSessionDelegate {

@IBOutlet weak var linkStatusLabel: WKInterfaceLabel!
    // Session Identifier
    var session : WCSession?

    // WK Connectivity
    func openSession () -> () {
        if(WCSession.isSupported()) {
            session = WCSession.defaultSession()
            session?.delegate = self
            session?.activateSession()
            print("watch: WC Session is SUPPORTED")
        } else {
            print("watch: WC Session is NOT SUPPORTED")
        }
    }

// Interval Timer
var intervalTimer = NSTimer()

    override func awakeWithContext(context: AnyObject?) {
        super.awakeWithContext(context)

    }

    override func willActivate() {
        // This method is called when watch view controller is about to be visible to user
        super.willActivate()

        // Let's set up a timer
        let interval:NSTimeInterval = 0.1
        if intervalTimer.valid{intervalTimer.invalidate()}
        intervalTimer = NSTimer.scheduledTimerWithTimeInterval(interval, target: self,
selector: "checkSensorStatus", userInfo: nil, repeats: true)
    }
```

```
// WatchKit Connectivity Delegate Methods

func session(session: WCSession, didReceiveMessage message: [String : AnyObject]) {
    if let status = message["CONNECT"] as? Bool {
        if (status == true) {
            linkStatusLabel.setText("connected")
            linkStatusLabel.setTextColor(UIColor .greenColor())
        } else {
            linkStatusLabel.setText("not connected")
            linkStatusLabel.setTextColor(UIColor .redColor())
        }
    }
}

//
// This is our custom function that gets called whenever the timer fires
// We check the sensorStatus and set the label as appropriate
//
func checkSensorStatus () -> () {
    // Get Data from phone using Watch Connectivity

    // First always try and open session if not already opened
    if let session = session where session.reachable {
        print("watch:WCSession with Watch is REACHABLE")
    } else {
        openSession()
    }}

override func didDeactivate() {
    // This method is called when watch view controller is no longer visible
    super.didDeactivate()
    intervalTimer.invalidate()
}

}
```

Once our dancer selects her performance option, she'll be confronted with either a waltz or a rumba controller interface. Let's assume she selects waltz. Although the typical place you might load your initialization code would be in the awakeWithContext method, because our dancer may go back and forth between options, we're going to put our key initial code into the willActivate function, shown in Listing 17-21. Much like we did in the main interface controller for checking sensor connectivity status, here we set up a timer to check for the type of heel lead the sensor is detecting. Remember, the iPhone code is agnostic in that it doesn't know what dance is being performed and only that a shoe (foot) is either angled up (heel lead) or down (toe lead). It is in the individual dance interface controller that the decision is made as to correctness of the movement.

Listing 17-21. Selecting a dance controller, loads the proper screen display for the user

```
override func willActivate() {
    // This method is called when watch view controller is about to be visible to user
    super.willActivate()
    // Let's set up a timer
    let interval:NSTimeInterval = 0.1
    if intervalTimer.valid{intervalTimer.invalidate()}
    intervalTimer = NSTimer.scheduledTimerWithTimeInterval(interval, target: self, selector:
    "checkForHeelLead", userInfo: nil, repeats: true)
}
```

Finally, when we get a type of lead coming into our WatchKit extension, we'll set the color to red or green while indicating the type of lead and, if the lead type is incorrect for the dance, we'll fire the haptic interface to vibrate a failure mode (Listing 17-22).

Listing 17-22. Determining What to Do When the Lead Type Comes in to the Watch

```
func session(session: WCSession, didReceiveMessage message: [String : AnyObject]) {
    if let status = message["LEAD_TYPE"] as? Bool {
        if (status == true) {
            leadStatusLabel.setText("TOE LEAD")
            leadStatusLabel.setTextColor(UIColor .redColor())
            // If we are doing the move incorrectly
            WKInterfaceDevice.currentDevice().playHaptic(.Failure)
        } else {
            leadStatusLabel.setText("HEEL LEAD")
            leadStatusLabel.setTextColor(UIColor .greenColor())
        }
    }
}
```

The rumba is very similar to waltz except that the lead types are reversed and the haptic feedback would be played when a heel lead was performed since a toe lead is required. The complete listing for the waltz interface controller is shown in Listing 17-23 and the rumba interface controller in Listing 17-24.

Listing 17-23. Waltz Interface Controller Swift Code

```
//
//  waltzInterfaceController.swift
//  Sensor Interface
//
//  Created by Molly Maskrey on 8/30/15.
//  Copyright (c) 2015 Global Tek Labs. All rights reserved.
//

import WatchKit
import Foundation
import WatchConnectivity
```

```swift
class waltzInterfaceController: WKInterfaceController, WCSessionDelegate {

    @IBOutlet weak var leadStatusLabel: WKInterfaceLabel!
    // Session Identifier
    var session : WCSession?

    // WK Connectivity
    func openSession () -> () {
        if(WCSession.isSupported()) {
            session = WCSession.defaultSession()
            session?.delegate = self
            session?.activateSession()
            print("watch: WC Session is SUPPORTED")
        } else {
            print("watch: WC Session is NOT SUPPORTED")
        }
    }

    // Interval Timer
    var intervalTimer = NSTimer()

    override func awakeWithContext(context: AnyObject?) {
        super.awakeWithContext(context)

        // Configure interface objects here.
        print("Waltz - awakeWithContext")

    }

    // WatchKit Connectivity Delegate Methods

    func session(session: WCSession, didReceiveMessage message: [String : AnyObject]) {
        if let status = message["LEAD_TYPE"] as? Bool {
            if (status == true) {
                leadStatusLabel.setText("TOE LEAD")
                leadStatusLabel.setTextColor(UIColor .redColor())
                // If we are doing the move incorrectly
                WKInterfaceDevice.currentDevice().playHaptic(.Failure)
            } else {
                leadStatusLabel.setText("HEEL LEAD")
                leadStatusLabel.setTextColor(UIColor .greenColor())
            }
        }
    }

    //
    // This is our custom function that gets called whenever the timer fires
    // All we're going to do is check and see if the session is open or not, and if not,
    open one
    //
    func checkForHeelLead () -> () {
        // Get Data from phone using Watch Connectivity
```

```
        // First always try and open session if not already opened
        if let session = session where session.reachable {
            print("watch:WCSession with Watch is REACHABLE")
        } else {
            openSession()
        }
    }

    override func willActivate() {
        // This method is called when watch view controller is about to be visible to user
        super.willActivate()
        // Let's set up a timer
        let interval:NSTimeInterval = 0.1
        if intervalTimer.valid{intervalTimer.invalidate()}
        intervalTimer = NSTimer.scheduledTimerWithTimeInterval(interval, target: self,
selector: "checkForHeelLead", userInfo: nil, repeats: true)
    }

    override func didDeactivate() {
        // This method is called when watch view controller is no longer visible
        super.didDeactivate()
        intervalTimer.invalidate()
    }

}
```

Listing 17-24. Rumba Interface Controller Swift Code

```
//
//  rumbaInterfaceController.swift
//  Sensor Interface
//
//  Created by Molly Maskrey on 8/30/15.
//  Copyright (c) 2015 Global Tek Labs. All rights reserved.
//

import WatchKit
import Foundation
import WatchConnectivity

class rumbaInterfaceController: WKInterfaceController, WCSessionDelegate {

    @IBOutlet weak var leadStatusLabel: WKInterfaceLabel!
    // Session Identifier
    var session : WCSession?

    // WK Connectivity
    func openSession () -> () {
        if(WCSession.isSupported()) {
            session = WCSession.defaultSession()
            session?.delegate = self
```

```
            session?.activateSession()
            print("watch: WC Session is SUPPORTED")
        } else {
            print("watch: WC Session is NOT SUPPORTED")
        }
    }

    // Interval Timer
    var intervalTimer = NSTimer()

    override func awakeWithContext(context: AnyObject?) {
        super.awakeWithContext(context)

        // Configure interface objects here.
        print("Rumba - awakeWithContext")
    }

    override func willActivate() {
        // This method is called when watch view controller is about to be visible to user
        super.willActivate()
        // Let's set up a timer
        let interval:NSTimeInterval = 0.1
        if intervalTimer.valid{intervalTimer.invalidate()}
        intervalTimer = NSTimer.scheduledTimerWithTimeInterval(interval, target: self,
        selector: "checkForToeLead", userInfo: nil, repeats: true)
    }

    // WatchKit Connectivity Delegate Methods

    func session(session: WCSession, didReceiveMessage message: [String : AnyObject]) {
        if let status = message["LEAD_TYPE"] as? Bool {
            if (status == true) {
                leadStatusLabel.setText("TOE LEAD")
                leadStatusLabel.setTextColor(UIColor .greenColor())
            } else {
                leadStatusLabel.setText("HEEL LEAD")
                leadStatusLabel.setTextColor(UIColor .redColor())
                // If we are doing the move incorrectly
                WKInterfaceDevice.currentDevice().playHaptic(.Failure)
            }
        }
    }

    //
    // This is our custom function that gets called whenever the timer fires
    // All we're going to do is check and see if the session is open or not, and if not,
open one
    //
    func checkForToeLead () -> () {
        // Get data from phone using Watch Connectivity
```

```
    // First, always try and open session if not already opened
    if let session = session where session.reachable {
        print("watch:WCSession with Watch is REACHABLE")
    } else {
        openSession()
    }
}

override func didDeactivate() {
    // This method is called when watch view controller is no longer visible
    super.didDeactivate()
    intervalTimer.invalidate()

}

}
```

Summary

This was just a very brief introduction to interfacing electronic technology—that is, accessories—to iOS devices and Apple Watch. As with any discussion of something outside the Apple/IOS ecosystem, I could literally write a book on each hardware project, as there are so many elements and technologies involved.

From our discussion in this chapter, I hope you'll see that there is a choice when deciding how to connect a device such as a sensor to your iOS application. In most cases, the choice will have already been made and will be outside your control. It really comes down to the data rate needed between the accessory and your Apple device. Higher speed data streams require an MFi-approved connection, either wired through the dock connector or using standard Bluetooth (BT 2.1+EDR).

Your job will be to make either of these function correctly in the applications with which you are working. For an MFi accessory, you'll use the External Accessory frameworks and NSStreams, as we saw in the first example in this chapter. These work great in that it does not matter whether your connection is wired or wireless. From the app's perspective, it's all the same.

What you will have to address and define is the exact formatting of the data stream using the NSStreams paths. This will usually come as a specification within the device or via an Interface Control Document (ICD) that you, or your engineering team, work out with the hardware/firmware developers.

For a Bluetooth 4.0 Low Energy accessory, you'll use the Core Bluetooth framework. While BTLE exists for simpler, lower frequency devices, setting up things in your app can be a bit tricky. Remember, you now need to understand the Bluetooth hierarchy, which means knowing the difference between a client and a server, or, in Apple-speak, the central and a peripheral.

A *peripheral* is an object in your code that represents the real device from which you are gathering data, or to which you are sending data such as commands. This nearly exactly maps to the architecture we talked about in Chapter 16 with our HomeKit accessory project.

However, you can't instantiate a peripheral object until it has been found and you connect to it. For that to happen, you first have to work with the CBCentralManager object.

The *central*, or, more specifically, the CBCentralManager object (we called it the manager), will go out and scan the airwaves looking for BTLE devices. Using delegate methods, you can peruse each peripheral found until you find the one, or several, for which you are searching. Since the delegate method returns a peripheral object, you use that object in your code to address it and get the services and characteristics it provides. Of course, you'll first need to set the delegate of that returned peripheral object in order to use the delegate methods.

Index

A

Accelerometer, 202
Analog-to-digital (A/D) convertor, 153
Analysis scheme, 191–192
Android-based point of
      sale (PoS) system, 222–223
Apple, 252, 255, 257
Apple App Store
    account distribution certificate, 236
    app identifier, 229
    app ID information, 232
    archive validation, 228
    distribution option, 235
    ID description, 230
    ID information, 231
    iOS distribution certificate, 237
    old archive, 233
    provisioning profile, 234, 239
Apple developer portal, 228
Apple's CloudKit framework, 19
Apple's Core Bluetooth framework, 109
Apple's Human Interface Guidelines, 258
Apple's MFi program, 206, 468
Apple Watch, 6, 21, 52, 193, 198
Apple watch interface
    checkSensorStatus
        convenience function, 546
    functional code, 545
    InterfaceController.swift File, 546
    rumba, 543–544
    Rumba Interface Controller
        Swift Code, 551
    storyboard, 545
    viewDidLoad function, 546
    waltz, 542–543
    Waltz Interface Controller Swift Code, 549
    Watch InterfaceController.swift File, 547
Arduino, 212–213
Assets.xcassets icon, 447

B

Balsamiq Mockups
    iOS and watch components, 168
    login UI design, 169
    multiple images, 170
    portrait and landscape UI layouts, 171
    rudimentary, 173
    simple UI simulations, 172
    wireframes, 167
Bluetooth-enabled embedded
        sensor system, 203
Bluetooth low energy (BTLE), 50–51,
        108, 370, 505–506
Bluetooth radio, 202
Business-to-Business (B2B) side, 225

C

Card sorting, 159
Career options
    adaptation, 30
    employee, 8
    entrepreneur
        agile development, 59
        business plan, 10, 57
        consulting company, 11
        consulting vs. product-oriented, 59
        contractor, 11
        ecosystem, 62
        incubators, 61
        IP's plans, 62

Get the eBook for only $5!

Why limit yourself?

Now you can take the weightless companion with you wherever you go and access your content on your PC, phone, tablet, or reader.

Since you've purchased this print book, we're happy to offer you the eBook in all 3 formats for just $5.

Convenient and fully searchable, the PDF version enables you to easily find and copy code—or perform examples by quickly toggling between instructions and applications. The MOBI format is ideal for your Kindle, while the ePUB can be utilized on a variety of mobile devices.

To learn more, go to www.apress.com/companion or contact support@apress.com.

All Apress eBooks are subject to copyright. All rights are reserved by the Publisher, whether the whole or part of the material is concerned, specifically the rights of translation, reprinting, reuse of illustrations, recitation, broadcasting, reproduction on microfilms or in any other physical way, and transmission or information storage and retrieval, electronic adaptation, computer software, or by similar or dissimilar methodology now known or hereafter developed. Exempted from this legal reservation are brief excerpts in connection with reviews or scholarly analysis or material supplied specifically for the purpose of being entered and executed on a computer system, for exclusive use by the purchaser of the work. Duplication of this publication or parts thereof is permitted only under the provisions of the Copyright Law of the Publisher's location, in its current version, and permission for use must always be obtained from Springer. Permissions for use may be obtained through RightsLink at the Copyright Clearance Center. Violations are liable to prosecution under the respective Copyright Law.

Printed in the United States
by Bookmasters

Printed in the United States
By Bookmasters